KING LEAR

WILLIAM SHAKESPEARE

TEXT & STUDY NOTES

KARL WHITE

FORUM PUBLICATIONS LTD.

Published by
Forum Publications Ltd.
23 Washington St., Cork.
Tel: (021) 4270525 · (021) 4270500
Fax: (01) 6335347

Edited by Billy Ramsell and Brian Forristal
Editorial Assistance: Siobhán Collins

Design and layout: Dominic Carroll & Jeremy Bowman

Film stills courtesy of Granada Television

ISBN: 978-1-906565-04-6

Laura Tunney 5C

WHO WAS WILLIAM SHAKESPEARE?

For all his fame and celebration, we know almost nothing about William Shakespeare. His father, John, was a glover and leather merchant who married Mary Arden, the daughter of the wealthy Robert Arden of Wilmecote, who owned a sixty-acre farm.

Shakespeare was born in 1564, though his precise date of birth is not known (traditionally, 23 April – St George's Day – has been Shakespeare's accepted birthday).

Shakespeare probably began his education at the age of six or seven at the Stratford grammar school. As was the case in all Elizabethan grammar schools, the focus would have been very much on Latin history, poetry and drama.

There are other fragmented and dubious details about Shakespeare's life growing up in Stratford. Many believe that after leaving school he worked as a butcher and in his father's glove business.

When Shakespeare was eighteen he married Anne Hathaway, who was twenty-six and already several months pregnant.

William's first child, Susanna, was baptised in Stratford sometime in May 1583. Baptism records reveal that twins Hamnet and Judith were born in February 1592.

Hamnet, William's only son, died in 1596, just eleven years old.

No one knows for certain how Shakespeare first started his career in the theatre, but by 1592 he had become an established actor.

By late 1594, Shakespeare was an actor, writer and part-owner of a playing company, known as the Lord Chamberlain's Men.

He went on to write many famous plays for this company including *Romeo and Juliet*, *Henry V*, *Julius Caesar* and *Hamlet*, and achieved great fame, fortune and the praise of Queen Elizabeth and King James I.

There is a general consensus among scholars that *King Lear* was written between 1604 and 1605. The great actor Richard Burbage played the title role, while Lear's three daughters were played by young boys, as women were not permitted to act. *King Lear* is now regarded as one of the greatest pieces of literature in the English language, and the old king has been the defining role in the career of many great actors. After writing *King Lear*, Shakespeare went on to write many other fine plays, cementing his reputation as the greatest dramatist of his age. He died on 23 April 1616 at the age of fifty-two.

CAST OF CHARACTERS

Lear *King of Britain*
Goneril *his eldest daughter*
Regan *his second daughter*
Cordelia *his youngest daughter*
Duke of Albany *married to Goneril*
Duke of Cornwall *married to Regan*
King of France
Duke of Burgundy
Earl of Gloucester
Edgar *his eldest son*
Edmund *his younger bastard son*
Earl of Kent
Fool
Oswald
Curan
Old Man

ACT 1 SCENE 1

King Lear's palace

Enter KENT, GLOUCESTER, and EDMUND. KENT and GLOUCESTER converse.
EDMUND stands back.

KENT I thought the King had more affected the Duke of Albany than Cornwall.

GLOUCESTER It did always seem so to us; but now, in the division of the kingdom, it appears not which of the Dukes he values most, for equalities are so weighed that curiosity in neither can make choice of either's moiety.

KENT Is not this your son, my lord?

GLOUCESTER His breeding, sir, hath been at my charge. I have so often blush'd to acknowledge him that now I am brazed to't.

KENT I cannot conceive you.

GLOUCESTER Sir, this young fellow's mother could; whereupon she grew round-womb'd, and had indeed, sir, a son for her cradle ere she had a husband for her bed. Do you smell a fault?

KENT I cannot wish the fault undone, the issue of it being so proper.

GLOUCESTER But I have, sir, a son by order of law, some year elder than this, who yet is no dearer in my account. Though this knave came something saucily into the world before he was sent for, yet was his mother fair, there was good sport at his making, and the whoreson must be acknowledged. Do you know this noble gentleman, Edmund?

EDMUND *[comes forward]* No, my lord.

GLOUCESTER My Lord of Kent: remember him hereafter as my honourable friend.

EDMUND My services to your lordship.

KENT I must love you, and sue to know you better.

EDMUND Sir, I shall study deserving.

GLOUCESTER He hath been out nine years, and away he shall again.

Sound a sennet.

The King is coming.

Enter one bearing a coronet; then LEAR; then the Dukes of ALBANY and CORNWALL; next, GONERIL, REGAN, CORDELIA, with Followers.

LEAR Attend the lords of France and Burgundy, Gloucester.

GLOUCESTER I shall, my liege.

Exeunt GLOUCESTER and EDMUND.

---

affected: *loved*

moiety: *portion*

10   **brazed:** *hardened*
conceive: *understand*

15   **fault:** *transgression*
issue: *offspring*

some year: *about a year*
knave: *fellow*
20   **saucily:** *wantonly*

whoreson: *bastard*

25

Services: *duty*
Sue: *seek*

30

out: *away*

Attend: *escort*

....

* 5–6   **equalities … moiety:** *shares are so measured that the most careful examination of the other person's share could not persuade either of the dukes to choose the other's portion above his own.*

† 12   **this young fellow's mother could:** *Gloucester puns on Kent's use of the word 'conceive' employing it in the sense of to become pregnant.*

‡ 30   **study deserving:** *work to earn your favour*

7

the love test

LEAR	Meantime we shall express our darker purpose.	35
	Give me the map there. Know we have divided	
	In three our kingdom; and 'tis our fast intent	
	To shake all cares and business from our age,	
	Conferring them on younger strengths while we	
	Unburthened crawl toward death. Our son of Cornwall,	40
	And you, our no less loving son of Albany,	
	We have this hour a constant will to publish	
	Our daughters' several dowers, that future strife	
	May be prevented now. The princes, France and Burgundy,	
	Great rivals in our youngest daughter's love,	45
	Long in our court have made their amorous sojourn,	
	And here are to be answered. Tell me, my daughters	
	(Since now we will divest us both of rule,	
	Interest of territory, cares of state),	
	Which of you shall we say doth love us most?	50
	That we our largest bounty may extend	
	Where nature doth with merit challenge. Goneril,	
	Our eldest-born, speak first.	
GONERIL	Sir, I love you more than words can wield the matter;	
	Dearer than eyesight, space, and liberty;	55
	Beyond what can be valued, rich or rare;	
	No less than life, with grace, health, beauty, honour;	
	As much as child e'er loved, or father found;	
	A love that makes breath poor, and speech unable.	
	Beyond all manner of so much I love you.	60
CORDELIA	[Aside] What shall Cordelia speak? Love, and be silent.	
LEAR	[to Goneril] Of all these bounds, even from this line to this,	
	With shadowy forests and with champains rich'd,	
	With plenteous rivers and wide-skirted meads,	
	We make thee lady. To thine and Albany's issue	65
	Be this perpetual. – What says our second daughter,	
	Our dearest Regan, wife to Cornwall? Speak.	
REGAN	Sir, I am made	
	Of the selfsame metal that my sister is,	
	And prize me at her worth. In my true heart	
	I find she names my very deed of love;	70
	Only she comes too short, that I profess	
	Myself an enemy to all other joys	
	Which the most precious square of sense possesses,	
	And find I am alone felicitate	
	In your dear Highness' love.	
CORDELIA	[Aside] Then poor Cordelia!	75
	And yet not so; since I am sure my love's	
	More richer than my tongue. N.B.	

Glossary (right margin):

35 darker: *hidden, secret*

fast: *fixed*

constant: *fixed*

sojourn: *journey*

Interest: *possession*

wield: *express*
space … : *freedom*
valued: *estimated*

breath: *expression*
all … much: *comparison*

this … this: *traces on map*

wide-skirted: *extensive*

perpetual: *continuous*

metal: *mettle, substance*
prize: *value*

square: *measure*
felicitate: *made happy*

---

* 47 answered: *given our decision*

† 51–2 **That we our largest bounty … merit challenge:** *That we may give the most generous share to the child whose expression of natural filial affection most earns it.*

‡ 63 **champains:** *unwooded land*

N.B Boosting his self-esteem.
His proposal to divide it
on the basis of an
artifical and contrived
love test can only be
described as an unforgiveable
egoism and idiocy

LEAR	To thee and thine hereditary ever	
	Remain this ample third of our fair kingdom,	
	No less in space, validity, and pleasure	80
	Than that conferred on Goneril. Now, our joy,	
	Although the last, not least; to whose young love	
	The vines of France and milk of Burgundy	
	Strive to be interess'd; what can you say to draw	
	A third more opulent than your sisters? Speak.	85
CORDELIA	Nothing, my lord.	
LEAR	Nothing?	
CORDELIA	Nothing.	
LEAR	Nothing can come of nothing. Speak again.	
CORDELIA	Unhappy that I am, I cannot heave	90
	My heart into my mouth. I love your Majesty	
	According to my bond; no more nor less.	
LEAR	How, how, Cordelia? Mend your speech a little,	
	Lest it may mar your fortunes.	
CORDELIA	Good my lord,	
	You have begot me, bred me, lov'd me; I	95
	Return those duties back as are right fit,	
	Obey you, love you, and most honour you.	
	Why have my sisters' husbands, if they say	
	They love you all? Haply, when I shall wed,	
	That lord whose hand must take my plight shall carry	100
	Half my love with him, half my care and duty.	
	Sure I shall never marry like my sisters,	
	To love my father all.	
LEAR	But goes thy heart with this?	
CORDELIA	Ay, good my lord.	
LEAR	So young, and so untender?	105
CORDELIA	So young, my lord, and true.	
LEAR	Let it be so! thy truth then be thy dower!	
	For, by the sacred radiance of the sun,	
	The mysteries of Hecate and the night;	
	By all the operation of the orbs	110
	From whom we do exist and cease to be;	
	Here I disclaim all my paternal care,	
	Propinquity and property of blood,	
	And as a stranger to my heart and me	
	Hold thee from this for ever. The barbarous Scythian,	115
	Or he that makes his generation messes	
	To gorge his appetite, shall to my bosom	
	Be as well neighboured, pitied, and relieved,	
	As thou my sometime daughter.	
KENT	Good my liege –	

validity: *value* (80)

bond: *kinship*

mar: *damage*

plight: *pledge* (100)

goes: *agrees*

dower: *inheritance, gift*

property of: *identity of blood*

messes: *food*
gorge: *swell*

sometime: *former*

---

*	78	**hereditary:** *by inheritance*
†	84	**interess'd:** *interested, closely connected*
‡	109	**Hecate:** *pagan goddess of the underworld and of night*
§	110	**operation of the orbs:** *influence of the celestial sphere*
₵	113	**Propinquity:** *close relationship*
**	115	**Scythian:** *inhabitant of regions of Asia, considered to be uncivilized*
††	116-7	**Or … messes:** *ref. to cannibalistic practice of eating one's child*

N.B. It is this misinterpatation and misjudgement on Lear's part which is one of the main springs of his own tradegy later in the play.

LEAR	Peace, Kent!
	Come not between the dragon and his wrath.
	I lov'd her most, and thought to set my rest
	On her kind nursery. Hence and avoid my sight!
	So be my grave my peace as here I give
	Her father's heart from her! Call France! Who stirs?
	Call Burgundy! Cornwall and Albany,
	With my two daughters' dowers digest this third;
	Let pride, which she calls plainness, marry her.
	I do invest you jointly in my power,
	Preeminence, and all the large effects
	That troop with majesty. Ourself, by monthly course,
	With reservation of an hundred knights,
	By you to be sustained, shall our abode
	Make with you by due turns. Only we still retain*
	The name, and all th' addition to a king. The sway,†
	Revenue, execution of the rest,
	Beloved sons, be yours; which to confirm,
	This coronet part betwixt you.
KENT	Royal Lear,
	Whom I have ever honoured as my king,
	Loved as my father, as my master followed,
	As my great patron thought on in my prayers, –
LEAR	The bow is bent and drawn; make from the shaft.‡
KENT	Let it fall rather, though the fork invade
	The region of my heart! Be Kent unmannerly
	When Lear is mad. What wouldst thou do, old man?
	Think'st thou that duty shall have dread to speak
	When power to flattery bows? To plainness honour's bound
	When majesty falls to folly. Reverse thy doom;
	And in thy best consideration check
	This hideous rashness. Answer my life my judgment,§
	Thy youngest daughter does not love thee least,
	Nor are those empty-hearted whose low sound
	Reverbs no hollowness.¶
LEAR	Kent, on thy life, no more!
KENT	My life I never held but as a pawn
	To wage against thine enemies; nor fear to lose it,
	Thy safety being the motive.
LEAR	Out of my sight!
KENT	See better, Lear, and let me still remain
	The true blank of thine eye.**
LEAR	Now by Apollo –
KENT	Now by Apollo, King,
	Thou swear'st thy gods in vain.
LEAR	O vassal! miscreant!

120

125

130

rest: *retirement*
nursery: *care;* Hence: *leave*

digest: *assimilate*
pride: *her only possession*

effects: *accompaniments*
Ourself: *royal plural*
reservation: *the retaining*
sustained: *paid for*

135

addition: *honours, titles*
Revenue: *income*

part: *divide*

140

it: *the arrow alluded to by Lear*

145

have dread: *be afraid*
plainness: *direct words*

150

low sound: *quite, modest words*

pawn: *chess piece of little value*
wage: *stake, risk*
motive: *cause*

155

Apollo: *pagan god of the sun*

160

vassal! miscreant: *servant! villain*

*	134	abode … turns: *he will stay with Goneril and Regan and their respective husbands each in turn.*
†	135	sway: *power of government*
‡	142	The bow … shaft: *the metaphorical arrow, representing Kent's words of criticism, is ready to shoot so proceed, in other words, state your reproach.*
§	150	Answer my life my judgment: *I will stake my life on my judgement.*
¶	153	Reverbs no hollowness: *echoes no insincerity*
**	158	See better … thine eye: *let me continue to guide you; sight is a recurrent motif in the play.*

Handwritten margin notes:
Symbolic moment

He intervens on cordelia's be half.

loyal + truthful adviser.

Lays his hand on his sword.

ALBANY }
CORNWALL }   Dear sir, forbear!

KENT   Do! Kill thy physician, and the fee bestow
Upon the foul disease. Revoke thy gift,
Or, whilst I can vent clamour from my throat,
I'll tell thee thou dost evil.

LEAR   Hear me, recreant!
On thine allegiance, hear me!
Since thou hast sought to make us break our vow –
Which we durst never yet – and with strained pride
To come between our sentence and our power, –
Which nor our nature nor our place can bear, –
Our potency made good, take thy reward.
Five days we do allot thee for provision
To shield thee from diseases of the world,
And on the sixth to turn thy hated back
Upon our kingdom. If, on the tenth day following,
Thy banished trunk be found in our dominions,
The moment is thy death. Away! By Jupiter,
This shall not be revoked.

KENT   Fare thee well, King. Since thus thou wilt appear,
Freedom lives hence, and banishment is here.
[To Cordelia] The gods to their dear shelter take thee, maid,
That justly think'st and hast most rightly said!
[To Regan and Goneril] And your large speeches may your deeds approve,
That good effects may spring from words of love.
Thus Kent, O princes, bids you all adieu;
He'll shape his old course in a country new.

Exit.

Flourish. Enter GLOUCESTER, with FRANCE and BURGUNDY; Attendants.

GLOUCESTER   Here's France and Burgundy, my noble lord.

LEAR   My Lord of Burgundy,
We first address toward you, who with this king
Hath rivalled for our daughter. What in the least
Will you require in present dower with her,
Or cease your quest of love?

BURGUNDY   Most royal Majesty,
I crave no more than hath your Highness offered,
Nor will you tender less.

LEAR   Right noble Burgundy,
When she was dear to us, we did hold her so;
But now her price is fallen. Sir, there she stands.
If aught within that little seeming substance,
Or all of it, with our displeasure pieced,
And nothing more, may fitly like your Grace,
She's there, and she is yours.

BURGUNDY   I know no answer.

LEAR   Will you, with those infirmities she owes,
Unfriended, new adopted to our hate,
Dower'd with our curse, and stranger'd with our oath,
Take her, or leave her?

[handwritten note:] Negative terms.

---

forbear: *hold back*

fee: *cost, consequence*
disease: *corruption (moral)*
vent: *utter*

165   **recreant:** *traitor*

vow: *word, promise*
strained: *forced, unnatural*

170   **place:** *status*
reward: *consequence, punishment*

diseases: *discomforts, disasters*

175

trunk: *body;* **dominions:** *lands*
Jupiter: *chief Roman god*

thus ... appear: *you will so act*
180   **hence:** *(from now) elsewhere*

approve: *prove true*
effects: *deeds*

185

course: *way of life*

190   **rivalled:** *competed*
present dower: *immediate gift*

tender: *give*

195   **dear:** *beloved / of high price (pun)*

pieced: *added*
fitly like: *please by its suitability*

200

owes: *owns*

....
* 196   **now her price is fallen:** *her worth
is measured in economics; she is as a
piece of property traded between men.*

† 203   **Dower'd ... stranger'd:** *gifted with
but a curse and disowned*

BURGUNDY   Pardon me, royal sir.
           Election makes not up on such conditions.   205
LEAR   Then leave her, sir; for, by the power that made me,
           I tell you all her wealth. *[To France]* For you, great King,
           I would not from your love make such a stray
           To match you where I hate; therefore beseech you
           To avert your liking a more worthier way   210
           Than on a wretch whom nature is ashamed
           Almost to acknowledge hers.
FRANCE   This is most strange,
           That she that even but now was your best object,
           The argument of your praise, balm of your age,
           Most best, most dearest, should in this trice of time   215
           Commit a thing so monstrous to dismantle
           So many folds of favour. Sure her offence
           Must be of such unnatural degree
           That monsters it, or your fore-vouched affection
           Fallen into taint; which to believe of her   220
           Must be a faith that reason without miracle
           Should never plant in me.
CORDELIA   I yet beseech your Majesty –
           If for I want that glib and oily art
           To speak and purpose not, since what I well intend,
           I'll do it before I speak – that you make known   225
           It is no vicious blot, murther, or foulness,
           No unchaste action or dishonoured step,
           That hath deprived me of your grace and favour;
           But even for want of that for which I am richer –
           A still-soliciting eye, and such a tongue   230
           As I am glad I have not, though not to have it
           Hath lost me in your liking.
LEAR   Better thou
           Hadst not been born than not to have pleased me better.
FRANCE   Is it but this – a tardiness in nature
           Which often leaves the history unspoken   235
           That it intends to do? My Lord of Burgundy,
           What say you to the lady? Love's not love
           When it is mingled with regards that stands
           Aloof from the entire point. Will you have her?
           She is herself a dowry.
BURGUNDY   Royal Lear,   240
           Give but that portion which yourself proposed,
           And here I take Cordelia by the hand,
           Duchess of Burgundy.

---

such a stray: *stray so far*
where I hate: *to Cordelia*
avert: *turn, redirect*

best object: *most prized, favoured*
argument: *subject, theme*
trice: *instant*
monstrous: *unnatural*

beseech: *beg*
for I want: *because I lack*
speak … not: *speak without intent*
make known: *let it be clear*
vicious blot: *moral stain*
dishonoured: *dishonourable*

even: *rather*
still-soliciting: *always imploring*

tardiness in nature: *natural reticence*
history: *narrative*

regards: *concerns*
Aloof: *detached*

---

* 205   Election … conditions: *such circum-
          stances allow for no choice.*

† 206   by the power that made me: *note
          how reluctant Lear is to relinquish his
          power and 'sway'.*

‡ 216–7 dismantle / So many folds of
          favour: *the image is of stripping away
          layers of clothes that enfold Cordelia
          in her father's love.*

§ 219–20 monsters it … into taint: *her offence
          must be so unnatural as to be mon-
          strous and demand your rejection, or
          else it is your sworn love for her that
          has become corrupted.*

❡ 221–2 faith … plant in me: *it would take a
          miracle for me to believe that Cordelia
          has committed a monstrous offence,
          reason suggests that the fault lies
          elsewhere.*

LEAR   Nothing! I have sworn; I am firm.

BURGUNDY   I am sorry then you have so lost a father   245
            That you must lose a husband.

CORDELIA   Peace be with Burgundy!
            Since that respects of fortune are his love,
            I shall not be his wife.

FRANCE   Fairest Cordelia, that art most rich, being poor;
            Most choice, forsaken; and most loved, despised!   250
            Thee and thy virtues here I seize upon.
            Be it lawful I take up what's cast away.
            Gods, gods! 'Tis strange that from their coldest neglect
            My love should kindle to inflamed respect.
            Thy dowerless daughter, King, thrown to my chance,   255
            Is Queen of us, of ours, and our fair France.
            Not all the dukes in waterish Burgundy
            Can buy this unprized precious maid of me.
            Bid them farewell, Cordelia, though unkind.
            Thou losest here, a better where to find.   260

LEAR   Thou hast her, France; let her be thine; for we
            Have no such daughter, nor shall ever see
            That face of hers again. Therefore be gone
            Without our grace, our love, our benison.
            Come, noble Burgundy.   265

Flourish. Exeunt LEAR, BURGUNDY, CORNWALL, ALBANY,
GLOUCESTER, and Attendants.

FRANCE   Bid farewell to your sisters.

CORDELIA   The jewels of our father, with washed eyes
            Cordelia leaves you. I know you what you are;
            And, like a sister, am most loath to call
            Your faults as they are named. Use well our father.   270
            To your professed bosoms I commit him;
            But yet, alas, stood I within his grace,
            I would prefer him to a better place!
            So farewell to you both.

GONERIL   Prescribe not us our duties.

REGAN   Let your study   275
            Be to content your lord, who hath received you
            At fortune's alms. You have obedience scanted,
            And well are worth the want that you have wanted.

CORDELIA   Time shall unfold what plighted cunning hides.
            Who cover faults, at last shame them derides.   280
            Well may you prosper!

FRANCE   Come, my fair Cordelia.

Exeunt FRANCE and CORDELIA.

GONERIL   Sister, it is not little I have to say of what most nearly
            appertains to us both. I think our father will hence to-night.

REGAN   That's most certain, and with you; next month with us.   285

GONERIL   You see how full of changes his age is. The observation we
            have made of it hath not been little. He always lov'd our
            sister most, and with what poor judgment he hath now cast her
            off appears too grossly.   290

---

lost … father: *implies lost a dowry*

respects: *care of*

I seize: *take possession*

inflamed: *impassioned*
thrown … chance: *cast by fortune*

waterish: *derisory, wet*

where: *place*

benison: *blessing*

washed: *with tears*

as … named: *by their proper names*
professed bosoms: *declared loves*

prefer: *recommend*

Prescribe: *advice*
study: *thought*

fortune's alms: *poor gift of fortune*
worth: *deserving of;* want: *lack*
plighted: *pleated with folds, complex*
at last: *in the end*

nearly: *closely*
will hence: *will go hence*

grossly: *is too apparent and obvious*

....

* 258   unprized precious: *oxymoron;*
         Cordelia is both unvalued in Lear's
         affection and without value, because
         she lacks a dowry, yet she is most pre-
         cious, most valuable.

† 277   scanted: *slighted;*

‡ 280–1 *see Proverbs 28.13: 'He that covereth*
         his sinnes, shall not prosper' (King
         James Authorised Bible, 1611).

REGAN   'Tis the infirmity of his age; yet he hath ever but slenderly
known himself.

GONERIL   The best and soundest of his time hath been but rash; then
must we look to receive from his age, not alone the   295
imperfections of long-ingraffed condition, but therewithal
the unruly waywardness that infirm and choleric years bring with
them.

REGAN   Such unconstant starts are we like to have from him as this
of Kent's banishment.   300

GONERIL   There is further compliment of leave-taking between France and
him. Pray you let us hit together:
If our father carry authority with such dispositions
as he bears, this last surrender of his will but
offend us.   305

REGAN   We shall further think on't.

GONERIL   We must do something, and in the heat.

Exeunt.

rash: *hasty, hot-headed*
age: *old age*
long-ingraffed: *deeply ingrained*
waywardness: *contrariness*

unconstant starts: *sudden fits*

compliment: *formality*

in the heat: *at once*

* 303–5 **If our … but offend us:** *If our father continues to exercise power in his characteristic way the recent giving up of his kingdom and will to us is not to be taken seriously.*

LEAR DIVIDES HIS KINGDOM

Gloucester and Kent speak about the king's decision to divide his kingdom. Gloucester introduces his illegitimate son Edmund to Kent.

Lear announces his abdication of the throne and says that he will divide his kingdom between his three daughters. He calls on each daughter to express their love for him. Goneril and Regan flatter the king and receive their share of his land. Cordelia cannot speak falsely and refuses to flatter the king. Lear flies into a rage and disowns her. Kent tells Lear that he is acting foolishly, and is subsequently banished.

The King of France takes Cordelia for his wife and they depart for France. Goneril and Regan speak together of the need to control Lear and limit his influence. Now that he has given away his kingdom he will be dividing his time between them.

ACTION

◈ LINES 1–6: SETTING THE SCENE

Kent, Gloucester and Edmund are conversing in the royal palace. Kent wonders whether the king prefers the Duke of Albany or the Duke of Cornwall. Gloucester says that the king is going to divide his kingdom and retire from active kingship.

◈ LINES 8–32: EDMUND

Kent asks Gloucester if the man with him is his son Edmund. Gloucester tells Kent that Edmund was born out of wedlock. His mother, he says, had 'a son for/ her cradle ere she had a husband for her bed'. (14–15) He then describes Edmund's conception in vulgar terms that suggest his socially inferior

status: 'there was/ good sport at his making, and the whoreson must be/ acknowledged'. (21–3)

Gloucester introduces Kent to Edmund as 'my honourable friend'. (27) Kent tells him that he will try to get to know him better, and Edmund responds by saying that he will try to earn Kent's favour: 'Sir, I shall study deserving'. (30) Gloucester tells Kent that Edmund has been abroad for nine years and will be departing again shortly. (31–2)

◈ LINES 33–54: LEAR'S DIVISION OF THE REALM

Lear enters with his three daughters: Goneril, Regan

and Cordelia. He announces his retirement as king, and the division of the kingdom. He says that he has divided the realm in three and intends to abdicate the throne so that the next generation can rule while he retires:

> 'Tis our fast intent
> To shake all cares and business from our age,
> Conferring them on younger strengths, while we
> Unburdened crawl toward death. (37–40)

Lear wants to grant each of his daughters their share of his land in public so 'that future strife/ May be prevented now'. (43–4) He also says that France and Burgundy have come to court to see which of them will marry Cordelia.

Each of his daughters will make a declaration of their love for him. The daughter with the most impressive declaration will receive the greatest share of the kingdom:

> Which of you shall we say doth love us most,
> That we our largest bounty may extend
> Where nature doth with merit challenge. (51–3)

LINES 54–82: GONERIL AND REGAN FLATTER LEAR
Goneril declares her love for Lear in flattering and elaborate terms. She says that words cannot express her feelings for her father: 'I love you more than words can wield the matter'. (55) Her love for him is dearer than 'eye-sight, space and liberty'. It is as much 'as child e'er lov'd, or father found;/ A love that makes breath poor and speech unable'. (59–60)

Goneril's declaration makes Cordelia uneasy. She feels that she will not be able to speak like her sister: 'What shall Cordelia do? Love, and be silent'. (62)

Lear is obviously pleased by the fulsome words of his eldest child. He gives her a portion of the kingdom 'with shadowy forests and with champains rich'd,/ With plenteous rivers and wide-skirted meads'. (64–5)

Regan speaks next, declaring that she feels the same as her sister: 'I am made as that self metal as my sister'. (69) She tries to top Goneril, however, by saying that her love for her father is the only thing that makes her happy: 'I am alone felicitate/ In your dear highness' love'. (75–6)

Cordelia is again distressed, but she knows that her

love for Lear is more real than any ability she might have to flatter him: 'my love's/ More richer than my tongue'. (77–8)

Lear seems as pleased with Regan as he was with Goneril. He gives her a share in the kingdom 'No less in space, validity and pleasure,/ Than that conferr'd on Goneril'. (81–2)

LINES 82–107: LEAR INVITES CORDELIA TO SPEAK
It is clear that Cordelia is Lear's favourite. He addresses her as 'our joy', and asks her what she can say to win a portion of the country even richer than that awarded her sisters. (86)

Cordelia's reply is bluntly honest: 'Nothing, my lord'. (87) Lear is disbelieving: 'Nothing?' (88) Cordelia repeats herself and Lear replies by saying that 'Nothing will come of nothing'. (90) He invites her to speak again and save herself.

Cordelia's reply is astoundingly honest. She declares herself incapable of expressing her feelings: 'I cannot heave/ My heart into my mouth'. (91–2) She says that she loves Lear as much as a daughter should: 'I love your majesty/ According to my bond; nor more nor less'. (92–3)

Lear warns her that she will lose everything if she does not say something more expressive: 'mend your speech a little,/ Lest you may mar your fortunes'.(94–5) Cordelia does indeed become more expansive, but not in the way that Lear would like:

- She repeats that she loves him in accordance with her duty as his daughter: 'You have begot me, bred me, lov'd me: I/ return those duties back as are right fit'. (96–7)
- She points out the hypocrisy of her sisters' speeches by asking why they have husbands if they claim that all their love belongs to their father: 'Why have my sisters husbands, if they say/ they love you all?' (99–100)
- She says that when she marries she will be obliged to divide her love equally between her husband and Lear: 'That lord whose hand must take my plight shall carry/ Half my love with him, half my care and duty'. (101–2)
- She will never make a marriage like those of Goneril and Regan's if she has to love her father exclusively: 'Sure I shall never marry like my sisters,/ To love my father all'. (103–4)

CHARACTER DEVELOPMENT

Lear is still incredulous and asks if she is being sincere: 'But goes thy heart with this?' (105) Cordelia says that she is. The king cannot believe her apparent lack of feeling: 'So young, and so untender?' (106) Cordelia reaffirms her honesty: 'So young, my lord, and true'. (107)

☙ LINES 108–20: CORDELIA IS BANISHED

Cordelia's honesty and bluntness has shocked and enraged Lear. His reaction is immediate and extreme: he disowns her. He sarcastically remarks that her only dowry will be her honesty: 'thy truth then be thy dower'. (108) He then calls on the heavens to witness his rejection of Cordelia:

> Here I disclaim all my paternal
> care,
> Propinquity and property of
> blood,
> And as a stranger to my heart
> and me
> Hold thee from this for ever.
> (113–16)

Lear tells Cordelia that she is no dearer to him now than barbarians who eat their own young. (116–20) He goes on to say how he loved Cordelia more than her sisters and had hoped to spend his retirement with her. Now peace will be found only in the grave. (124–5)

LEAR

AN AGROGANT AND VAIN KING

Although King Lear is the hero of the play, it has to be said that he does not make a very favourable first impression. He appears as a very arrogant and domineering figure. The most off-putting feature of his character is the manner by which he divides the kingdom. He wishes to be flattered in public in what is an egotistical and vain exercise: 'Which of you shall we say doth love us most?' (51)

He accepts the flattering declarations of his two eldest daughters without question, never seeming to suspect that they may be playing on his vanity for their own ends. Lear's high opinion of himself is also reflected in the language he uses to warn Kent to hold his tongue: 'Come not between the dragon and his wrath'. (123)

The king appears to expect everyone around him to serve him without question. If they do not, he regards them as being of no value. This is indicated by his condemnation of Cordelia: 'Better thou/ Hadst not been born than not to have pleas'd me/ better'. (235) The language he uses to humiliate her is also brutal and unforgiving. He describes her as 'that little-seeming substance' and as 'a wretch whom nature is asham'd/ Almost to acknowledge hers'. He is determined to debase her publicly for embarrassing him before his court.

RASH AND IMPETUOUS

Lear is also an extremely rash and hot-headed individual. He appears to have very little control over his temper. He cannot seem to recognise that Cordelia is simply incapable of translating her genuine love for him into flattering words, and he banishes her in a merciless and unsympathetic fashion.

The same traits are shown when he banishes Kent. Although the latter has clearly been a lifelong and selflessly devoted servant, Lear threatens him with violence and promises him death if he has not left the kingdom after ten days. The king cannot distinguish between those who genuinely love and care for him, and those who flatter and fawn over him for their own advancement. Regan confirms that this is not merely a product of the king's advanced age; he has always been like this: 'yet he hath ever but/ slenderly known himself'. (292)

POLITICALLY NAIVE?

Although on the surface Lear's plan to divide the kingdom between his three daughters may appear to be politically astute, upon closer examination it appears flawed. Lear says he is doing it so 'that future strife/ May be prevented now'. (44) Yet he also makes it clear that, if she speaks correctly, Cordelia will receive the most valuable section of the land: 'what can you say to draw/ A third more opulent than your sisters?' (85) This hardly appears to be a formula that will ensure future peace amongst his daughters.

INCAPABLE OF RELINQUISHING POWER

Lear divides his kingdom between his daughters, but appears incapable of letting go of power completely. He will 'retain/ The name and all th' addition to a king'. (135) He tells Goneril and Regan that they will take turns to accommodate him and his retinue of knights a month at a time, oblivious to the fact that since he has now relinquished power they are under no technical obligation to do so. Although we may say that he has no obvious reason to doubt his daughters' love for him, he does seem unaware of the fact that he has now thrown himself completely on their mercy and goodwill.

LEAR

LINES 121–38: THE NEW ARRANGEMENT

Lear divides what was to be Cordelia's share of the kingdom between Cornwall and Albany. He declares that he will spend one month at a time with Goneril and Regan, who will accommodate him and his retinue of one hundred knights. He will continue to hold the name of King and all of the external honours that go with it: 'Only we shall retain/ The name and all th' addition to a king'. (134–5) He gives Albany and Cornwall a coronet that they are to divide between them as a symbol of the new arrangement.

LINES 139–88: KENT IS BANISHED

Kent attempts to intervene on Cordelia's behalf, but Lear stops him immediately: 'Come not between the dragon and his wrath'. (123) Kent insists on speaking, regardless of the consequences for him personally.

He tells Lear to keep his kingdom ('Reserve thy state') and says that Cordelia does not love Lear less than her sisters just because she refused to flatter him: 'Nor are those empty-hearted whose low sound/ Reverbs no hollowness'. (153–4) He accuses Lear of being a 'mad' old man. (145)

Lear is furious and orders Kent to leave: 'Kent, on thy life, no more … Out of my sight!' (157) When Kent refuses, Lear is enraged and puts his hand on his sword, threatening violence. Albany and Cornwall intervene, asking the king to calm down. (164)

Kent persists, and asks Lear to let him stay as his loyal and truthful adviser: 'The true blank of thine eye'. (159) He says that his only desire was to protect and serve Lear. (154–6)

He once again urges Lear not to divide his kingdom, telling the king that he will protest as long as he can speak: 'Or, whilst I can vent clamour from my throat,/ I'll thee thou dost evil'. (163–4)

Lear's rage is now beyond control. He calls Kent a traitor ('recreant') and tells him that he has five days to prepare himself for exile. (174–5) If he is still in the kingdom on the tenth day, he will be killed: 'thy moment is death'. (179)

CHARACTER DEVELOPMENT

Kent appears to accept his banishment unquestioningly: 'thus thou wilt appear/ Freedom lives hence, and banishment is here'. (181–2) He bids farewell to Cordelia, commending her safety to the gods and telling her that she spoke honestly. (184) He tells Goneril and Regan that he hopes they will live true to their vows of love for Lear: 'And your large speeches may/ your deeds approve'. (186) He exits, saying that he will begin a new life in a new land: 'He'll shape his old course in a country new'. (188)

✏ LINES 189–214: BURGUNDY REJECTS CORDELIA

CORDELIA

Gloucester reenters with France and Burgundy. Lear addresses Burgundy first. He asks him what dowry he will accept for Cordelia. (193–4) Burgundy replies that he will only accept what Lear has previously promised: 'I crave no more than hath your highness offer'd,/ Nor will you tender less'. (194–5)

Lear tells him her 'price is fall'n' and that there is no dowry. (198) He says that if there is anything within her 'little-seeming substance' that he wants he may take her. (199–202) Lear describes his daughter in extremely negative terms: 'Unfriended, new-adopted to our hate,/ Dower'd with our curse, and stranger with our oath'. (205–6)

CORDELIA

TOTALLY HONEST
Unlike her sisters, Cordelia is completely honest and incapable of flattery. As soon as she hears Goneril begin to flatter Lear, she knows there is trouble in store for her: 'What shall Cordelia do? Love, and be silent'. (62) She knows her love for Lear is more real and genuine than any glittering words: 'my love's/ More richer than my tongue'. (78) She knows that she lacks 'that glib and oily art' of flattery.

PROUD AND TACTLESS?
Although Cordelia's honesty is admirable on one level, we might ask ourselves if she displays a lack of tact. She must know her father is a vain man, and could have chosen to humour him if she wished. Her declaration of love appears very unfeeling and clinical: 'I love your majesty/ According to my bond, nor more nor less'. (92–3)

She also has no hesitation in pointing out the hypocrisy of her sisters. She asks why they have husbands if they claim to love Lear so much: 'Why have my sisters husbands, if they say/ They love you all?' (99–100) She is perfectly clear that if she marries, her love will be equally divided amongst her husband and father. (101–2) Cordelia seems unaware of the intense humiliation that such clinical honesty will cause a proud man like Lear.

It can also be said that Cordelia displays some of her father's pride. She is eager to have France know that she has not been disowned on account of a sexual impropriety. (227–30) She is also keen to let Burgundy know that although he rejects her, she has no interest in him either: 'Since that respects of fortune are his love,/ I shall not be his wife'. (249–50)

A LOVING DAUGHTER
Whatever about the bluntness of her honesty, it is also apparent that Cordelia deeply loves her father. She declares her sadness at having to leave him, and expresses her fears for his safety at the hands of her sisters: 'stood I within his grace,/ I would prefer him to a better place'. (274–5) We may also suspect that her desire to have France know that she is still pure comes from a long-term aim. If France takes her as his wife, she will be in a strong position to intervene on Lear's behalf if her suspicions concerning Regan and Goneril are confirmed.

Burgundy is shocked, having clearly expected to gain land and wealth when he married Cordelia: 'I know no answer'. (203) He tells Lear that he will not marry her without a dowry. Lear tells him to forget about her and turns to France.

LINES 215–67: FRANCE ACCEPTS CORDELIA

Lear advises France out of friendship that he should reject Cordelia: 'I would not from your love make such a stray'. (210) He describes her as a 'wretch whom nature is asham'd/ Almost to acknowledge hers'. (213–14) France is baffled by Lear's hatred of his daughter, who was once his 'best object'. (216) He says that her crime must have been hideous.

Cordelia speaks up, asking Lear to tell France that she has not fallen into disfavour because of any disgraceful or dishonourable act. (227–9) She wants France to know that she has been disowned because of her lack of greed and ambition ('a still-soliciting eye') and her inability to flatter her father: 'and such a tongue/ That I am glad I have not'. (232–3)

France cannot believe that Cordelia has fallen from grace on account of so trivial a fault: 'Is it but this?' (236) He is obviously enchanted by her and announces that he will take her as his wife: 'She is herself a dowry'. (242) He tells Cordelia to say farewell to her family. (260)

Lear gladly gives Cordelia to France and repeats that he has disowned her: 'let her be thine, for we/ Have no such daughter, nor shall ever see/ That face of hers again'. (263–5) He and the court exit, leaving France and his daughters behind.

LINES 268–84: CORDELIA LEAVES HER SISTERS

Cordelia makes her farewell speech to Goneril and Regan. She seems to know that her sisters are wicked people with evil intentions: 'I know what you are;/ And like a sister am most loath to call/ Your faults as they are nam'd'. (270–2) She asks that they look after Lear, but suspects that they will not. (274–5)

Regan's reply is cold: 'Prescribe us not our duties'. (275) Goneril tells Cordelia that she got what she deserved on account of her lack of love for Lear: 'you have obedience scanted/ And

---

SOME LINES TO LEARN

Nothing will come of nothing
Lear (90)

To plainness honour's bound
When majesty falls to folly
Kent (148)

Kill thy physician, and the fee bestow
Upon the foul disease
Kent (163)

Time shall unfold what plighted cunning hides
Who covers faults, at last shame them derides
Cordelia (281–2)

CHARACTER DEVELOPMENT

GONERIL

FLATTERING

Lear's eldest daughter comes across as highly astute and calculating in this scene. She knows what her father wishes to be told in the love-test, and feeds his ego shamelessly: 'Sir, I love you more than words can wield the matter'. (55) Whatever her real feelings may be for Lear, she is happy to manipulate the old man's vanity for her own purposes.

A SELF-CENTRED SCHEMER

It is Goneril who instigates the sisters' plotting against Lear. She takes Regan aside after the king leaves and tells her 'it is not little I have to say what most nearly/ appertains to us both'. (285) She encourages Regan's distrust of Lear by pointing out the king's inconstant nature ('You see how full of changes his age is') and tells her that they must expect, like Cordelia and Kent, to suffer on account of Lear's egotism: 'this last surrender of his will but offend us'. (304) She is determined to act against her father quickly: 'We must do something, and i' the heat'. (306) She also has no mercy for Cordelia. She tells her she deserves her fate: 'you have obedience scanted/ And well are worth the want that you have/ wanted'. (280) Goneril is ambitious and without pity.

REGAN

EQUALLY FLATTERING

Regan is also clearly determined to manipulate her father's vanity. She even tries to outdo Goneril in the love-test: 'Only she comes too short'. (72) She shamelessly declares that only her father's love makes her happy, in spite of the fact that she is married to Cornwall. (75)

CO-CONSPIRATOR

Although it is Goneril who begins the plotting against Lear, Regan does not need much encouragement. She echoes her sister's fear of Lear's unpredictable temperament: 'Such unconstant starts are we like to have from him/ as this of Kent's banishment'. (300) It is clear that she also has no moral scruples about acting against Lear.

well are worth the want that you have/ wanted'. (278–80) Cordelia answers by saying that time will uncover their hypocrisy: 'Time shall unfold what plighted cunning hides'. (281) She departs with France.

LINES 284–306: GONERIL AND REGAN BEGIN TO SCHEME

Goneril and Regan speak about their father:

- They say that Lear is unpredictable and rash. (288–2)
- They say that he has always lacked self-knowledge: 'yet he hath ever but/ slenderly known himself'. (293–4)
- They say that age has made him angry and unstable: 'the unruly waywardness that infirm/ and choleric years bring with them'. (297–8)
- They cite Kent's banishment and his disowning of Cordelia as examples of his difficult and unpredictable behaviour.

CHARACTER DEVELOPMENT

KENT

A LOYAL SERVANT

Kent is Lear's completely loyal and loving servant. He tries to prevent Lear's surrender of power although he knows he risks his life in doing so. He breaks court decorum by addressing his master as 'old man' in attempting to dissuade the king from what he knows to an impetuous and foolish act: 'check/ this hideous rashness'. (150–1)

He also knows that Cordelia is the most genuine of his daughters: 'Thy youngest daughter does not love thee least'. (152) Kent's only interest is Lear's welfare, and he is willing to lay down his life for his master: 'My life I never held but as a pawn/ To wage against thine enemies; nor fear to lose it,/ Thy safety being the motive'. (154–5) He refuses to flatter Lear's ego: 'whilst I can vent clamour from my throat,/ I'll tell thou dost evil'. (166)

GONERIL & REGAN

They feel that if Lear continues to exert power, they will suffer: 'if our/ father carry authority with such disposition as he/ bears, this last surrender of his will but offend us'. (303–4) They agree to make sure that the retired king will have no more influence over what is now their kingdom. Goneril says that they must act quickly. (306)

FRANCE

A GENUINE SUITOR

France comes across as a genuine and morally upright figure in the opening scene. He cannot believe that Cordelia could have done anything worthy of her father's vicious wrath: 'which to believe of her/ must be a faith that reason without miracle/ Could never plant in me'. (222–4) He knows that true love is unconditional and does not depend on material circumstances: 'Love is not love/ When it is mingled with regards that stand/ Aloof from the entire point'. (239–41) He loves Cordelia regardless of the fact that she lost her dowry, and her description of her stands in stark contrast to Lear's brutal condemnations: 'thou art most rich, being poor;/ Most choice, forsaken; and most lov'd, despis'd!' (251–2)

BURGUNDY

A FALSE SUITOR

Burgundy appears as a completely materialistic and self-interested suitor of Cordelia's. He is willing to accept her only on condition that she comes with the portion of the kingdom he had been led to believe she would inherit. Once it becomes apparent that Cordelia will have no dowry, he has no interest in her.

GLOUCESTER

A TACTLESS FATHER

We do not learn a great deal about Gloucester in the opening scene, but his description of Edmund to Kent does appear tactless and insensitive. He says that he has 'often blushed to acknowledge' his son, but clearly enjoys describing the illegitimate nature of Edmund's conception. He also labels him a 'whoreson' in his presence. Gloucester's lack of tact and apparent thoughtlessness will soon come back to haunt him.

EDMUND

AN ILLEGITIMATE SON

Edmund appears as a quiet and courteous young man in this scene. He does not say a great deal, but we learn the key fact about him, which is his illegitimacy. In a feudal system, to be illegitimate (a 'bastard') was to suffer social stigma and a denial of normal rights of inheritance and privilege. We may suspect that Edmund has plans of his own from his words to Kent: 'Sir, I shall study deserving'. (30)

[handwritten: 2 sons — Edgar (legitimate), Gloucester, Edmund (illegitimate)]

[handwritten: Soliloquy – on stage by yourself.]

[handwritten: Sub plot]

Enter EDMUND, with a letter.

EDMUND	Thou, Nature, art my goddess; to thy law
	My services are bound. Wherefore should I
	Stand in the plague of custom, and permit
	The curiosity of nations to deprive me,
	For that I am some twelve or fourteen moonshines
	Lag of a brother? Why bastard? wherefore base?
	When my dimensions are as well compact,
	My mind as generous, and my shape as true,
	As honest madam's issue? Why brand they us
	With base? with baseness? bastardy? base, base?
	Who, in the lusty stealth of nature, take
	More composition and fierce quality
	Than doth, within a dull, stale, tired bed,
	Go to the creating a whole tribe of fops
	Got 'tween asleep and wake? Well then,
	Legitimate Edgar, I must have your land.
	Our father's love is to the bastard Edmund
	As to th' legitimate. Fine word – 'legitimate'!
	Well, my legitimate, if this letter speed,
	And my invention thrive, Edmund the base
	Shall top th' legitimate. I grow; I prosper.
	Now, gods, stand up for bastards!

[handwritten left margin: · nature. · angry social stigma (illegitimate) · condems social conventions that do not allow illegitimate sons to inheratance.]

[handwritten middle: more daring + adventurous than legitim...]

Enter GLOUCESTER.

GLOUCESTER	Kent banished thus? and France in choler parted?
	And the King gone to-night? subscribed his power?
	Confined to exhibition? All this done
	Upon the gad? Edmund, how now? What news?
EDMUND	So please your lordship, none.

Puts up the letter.

GLOUCESTER	Why so earnestly seek you to put up that letter?
EDMUND	I know no news, my lord.
GLOUCESTER	What paper were you reading?
EDMUND	Nothing, my lord.
GLOUCESTER	No? What needed then that terrible dispatch of it into your pocket? The quality of nothing hath not such need to hide itself. Let's see. Come, if it be nothing, I shall not need spectacles.

Line numbers: 5, 10, 15, 20, 25, 30, 35

Glosses (right margin):

curiosity: *particularity*
For that: *because*
moonshines lag: *months behind*
dimensions: *proportions*
generous: *as befitting noble birth*

lusty … nature: *natural, furtive, sexual activity*
More: *fuller;* **fierce:** *ardent*
tired bed: *marital, therefore law-abiding, bed*
fops: *fools*
Got: *begot*
Legitimate: *lawful;* **Edgar:** *his half-brother*

speed: *succeed*
invention: *made-up scheme*

choler: *anger*
subscribed: *signed away*
Confined: *reduced, limited*
Upon the gad: *so suddenly*

Puts up: *puts away (into his pocket)*

terrible: *hurried, fearful*

---

* 1–2 **Nature … bound:** *Nature is a key theme of the play. Though 'nature' often refers to natural human feeling and kinship, used here by Edmund it seems to refer to the self or individual will as it exists outside of the bounds of man-made laws. Nature is Edmund's deity, it is her laws, rather than those of society, that he honours.*

† 3 **plague of custom:** *referring to the law by which a 'bastard' child could not inherit his father's property*

‡ 9 **honest madam's issue:** *married woman's child*

EDMUND	I beseech you, sir, pardon me. It is a letter from my brother that I have not all o'er-read; and for so much as I have perused, I find it not fit for your o'erlooking.
GLOUCESTER	Give me the letter, sir.
EDMUND	I shall offend, either to detain or give it. The contents, as in part I understand them, are to blame.
GLOUCESTER	Let's see, let's see!
EDMUND	I hope, for my brother's justification, he wrote this but as an essay or taste of my virtue.
GLOUCESTER	[Reads] 'This policy and reverence of age makes the world bitter to the best of our times; keeps our fortunes from us till our oldness cannot relish them. I begin to find an idle and fond bondage in the oppression of aged tyranny, who sways, not as it hath power, but as it is suffered. Come to me, that of this I may speak more. If our father would sleep till I wak'd him, you should enjoy half his revenue for ever, and live the beloved of your brother, 'EDGAR.' Hum! Conspiracy? 'Sleep till I wak'd him, you should enjoy half his revenue.' My son Edgar! Had he a hand to write this? a heart and brain to breed it in? When came this to you? Who brought it?
EDMUND	It was not brought me, my lord: there's the cunning of it. I found it thrown in at the casement of my closet.†
GLOUCESTER	You know the character to be your brother's?
EDMUND	If the matter were good, my lord, I durst swear it were his; but in respect of that, I would fain think it were not.
GLOUCESTER	It is his.
EDMUND	It is his hand, my lord; but I hope his heart is not in the contents.
GLOUCESTER	Hath he never before sounded you in this business?
EDMUND	Never, my lord. But I have heard him oft maintain it to be fit that, sons at perfect age, and fathers declining, the father should be as ward to the son, and the son manage his revenue.
GLOUCESTER	O villain, villain! His very opinion in the letter! Abhorred villain! Unnatural, detested, brutish villain! worse than brutish! Go, sirrah, seek him. I'll apprehend him. Abominable villain! Where is he?
EDMUND	I do not well know, my lord. If it shall please you to suspend your indignation against my brother till you can derive from him better testimony of his intent, you should run a certain course; where, if you violently proceed against him, mistaking his purpose, it would make a great gap in your own honour and shake in pieces the heart of his obedience. I dare pawn down my life for him that he hath writ this to feel my affection to your honour, and to no other pretence of danger.
GLOUCESTER	Think you so?
EDMUND	If your honour judge it meet, I will place you where you shall hear us confer of this and by an auricular assurance have your satisfaction, and that without any further delay than this very evening.
GLOUCESTER	He cannot be such a monster.

Margin glosses:

perused: *read carefully*

essay or taste: *test*

best of our times: *our youth*
relish: *enjoy;* idle: *wasted*
fond bondage: *foolish slavery*

hand: *capacity*
breed: *imagine*

character: *handwriting*
matter: *content, subject*

perfect age: *fully mature*
ward: *dependent*

apprehend: *arrest*

violently: *rashly*

pawn down: *risk*
feel: *test*
pretence of danger: *dangerous intent*

auricular: *heard*

Line numbers: 40, 45, 50, 55, 60, 65, 70, 75, 80, 85, 90

Handwritten margin note: Gloucester's total outrage like Lear

* 49 sways ... suffered: *age rules not by its strength but because we allow it*

† 59 casement of my closet: *window of my room*

EDMUND	Nor is not, sure.	
GLOUCESTER	To his father, that so tenderly and entirely loves him.	
	Heaven and earth! Edmund, seek him out; wind me into him,	
	I pray you; frame the business after your own wisdom.	95
	I would unstate	
	myself to be in a due resolution.	
EDMUND	I will seek him, sir, presently; convey the business as I	
	shall find means, and acquaint you withal.	
GLOUCESTER	These late eclipses in the sun and moon portend no good to	100
	us. Though the wisdom of nature can reason it thus and thus, yet	
	nature finds itself scourged by the sequent effects. Love cools,	
	friendship falls off, brothers divide. In cities, mutinies; in	
	countries, discord; in palaces, treason; and the bond cracked	105
	'twixt son and father. This villain of mine comes under the	
	prediction; there's son against father: the King falls from bias	
	of nature; there's father against child. We have seen the best	
	of our time. Machinations, hollowness, treachery, and all	
	ruinous disorders follow us disquietly to our graves.	110
	Find out this villain, Edmund; it shall lose thee nothing; do it	
	carefully. And the noble and true-hearted Kent banished! his	
	offence, honesty! 'Tis strange.	

Exit.

EDMUND	This is the excellent foppery of the world, that, when we are	115
	sick in fortune, often the surfeit of our own behaviour, we make	
	guilty of our disasters the sun, the moon, and the stars; as if	
	we were villains on necessity; fools by heavenly compulsion;	
	knaves, thieves, and treachers by spherical pre-dominance;	120
	drunkards, liars, and adulterers by an enforced obedience of	
	planetary influence; and all that we are evil in, by a divine	
	thrusting on. An admirable evasion of whore-master man, to lay	
	his goatish disposition to the charge of a star! My father	125
	compounded with my mother under the Dragon's Tail, and my	
	nativity was under Ursa Major, so that it follows I am rough and	
	lecherous. Fut! I should have been that I am, had the	
	maidenliest star in the firmament twinkled on my bastardizing.	
	Edgar –	130

Enter EDGAR.

	and pat! he comes, like the catastrophe of the old comedy. My	
	cue is villainous melancholy, with a sigh like Tom o' Bedlam.	
	O, these eclipses do portend these divisions! Fa, sol, la, mi.	
EDGAR	How now, brother Edmund? What serious contemplation	135
	are you in?	
EDMUND	I am thinking, brother, of a prediction I read this other day,	
	what should follow these eclipses.	
EDGAR	Do you busy yourself with that?	

Glossary (margin):

wind: *indirectly advance*
frame: *fashion, manage*
unstate: *forfeit my rank*

convey: *conduct, manage*
withal: *therewith*
late: *recent;* portend: *foretell*
wisdom: *science;* reason: *explain*

mutinies: *riots*
bond: *of kinship*
villain of mine: *Edgar*
bias: *natural partiality*

foppery: *stupidity*
surfeit: *result*
make guilty of: *blame*

treachers: *traitors*

divine: *heavenly*
whore-master: *lecherous*
goatish: *lustful*
Dragon's Tail: *astrological sign*
nativity: *birth*
Fut!: *Rubbish!*
bastardizing: *extra-marital conception*

catastrophe: *concluding episode*

divisions: *conflicts*

Handwritten margin notes:

nature's upheaval

the good old days gone — evil + decline are here

Edmund's contempt.

Gloucester
• Rash
• Gullible
• Superstitous

Footnotes:

* 102   **nature finds itself scourged by the sequent effects:** *human nature is nevertheless afflicted by the consequences of lunar movement. This passage shows Gloucester to be of a superstitious mind.*

† 120   **spherical pre-dominance:** *the dominance of a particular planet at the time of our birth*

‡ 133   **cue … like Tom o' Bedlam:** *Edmund adopts theatrical language in keeping with his role-playing and inventiveness; Tom was the name commonly given to a madman (bedlam was a London lunatic asylum).*

| EDMUND | I promise you, the effects he writes of succeed unhappily: as | 140 | succeed: *turn out* |

EDMUND   I promise you, the effects he writes of succeed unhappily: as   140
of unnaturalness between the child and the parent; death,
dearth, dissolutions of ancient amities; divisions in state,
menaces and maledictions against king and nobles; needless
diffidences, banishment of friends, dissipation of cohorts,   145
nuptial breaches, and I know not what.

EDGAR   How long have you been a sectary astronomical?*

EDMUND   Come, come! When saw you my father last?

EDGAR   The night gone by.

EDMUND   Spake you with him?   150

EDGAR   Ay, two hours together.

EDMUND   Parted you in good terms? Found you no displeasure in him by
word or countenance

EDGAR   None at all.

EDMUND   Bethink yourself wherein you may have offended him;   155
and at my entreaty forbear his presence until some little time
hath qualified the heat of his displeasure, which at this instant so
rageth in him that with the mischief of your person it would
scarcely allay.†   160

EDGAR   Some Villain hath done me wrong.

EDMUND   That's my fear. I pray you have a continent forbearance till‡
the speed of his rage goes slower; and, as I say, retire with me
to my lodging, from whence I will fitly bring you to hear my
lord speak. Pray ye, go! There's my key. If you do stir abroad,   165
go arm'd.

EDGAR   Arm'd, brother?

EDMUND   Brother, I advise you to the best. Go arm'd. I am no honest
man if there be any good meaning toward you. I have told   170
you what I have seen and heard; but faintly, nothing like the
image and horror of it. Pray you, away!

EDGAR   Shall I hear from you anon?

EDMUND   I do serve you in this business.   175

Exit EDGAR.

A credulous father! and a brother noble,
Whose nature is so far from doing harms
That he suspects none; on whose foolish honesty
My practices ride easy! I see the business.
Let me, if not by birth, have lands by wit;   180
All with me's meet that I can fashion fit.§

Exit.

Marginal glosses:

succeed: *turn out*

amities: *friendships*

dissipation: *dispersal*

forbear ... presence: *avoid meeting him*
qualified: *mitigated, toned down*

fitly: *opportunely, at a suitable time*

arm'd: *carry a weapon*

faintly: *in a subdued way*

anon: *soon*

practices: *intrigues*

Footnotes:

* 147   sectary astronomical: *student of astronomy*

† 159–60 with the mischief ... scarcely allay: *even injury to you would hardly be enough to calm his anger*

‡ 162   continent forbearance: *ability to exercise restraint;*

§ 181   All with me's meet that I can fashion fit: *all is fine and permissible with me once I can frame it to serve my own purpose*

Edmund speaks about the social stigma attached to being an illegitimate child and how custom will not permit him to inherit his father's land (Gloucester's land will go to his legitimate son, Edgar). He reveals how he intends to trick his father into giving him Edgar's inheritance. When Gloucester arrives, Edmund makes to hide a letter, which he says he received from Edgar. The false letter outlines Edgar's desire to kill his father and gain his inheritance. Gloucester believes the letter is genuine and is filled with rage. When Edmund later meets Edgar, he alarms his brother by telling him that he has offended his father and that his life is now in danger. He advises Edgar to hide himself away in Edmund's lodgings and to arm himself.

EDMUND

A KEY MOMENT

This scene kicks off the sub-plot of the play. Edmund's scheming to dupe his father and have Edgar eliminated mirror the treachery and guiles of Goneril and Regan. From this point on, the two plots will run parallel and intertwine at crucial moments.

ACTION

🌮 LINES 1–22: EDMUND SHOWS HIS TRUE COLOURS

We are in a room in Gloucester's palace. Edmund enters with a letter. He makes a speech that reveals his true character and sinister intent:

· He declares Nature to be his goddess: 'to thy law/ My services are bound'. (1–2)

· Edmund is angry at the social stigma attached to being illegitimate. He cannot understand why he should be regarded as any less worthy of respect than someone born in wedlock: 'When my dimensions are as well compact,/ My mind as generous, and my shape as true,/ As honest madam's issue?' (7–9)

· He condemns the social conventions that prevent illegitimate children inheriting property: 'the plague of custom'. (3)

· He regards the conception of illegitimate children as being more daring and adventurous than the run-of-the-mill production of legitimate children: 'Who in the lusty stealth of nature take/ More composition and fierce quality/ Than doth, within a dull, stale, tired bed,/ Go to the creating a whole tribe of fops'. (11–14)

He declares that he intends to gain the land his brother is due to inherit: 'Legitimate Edgar, I must have your land'. (16) He has a scheme in mind that involves the letter he is holding. Edmund sees himself as a representative of wronged illegitimate children everywhere: 'I grow, I prosper;/ Now, gods, stand up for bastards!' (21–2)

GLOUCESTER & EDMUND

CHARACTER DEVELOPMENT

EDMUND

AN AMBITIOUS VILLAIN

Edmund reveals his true self in this scene. He is determined to gain his father's land and to destroy his brother. The source of his anger and ambition is the unfair treatment meted out to illegitimate sons. He fails to see why he should be disadvantaged on account of a mere accident of birth:

> *Why bastard? Wherefore*
> *   base?*
> *When my dimensions are as*
> *   well compact,*
> *My mind as generous, and my*
> *   shape as true,*
> *As honest madam's issue?* (6–9)

CLEVER AND MANIPULATIVE

Edmund's intelligence and cunning is made very clear in this scene. He artfully uses the forged letter to convince Gloucester that Edgar is his enemy. His expression of hope that Edgar may only be testing his virtue is a cunning psychological means of fuelling his father's suspicions. He is also easily able to fool his brother with his feigned concern for his safety.

ADMIRABLE?

Although Edmund's motives are entirely selfish, it has to be said that he does possess a certain charm. We can easily feel sympathy for his complaints about the social stigma he suffers on account of his illegitimacy. His condemnation of the way men abdicate responsibility for their actions and blame the heavens is also admirable for its bluntness. It is part of Shakespeare's great dramatic skill that he can arouse sympathy in us for a character whose aims are entirely self-centred and whose methods are ruthless.

❧ LINES 20–74: THE SET-UP

Gloucester enters, lamenting the events at court. Edmund makes to hide the letter he's holding, and Gloucester asks him what it contains. Edmund says there is nothing in it. (28–31) Gloucester's suspicions are aroused, however, and he demands to know the letter's contents: 'the quality of nothing hath not such/ need to hide itself'. (33–4)

Edmund says it is a disturbing letter from Edgar that he has not read through properly: 'I find it not fit for your o'er-looking'. (38) He pretends to be reluctant to hand it over to his father, and says he hopes Edgar wrote the letter as a test of his (Edmund's) virtue. (39–43)

Gloucester reads the letter in which Edgar expresses his frustration that he must wait till his father dies before coming into his inheritance. He says he is sick of living under his father's 'aged tyranny'. He wants to murder Gloucester and claim his inheritance now. He asks Edmund to join him in this diabolical plot:

> *If our father would sleep till I waked him,*
> *You should enjoy half his revenue for ever, and live*
> *The beloved of your brother.* (52–4)

Gloucester asks if it is really Edgar's handwriting. Edmund cleverly says he thinks it is, but wishes it were not. (62–3) Gloucester then asks if Edgar has said anything about these issues to Edmund before. Edmund says no, but adds that he has heard Edgar say that at a certain age fathers should grant control of their estates to their sons: 'the father should be as ward to the son, and/ the son manage his revenue'. (73)

LINES 74–120: GLOUCESTER'S ANGER

Gloucester is furious. He condemns Edgar in terms that remind us of Lear's anger toward Cordelia: 'Abhorred villain! Unnatural, detested, brutish villain!/ worse than brutish!' (75–6)

Edmund continues to scheme. He tells his father that he shouldn't condemn Edgar until he has proof of his evil intentions. He says that he is convinced that Edgar has only written the letter to test his own love for Gloucester: 'I dare pawn down my life for him, that he hath writ this to feel my/ affection to your honour, and to no other pretence of/ danger'. (84–6)

Edmund tells Gloucester that he will arrange to meet Edgar that evening. Gloucester can listen in on their discussion and discover Edgar's true intentions. (89–93) Gloucester agrees, saying that he cannot believe that Edgar would betray him when he loves his son so dearly. He says that he would be willing to give up everything to have the matter resolved: 'I would unstate myself to be in a due resolution'. (99)

Gloucester then launches into a long lament in which he blames astrological phenomena for the current upheaval in the land: 'These late eclipses in the sun and moon portend no/ good to us'. (102) He lists the recent events that have overthrown the natural order of things:

> Love cools, friendship falls off, brothers divide: in cities, mutinies; in countries, discord; in palaces, treason; and the bond cracked between son and father. (105–8)

The best period of the age is over and only evil and decline remains: 'We have the seen the best of our time: machinations,/ hollowness, treachery, and all ruinous disorders,/ follow us disquietly to our graves'. (111–12) Gloucester exits, urging Edmund to do his best in regard to Edgar. (115)

LINES 117–31: EDMUND'S CONTEMPT

Edmund is disgusted by Gloucester's lament, describing it as 'foppery', or foolishness. (118) He believes it is stupid to blame 'the sun,/ the moon and the stars' for misfortunes we all too often bring upon ourselves. (118–19) Such an attitude ignores the moral responsibility we have for our own behaviour: 'as if we were villains by/ necessity, fools by heavenly compulsion, knaves,/ thieves, and treachers by spherical pre-dominance …' (120–2) He believes that only people of low character blame the stars for the consequences of their freely chosen actions: 'an admirable evasion/ of whoremaster man, to lay his goatish disposition/ to the charge of a star!' (125–6)

CHARACTER DEVELOPMENT

GLOUCESTER

A GULLIBLE FATHER

Gloucester does not make a very good impression in this scene. He is too easily fooled by Edmund and is ready to think the worst of Edgar. He does not stop to ask why Edgar would write such damning sentiments in a letter rather than approach Edmund in person. His belief that astronomical phenomena are responsible for the upheavals in the land also strikes us as naive and as being an abdication of moral responsibility.

RASH

Gloucester's anger and lack of perception mirror that of King Lear. The language he uses to condemn his son reminds us of the king's damning of Cordelia: 'Abhorred villain! Unnatural, detested, brutish villain!/ worse than brutish! (75–6) He has very little hesitation in believing the worst of Edgar.

EDGAR

DUPED

It is difficult not to feel sympathy for Edgar in this scene. He is completely duped by Edmund as a result of the good faith he has in his brother. He is in a state of shock once he is told that his father is angry with him, and is easy prey for Edmund's wiles. We know from Edmund that Edgar has a good and upright character: 'a brother noble,/ Whose nature is so far from doing harms/ That he suspects none'. (177–8)

✍ LINES 138–81: EDGAR IS DECEIVED

Edgar greets his brother and asks him what he is doing. Edmund tells him he has been reading astrological predictions. (140–2) Edgar expresses surprise, but Edmund, mimicking his father's speech of earlier, goes on to outline a series of disasters that have shaken the land: 'unnaturalness between the child/ and the parent; death, dearth, dissolutions of amities'. (144–5)

Edmund asks Edgar when he last saw Gloucester and if he spoke with him. (150–3) Edgar says that they spoke for two hours and that they parted on good terms. Edmund tells him that he must have unintentionally offended their father, as Gloucester is in a terrible rage and should be avoided. (157–61) Edgar is puzzled by this and believes that 'Some villain' must have turned Gloucester against him. (162)

EDGAR & EDMUND

SOME LINES TO LEARN

Now, gods, stand up for bastards!
Edmund (22)

We have seen the best of our time: machinations, hollowness, treachery, and all ruinous disorders, follow us disquietly to our graves
Gloucester (111–12)

This is the excellent foppery of the world, that, when we are sick in fortune, – often the surfeit of our own behaviour, – we make guilty of our disasters the sun, the moon, and the stars
Edmund (117–20)

Let me, if not by birth, have lands by wit:
All with me's meet that I can fashion fit
Edmund (180–1)

Edmund advises Edgar to take refuge from his father's rage in Edmund's lodging. (163–9) He also advises him to arm himself. (163–7) Edgar is shocked at the last suggestion, but Edmund insists it is for his own good because someone is obviously out to get him. (170–2) He tells him to leave and that he will be with him shortly. (168–75)

Edmund is pleased by his cunning. He has 'A credulous father, and a brother noble,/ Whose nature is so far from doing harms/ That he suspects none'. (175–7) He intends to be merciless in order to gain his ends: 'Let me, if not by birth, have lands by wit:/ All with me's meet that I can fashion fit'. (180–1)

EDGAR & EDMUND

The Duke of Albany's palace

Enter GONERIL and her Steward, OSWALD.

GONERIL	Did my father strike my gentleman for chiding of his fool?
OSWALD	Ay, madam.
GONERIL	By day and night, he wrongs me! Every hour
	He flashes into one gross crime or other
	That sets us all at odds. I'll not endure it.
	His knights grow riotous, and himself upbraids us
	On every trifle. When he returns from hunting,
	I will not speak with him. Say I am sick.
	If you come slack of former services,
	You shall do well; the fault of it I'll answer.

Horns within.

OSWALD	He's coming, madam; I hear him.
GONERIL	Put on what weary negligence you please,
	You and your fellows. I'd have it come to question.
	If he distaste it, let him to our sister,
	Whose mind and mine I know in that are one,
	Not to be overruled. Idle old man,
	That still would manage those authorities
	That he hath given away! Now, by my life,
	Old fools are babes again, and must be used
	With checks as flatteries, when they are seen abused.
	Remember what I have said.
OSWALD	Very well, madam.
GONERIL	And let his knights have colder looks among you.
	What grows of it, no matter. Advise your fellows so.
	I would breed from hence occasions, and I shall,
	That I may speak. I'll write straight to my sister
	To hold my very course. Prepare for dinner.

Exeunt.

Handwritten note: Her comments on lear's childishness + senile

Line numbers and glossary:

5

chiding: *reprimanding*

crime: *offence*

10 **slack ... services:** *careless of services to Lear*
fault: *responsibility*

it: *the negligence*
15 **distaste:** *doesn't like*

Idle: *foolish*

20

25 **breed ... occasions:** *generate ... opportunities*

hold ... course: *secure my plan*

* 21 **checks as flatteries, when they are seen abused:** *treated by correction or rebuke (instead of, or as well as) indulgences when they are seen to be spoilt and deluded*

GONERIL & OSWALD

Goneril speaks to Oswald about how Lear and his retinue are proving troublesome. She instructs Oswald to be rude and cold when dealing with the King. She says that she will write to Regan to advise her to act the same.

GONERIL

BEGINNING TO PLOT
Goneril starts her machinations against Lear in this scene by adopting a policy of rudeness toward him. Again, as in the first scene, she is the sister who takes the initiative.

Goneril claims she has been forced to do so by the unruly behaviour of Lear and his knights. Yet she is also distressed that Lear continues to act as if he still ruled the country.

She wishes to 'occasion' or provoke a conflict that will allow her to remove Lear as a threat to her and Regan's authority.

LEAR

A DIFFICULT GUEST?
We have only Goneril's negative report on Lear's behaviour to tell us how the king is handling his retirement. According to Goneril, he is demanding, arrogant and self-centred.

He is still active, hunting and giving orders. In fact, he behaves as if he is still ruler of the country. Whether he is as troublesome as his daughter claims is difficult to know. There is every possibility that his behaviour is being exaggerated by Goneril to justify her own selfish motives.

OSWALD

OBEDIENT SERVANT
Oswald says little in this scene. He merely obeys Goneril's orders without question. He will have more to do shortly.

ACTION

✍ LINES 1–28: A TROUBLESOME GUEST

Goneril is talking with her servant Oswald. The scene takes place in a room in Albany's castle, where Lear has been staying with Goneril and Albany. Oswald confirms that Lear hit one of Goneril's attendants. (1) Lear was annoyed because the servant 'chided' his fool. (1) Goneril launches into a tirade against her father, who has, it seems, been a difficult guest:

> By day and night he wrongs me; every hour
> He flashes into one gross crime or other,
> That sets us all at odds. (4–6)

CHARACTER DEVELOPMENT

SOME LINES TO LEARN

Old fools are babes again,
and must be us'd
With checks as flatteries, when
they are seen abus'd
Goneril (20–1)

Lear complains regularly to Goneril and her husband, and his knights are proving troublesome ('riotous'). Goneril is infuriated by Lear's inability to stop acting as if he were still in power: 'Idle old man,/ That would still manage those authorities/ That he hath given away!' (17–18) She compares the behaviour of elderly people to children: both need to be disciplined as well as humoured. (20–1)

Goneril says she will no longer put up with Lear's bad behaviour: 'I'll not endure it'. (6) She decides that she will refuse to see Lear when he returns from hunting. She tells Oswald to be rude when dealing with the king. (9–10) The servants should be rude when dealing with his knights, regardless of the consequences. (24–5) She will write to Regan to advise her to adopt a similar policy of rudeness toward their father. (27–8)

The Duke of Albany's palace

Enter KENT, disguised.

KENT If but as well I other accents borrow,
That can my speech defuse, my good intent
May carry through itself to that full issue
For which I razed my likeness. Now, banished Kent,
If thou canst serve where thou dost stand condemned,   5
So may it come, thy master, whom thou lov'st,
Shall find thee full of labours.

Horns within. Enter LEAR, Knights, and Attendants.

LEAR Let me not stay a jot for dinner; go get it ready.

Exit an Attendant.

How now? What art thou?

KENT A man, sir.   10

LEAR What dost thou profess? What wouldst thou with us?

KENT I do profess to be no less than I seem, to serve him truly
that will put me in trust, to love him that is honest, to
converse with him that is wise and says little, to fear   15
judgment, to fight when I cannot choose, and to eat no fish.

LEAR What art thou?

KENT A very honest-hearted fellow, and as poor as
the King.   20

LEAR If thou be as poor for a subject as he's for a king, thou
art poor enough. What wouldst thou?

KENT Service.

LEAR Who wouldst thou serve?

KENT You.   25

LEAR Dost thou know me, fellow?

KENT No, sir; but you have that in your countenance which I would
fain call master.

LEAR What's that?

KENT Authority.   30

LEAR What services canst thou do?

KENT I can keep honest counsel, ride, run, mar a curious tale in
telling it and deliver a plain message bluntly. That which
ordinary men are fit for, I am qualified in, and the best of me
is diligence.   35

LEAR How old art thou?

KENT Not so young, sir, to love a woman for singing, nor so old to
dote on her for anything. I have years on my back forty-eight.

LEAR Follow me; thou shalt serve me. If I like thee no worse after   40
dinner, I will not part from thee yet. Dinner, ho, dinner!
Where's my knave? my Fool? Go you and call my Fool hither.

Exit an attendant.

---

defuse: *disguise*

full issue: *complete outcome*

razed: *obliterated*

thy master: *ref. to Lear*

stay a jot: *wait a minute*

profess: *practice as your trade*

countenance: *bearing*

mar: *ruin*

bluntly: *directly*

Fool: *court jester*

* 1–4 **If but as well … razed my likeness:** *If I can as successfully alter my accent as I have my appearance, I may well be able to carry out fully my good intentions.*

Enter OSWALD the Steward.

	You, you, sirrah, where's my daughter?	
OSWALD	So please you – *[Exit]*	45
LEAR	What says the fellow there? Call the clotpoll back.	**clotpoll:** *blockhead*

Exit a Knight.

Where's my Fool, ho? I think the world's
asleep.

Enter KNIGHT.

	How now? Where's that mongrel?	
KNIGHT	He says, my lord, your daughter is not well.	
LEAR	Why came not the slave back to me when I called him?	50
KNIGHT	Sir, he answered me in the roundest manner, he would not.	**roundest:** *plainest, rudest*
LEAR	He would not?	
KNIGHT	My lord, I know not what the matter is; but to my judgment your Highness is not entertained with that ceremonious affection as you were wont. There's a great abatement of kindness appears as well in the general dependants as in the Duke himself also and your daughter.	55 / **entertained:** *treated* / **ceremonious:** *formal;* **wont:** *used to* / **abatement:** *reduction* / **dependants:** *servants* / 60
LEAR	Ha! say'st thou so?	
KNIGHT	I beseech you pardon me, my lord, if I be mistaken; for my duty cannot be silent when I think your Highness wronged.	
LEAR	Thou but rememb'rest me of mine own conception. I have perceived a most faint neglect of late, which I have rather blamed as mine own jealous curiosity than as a very pretence and purpose of unkindness. I will look further into't. But where's my Fool? I have not seen him this two days.	65 / **rememb'rest:** *remind* / **most faint:** *barely perceptible* / **jealous curiosity:** *sensitivity* / 70
KNIGHT	Since my young lady's going into France, sir, the Fool hath much pined away.	**young lady:** *Cordelia*
LEAR	No more of that; I have noted it well. Go you and tell my daughter I would speak with her. *[Exit Knight]* Go you, call hither my Fool.	75

Exit an Attendant.

Enter OSWALD the Steward.

	O, you, sir, you! Come you hither, sir. Who am I, sir?	
OSWALD	My lady's father.	
LEAR	'My lady's father'? My lord's knave! You whoreson dog! you slave! you cur!	80
OSWALD	I am none of these, my lord; I beseech your pardon.	
LEAR	Do you bandy looks with me, you rascal? *[Strikes him]*	**bandy:** *exchange insolent glances*
OSWALD	I'll not be strucken, my lord.	**Strucken:** *struck*
KENT	Nor tripped neither, you base football player? *[Trips up his heels]*	
LEAR	I thank thee, fellow. Thou serv'st me, and I'll love thee.	85
KENT	Come, sir, arise, away! I'll teach you differences. Away, away! If you will measure your lubber's length again, tarry; but away! Go to! Have you wisdom?	**differences:** *of rank* / **lubber:** *lout*

Exit OSWALD.

	So.	90
LEAR	Now, my friendly knave, I thank thee. There's earnest of thy service. *[Gives money]*	**earnest:** *sum paid to secure service*

Enter FOOL.

FOOL	Let me hire him too. Here's my coxcomb. *[Offers Kent his cap]*	**coxcomb:** *cap of the professional fool*
LEAR	How now, my pretty knave? How dost thou?	
FOOL	Sirrah, you were best take my coxcomb.	95
KENT	Why, Fool?	

Handwritten margin notes:

Lear admits he ha noticed disrespect in Goneril's attidude + household.

Evidence of Lears bad behaviour

FOOL	Why? For taking one's part that's out of favour. Nay, and thou canst not smile as the wind sits, thou'lt catch cold shortly. There, take my coxcomb! Why, this fellow hath banished two on's daughters, and did the third a blessing against his will. 100 If thou follow him, thou must needs wear my coxcomb – How now, nuncle? Would I had two coxcombs and two daughters!
LEAR	Why, my boy? 105
FOOL	If I gave them all my living, I'd keep my coxcombs myself. There's mine; beg another of thy daughters.
LEAR	Take heed, sirrah – the whip.
FOOL	Truth's a dog must to kennel; he must be whipped out, when Lady the brach may stand by the fire and stink. 110
LEAR	A pestilent gall to me!
FOOL	Sirrah, I'll teach thee a speech.
LEAR	Do.
FOOL	Mark it, nuncle. 115

> Have more than thou showest,
> Speak less than thou knowest,
> Lend less than thou owest,
> Ride more than thou goest,
> Learn more than thou trowest,   120
> Set less than thou throwest;
> Leave thy drink and thy whore,
> And keep in-a-door,
> And thou shalt have more
> Than two tens to a score.   125

KENT	This is nothing, fool.
FOOL	Then 'tis like the breath of an unfee'd lawyer; you gave me nothing for it. Can you make no use of nothing, nuncle?
LEAR	Why, no, boy. Nothing can be made out of nothing. 130
FOOL	[to Kent] Prithee tell him, so much the rent of his land comes to. He will not believe a fool.
LEAR	A bitter fool!
FOOL	Dost thou know the difference, my boy, between a bitter fool and a sweet fool? 135
LEAR	No, lad; teach me.
FOOL	That lord that counselled thee

> To give away thy land,
> Come place him here by me –
> Do thou for him stand.   140
> The sweet and bitter fool
> Will presently appear;
> The one in motley here,
> The other found out there.

| LEAR | Dost thou call me fool, boy?   145 |
| FOOL | All thy other titles thou hast given away; that thou wast born with. |

Handwritten note (line 105): notes line 100–101

Handwritten note (bottom): The fool believes that Lear has given everything away and needs to be taught self-control + prudence.

banished: *expelled their love and respect*
on's: *of his*

nuncle: *contracted from mine uncle*

Lady the brach: *bitch called Lady*
pestilent gall: *poisonous irritant*

showest: *show, display*
knowest: *know*
owest: *owe (or, own)*
goest: *walk*

in-a-door: *indoors*

unfee'd: *unpaid*

counselled: *advised*

motley: *fool's costume*
there: *indicates Lear as the bitter one*

* 109–10 **Truth's a dog … fire and stink:** *truth is imagined as an unwelcome dog forced into the doghouse, whereas the bitch, called Lady, enjoys a place of privilege.*

† 120 **Learn … trowest:** *'don't believe all that you hear'*

‡ 121 **Set less than thou throwest:** *don't risk all your winnings on a single throw.*

§ 116–25 *the speech is set in sing-song rhyme to emphasise its proverbial wisdom.*

KENT	This is not altogether fool, my lord.
FOOL	No, faith; lords and great men will not let me. If I had a monopoly out, they would have part on't. And ladies too, they will not let me have all the fool to myself; they'll be snatching. Give me an egg, nuncle, and I'll give thee two crowns.
LEAR	What two crowns shall they be?
FOOL	Why, after I have cut the egg in the middle and eat up the meat, the two crowns of the egg. When thou clovest thy crown i' th' middle and gav'st away both parts, thou bor'st thine ass on thy back o'er the dirt. Thou hadst little wit in thy bald crown† when thou gav'st thy golden one away. If I speak like myself in this, let him be whipped that first finds it so.

[Sings]   Fools had ne'er less grace in a year,
             For wise men are grown foppish;
             They know not how their wits to wear,
             Their manners are so apish.

LEAR	When were you wont to be so full of songs, sirrah?
FOOL	I have used it, nuncle, ever since thou mad'st thy daughters thy mother; for when thou gav'st them the rod, and put'st down thine own breeches,

[Sings]   Then they for sudden joy did weep,
             And I for sorrow sung,
             That such a king should play bo-peep
             And go the fools among.

Prithee, nuncle, keep a schoolmaster that can teach thy fool to lie. I would fain learn to lie.

LEAR	And you lie, sirrah, we'll have you whipped.
FOOL	I marvel what kin thou and thy daughters are. They'll have me whipped for speaking true; thou'lt have me whipped for lying; and sometimes I am whipped for holding my peace. I had rather be any kind o' thing than a fool! And yet I would not be thee, nuncle. Thou hast pared thy wit o' both sides and left nothing i' th' middle. Here comes one o' the

Enter GONERIL.

LEAR	How now, daughter? What makes that frontlet on? Methinks you are too much o' late i' th' frown.
FOOL	Thou wast a pretty fellow when thou hadst no need to care for her frowning. Now thou art an O without a figure. I am better than thou art now: I am a fool, thou art nothing.

[To Goneril] Yes, forsooth, I will hold my tongue. So your face bids me, though you say nothing.

        Mum, mum!
        He that keeps nor crust nor crum,
        Weary of all, shall want some.

[Points at Lear] That's a sheal'd peascod.

Line numbers: 150, 155, 160, 165, 170, 175, 180, 185, 190, 195

Handwritten margin note: Lear has placed himself in his daughters power

---

altogether fool: *completely foolish*

like myself: *like a fool*

foppish: *foolish*

apish: *imitative*

the rod: *symbol of power and control*

frontlet: *bandage wore on forehead*

O: *nought*

forsooth: *expletive, truly*

---

* 149–51 … they will not let me have all the fool … they'll be snatching: *the fool's speech is a punning response to Kent's words 'altogether fool'.*

† 156–8 When thou clovest thy crown … o'er the dirt: *alludes to Lear's division of the kingdom, symbolised by the crown, compares Lear to the foolish man who, out of a mistaken sense of kindness, carried his ass on his back instead of letting it carry him. Fool suggests that the natural hierarchical order has been inverted.*

‡ 187 too much o' late i' th' frown: *frowning too much of late*

GONERIL	Not only, sir, this your all-licensed fool,	
	But other of your insolent retinue	
	Do hourly carp and quarrel, breaking forth	200
	In rank and not-to-be-endured riots. Sir,	
	I had thought, by making this well known unto you,	
	To have found a safe redress, but now grow fearful,	
	By what yourself, too, late have spoke and done,	
	That you protect this course, and put it on	205
	By your allowance; which if you should, the fault	
	Would not scape censure, nor the redresses sleep,	
	Which, in the tender of a wholesome weal,	
	Might in their working do you that offence	
	Which else were shame, that then necessity	210
	Must call discreet proceeding.	
FOOL	For you know, nuncle,	
	The hedge-sparrow fed the cuckoo so long	
	That it had it head bit off by it young.	
	So out went the candle, and we were left darkling.	215
LEAR	Are you our daughter?	
GONERIL	Come, sir,	
	I would you would make use of that good wisdom	
	Whereof I know you are fraught, and put away	
	These dispositions that of late transport* you	
	From what you rightly are.	220
FOOL	May not an ass know when the cart draws the horse?	
	Whoop, Jug, I love thee!	
LEAR	Doth any here know me? This is not Lear.	
	Doth Lear walk thus? speak thus? Where are his eyes?	
	Either his notion weakens, his discernings	225
	Are lethargied – Ha! waking? 'Tis not so!	
	Who is it that can tell me who I am?	
FOOL	Lear's shadow.	
LEAR	I would learn that; for, by the marks of sovereignty,	
	Knowledge, and reason, I should be false persuaded	230
	I had daughters.	
FOOL	Which they will make an obedient father.	
LEAR	Your name, fair gentlewoman?	

Handwritten annotation (left margin, next to Fool's lines 213–215): shocked at her tone

Glossary (right column):

all-licensed: *free to say anything*
retinue: *attendants*
carp: *grumble*
rank: *gross*

safe redress: *sure remedy*
late: *recently*
put it on: *encourage it*
allowance: *approval*
scape: *escape*
wholesome weal: *healthy state*

proverbial tale of warning

darkling: *in the dark*

fraught: *furnished*
dispositions: *moods, humours*

Jug: *nickname for whore*

notion: *understanding*
Lethargied: *exhausted, weakened*

shadow: *pale imitation of himself*

Handwritten annotation (lower portion):

loosing self identity beginning to Relaise Goneril is showing no mercy.

NB. Lear loosing self identity crumbling lose of dignity entire life built on social Respect + obedience + he wa King now powerless Robbed of st cannot adjust to his Real His confusion touching f

* 206–11 Which if you should … discreet proceeding: *If you should approve this, then you are at fault and I will censure you and redress the riotous behaviour of your knights. My disciplinary measures, which would in other circumstances be considered as an offence to you and thus shameful, in this instance will be seen as necessary for the maintenance of a healthy state.*

GONERIL	This admiration, sir, is much o' th' savour
	Of other your new pranks. I do beseech you
	To understand my purposes aright.
	As you are old and reverend, you should be wise.
	Here do you keep a hundred knights and squires;
	Men so disordered, so deboshed, and bold
	That this our court, infected with their manners,
	Shows like a riotous inn. Epicurism and lust
	Make it more like a tavern or a brothel
	Than a graced palace. The shame itself doth speak
	For instant remedy. Be then desired
	By her that else will take the thing she begs
	A little to disquantity your train,
	And the remainder that shall still depend
	To be such men as may besort your age,
	Which know themselves, and you.
LEAR	Darkness and devils!
	Saddle my horses! Call my train together!
	Degenerate bastard, I'll not trouble thee;
	Yet have I left a daughter.
GONERIL	You strike my people, and your disordered rabble
	Make servants of their betters.

Enter ALBANY.

LEAR	Woe that too late repents! – O, sir, are you come?
	Is it your will? Speak, sir! – Prepare my horses.
	Ingratitude, thou marble-hearted fiend,
	More hideous when thou show'st thee in a child
	Than the sea-monster!
ALBANY	Pray, sir, be patient.
LEAR	*[to Goneril]* Detested kite, thou liest!
	My train are men of choice and rarest parts,
	That all particulars of duty know
	And in the most exact regard support
	The worships of their name. – O most small fault,
	How ugly didst thou in Cordelia show!
	Which, like an engine, wrenched my frame of nature
	From the fixed place; drew from my heart all love
	And added to the gall. O Lear, Lear, Lear!
	Beat at this gate that let thy folly in *[Strikes his head]*
	And thy dear judgment out! Go, go, my people.
ALBANY	My lord, I am guiltless, as I am ignorant
	Of what hath moved you.
LEAR	It may be so, my lord.
	Hear, Nature, hear! dear goddess, hear!
	Suspend thy purpose, if thou didst intend
	To make this creature fruitful.
	Into her womb convey sterility;
	Dry up in her the organs of increase;
	And from her derogate body never spring
	A babe to honour her! If she must teem,
	Create her child of spleen, that it may live
	And be a thwart disnatured torment to her.
	Let it stamp wrinkles in her brow of youth,
	With cadent tears fret channels in her cheeks,
	Turn all her mother's pains and benefits
	To laughter and contempt, that she may feel
	How sharper than a serpent's tooth it is
	To have a thankless child! Away, away! *[Exit]*

Right-hand glossary column:

235 admiration: *wonderment*

deboshed: *debauched*

240 Epicurism: *focus on pleasure*

speak: *ask*
desired: *requested*
245 her: *referring to herself*
disquantity: *reduce;* train: *attendants*

besort: *befit*

250

a daughter: *ref. to Regan*

betters: *superiors*

255 Woe: *woe to one who*

kite: *carrion bird*
260 choice: *select*

worships: *dignity*
265 didst thou: *the small fault*
like an engine: *the rack*
the fixed place: *foundations of his being*
gall: *bitterness*

270

thy purpose: *to reproduce*

275

derogate: *debased*
teem: *have children*
280 spleen: *of foul temperament*
thwart: *perverse*

cadent: *falling;* fret: *wear away*

285
....
* 234–5   o' th' savour … pranks: *this is characteristic of your recent childish behaviour.*

† 281   disnatured: *without natural affection*

Handwritten margin notes (left): "Key moment Lear's Realisation + acknowledgement of his foolish actions in banishing Cordelia NB knavery + haste"; "(Cordelia)"

ALBANY	Now, gods that we adore, whereof comes this?
GONERIL	Never afflict yourself to know the cause;
	But let his disposition have that scope
	That dotage gives it.

Enter LEAR.

LEAR	What, fifty of my followers at a clap?
	Within a fortnight?
ALBANY	What's the matter, sir?
LEAR	I'll tell thee. *[To Goneril]* Life and death! I am ashamed
	That thou hast power to shake my manhood thus;
	That these hot tears, which break from me perforce,
	Should make thee worth them. Blasts and fogs upon thee!
	Th' untented woundings of a father's curse
	Pierce every sense about thee! – Old fond eyes,
	Beweep this cause again, I'll pluck ye out,
	And cast you, with the waters that you loose,
	To temper clay. Yea, is it come to this?
	Let it be so. Yet have I left a daughter,
	Who I am sure is kind and comfortable.
	When she shall hear this of thee, with her nails
	She'll flay thy wolvish visage. Thou shalt find
	That I'll resume the shape which thou dost think
	I have cast off for ever; thou shalt, I warrant thee.

Exeunt LEAR, KENT, and Attendants.

GONERIL	Do you mark that, my lord?
ALBANY	I cannot be so partial, Goneril,
	To the great love I bear you –
GONERIL	Pray you, content. – What, Oswald, ho!
	[To the Fool] You, sir, more knave than fool, after
	your master!
FOOL	Nuncle Lear, nuncle Lear, tarry! Take the fool with thee.
	A fox when one has caught her,
	And such a daughter,
	Should sure to the slaughter,
	If my cap would buy a halter.
	So the fool follows after. *[Exit]*
GONERIL	This man hath had good counsel! A hundred knights?
	'Tis politic and safe to let him keep
	At point a hundred knights; yes, that on every dream,
	Each buzz, each fancy, each complaint, dislike,
	He may enguard his dotage with their powers
	And hold our lives in mercy. – Oswald, I say!
ALBANY	Well, you may fear too far.
GONERIL	Safer than trust too far.
	Let me still take away the harms I fear,
	Not fear still to be taken. I know his heart.
	What he hath uttered I have writ my sister.
	If she sustain him and his hundred knights,
	When I have show'd th' unfitness –

Enter OSWALD the Steward.

	How now, Oswald?
	What, have you writ that letter to my sister?

---

290   **disposition:** *mood, humour*

at a clap: *at one stroke*

295

Blasts: *gusts of foul air*
untented: *deep, unattended, thus infectious*
fond: *foolish*
300   **Beweep:** *if you weep for*
loose: *release*
temper clay: *to moisten earth with water*

comfortable: *able to comfort*

305   **visage:** *face*
the shape: *of kingship*

310   **partial:** *biased*

315

halter: *hangman's noose*

320

This man … : *speaks sarcastically*

At point: *in armed readiness*
buzz: *rumour*
325   **enguard:** *protect*
in mercy: *at his mercy*

330

---

* 296–7   **That these hot tears … worth them:** *that the tears that fall by force of the circumstances whereby you have power over me should suggest that you are worth them, that they are a sign that I care for you.*

† 312   **Pray you, content:** *Goneril cuts Albany off in mid-sentence.*

‡ 329   **Not fear still to be taken:** *rather than live in the fear of being overtaken*

OSWALD	Yes, madam.	
GONERIL	Take you some company, and away to horse!	335
	Inform her full of my particular fear,	
	And thereto add such reasons of your own	
	As may compact it more. Get you gone,	
	And hasten your return. [Exit Oswald] No, no, my lord!	
	This milky gentleness and course of yours,	340
	Though I condemn it not, yet, under pardon,	
	You are much more at task for want of wisdom	
	Than praised for harmful mildness.	
ALBANY	How far your eyes may pierce I cannot tell.	
	Striving to better, oft we mar what's well.	345
GONERIL	Nay then –	
ALBANY	Well, well; th' event.	

Exeunt.

full: *fully*; particular: *own*

compact it: *give it more weight*

milky: *mild and womanly*
under pardon: *with your pardon*
at task: *at fault*

may pierce: *see into the future*

th' event: *we shall see*

Handwritten notes:

Goneril acting independitly of her husband in the dark as she continues plotting. Dominint figure + distrust in everyone.

° Opening Goneril hostile heartless cold

Lear's chattering experience at Goneril's hands help to open Lear's eyes to the truth about himself + other's.

first public step to eleminal her father cruel making clear she has swaped rolls with her father.

This scene marks a sharp downward turn in Lear's fortunes the fools main function is make Lear Reconise his true position to make him relaise the he is out of favour with the 2 daughters to whom his

* 343   harmful mildness: *this oxymoron suggests that Albany's mild and gentle way may be harmful and dangerous under the circumstances*

Kent disguises himself and goes to Goneril's castle to be with Lear. He presents himself to Lear as a poor man who wishes to serve the king and his services are accepted. Oswald is disrespectful to the king and is subsequently beaten by Lear and Kent. The king's Fool appears and mocks Lear for being foolish enough to give away his kingdom. Goneril confronts Lear and tells him that his men are poorly behaved and that their numbers will have to be reduced. Lear, shocked and enraged that his own daughter would treat him this way, curses Goneril and laments his decision to banish Cordelia and give away his land. He says that he will leave Goneril's castle and go to stay with Regan. Goneril writes to Regan to advise her of events. Albany suggests to Goneril that she is acting harshly towards her father, but his words are ignored.

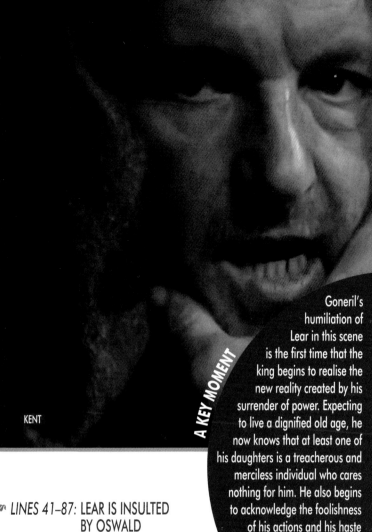

KENT

A KEY MOMENT

Goneril's humiliation of Lear in this scene is the first time that the king begins to realise the new reality created by his surrender of power. Expecting to live a dignified old age, he now knows that at least one of his daughters is a treacherous and merciless individual who cares nothing for him. He also begins to acknowledge the foolishness of his actions and his haste in banishing Cordelia. Unfortunately for Lear, it is only the first step on his long road to enlightenment.

ACTION

LINES 1–41: KENT REJOINS LEAR

Kent has entered Goneril's castle in disguise. He hopes that his disguise will be successful in order that he can continue to serve Lear: 'So may it come, thy master, whom thou lov'st,/ Shall find thee full of labours'. (6–7) Lear enters with his knights and servants. The king proves he is still in autocratic form by ordering a servant to fetch his dinner immediately: 'Let me stay not a jot for dinner: go, get it ready'. (8)

Kent asks Lear if he can be his servant. (12–13) He claims he does not know who Lear is, but wishes to serve him because of his authoritative appearance. (21–6) He says he is an honest and diligent man who can provide several services. (30–7) Lear agrees to take him on as a servant, displaying a touch of his moodiness in his answer: 'if I like thee no worse/ after dinner I will not part from thee yet'. (38–9)

He says that he is 'as poor as the king'. (18) Lear appears to display a glimmer of insight into the reality of his new position in his answer: 'If thou be as poor for a subject as he is for a king,/ thou art poor enough'. (19–20)

LINES 41–87: LEAR IS INSULTED BY OSWALD

Lear asks Oswald where Goneril is, but Oswald refuses to answer and walks off. (41–2) Lear sends a knight after him, but he refuses to return and answer the king's question: 'Sir, he answered me in the roundest manner,/ he would not'. (50–1) Lear is shocked at this insulting behaviour. One of his knight's tells him he has observed a general disrespect in the attitude of Goneril and her house. (55–8) Lear admits he has noticed something similar, although he was unsure if he was merely imagining it:

I have perceived a most faint neglect of late; which I have rather blamed as mine own jealous curiosity than as a very pretence and purpose of unkindness. (64–6)

Oswald re-enters. Lear asks him if he knows who he is. (74) Oswald's answer is highly discourteous: 'My lady's father'. (75) Lear is outraged that Oswald would describe him as Goneril's father rather than as king:

'My lady's father!' my lord's knave: you whoreson/ dog! You slave! You cur!' (76–7) Oswald offers a mocking, insincere apology and Lear strikes him. (79) Kent joins in, tripping Oswald, pushing him away and vowing to teach him some manners: 'I'll teach you differences'. (83) Lear thanks Kent and gives him money as a reward. (86)

Lear asks where the Fool is. The knight tells him that the Fool has been pining since Cordelia left for France. (70) His answer strikes a chord with Lear, who wishes to hear no more about his banished daughter: 'No more of that; I have noted it well'. (71) He sends an attendant to tell Goneril that he wishes to speak with her, and sends another to summon his fool.

LINES 87–172: THE FOOL

The Fool enters and offers Kent his clown's cap (the coxcomb). (86) He says that Kent is a fool for following a man who has surrendered his power: 'if thou follow him thou/ must needs wear my coxcomb'. (94–5) Initially Kent is not impressed with the fool's utterances: 'This is nothing, fool'. Eventually, however, he sees some wisdom in the Fool's words: 'This is not altogether fool, my lord'. (139)

The fool turns his attention to Lear. He mocks Lear in various ways for having been foolish enough to give away his kingdom:

- He says that if we were to give his possessions to his daughters he would at least keep two clown-caps, unlike Lear, who gave everything away. (96–102)
- He says he will teach Lear a speech about self-control and prudence: 'Have more than thou showest,/ Speak less than thou knowest,/ Lend less than thou owest'. (107–9) The Fool is obviously criticising Lear's temper and rash actions.
- He patronises Lear, addressing him as 'my boy' and reciting a ditty that suggests he's a 'sweet and bitter fool' for giving away his kingdom. (129–36) He says Lear 'hadst little wit in thy bald crown when thou/ gavest thy golden one away'. (150–2)
- When Lear asks him if he is calling him a fool, his reply is bitterly comic. Lear, he says, has given away all his other titles; 'Fool' is the only title he has left, a title that will be with him for life: 'All thy other titles thou hast given away; that thou/ wast born with'. (138–9)
- He suggests Lear's stupidity by singing a song about how wise men have grown foolish. (151–4)
- He says Lear has placed himself in his daughters' power: 'thou madest thy/ daughters thy mothers;

THE FOOL & LEAR

for when thou gavest them/ the rod and puttest down thine own breeches'. (157–8)

Lear seems genuinely fond of the fool. However, there are times during this exchange when he becomes annoyed at the fool's insolence. He calls him a 'pestilent gall', and threatens to have him whipped. (102) The Fool says he has no choice but to tell the truth. (103–4)

He sarcastically remarks that Lear should hire someone to teach his Fool to lie. (166–7) Lear responds by saying that if the Fool starts lying he'll have him whipped. The Fool comments on how alike Lear and his daughters are as they all want to have him whipped. Goneril wants to have him whipped for telling the truth, while Lear threatens to have him whipped for lying. (169–71)

LINES 184–241: GONERIL CONFRONTS LEAR

Goneril enters and Lear asks her why she looks so angry: 'Methinks you are too much of late i' the frown'. (174) The Fool remarks on how he cared nothing for Goneril's moods before because he had no need to. He says that he is in a better position than Lear: 'I am better than thou art now; I am a fool, thou/ art nothing'. (178) The Fool registers Goneril's disapproval and says he will keep silent. (179–80) Goneril begins to attack Lear in cold and formal language:

· She complains that he has hit her servants: 'You strike my people'. (240)

· She sarcastically suggests that he should use his 'good wisdom' to stop being so difficult and temperamental. (204–7)

· She says his fool is insulting and disrespectful.

· She says Lear's knights treat her

CHARACTER DEVELOPMENT

LEAR

AUTOCRATIC

At the beginning of this scene, we see that Lear is still acting and talking like a man in power. He orders his food to be fetched immediately after his return from hunting: 'Let me not stay a jot for dinner: go, get it ready'. (8) Likewise, the way he talks to the disguised Kent also displays his imperious nature: 'if I like thee no worse/ after dinner I will not part from thee yet'. (38) Lear still commands and expects his orders to be obeyed instantly. He cannot understand why those around him are not treating him with the respect they once used to: 'I think the world's/ asleep'. (45)

Lear seems to only vaguely realise that things in the kingdom have changed, that he has gone from being someone who was all powerful to someone who has no real power at all: 'I have perceived a most faint neglect of late; which I/ have rather blamed as mine own jealous curiosity/ than as a very pretence and purpose of unkindness'. (64–6) Unfortunately for Lear, he is now at the mercy of his daughters.

SELF-IDENTITY SHATTERED

The most striking aspect of Lear's reaction to his humiliation at the hands of Goneril is that his self-identity begins to show signs of crumbling. His entire life has been built on a system of social respect and obedience in which Lear occupied the highest point. But now that he has given away his power, his status is gone too.

Lear cannot adjust to this reality, and is incredulous at the treatment he receives. He asks Goneril 'Are you our daughter?' (203) People and the world suddenly seem strange to him. He is baffled and confused by the new order, and cannot come to terms with his lowly position in it: 'Does any here know me?/ This is not Lear'. (210) Lear's confusion is touching and pathetic. Although the king's arrogance may be unappealing, it is difficult not to feel sympathy for the confused old man we now see. His helplessness is best summed up by his cry 'Who is it that can tell me who I am?' (214)

SELF-KNOWLEDGE

Only now does Lear finally begin to realise his enormous foolishness in having given power to Regan and Goneril, and of having banished Cordelia: 'Woe, that too late repents'. (242) He knows now the stupidity of the love-test charade in the opening scene: 'O Lear, Lear, Lear!/ Beat at this gate, that let thy folly in/ And thy dear judgement out!' (257–9) Unfortunately for Lear, his trials have only just begun. He still has misplaced faith in Regan: 'I have another daughter,/ Who, I am sure, is kind and comfortable'. (291–2) We sense that Lear has enormous suffering to undergo before he truly realises the folly of his behaviour.

PRIDE AND ANGER

Once Lear finally sees that Goneril is now his enemy, his anger asserts itself in a ferocious tirade of hatred. He calls on Nature to make Goneril barren: 'Suspend thy purpose, if thou didst intend/ To make this creature fruitful! Into her womb convey sterility!' (263–5) He asks that if she should conceive, for her child to become her bitter enemy: 'if she must teem,/ Create her child of spleen, that it may live/ And be a thwart disnatur'd torment to her!' (267–9)

Lear wants Nature to avenge him, as he feels that Goneril has betrayed the natural duties of filial gratitude that children have toward their parents. He is so shook by Goneril's heartless treachery that he is moved to 'hot tears' in spite of himself. (283) Throughout the play, Lear will come to learn that Nature is a merciless force that takes pity on no-one.

palace like a tavern or a brothel, and treat her own people like their servants. (226–9)

· She says they fight and riot all the time: 'other of your insolent retinue/ Do hourly carp and quarrel, breaking forth/ In rank and not-to-be-endured riots'. (187)

· She says that if Lear and his retinue don't behave she will have to take action against them: 'that then necessity/ Will call discreet proceeding'. (198)

· She says that if he does not reduce the number of his retinue, she will dismiss some of them herself, and leave him with an escort that is appropriate to his age. (232–5)

Lear is shocked and baffled by Goneril's tone. He cannot believe that one of his daughters could talk to him like this: 'Are you our daughter?' (203) Lear now sees Goneril as a stranger, and asks her who she is: 'Your name, fair gentlewoman?' (220) Goneril pretends that Lear's astonishment is another part of his disruptive behaviour: 'This admiration, sir, is much 'o the favour/ Of other your new pranks'. (221–2)

Lear says he's confused and needs someone to tell him who he is: 'Who is it that can tell me who I am?' (214) Lear seems not to know who he is or what's going on: 'Does any here know me? This is not Lear:/ Does Lear walk thus? Speak thus? Where are his/ eyes?' (210–11) The Fool tells him that he is now only 'Lear's shadow'. (215)

The king is beginning to realise that Goneril is going to show him no mercy: 'I should be false persuaded I/ had daughters'. (218) Lear is seized with anger and orders his men to be called together for departure. He calls Goneril a 'degenerate bastard', and expresses his faith in Regan: 'I'll not trouble thee:/ Yet have I left a daughter'. (238–9)

LINES 242–96: LEAR'S REMORSE AND ANGER

Lear appears to realise that he has made a massive error of judgement in regard to his daughters: 'Woe, that too late repents'. (242) It dawns on him that he has wronged Cordelia for her inability to flatter him, which was ultimately an insignificant failing: 'O most small fault,/ How ugly didst thou in Cordelia show!' (252–3) The king cannot believe his own stupidity: 'O Lear, Lear, Lear!/ Beat at this gate, that let thy folly in/ And thy dear judgement out!' (256–8)

Lear flies into a rage with Goneril. He accuses her of slandering his retinue: 'My train are men of choice and rarest parts'. (249) He curses her cruelty, saying she has a heart as cold as marble: 'In gratitude, thou marble-hearted fiend,/ More hideous, when thou show'st thee in a child,/ Than

GONERIL

A HEARTLESS DAUGHTER

In this scene Goneril takes the first public step in her plan to eliminate her father. In doing so, she displays complete heartlessness and cruelty. She initially addresses Lear in extremely cold and unfeeling language ('That you protect his course, and put it on ...'). Lear is so taken aback that he wonders who Goneril has become: 'Are you our daughter?' (203)

Goneril uses the pretext of Lear's riotous knights as an opening by which to destroy her father. She knows that by threatening to reduce their number, she is publicly asserting her new power and the real helplessness of Lear. She is making it clear for all to see that she and her father have now swapped roles. Goneril puts on the necessary diplomatic airs by making patronising references to Lear's advanced age and the small allowances that he is thereby due, knowing full well that this is only likely to inflame him and make him look ridiculous.

AN ASSERTIVE WIFE

Goneril's assertive qualities are also illustrated by the fact that she appears to be acting completely independently of her husband Albany. The latter has no idea what is going on when he enters, and it becomes apparent that Goneril has been keeping him in the dark as regards to her plotting.

She also feels that he does not need to know the reasons behind her manoeuvring: 'Never afflict yourself to know the cause'. (277) Her dominance is also illustrated by the instances where she cuts Albany off in mid-sentence. (300, 315) Goneril tells him straight out that he suffers from 'want of wisdom'. (330) It is clear in this scene that, at the moment, Goneril is the dominant partner in her marriage.

DISTRUSTFUL

Goneril's distrust of others is total. It is quite noticeable that she seems to lack complete faith even in her partner-in-crime Regan. She has written her a letter warning her of Lear's arrival, but cannot be sure in her own mind if Regan will go along with her plan: 'If she sustain him and his hundred knights,/ When I have show'd the unfitness.' (319–20) The seeds of further betrayal and plotting are already present even at this early stage of the play.

ALBANY, GONERIL & LEAR

the sea-monster'. (245–7) Lear calls on Nature to punish Goneril by making her infertile:

> Suspend thy purpose, if thou didst intend
> To make this creature fruitful!
> Into her womb convey sterility!' (263–5)

He asks that if she does reproduce, her child should be a torment to her, just as she is to Lear. (267–9) Lear wants her to know the pain of having a thankless child: 'that she may feel/ How sharper than a serpent's tooth it is/ To have a thankless child!' (273–5)

Lear exits briefly but re-enters in a rage. He has discovered that Goneril has dismissed fifty of his knights. (280–1) Lear is now distraught and weeping, and is ashamed of his emotion: 'I am asham'd/ That thou hast power to shake my manhood thus'. (283–4) He says that he will pluck out his eyes rather than continue to cry. (287–90)

His last hope is Regan. He still believes that she will treat him well: 'I have another daughter,/ Who, I am sure, is kind and comfortable'. (291–2) Regan will avenge him: 'with her nails/ She'll flay thy wolvish visage'. (293–4) Lear threatens to somehow regain his power so that he can punish Goneril: 'I'll resume the shape which thou dost think/ I have cast off for ever; thou shalt, I warrant thee'. (294–6) He exits with his attendants. The Fool remains behind until Goneril tells him to leave. (301–8)

LINES 297–335: GONERIL'S SCHEMES

Goneril asks Albany if he has seen what has occurred. She clearly expects him to side with her. Albany, however, is not prepared to blindly follow her: 'I cannot be so partial, Goneril,/ To the great love I bear you'. (298–9) Goneril attempts to justify her halving of Lear's retinue. She says that if her father were to keep

CHARACTER DEVELOPMENT

THE FOOL

THE TRUTH-TELLER

The figure of the Fool traditionally had two roles: that of entertaining the audience with slapstick knockabout comedy, and that of acting as the voice of truth through means of songs and riddles. The Fool can tell the truth because he is officially at the bottom of society and can go no lower. He is therefore immune from punishment. Paradoxically, the low regard with which the Fool is held gives him the power to speak truthfully in a manner that is denied to other characters, who must obey society's rules in order to protect their position.

Telling the truth is certainly the Fool's main role in the play. He speaks frankly about Lear's powerlessness now that he has given his kingdom away. He says that Kent is a fool for volunteering to follow Lear, a man who wields no power: 'if thou follow him thou/ must needs wear my coxcomb'. (94–5) He is particularly relentless in telling Lear how stupid he was to relinquish power to his daughters. When Lear asks him if he is calling him a fool, the Fool's response is sharp and cutting: 'All thy other titles thou hast given away; that thou/ wast born with'. (138)

The Fool also perceives the true nature of Goneril long before Lear does. He sees that Lear has now 'madest thy/ daughters thy mothers'. (157) He also knows that Lear's children intend him harm: 'The hedge-sparrow fed the cuckoo so long,/ That it had it head bit off by it young'. (200–1)

Although the Fool may sometimes appear to be a little cruel in the way he seems to taunt Lear, we know that he loves his master and is only trying to awaken him to the reality of the new situation. For this he is not thanked. Lear threatens to have him whipped, as does Goneril. The Fool knows his task is a thankless one: 'Truth's a dog must to kennel; he must be whipped out/ when Lady the brach may stand by the fire and stink'. (101–2)

a hundred armed knights, their lives would be in danger due to the king's unpredictable moods:

> *Each buzz, each fancy, each complaint, dislike,*
> *he may enguard his dotage with their powers,*
> *And hold our lives in mercy.* (312–14)

She says she will send a letter to Regan describing her father's behaviour. Significantly, she displays the first small sign of distrust in her sister: 'If she sustain him and his hundred knights,/ When I have show'd the unfitness'. (319–20) Oswald enters and tells Goneril he has written the letter as ordered. (321–3) She tells him to go to Regan, deliver the letter, and add whatever details he thinks may support her cause (324–7)

Albany feels that Goneril is being a little paranoid about Lear's knights: 'Well, you may fear too far'. (315) He has reservations about his wife's treatment of her father: 'How far your eyes may pierce I cannot tell:/ Striving to better, oft we mar what's well'. (332–3) Goneril says that it is better to be cautious: 'Safer than trust too far'. (316) She says her husband is a kind and gentle person but perhaps lacks wisdom. (328–30) Albany says they will await the outcome of her actions: 'Well, well, the event'. (334–5)

SOME LINES TO LEARN

Truth's a dog must to kennel; he must be whipped out when Lady the brach may stand by the fire and stink
The Fool (101)

Who is it that can tell me who I am?
Lear (215)

Hear, Nature, hear! Dear goddess, hear! Suspend thy purpose, if thou didst intend To make this creature fruitful! Into her womb convey sterility!
Lear (262–5)

How sharper than a serpent's tooth it is To have a thankless child!
Lear (274–5)

CHARACTER DEVELOPMENT

KENT

A LOYAL SERVANT
Kent proves his unquestioning loyalty to Lear in this scene. He has risked his life to return in disguise so that he may serve and protect the man who banished him and threatened him with death: 'if thou canst serve where thou dost stand condemn'd,/ So may it come, thy master, whom thou lov'st,/ Shall find thee full of labours'. (4–6)

He immediately becomes involved in the drama of the scene when he trips up Oswald in retaliation for the latter's insolence toward Lear. (81) This act earns him the king's trust: 'I thank thee, fellow; thou servest me, and I'll love thee'. (82)

Kent receives a small bit of abuse from the Fool for being loyal to a man who has voluntarily surrendered his power, but he does come to see that the Fool's warnings to Lear are accurate and deserve to be listened to: 'This is not altogether fool, my lord'. (139) Kent will prove to be a beacon of loyalty throughout the ordeals that await Lear.

ALBANY

IN THE DARK
It is made quickly apparent that Albany is not party to Goneril's scheming. When he enters, he is baffled as to the reason for Lear's anger: 'My lord, I am guiltless, as I am ignorant/ Of what hath mov'd you'. (259–60) He continually asks Lear what is troubling him, but Lear's rage at Goneril stops him from explaining.

THE VOICE OF MODERATION
Albany attempts to be the voice of reason in this scene. He tells his wife that his love for her will not bias him: 'I cannot be so partial, Goneril,/ To the great love I bear you'. (298–9) He also tells Goneril that she may be suffering from paranoia in regard to Lear: 'Well, you may fear too far'. (315) He is continually interrupted by Goneril, until the last words in the scene, when he tells her they will wait to see how things develop. (335)

OSWALD

GONERIL'S LOYAL SERVANT
Oswald acts as a sort of counterpart to Kent by unquestionably obeying his mistress' orders. He is rude to Lear, and insults him by calling him 'My lady's father'. (75) He is struck by Lear and tripped up by Kent for his troubles. His last act in the scene is to act as a messenger boy for Goneril's letter to Regan.

ACT 1 SCENE 5

Court before the Duke of Albany's palace

Enter LEAR, KENT, and FOOL.

LEAR	Go you before to Gloucester with these letters. Acquaint my daughter no further with anything you know than comes from her demand out of the letter. If your diligence be not speedy, I shall be there afore you.	5
KENT	I will not sleep, my lord, till I have delivered your letter.	

Exit.

FOOL   If a man's brains were in's heels, were't not in danger of kibes?

LEAR   Ay, boy.

FOOL   Then I prithee be merry. Thy wit shall not go slip-shod.   10

LEAR   Ha, ha, ha!

FOOL   Shalt see thy other daughter will use thee kindly; for though she's as like this as a crab's like an apple, yet I can tell what I can tell.   15

LEAR   What canst tell, boy?

FOOL   She'll taste as like this as a crab does to a crab. Thou canst tell why one's nose stands i' th' middle on's face?

LEAR   No.   20

FOOL   Why, to keep one's eyes of either side's nose, that what a man cannot smell out, he may spy into.

LEAR   *N.B* I did her wrong. *Cordelia.*

FOOL   Canst tell how an oyster makes his shell?   25

LEAR   No.

FOOL   Nor I neither; but I can tell why a snail has a house.

LEAR   Why?

FOOL   Why, to put his head in; not to give it away to his daughters, and leave his horns without a case.   30

LEAR   I will forget my nature. So kind a father! – Be my horses ready?

FOOL   Thy asses are gone about 'em. The reason why the seven stars are no moe than seven is a pretty reason.

LEAR   Because they are not eight?   35

FOOL   Yes indeed. Thou wouldst make a good fool.

LEAR   To take it again perforce! Monster ingratitude!

FOOL   If thou wert my fool, nuncle, I'ld have thee beaten for being old before thy time.

LEAR   How's that?   40

FOOL   Thou shouldst not have been old till thou hadst been wise.

LEAR   O, let me not be mad, not mad, sweet heaven! Keep me in temper; I would not be mad!

Enter a GENTLEMAN.

LEAR   How now? Are the horses ready?   45

GENTLEMAN   Ready, my lord.

LEAR   Come, boy.

FOOL   She that's a maid now, and laughs at my departure, Shall not be a maid long, unless things be cut shorter.

Exeunt.

Gloucester: *the town of*

demand: *enquiries*

kibes: *chilblains*

slip-shod: *in slippers*

crab: *crab-apple, a sour wild apple*

as like this: *as like Goneril*
on's: *of his*

her: *refers to Cordelia*

forget: *lose;* **nature:** *fatherly instinct*

asses: *servants*

it: *the sway of kingship*

in temper: *in balance*

....
* 12   **kindly:** *pun on kind, suggests both affectionately and according to her kind (she is like her kin, Goneril).*

† 42   **let me not be mad:** *Lear's passion is increasing*

LEAR & THE FOOL

Lear sends Kent ahead to Regan with a letter in which he outlines his side of the story. The Fool jokes with Lear and criticises him for his lack of wisdom. Lear suddenly fears that he will lose his sanity.

ACTION

LINES 1–6: LEAR ACTS

We are outside Goneril's palace. Lear has decided to send a letter to Regan telling her of his humiliation at Goneril's hands. He still has faith in his other daughter, and intends to pre-empt Goneril by getting his side of the story to Regan before she does: 'Acquaint my daughter no further with any thing you/ know than comes from her demand out of the letter'. (2–3) He sends Kent in all haste with the letter.

LINES 6–47: THE FOOL AND LEAR

Lear and the Fool are left alone. The Fool attempts to cheer his master up by telling him jokes, which also serve as warnings to Lear about his actions. His first witticism about a man's brains being in his heels refers to the Fool's belief that Lear is misguided in seeking refuge with Regan. (6–11)

The Fool then tries to warn Lear that his daughters are identical in their malice: 'Shalt see thy other daughter will use thee kindly; for/ though she's as like this as a crab is like an apple, yet/ I can tell what I can tell'. (13–15) When Lear asks him to explain his meaning, the Fool says that Regan will treat him no differently than Goneril: 'She will taste as like this as a crab does to a crab'. (17) The Fool continues with his riddles, comparing Lear's surrender of the throne to a snail giving up his shell. (26–9)

Thou shouldst not have been old before thou
hadst been wise

The Fool (41–2)

O! let me not be mad, not mad, sweet heaven;
Keep me in temper; I would not be mad!

Lear (43–4)

SOME LINES TO LEARN

CHARACTER DEVELOPMENT

Lear is only half listening to the Fool's jesting. He is very distracted, and acknowledges the injustice he perpetrated against Cordelia: 'I did her wrong'. (23) Lear, however, is still remonstrating with himself: 'I will forget my nature. So kind a father!' (30) He dreams of regaining his power and clearly still cannot come to terms with Goneril's behaviour: 'To take it again perforce! Monster ingratitude!' (37)

The Fool becomes more direct in his criticism, telling Lear he would have him beaten if he could for his lack of wisdom: 'shouldst not have been old before thou hadst/ been wise'. (41–2) Lear now has a terrifying premonition of what awaits him. He suddenly fears he may lose his sanity: 'O! let me not be mad, not mad, sweet heaven;/ Keep me in temper; I would not be mad!' (43–4) A servant comes to tell him his horses are ready and he departs with the Fool. (45–7)

LEAR

CONFUSED

In this scene we see that Lear is still in a state of shock after his humiliation at the hands of his daughter. He is obviously very distracted and confused. He only half-listens to the Fool's riddles and witticisms, and mumbles his thoughts aloud.

SELF-AWARENESS

The king is gradually realising the terrible consequences of his actions. He knows now that he treated Cordelia in a monstrously unjust manner: 'I did her wrong'. (23) More tellingly, he has a sudden intuition of his fate and is terrified by the prospect: 'O! let me not be mad, not mad, sweet heaven;/ Keep me in temper; I would not be mad!' (43–4) Our sympathy for Lear grows as we now see him teetering toward madness.

THE FOOL

CRUELLY KIND

The Fool shows his affection and love for Lear in this scene by trying to gently awaken him to the awful truth of his situation. His riddles and jokes, as well as being an attempt to cheer up the king, are an indirect means of warning his master about Regan in order that he may protect himself. The Fool shows that he is shrewd; he knows that Regan will act no differently than Goneril: 'She will taste as like this as a crab does to a crab'. (17) The Fool cares only for Lear's welfare.

A court within the castle of the Earl of Gloucester

Enter EDMUND and CURAN, meeting.

EDMUND	Save thee, Curan.
CURAN	And you, sir. I have been with your father, and given him notice that the Duke of Cornwall and Regan his Duchess will be here with him this night.
EDMUND	How comes that?
CURAN	Nay, I know not. You have heard of the news abroad? I mean the whispered ones, for they are yet but ear-kissing arguments?
EDMUND	Not I. Pray you, what are they?
CURAN	Have you heard of no likely wars toward 'twixt the two Dukes of Cornwall and Albany?
EDMUND	Not a word.
CURAN	You may do, then, in time. Fare you well, sir. *[Exit]*
EDMUND	The Duke be here to-night? The better! Best!

This weaves itself perforce into my business.
My father hath set guard to take my brother;
And I have one thing, of a queasy question,
Which I must act. Briefness and fortune, work!
Brother, a word! Descend: Brother, I say!

Enter EDGAR.

My father watches. O sir, fly this place!
Intelligence is given where you are hid.
You have now the good advantage of the night.
Have you not spoken 'gainst the Duke of Cornwall?
He's coming hither; now, i' th' night, i' th' haste,
And Regan with him. – Have you nothing said
Upon his party 'gainst the Duke of Albany?
Advise yourself.

EDGAR	I am sure on't, not a word.
EDMUND	I hear my father coming. Pardon me!

In cunning I must draw my sword upon you.
Draw, seem to defend yourself; now quit you well.
Yield! Come before my father. Light, ho, here!
Fly, brother. – Torches, torches! – So farewell.

Exit EDGAR.

Some blood drawn on me would beget opinion
Of my more fierce endeavour. *[Stabs his arm]* I have seen drunkards
Do more than this in sport. – Father, father! –
Stop, stop! No help?

Enter GLOUCESTER, and Servants with torches.

GLOUCESTER	Now, Edmund, where's the villain?

Line numbers: 5, 10, 15, 20, 25, 30, 35

Save thee: *God save thee*

news abroad: *news traveling around*

ear-kissing arguments: *rumours*

toward: *about to happen*

queasy: *sensitive nature*
Briefness: *speed*

Intelligence: *information*

Upon his party: *on his side*
Advise: *think on it*

cunning: *device, pretence*
quit: *behave*

beget opinion: *create a false impression*

* 23–7 spoken 'gainst … Advise yourself: *Edmund is planting seeds of doubt and suspicion in Edgar's mind regarding his safety;*

† 29 In cunning I must draw my sword upon you: *his cunning is used against rather than for Edgar.*

N.B. The subplot mirrors the main plot in the deception of Gloucester by his hypicrital son edmund +

EDMUND	Here stood he in the dark, his sharp sword out,
	Warbling of wicked charms, conjuring the moon
	To stand auspicious mistress.
GLOUCESTER	But where is he?
EDMUND	Look, sir, I bleed.
GLOUCESTER	Where is the villain, Edmund?
EDMUND	Fled this way, sir. When by no means he could –
GLOUCESTER	Pursue him, ho! Go after.

Exeunt some Servants.

	By no means what?
EDMUND	Persuade me to the murther of your lordship;
	But that I told him the revenging gods
	'Gainst parricides did all their thunders bend;
	Spoke with how manifold and strong a bond
	The child was bound to th' father – sir, in fine,
	Seeing how loathly opposite I stood
	To his unnatural purpose, in fell motion
	With his prepared sword he charges home
	My unprovided body, lanc'd mine arm;
	But when he saw my best alarum'd spirits,
	Bold in the quarrel's right, rous'd to th' encounter,
	Or whether gasted by the noise I made,
	Full suddenly he fled.
GLOUCESTER	Let him fly far.
	Not in this land shall he remain uncaught;
	And found – dispatch. The noble Duke my master,
	My worthy arch and patron, comes to-night.
	By his authority I will proclaim it
	That he which find, him shall deserve our thanks,
	Bringing the murderous caitiff to the stake;
	He that conceals him, death.
EDMUND	When I dissuaded him from his intent
	And found him pight to do it, with curst speech
	I threaten'd to discover him. He replied,
	'Thou unpossessing bastard, dost thou think,
	If I would stand against thee, would the reposal
	Of any trust, virtue, or worth in thee
	Make thy words faith'd? No. What I should deny
	(As this I would; ay, though thou didst produce
	My very character), I'ld turn it all
	To thy suggestion, plot, and damned practice;
	And thou must make a dullard of the world,
	If they not thought the profits of my death
	Were very pregnant and potential spurs
	To make thee seek it.'
GLOUCESTER	Strong and fastened villain!
	Would he deny his letter? I never got him.

Tucket within.

	Hark, the Duke's trumpets! I know not why he comes.
	All ports I'll bar; the villain shall not scape;
	The Duke must grant me that. Besides, his picture
	I will send far and near, that all the kingdom
	May have due note of him, and of my land,
	Loyal and natural boy, I'll work the means
	To make thee capable.

Line numbers: 40, 45, 50, 55, 60, 65, 70, 75, 80

Glossary (right column):

Warbling: *singing, chanting*
mistress: *allusion to Hecate*

parricides: *killing of fathers*
manifold: *many-sided*
in fine: *in short, to sum up*
loathly opposite: *grossly opposed*
fell motion: *fierce movement*
prepared: *drawn*
unprovided: *unprotected*

gasted: *frightened (aghast)*

dispatch: *death*
arch: *superior*

caitiff: *miserable wretch*

pight: *determined;* curst: *angry*

unpossessing: *no rights of inheritance*
reposal: *placing*

faith'd: *believed*

character: *handwriting*

dullard: *fool*

pregnant: *full of potential*

fastened: *fixed, complete*

scape: *escape*

natural: *two senses: illegitimate / loving*
capable: *of inheriting*

* 37–8   Warbling … mistress: *Edgar's description of Edmund's occult activities
feeds Gloucester's fear of supernatural
forces.*

† 45   thunders bend: *aim their thunderbolts*

Handwritten annotations (bottom left):

• the meanness of Regan shunning her father's visit.

N.B. • Lear has unleashed a monster in dividing his kingdom
• Rivalry between Cornwall + Albany (mistake of Lear to divide kingdom)
• Gloucester's easy acceptance of his loyal son Edgar betraying him

Enter CORNWALL, REGAN, and Attendants.

CORNWALL	How now, my noble friend? Since I came hither	85
	(Which I can call but now) I have heard strange news.	
REGAN	If it be true, all vengeance comes too short	
	Which can pursue th' offender. How dost, my lord?	
GLOUCESTER	O madam, my old heart is crack'd, it's crack'd!	
REGAN	What, did my father's godson seek your life?	90
	He whom my father nam'd? Your Edgar?	
GLOUCESTER	O lady, lady, shame would have it hid!	
REGAN	Was he not companion with the riotous knights	
	That tend upon my father?	
GLOUCESTER	I know not, madam. 'Tis too bad, too bad!	95
EDMUND	Yes, madam, he was of that consort.	
REGAN	No marvel then though he were ill affected.	
	'Tis they have put him on the old man's death,	
	To have th' expense and waste of his revenues.	
	I have this present evening from my sister	100
	Been well inform'd of them, and with such cautions	
	That, if they come to sojourn at my house,	
	I'll not be there.	
CORNWALL	Nor I, assure thee, Regan.	
	Edmund, I hear that you have shown your father	105
	A childlike office.	
EDMUND	'Twas my duty, sir.	
GLOUCESTER	He did betray his practice, and received	
	This hurt you see, striving to apprehend him.	
CORNWALL	Is he pursued?	
GLOUCESTER	Ay, my good lord.	
CORNWALL	If he be taken, he shall never more	
	Be fear'd of doing harm. Make your own purpose,	110
	How in my strength you please. For you, Edmund,	
	Whose virtue and obedience doth this instant	
	So much commend itself, you shall be ours.	
	Natures of such deep trust we shall much need;	
	You we first seize on.	115
EDMUND	I shall serve you, sir,	
	Truly, however else.	
GLOUCESTER	For him I thank your Grace.	
CORNWALL	You know not why we came to visit you	
REGAN	Thus out of season, threading dark-ey'd night.	
	Occasions, noble Gloucester, of some prize,	
	Wherein we must have use of your advice.	120
	Our father he hath writ, so hath our sister,	
	Of differences, which I best thought it fit	
	To answer from our home. The several messengers	
	From hence attend dispatch. Our,	
	Lay comforts to your bosom, and bestow	
	Your needful counsel to our business,	
	Which craves the instant use.	
GLOUCESTER	I serve you, madam.	
	Your Graces are right welcome.	

Exeunt. Flourish.

Side glossary:

How now: *how is it now*

consort: *company*
ill affected: *badly influenced*
put: *encouraged*
revenues: *wealth*

assure thee: *be assured*

childlike office: *filial service*

practice: *plans*

ours: *use of the royal plural*

threading: *passing through (as in a needle)*
Occasions: *business*

attend: *await orders to be sent back*

....

* 90   **What, did my father's godson seek your life?** : *Edgar is Lear's godson. Their connection highlighted by Regan, also suggests how their fates are linked as both suffer from political and familial deception and disorder.*

† 111   **How in my strength you please:** *Use my authority and power as you see fit.*

‡ 123–4 **I best thought it fit / To answer from our home:** *Regan's decision to leave her home makes it easier for her to both avoid accepting Lear into her home and consult with Goneril.*

Handwritten annotations:

He uses Cornwall to achieve more status + power.

* Edgar cunning, meanipathshrewd, knowledge of human nature (greatest asset).
* Regan - strong women dominent, evil minded, able to express clearly her opoions (calls for edgar to be punished) * Gloucester blind but respected unforgiving like Lear, harsh Openly disowns his

EDGAR & EDMUND

Edmund makes Edgar appear guilty by convincing him to flee Gloucester's castle just as his father is arriving. Edmund then tells Gloucester that Edgar was plotting to murder him. Gloucester believes everything that Edmund tells him. When Cornwall and Regan arrive at Gloucester's castle, they commend Edmund for taking action against Edgar, and ask him to serve them. Regan asks Gloucester for advice regarding Lear.

ACTION

✎ LINES 1–13: CIVIL UNREST?

Edmund and his servant Curren are talking in Gloucester's castle. Curren informs Edmund that Cornwall and Regan are on their way to the castle. (2–4) Curran also tells Edmund that there are whispers of a war brewing between Cornwall and Albany. (10–11) Curran exits.

Edmund is pleased by Curran's news. He thinks that Cornwall's arrival might fit into his plans to make Edgar flee: 'This weaves itself perforce into my business'. (15) He calls out for Edgar. (15–17)

✎ LINES 14–36: EDMUND ENSNARES EDGAR

Edmund wants to make Edgar look guilty. He plans to confuse and bamboozle Edgar so that he will panic and flee Gloucester's castle. Edmund knows that if

Edgar flees the castle, he will appear guilty in the eyes of his father.

When Edgar appears, Edmund pretends to be in a state of distress. He advises Edgar to flee. (20–2) He tells Edgar that Gloucester is looking for him, and suggests that Cornwall is rushing to the castle because Edgar spoke out against him: 'Have you not spoken 'gainst the Duke of Cornwall?' (23) He confuses Edgar further by asking him if he has spoken out against Albany. (26)

Edgar is now thoroughly puzzled: 'I am sure on't, not a word'. (27) Edgar is in such a state of confusion that he does whatever Edmund tells him. Firstly, he obeys Edmund's instruction to draw his sword. He then obeys Edmund's instruction to run away.

Edmund makes it seem that he is defending Gloucester from Edgar. (31) He shouts out 'Yield! – come before my father', and calls for servants to come with torches. (31) He cuts himself to make it look as if Edgar has wounded him. (33)

LINES 37–85: GLOUCESTER IS FOOLED

Gloucester and his servants enter to investigate what is happening. Edmund now begins to spin his web:

· He says that Edgar tried to persuade him to murder Gloucester.
· He tells his father that Edgar was standing in the dark with his sword drawn, and calling upon dark forces to help him ('Mumbling of wicked charms, conjuring the moon/ To stand auspicious mistress').
· He says that he refused to cooperate with Edgar's dastardly plan. To kill one's father is to sin against the will of the gods and natural law. (48–51)
· Edmund says that Edgar was enraged by his refusal to co-operate, drew his sword and wounded his arm before fleeing. (53–6)
· He points to where Edgar fled (presumably in a false direction, so as to give Edgar time to make his escape).

CHARACTER DEVELOPMENT

EDMUND

A CAPABLE VILLAIN

In this scene, Edmund displays his great intelligence and cunning. He is a master actor and manipulator. He effortlessly persuades Edgar to participate in the mock fight, and arranges the timing of Gloucester's entry perfectly. His determination to achieve his ends is proven by his willingness to cut himself in order to lend plausibility to his story.

A MASTER MANIPULATOR

Edmund also shows he has great insight into human nature with his masterful psychological manipulation. He confuses Edgar with his suggestions that he has offended either Cornwall or Albany, and allows his brother no time to pause or reflect on events.

He cleverly plays on Gloucester's superstitious nature by claiming that he overheard Edgar 'mumbling of wicked charms, conjuring the moon/ To stand auspicious mistress'. (39–40) He adds to this by pretending to have told his brother that 'the revenging gods/ 'Gainst parricides did all their thunders bend'. (48–9)

His cleverest stroke, however, is probably when he anticipates the suspicion that may fall on him by claiming that Edgar said that no one would take his word as truth because he stood to gain so much by his brother's death. (72–7) It is a brilliant piece of psychology.

Edmund also seizes the opportunity to ingratiate himself with Cornwall and Regan. He lends support to Regan's (presumably false) claim that Edgar was friendly with Lear's unruly entourage, and that this caused him to plot against his father: 'Yes, madam, he was of that consort'. (97) Edmund shows that he is a brilliant opportunist.

GLOUCESTER & EDMUND

But I told him, the revenging gods
'Gainst parricides did all their thunders bend;
Spoke with how manifold and strong a bond
The child was bound to the father
Edmund (45–8)

SOME LINES TO LEARN

Edmund knows that two things might cause people to doubt his story: 1) As an illegitimate child he is automatically perceived as untrustworthy; 2) He stands to gain from Edgar's fall from grace. He cleverly mentions these issues himself in order to minimise the impact they would have on his credibility.

Gloucester completely swallows Edmund's story. He disowns Edgar, saying he never fathered him: 'I never got him'. (78) He says that he will arrange for Edmund to be his heir: 'and of my land,/ Loyal and natural boy, I'll work the means/ To make thee capable'. (83–5)

Gloucester says that no matter how far Edgar gets, he will be found and killed ('dispatch'). (58) A bounty will be put on his head, and anyone who shields him will be put to death.

LINES 86–104: EDGAR IS SLANDERED
Cornwall, Regan and their attendants enter. Somehow, news has already spread of the dramatic events. Regan calls for Edgar to be punished: 'If it be true, all vengeance comes too short/ Which can pursue the offender'. (88–9)

Regan wants to strip Lear of his troops and undermine whatever power the old king has left. She therefore falsely suggests that Lear's 'riotous knights' might have influenced Edgar to attack Gloucester: 'Was he not companion with the riotous knights/ That tend upon my father?' (94–5) Edmund confirms this suggestion even though he knows it to be false: 'Yes, madam, he was of that consort'. (97)

Cornwall tells Edmund that he has heard of his 'brave deeds': 'I hear that you have shown your father/ A child-like office'. (106–7) He is so impressed that he asks Edmund to serve him. (112–14) Edmund agrees to enter Cornwall's service, and pledges his allegiance; 'I shall serve you, sir,/ Truly, however else'. (114–16)

LINES 118–30: REGAN SEEKS ADVICE
Regan tells Gloucester that she has received letters from both her sister and her father, each telling their version of events at Goneril's palace. She wants Gloucester's advice on how best to respond: 'Our good old friend,/ Lay comforts to your bosom, and bestow/ Your needful counsel to our businesses,/ Which craves the instant use'. (125–8) Gloucester says that he is at her disposal. (129–30)

CHARACTER DEVELOPMENT

GLOUCESTER

GULLIBLE
Gloucester again shows his gullibility in this scene. Admittedly, he is confronted with the spectacle of a wounded Edmund, but he does not appear to pause for a second to consider the plausibility of his son's story.

UNFORGIVING
One of the key features of this scene is the way in which strong parallels are established between Gloucester and Lear. Not only do both display complete faith in their treacherous children and banish the innocent parties, but they also display a harsh and unforgiving temper. Gloucester has no interest in sparing Edgar. He immediately hands down a death sentence on him: 'Not in this land shall he remain uncaught;/ And found – dispatch'. (57–8) Such is his anger that he decrees that anyone found sheltering Edgar will also be killed. (63)

Like Lear, he openly disowns the child who really loves him: 'I never got him'. (78) Both Gloucester and Lear are easy prey for their selfish and manipulative children.

A MAN OF STATURE
Although Gloucester may be gullible, we also get indications in this scene that he is a well-respected figure. Even the selfish Regan appears genuinely concerned at the 'plot' against his life. She seems to sincerely seek his advice. She refers to him as 'Our good old friend', and seeks his 'needful counsel'. (127)

EDGAR

INNOCENT VICTIM
Edgar is completely manipulated by Edmund in this scene. Although we may be tempted to suggest that he is too easily fooled, we should also bear in mind that he has no real reason to doubt his brother's sincerity. He is a victim of Edmund's skilful cunning and deception. His fate parallels, to a certain extent, that of the banished Cordelia.

CORNWALL & REGAN

CORNWALL

TRYING TO APPEAR STRONG

Cornwall appears to be somewhat
under the thumb of his wife in this
scene. He is eager to declare that
he also will not receive Lear: 'Nor
I, assure thee, Regan'. (105) In order
to make up for this, he is keen to
assert his own rank and authority
by telling Gloucester that he may
act against Edgar in whatever way
he pleases with all of his support:
'make your own purpose,/ How in
my strength you please'. (111–12) He
is assertive also in his quick recruit-
ment of Edmund ('you shall be
ours'). However, as we saw, this does
not prevent his wife from taking the
lead in explaining why they have
come to Gloucester.

REGAN

SELF-SERVING

Regan shows in this scene that she is as manipulative and
self-serving as Edmund. She takes advantage of the news of
Edgar's 'treachery' to blacken Lear further by suggesting that
Edgar was corrupted by her father's retinue: 'No marvel then
though he were ill affected;/ 'Tis they have put him on the old
man's death'. (38–9) By connecting a would-be murderer with
Lear, she is paving the way to make her later brutal treatment
of her father seem justified.

A STRONG WOMAN

Like her sister, Regan shows in this scene that she is a strong-
minded female who has no difficulty expressing her opinions.
She immediately calls for Edgar to be harshly punished: 'If it
be true, all vengeance comes too short/ Which can pursue the
offender'. (88–9) Also like Goneril, she has no problem cutting
across her husband in order to explain why they have come to
Gloucester's castle. (118–19)

A RELUCTANT VILLAIN?

One interesting question that emerges from this scene is
the issue of how willing a participant Regan is in Goneril's
scheming. Is she genuinely uncertain about how she should
respond to the spat between Goneril and King Lear? We
should remember that Goneril voiced a little doubt in her
sister in Act 1, Scene 4 ('If she sustain him and his hundred
knights,/ When I have show'd the unfitness'). The interplay
between the two sisters in the remainder of the play will prove
that theirs is an uneasy alliance.

Enter KENT and OSWALD the Steward, severally.

OSWALD	Good dawning to thee, friend. Art of this house?
KENT	Ay.
OSWALD	Where may we set our horses?
KENT	I' the mire.
OSWALD	Prithee, if thou lov'st me, tell me.
KENT	I love thee not.
OSWALD	Why then, I care not for thee.
KENT	If I had thee in Lipsbury Pinfold, I would make thee care for me.
OSWALD	Why dost thou use me thus? I know thee not.
KENT	Fellow, I know thee.
OSWALD	What dost thou know me for?
KENT	A knave; a rascal; an eater of broken meats; a base, proud, shallow, beggarly, three-suited, hundred-pound, filthy, worsted-stocking knave; a lily-liver'd, action-taking, whoreson, glass-gazing, super-serviceable, finical rogue; one-trunk-inheriting slave; one that wouldst be a bawd, in way of good service, and art nothing but the composition of a knave, beggar, coward, pander, and the son and heir of a mongrel bitch; one whom I will beat into clamorous whining, if thou deny the least syllable of thy addition.
OSWALD	Why, what a monstrous fellow art thou, thus to rail on one that's neither known of thee nor knows thee!
KENT	What a brazen-faced varlet art thou, to deny thou knowest me! Is it two days ago since tripp'd up thy heels and beat thee before the King? *[Draws his sword]* Draw, you rogue! for, though it be night, yet the moon shines. I'll make a sop o' the moonshine o' you. Draw, you whoreson, cullionly, barber-monger! draw!
OSWALD	Away! I have nothing to do with thee.
KENT	Draw, you rascal! You come with letters against the King, and take Vanity the puppet's part against the royalty of her father. Draw, you rogue, or I'll so carbonado your shanks! Draw, you rascal! Come your ways!

Line markers: 5, 10, 15, 20, 25, 30, 35

mire: *mud*

Lipsbury Pinfold: *dog pound*

use: *treat*

broken meats: *scraps*

worsted: *woollen (rather than silk)*
glass-gazing: *vain (glass = mirror)*
super-serviceable: *officious;* **finical:** *fussy*
bawd: *pimp*
composition: *compound*

addition: *titles*

varlet: *rascal*

sop: *sponge*
cullionly: *contemptible*

* 1   **Art of this house?:** *Are you a servant here?*

† 31   **barber-monger:** *frequenter of barber shops, vain fool, dandy*

‡ 33   **Vanity the puppet's part:** *Vanity is traditionally personified as a proud, self-admiring woman. The term 'puppet' was also used for a vain, 'dolled-up' woman. Kent is referring to Goneril when he accuses Oswald of taking 'Vanity the puppet's part' against the king.*

OSWALD	Help, ho! murder! help!
KENT	Strike, you slave! Stand, rogue! Stand, you neat slave!
	Strike! [Beats him]
OSWALD	Help, ho! murder! murder!

Enter EDMUND, with his rapier drawn, GLOUCESTER, CORNWALL,
REGAN, Servants.

EDMUND	How now? What's the matter? [Parts them]
KENT	With you, goodman boy, if you please! Come,
	I'll flesh ye! Come on, young master!
GLOUCESTER	Weapon? arms? What's the matter here?
CORNWALL	Keep peace, upon your lives!
	He dies that strikes again. What is the matter?
REGAN	The messengers from our sister and the King
CORNWALL	What is your difference? Speak.
OSWALD	I am scarce in breath, my lord.
KENT	No marvel, you have so bestirr'd your valour. You
	Cowardly rascal, nature disclaims in thee; a tailor
	made thee.
CORNWALL	Thou art a strange fellow. A tailor make a man?
KENT	Ay, a tailor, sir. A stone-cutter or a painter could not have
	made him so ill, though be had been but two
	hours o' the trade.
CORNWALL	Speak yet, how grew your quarrel?
OSWALD	This ancient ruffian, sir, whose life I have spar'd
	at suit of his grey beard –
KENT	Thou whoreson zed! thou unnecessary letter! My lord, if
	you'll give me leave, I will tread this unbolted
	villain into mortar and daub the walls of a jakes with him.
	'Spare my grey beard,' you wagtail?
CORNWALL	Peace, sirrah!
	You beastly knave, know you no reverence?
KENT	Yes, sir, but anger hath a privilege.
CORNWALL	Why art thou angry?
KENT	That such a slave as this should wear a sword,
	Who wears no honesty. Such smiling rogues as these,
	Like rats, oft bite the holy cords a-twain,
	Which are too intrinse t' unloose; smooth every passion
	That in the natures of their lords rebel,
	Bring oil to fire, snow to their colder moods;
	Renege, affirm, and turn their halcyon beaks
	With every gale and vary of their masters,
	Knowing naught (like dogs) but following.
	A plague upon your epileptic visage!
	Smile you my speeches, as I were a fool?
	Goose, an I had you upon Sarum plain,
	I'd drive ye cackling home to Camelot.
CORNWALL	What, art thou mad, old fellow?
GLOUCESTER	How fell you out? Say that.
KENT	No contraries hold more antipathy
	Than I and such a knave.
CORNWALL	Why dost thou call him knave? What is his fault?
KENT	His countenance likes me not.

Glossary (right margin):

40

goodman boy: *scornful address*
flesh ye: *initiate blood (teach you to fight)*

45

50 difference: *quarrel*

disclaims: *denies*

55

60 suit: *out of pity / respect for*

unbolted: *effeminate*
jakes: *privy (bathroom)*
65 wagtail: *inconstant bird*

a privilege: *a right to speak*

70 sword: *gentleman's weapon*

a-twain: *in two*
intrinse: *intrinsic, tight*
rebel: *against reason*
75 oil to fire: *feeding passion*
halcyon: *kingfisher, used as weathervane*
vary: *whim*

epileptic visage: *distorted face*
80 Smile: *deride*
Sarum: *Salisbury*

85

likes: *pleases*

---

* 62 **Thou whoreson zed! thou unnecessary letter:** *The letter 'z' is unnecessary because it is not used in Latin, nor in English dictionaries of the time, its function being replaced by 's'.*

CORNWALL	No more perchance does mine, or his, or hers.	
KENT	Sir, 'tis my occupation to be plain.	90 plain: *candid*
	I have seen better faces in my time	
	Than stands on any shoulder that I see	
	Before me at this instant.	
CORNWALL	This is some fellow,	
	Who, having been prais'd for bluntness, doth affect	95 bluntness: *curtness*
	A saucy roughness, and constrains the garb	saucy: *insolent*; constrains: *distorts*
	Quite from his nature. He cannot flatter, he!	nature: *true (natural) meaning*
	An honest mind and plain, he must speak truth!	
	An they will take it, so; if not, he's plain.	
	These kind of knaves I know which in this plainness	
	Harbour more craft and more corrupter ends	100 Harbour: *hide, conceal*
	Than twenty silly-ducking observants,	observants: *servants*
	That stretch their duties nicely.	
KENT	Sir, in good faith, in sincere verity,	verity: *Latinate word for truth*
	Under th' allowance of your great aspect,	allowance: *approval*; aspect: *state*
	Whose influence, like the wreath of radiant fire	105 influence: *astrological term*
	On flickering Phoebus' front,	Phoebus: *sun god*
CORNWALL	What mean'st by this?	
KENT	To go out of my dialect, which you discommend so	dialect: *usual way of speaking*
	much. I know, sir, I am no flatterer. He that beguiled	beguiled: *fooled*
	you in a plain accent was a plain knave, which, for my	
	part, I will not be, though I should win your	110
	displeasure to entreat me to't.	entreat: *persuade*
CORNWALL	What was the offence you gave him?	
OSWALD	I never gave him any.	
	It pleas'd the King his master very late	
	To strike at me, upon his misconstruction;	115 misconstruction: *misunderstanding*
	When he, conjunct, and flattering his displeasure,	conjunct: *in league with him*
	Tripp'd me behind; being down, insulted, rail'd	
	And put upon him such a deal of man	a deal of man: *a manly attitude*
	That worthied him, got praises of the King	worthied: *made him appear worthy*
	For him attempting who was self-subdu'd;	120
	And, in the fleshment of this dread exploit,	fleshment: *excitement*
	Drew on me here again.	
KENT	None of these rogues and cowards	
	But Ajax is their fool.	Ajax: *foolish Greek commander*
CORNWALL	Fetch forth the stocks!	
	You stubborn ancient knave, you reverent braggart,	reverent: *venerable (sarcastic tone)*
	We'll teach you –	125
KENT	Sir, I am too old to learn.	
	Call not your stocks for me. I serve the King;	
	On whose employment I was sent to you.	
	You shall do small respect, show too bold malice	
	Against the grace and person of my master,	
	Stocking his messenger.	130
CORNWALL	Fetch forth the stocks! As I have life and honour,	
	There shall he sit till noon.	

---

* 104   discommend: *find fault with*

† 110–11   though I should win ... entreat me to't: *Even the threat of Cornwall's displeasure could not persuade Kent to be the kind of 'plain knave' that Cornwall has described.*

‡ 120   For him attempting who was self-subdu'd: *for attacking a man who was already cowed into submission.*

§ 123   Fetch forth the stocks! : *Cornwall calls for the stocks because he thinks that Kent identifies him with Ajax.*

Regan - Dominant demands that Kent stays in the stocks all night ~~contradicts~~. her husbands order + wishes to out do her sister in her cruelty.

REGAN	Till noon? Till night, my lord, and all night too!	
KENT	Why, madam, if I were your father's dog,	
	You should not use me so.	135
REGAN	Sir, being his knave, I will.	
CORNWALL	This is a fellow of the self-same colour	
	Our sister speaks of. Come, bring away the stocks!	

Stocks brought out.

GLOUCESTER	Let me beseech your Grace not to do so.	
	His fault is much, and the good King his master	
	Will check him for't. Your purposed low correction	140
	Is such as basest and contemned'st wretches	
	For pilferings and most common trespasses	
	Are punish'd with. The King must take it ill	
	That he, so slightly valued in his messenger,	
	Should have him thus restrain'd.	145
CORNWALL	I'll answer that.	
REGAN	My sister may receive it much more worse,	
	To have her gentleman abus'd, assaulted,	
	For following her affairs. Put in his legs.	

KENT is put in the stocks.

| | Come, my good lord, away. | |

Exeunt all but GLOUCESTER and KENT.

GLOUCESTER	I am sorry for thee, friend. 'Tis the Duke's pleasure,	150
	Whose disposition, all the world well knows,	
	Will not be rubb'd nor stopp'd. I'll entreat for thee.	
KENT	Pray do not, sir. I have watch'd and travell'd hard.	
	Some time I shall sleep out, the rest I'll whistle.	155
	A good man's fortune may grow out at heels.	
	Give you good morrow!	
GLOUCESTER	The Duke's to blame in this; 'twill be ill taken. *[Exit]*	
KENT	Good King, that must approve the common saw,	
	Thou out of heaven's benediction com'st	
	To the warm sun!	160
	Approach, thou beacon to this under globe,	
	That by thy comfortable beams I may	
	Peruse this letter. Nothing almost sees miracles	
	But misery. I know 'tis from Cordelia,	
	Who hath most fortunately been inform'd	165
	Of my obscured course – and *[reads]* 'shall find time	
	From this enormous state, seeking to give	
	Losses their remedies' – All weary and o'erwatch'd,	
	Take vantage, heavy eyes, not to behold	
	This shameful lodging.	170
	Fortune, good night; smile once more, turn thy wheel.	

He sleeps.

colour: *character*

low correction: *shameful punishment*
contemned'st: *despised*

restrain'd: *confined (in the stocks)*

disposition: *character*
rubb'd: *hindered*

… heels: *change for the worse*

under globe: *sphere of the earth*

Peruse: *read;* **Nothing almost:** *????*

obscured: *hidden, secret*
enormous state: *irregular, disordered state*
o'erwatch'd: *exhausted*
vantage: *advantage*

Kent

Cornwall – concious of his image + anxious to inhance his reputation, degrades Kent by sentencing him to the stocks.
GLOUCESTER – he inhances his reputation by protesting against the degrading punishment of Kent + remains behind to console him

* 158–60 **approve the common saw … warm sun:** *the king's circumstances confirms the proverbial truth of Fortune's movement from good to bad, as he moves from the light of heaven to the heat of earth's sun.*

† 171 **Fortune … wheel:** *Fortune was imaged as a wheel that ever turns*

KENT & OSWALD

Kent meets Oswald outside Gloucester's castle, and they argue. When Cornwall intervenes, Kent insults him is placed in the stocks as punishment. Gloucester attempts to intervene, telling Cornwall that it is disrespectful to Lear to put his servant in the stocks, but his plea for lenience is ignored. Kent is left alone in the stocks. He reads a letter he has received from Cordelia.

ACTION

✒ LINES 1–42: KENT ATTACKS OSWALD

Kent and Oswald meet in front of Gloucester's castle. Kent is very rude to Oswald. He tells him to tether his horses 'I' the mire'. (4) He calls him a string of names ('A knave, a rascal, an eater of broken meats') and threatens him with violence. (22) Oswald is shocked by the abuse of a man who appears to be a stranger: 'Why, what a monstrous fellow art thou, thus to rail on/ one that is neither known of thee nor knows thee!' (24–5)

Kent is enraged that Oswald is acting on behalf of Goneril against Lear: 'you come with letters against the king, and take vanity the puppet's part against the royalty of her father'. (34–6) He draws his sword, but Oswald does not wish to fight: 'Away! I have nothing to do with thee'. (33) Oswald is now clearly terrified and calls for help: 'Help, ho! Murder! Help!' (39)

✒ LINES 43–87: CORNWALL INTERVENES

Edmund enters, swiftly followed by Cornwall, Regan, Gloucester and their servants. They are shocked by the sight of Kent and Oswald fighting. Cornwall immediately attempts to assert his authority, instructing them to stop fighting or die: 'He dies that strikes again'. (48) He asks them to explain why the fight started. (51)

Kent says that he is angry because a dishonest man like Oswald should be allowed to bear a sword. (70–1) He says that Oswald is a fawning servant who panders to his master's every whim. (77–9) Kent notices Oswald smiling at this description and threatens him again. (81–2) Kent says he and Oswald are complete opposites: 'No contraries hold more antipathy/ Than I and such a knave. (85–6)

LINES 87–124: KENT INSULTS CORNWALL

Cornwall tries to get to the bottom of the fight, but Kent insults him. Kent tells him he has no choice but to speak honestly and plainly. He will not behave like other servants, even if this means incurring Cornwall's wrath. (110–11)

- He suggests that Cornwall and the other nobles are ugly: 'I have seen better faces in my time'. (91)
- He suggests that Cornwall is foolish: 'None of these rogues and cowards/ But Ajax is their fool'. (122–3)
- He mocks Cornwall by pretending to flatter him. (103–6)

LINES 124–38: KENT IS PUT IN THE STOCKS

Cornwall is enraged by Kent's insolence. He calls for the stocks to be brought out and tells Kent that he will teach him a lesson: 'You stubborn ancient knave, you reverend braggart,/ We'll teach you'. (124–5) Kent says that they shouldn't insult Lear by putting his servant in the stocks:

You shall do small respect, show too bold malice
Against the grace and person of my master,
Stocking his messenger. (128–30)

Cornwall declares that Kent must be one of Lear's troublesome companions. (137–8) He calls for the stocks again, and tells Kent that he will sit in them until noon. (131–2) Regan then displays her cruelty by saying that Cornwall is being too lenient: 'Till noon! Till night, my lord; and all night too'. (133) Kent is disgusted by her malice: 'Why, madam, if I were your father's dog,/ You should not use me so'. (134–5)

LINES 139–57: GLOUCESTER ATTEMPTS TO INTERVENE

Gloucester is disturbed by the way that Cornwall and Regan are treating Kent. He says that Lear will punish his own servant: 'the good king his master/ Will check him for't'. (139–40) He says that the stocks are fit punishment only for low criminals, and that the king will be offended if his man is treated as such:

A KEY MOMENT

Kent's revelation that Cordelia may be on her way to help Lear shows the first glimmer of light for the king in the play. The question now is whether she will intervene in time to save her father from a terrible fate.

KENT

'the king must take it ill,/ That he, so slightly valu'd in his messenger,/ Should have him thus restrained'. (143–5)

Gloucester's plea for lenience is ignored. He is clearly embarrassed by the punishment meted out to Kent. He apologises to him, and blames Cornwall's stubborn mindset: "tis the duke's pleasure,/ Whose disposition, all the world well knows,/ Will not be rubb'd nor stopp'd'. (151–2) He promises to try and help Kent again: 'I'll entreat for thee'. (152)

Kent declines Gloucester's offer, and tells him that he will spend his time in the stocks sleeping and whistling. He appears resigned to his fate: 'A good man's fortune may grow out at heels'. (155) Gloucester is still upset, and fears the consequences of Kent's stocking: 'The duke's to blame in this; 'twill be ill taken'. (157) He exits.

LINES 158–71: A LETTER FROM CORDELIA

Kent is left alone in the stocks. He asks for some sunshine so that he may read a letter he has received from Cordelia. (161–3) She knows Kent is trying to help her father. He hopes that she too will come to Lear's aid. Kent then expresses a longing for sleep, and calls for Fate to intervene on his behalf: 'Fortune, good night, smile once more; turn thy wheel!' (171)

KENT

LOYAL
Kent continues to display unswerving loyalty to Lear in this scene. His anger toward Oswald comes from the fact that Goneril's servant showed his master a lack of respect a short time ago, and Kent is unwilling to forgive him for this. He also seeks to protect Lear from Goneril's schemes: 'you come with letters against the/ king, and take vanity the puppet's part against the/ royalty of her father'. (34–6)

Kent expects others to respect Lear, even though the king no longer holds power. He tells Cornwall that to put him in the stocks would be an insult against his wife's father: 'You shall do small respect, show too bold malice/ Against the grace and person of my master,/ Stocking his messenger'. (128–30) He is disgusted by Regan's malice: 'Why, madam, if I were your father's dog,/ You should not use me so'. (134–5) Kent's loyalty and reverence for Lear is absolute and unquestioning.

TACTLESS?
Kent is honest to the point of being tactless. He is determined to speak his mind, regardless of the consequences. His insulting of Cornwall and the others seems almost insane given his lowly status: 'I have seen better faces in my time/ Than stands on any shoulder that I see/ Before me at this instant'. (91–3)

Although Kent's forthrightness is obviously admirable on one level, we might ask ourselves if he is really serving Lear's best interests by being so blunt. He knows he runs the risk of being punished by the king's enemies for his behaviour, yet he refuses to stop. By getting himself put in the stocks, he is rendered powerless to serve his master, who is now left with one less ally.

CORNWALL

IN COMMAND
Cornwall comes across as a very assertive figure in this scene. He is possibly attempting to assert his authority in front of his wife. He immediately tries to defuse the quarrel between Kent and Oswald by threatening death: 'he dies that strikes again'. (48) He repeatedly asks Kent to explain himself, and grows angry when he does not: 'You beastly knave, know you no reverence?' (67) He ignores Kent when he tells him that his action will be seen as an insult to Lear. Cornwall feels the need to assert his authority in the face of Kent's impudence.

REASONABLE
It has to be said in Cornwall's defence that he does give Kent plenty of opportunities to explain himself. His patience only cracks when Kent suggests that he is a fool: 'None of these rogues and cowards,/ But Ajax is their fool'. (123–4)

GLOUCESTER

DEFENDING LEAR
Gloucester makes a good impression in this scene when he attempts to save Kent from the stocks. He thinks Cornwall is being hasty and extreme in subjecting Kent to this punishment, a fate usually reserved only for petty criminals. He promises Kent that he will try to intervene on his behalf again. (152)

The fact that Lear has no real power does not seem to have affected Gloucester's respect for him: 'the king must take it ill,/ That he, so slightly valu'd in his messenger,/ Should have him thus restrain'd'. (143-5) Gloucester is clearly baffled by the shifts in power that are taking place all around him. Little does he realise that he will soon become a victim of the new order.

REGAN

CRUEL AND INSULTING
Regan does not say a great deal in this scene, but what she does say illustrates her cruel and pitiless manner. When her husband proposes that Kent be held in the stocks until noon, Regan immediately increases the sentence: 'Till noon! Till night, my lord; and all night too'. (133) Cornwall apparently goes along with this.

In response to Kent's protest at this treatment ('if I were your father's dog,/ you should not use me so'), she is heartless: 'Sir, being his knave, I will'. (136) When Gloucester points out how offended Lear will be, Regan makes it clear that her father's feelings are completely irrelevant. She is concerned only about Goneril's reaction: 'My sister may receive it much more worse/ To have her gentleman abus'd, assaulted./ For following her affairs'. (145-7) Her contempt for Lear is now on clear display.

OSWALD

INNOCENT?
Although Oswald is a servant of Lear's enemies, it is difficult not to feel a little sympathy for him in this scene. Much to his amazement, he is mercilessly insulted and set upon by Kent, who tries to make him fight a duel. We may think that, like Kent, he is only obeying his mistress and showing total loyalty.

A LIAR
Whatever sympathy we may or may not feel for Oswald is reduced by the fact that he lies to Cornwall about the fracas between him and Kent. He claims that he spared Lear's man out of pity for his old age: 'This ancient ruffian, sir, whose life I have spar'd/ at suit of his grey beard'. (60-1) Clearly, Oswald is concerned with protecting his reputation.

CORDELIA

TO THE RESCUE?
Although she does not appear in this scene, the letter Kent speaks about in the stocks indicates that she has heard of the mistreatment being perpetrated against her father, and is preparing to come to his aid. Kent hopes that she 'shall find time/ From this enormous state, seeking to give/ Losses their remedies'. (166-8)

SOME LINES TO LEARN

Thou whoreson zed! Thou unnecessary letter!

Kent (62)

I have seen better faces in my time
Than stands on any shoulder that I see
Before me at this instant

Kent (91-3)

A good man's fortune may grow out at heels

Kent (155)

Fortune, good night, smile once more; turn thy wheel!

Kent (171)

ACT 2 SCENE 3

The open country

Enter EDGAR.

EDGAR   I heard myself proclaim'd,
And by the happy hollow of a tree
Escap'd the hunt. No port is free, no place
That guard and most unusual vigilance
Does not attend my taking. While I may scape, 5
I will preserve myself; and am bethought
To take the basest and most poorest shape
That ever penury, in contempt of man,
Brought near to beast. My face I'll grime with filth,
Blanket my loins, elf all my hair in knots, 10
And with presented nakedness outface
The winds and persecutions of the sky.
The country gives me proof and precedent
Of Bedlam beggars, who, with roaring voices,
Strike in their numb'd and mortified bare arms 15
Pins, wooden pricks, nails, sprigs of rosemary;
And with this horrible object, from low farms,
Poor pelting villages, sheep-cotes, and mills,
Sometime with lunatic bans, sometime with prayers,
Enforce their charity. 'Poor Turlygod! poor Tom!' 20
That's something yet! Edgar I nothing am.

Exit.

proclaim'd: *publicly outlawed*
happy: *lucky*
port:

While: *until*; scape: *escape*
am bethought: *I have thought*

penury: *poverty*

elf: *tangle*
presented: *exposed*

proof: *example*
Bedlam beggars: *former inmates of asylum*
numb'd: *with the cold*

object: *manifestation*
sheep-cotes: *shepherd's cottages*
bans: *curses*

handwritten note:

* <u>New identity</u> *

Symbolic reduced to basic elemental level of existence. feigned madness. prepares us for + softens the shock of Lear's real madness later in the play (Lear. neath confronting storm)

* 14 **Of Bedlam beggars:** *beggars so called because they were either former inmates of Bedlam lunatic asylum, or they feigned madness in order to beg.*

† 20–21 **poor Tom … I nothing am:** *Edgar has taken on the disguise of a 'Tom o' Bedlam', and suggests that such a character, no matter how base, is at least something. His identity as Edgar, being renounced, has become nothing.*

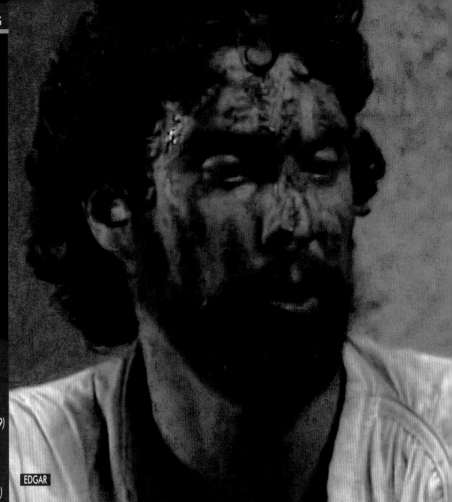

Edgar knows that his life is now in danger. He decides to disguise himself as a beggar and to go by the name of 'poor Tom'. He believes that his new identity will lend him more safety.

SOME LINES TO LEARN

I will preserve myself; and am bethought
To take the basest and most poorest shape
That ever penury, in contempt of man,
Brought near to beast

Edgar (6–9)

Poor Turlygood! Poor Tom!
That's something yet: Edgar I nothing am

Edgar (21)

EDGAR

ACTION

⁊ LINES 1–21: EDGAR DISGUISES HIMSELF

Edgar enters and tells how he escaped the pursuit of Gloucester's men by hiding in the hollow of a tree. (1–3) He knows that he is in grave danger: 'No port is free; no place,/ That guard, and most unusual vigilance,/ Does not attend my taking'. (3–5) He decides that he will disguise himself as a mad beggar: 'To take the basest and most poorest shape/ That ever penury, in contempt of man,/ Brought near to beast'. (7–9)

Edgar says he will blacken his hair, face and body. (9–10) With this new identity, he will 'with presented nakedness outface/ The winds and persecutions of the sky'. (11–12) He says he is following the example of beggars that wander the countryside with objects stuck in their arms, roaring and begging for charity. (13–20) His new name will be 'poor Tom', and his new identity will lend him more safety than his old one: 'That's something yet: Edgar I nothing am'. (21)

CHARACTER DEVELOPMENT

EDGAR

INGENUITY
Although until now Edgar has been a dupe of Edmund, he shows in this scene that he is capable and resourceful. He has avoided capture, and hits upon a disguise that is unlikely to arouse suspicion.

A NEW IDENTITY
Edgar's new role as poor Tom is symbolic on a number of levels. It shows a man being reduced to a basic elemental level of existence, and reflects on how the new order of power in the kingdom has turned everything upside down. In terms of the play's development, Edgar's disguise foreshadows the madness that will shortly descend on Lear.

Before Gloucester's castle; Kent in the stocks

Enter LEAR, FOOL, and GENTLEMAN.

LEAR	'Tis strange that they should so depart from home,
	And not send back my messenger.
GENTLEMAN	As I learn'd,
	The night before there was no purpose in them
	Of this remove.
KENT	Hail to thee, noble master!
LEAR	Ha!
	Mak'st thou this shame thy pastime?
KENT	No, my lord.
FOOL	Ha, ha! look! he wears cruel garters. Horses are tied by the
	head, dogs and bears by th' neck, monkeys by
	th' loins, and men by th' legs. When a man's over-lusty
	at legs, then he wears wooden nether-stocks.
LEAR	What's he that hath so much thy place mistook
	To set thee here?
KENT	It is both he and she,
	Your son and daughter.
LEAR	No.
KENT	Yes.
LEAR	No, I say.
KENT	I say yea.
LEAR	No, no, they would not!
KENT	Yes, they have.
LEAR	By Jupiter, I swear no!
KENT	By Juno, I swear ay!
LEAR	They durst not do't;
	They would not, could not do't. 'Tis worse than murther
	To do upon respect such violent outrage.
	Resolve me with all modest haste which way
	Thou mightst deserve or they impose this usage,
	Coming from us.

5

10

15

20

25

they: *Cornwall and Regan*
messenger: *Kent*

purpose: *intent*
remove: *departure*

this shame: *of being in the stocks*

cruel garters: *the stocks*

over-lusty: *too eager*
at legs: *at legging it, running away*

Jupiter: *king of the Roman gods*
Juno: *Roman goddess*

Resolve: *explain to me;* **modest:** *moderate*
mightst: *might have*
us: *royal plural*

....
* 23–4   **'Tis worse … such violent outrage:**
*It is worse than murder to so violently
disregard the respect due to a king's
messenger.*

KENT	My lord, when at their home
	I did commend your Highness' letters to them,
	Ere I was risen from the place that show'd
	My duty kneeling, came there a reeking post,
	Stew'd in his haste, half breathless, panting forth
	From Goneril his mistress salutations;
	Deliver'd letters, spite of intermission,
	Which presently they read; on whose contents,
	They summon'd up their meiny, straight took horse,
	Commanded me to follow and attend
	The leisure of their answer, gave me cold looks,
	And meeting here the other messenger,
	Whose welcome I perceiv'd had poison'd mine –
	Being the very fellow which of late
	Display'd so saucily against your Highness –
	Having more man than wit about me, drew.
	He rais'd the house with loud and coward cries.
	Your son and daughter found this trespass worth
	The shame which here it suffers.
FOOL	Winter's not gone yet, if the wild geese fly that way.
	Fathers that wear rags
	Do make their children blind;
	But fathers that bear bags
	Shall see their children kind.
	Fortune, that arrant whore,
	Ne'er turns the key to th' poor.
	But for all this, thou shalt have as many dolours for thy
	daughters as thou canst tell in a year.
LEAR	O, how this mother swells up toward my heart!
	Hysterica passio! Down, thou climbing sorrow!
	Thy element's below! Where is this daughter?
KENT	With the Earl, sir, here within.
LEAR	Follow me not;
	Stay here.
	Exit.
GENTLEMAN	Made you no more offence but what you speak of?
KENT	None.
	How chance the King comes with so small a number?
FOOL	And thou hadst been set i' th' stocks for that question,
	thou'dst well deserv'd it.
KENT	Why, fool?

Handwritten margin note: Overcome with. Lear - grief + Sorrow

Right-hand glossary column:

30

commend: *deliver*

post: *messenger*
Stew'd: *his sweat steaming from the heat*
salutations: *Goneril's greetings*

whose: *the letter's*
meiny: *servants*

35

other messenger: *Oswald*

40

drew: *drew his sword*

trespass: *offence*

45

blind: *to their father's needs*
bags: *money bags*

50

turns the key: *opens the door*
dolours: *sorrows*

mother: *hysteria, associated with women*

55

this daughter: *Regan*
Earl: *Gloucester*

60

And thou: *and if you*

* 32   spite of intermission: *in spite of interrupting me (which Regan and Cromwell permitted).*

† 41   more man than wit: *more manly (brave) instinct than judgement;*

‡ 45   Winter's not gone yet, if the wild geese fly that way: *we have not seen the worst of bad and lean times yet, if that is the way Regan and Cromwell are acting.*

§ 56   Thy element's below: *the element or sphere associated with hysteria is positioned in the lower part of the body, which is now threatening to rebel against the higher faculty of judgement located in the brain.*

FOOL	We'll set thee to school to an ant, to teach thee there's	65
	no labouring i' th' winter. All that follow their noses are	
	led by their eyes but blind men, and there's	
	not a nose among twenty but can smell him that's	
	stinking. Let go thy hold when a great wheel runs	
	down a hill, lest it break thy neck with following	70
	it; but the great one that goes upward, let him draw	
	thee after. When a wise man gives thee better counsel,	
	give me mine again. I would have none but knaves	
	follow it, since a fool gives it.	
	That sir which serves and seeks for gain,	75
	And follows but for form,	
	Will pack when it begins to rain	
	And leave thee in the storm.	
	But I will tarry; the fool will stay,	
	And let the wise man fly.	80
	The knave turns fool that runs away;	
	The fool no knave, perdy.	
KENT	Where learn'd you this, fool?	
FOOL	Not i' th' stocks, fool.	

Enter LEAR and GLOUCESTER.

LEAR	Deny to speak with me? They are sick? they are weary?	85
	They have travell'd all the night? Mere fetches,	
	The images of revolt and flying off!	
	Fetch me a better answer.	
GLOUCESTER	My dear lord,	
	You know the fiery quality of the Duke,	
	How unremovable and fix'd he is	90
	In his own course.	
LEAR	Vengeance! plague! death! confusion!	
	Fiery? What quality? Why, Gloucester, Gloucester,	
	I'ld speak with the Duke of Cornwall and his wife.	
GLOUCESTER	Well, my good lord, I have inform'd them so.	95
LEAR	Inform'd them? Dost thou understand me, man?	
GLOUCESTER	Ay, my good lord.	

---

great wheel: *image represents Lear's fortune*

sir: *man*
form: *outward show*

Perdy: *Par Dieu, by God*

fetches: *excuses*
flying off: *desertion*

quality: *character*
unremovable and fix'd: *stubborn*

---

* 65–6   **to school … winter:** *the ant, as in Aesop's tales, knows to gather food in harvest time not in winter. Lear is now metaphorically in his time of winter, with regard to both his age and his wealth, thus, the Fool suggests, he has fewer men, which Kent ought to recognise.*

LEAR	The King would speak with Cornwall; the dear father	
	Would with his daughter speak, commands her service.	
	Are they inform'd of this? My breath and blood!	100
	Fiery? the fiery Duke? Tell the hot Duke that –	
	No, but not yet! May be he is not well.	
	Infirmity doth still neglect all office	
	Whereto our health is bound. We are not ourselves	
	When nature, being oppress'd, commands the mind	105
	To suffer with the body. I'll forbear;	
	And am fallen out with my more headier will,	
	To take the indispos'd and sickly fit	
	For the sound man. – Death on my state!	
	[looking at Kent] Wherefore	
	Should he sit here? This act persuades me	110
	That this remotion of the Duke and her	
	Is practice only. Give me my servant forth.	
	Go tell the Duke and's wife I'd speak with them –	
	Now, presently. Bid them come forth and hear me,	
	Or at their chamber door I'll beat the drum	115
	Till it cry sleep to death.	
GLOUCESTER	I would have all well betwixt you. [Exit]	
LEAR	O me, my heart, my rising heart! But down!	
FOOL	Cry to it, nuncle, as the cockney did to the eels	
	when she put 'em i' th' paste alive. She	120
	knapp'd 'em o' th' coxcombs with a stick and	
	cried 'Down, wantons, down!' 'Twas her brother	
	that, in pure kindness to his horse, buttered his hay.	

Enter CORNWALL, REGAN, GLOUCESTER, Servants.

LEAR	Good morrow to you both.	
CORNWALL	Hail to your Grace!	125

KENT is set at liberty.

REGAN	I am glad to see your Highness.	
LEAR	Regan, I think you are; I know what reason	
	I have to think so. If thou shouldst not be glad,	
	I would divorce me from thy mother's tomb,	
	Sepulchring an adultress. [To Kent] O, are you free?	
	Some other time for that. Beloved Regan,	130
	Thy sister's naught. O Regan, she hath tied	
	Sharp-tooth'd unkindness, like a vulture, here!	

Lays his hand on his heart.

	I can scarce speak to thee. Thou'lt not believe	
	With how deprav'd a quality – O Regan!	
REGAN	I pray you, sir, take patience. I have hope	135
	You less know how to value her desert	
	Than she to scant her duty.	

Glossary (right column):

hot: *quibble on 'fiery'*

headier will: *rash, hasty impulse*

sound: *healthy*

remotion: *departure*
practice: *deliberate cunning*

presently: *immediately*

sleep to death: *kills sleep*

rising heart: *increasing hysteria*

Sepulchring: *entombing*

naught: *nothing, worthless*

deprav'd: *degenerate nature*

take patience: *be calm*

desert: *worth*

....

* 103–6 Infirmity doth still … the body: *illness makes us neglect our duties, which we would not hesitate to perform when well. We are not ourselves when we are sick, our mind suffers with the body.*

† 119–23 cockney … hay: *the Fool gives examples of foolish kindness.*

‡ 132 Sharp-tooth'd … vulture, here: *presents an image of Goneril as a scavenger, as a bird of prey gnawing at Lear's heart with her sharp teeth.*

§ 135–7 I have hope … her duty: *I more believe that you are less able to value Goneril and recognise her value than that she has been negligent of her duty towards you.*

LEAR	Say, how is that?
REGAN	I cannot think my sister in the least
	Would fail her obligation. If, sir, perchance
	She have restrain'd the riots of your followers,
	'Tis on such ground, and to such wholesome end,
	As clears her from all blame.
LEAR	My curses on her!
REGAN	O, sir, you are old!
	Nature in you stands on the very verge
	Of her confine. You should be ruled, and led
	By some discretion that discerns your state
	Better than you yourself. Therefore I pray you
	That to our sister you do make return;
	Say you have wrong'd her, sir.
LEAR	Ask her forgiveness?
	Do you but mark how this becomes the house:
	'Dear daughter, I confess that I am old. *[Kneels]*
	Age is unnecessary. On my knees I beg
	That you'll vouchsafe me raiment, bed, and food.'
REGAN	Good sir, no more! These are unsightly tricks.
	Return you to my sister.
LEAR	*[rises]* Never, Regan!
	She hath abated me of half my train;
	Look'd black upon me; struck me with her tongue,
	Most serpent-like, upon the very heart.
	All the stor'd vengeances of heaven fall
	On her ingrateful top! Strike her young bones,
	You taking airs, with lameness!
CORNWALL	Fie, sir, fie!
LEAR	You nimble lightnings, dart your blinding flames
	Into her scornful eyes! Infect her beauty,
	You fen-suck'd fogs, drawn by the pow'rful sun,
	To fall and blast her pride!
REGAN	O the blest gods! so will you wish on me
	When the rash mood is on.
LEAR	No, Regan, thou shalt never have my curse.
	Thy tender-hefted nature shall not give
	Thee o'er to harshness. Her eyes are fierce; but thine
	Do comfort, and not burn. 'Tis not in thee
	To grudge my pleasures, to cut off my train,
	To bandy hasty words, to scant my sizes,
	And, in conclusion, to oppose the bolt
	Against my coming in. Thou better know'st
	The offices of nature, bond of childhood,
	Effects of courtesy, dues of gratitude.
	Thy half o' th' kingdom hast thou not forgot,
	Wherein I thee endow'd.
REGAN	Good sir, to th' purpose.

Tucket within.

Glosses:

140

obligation: *her filial duty*

wholesome end: *good of the state*

145

confine: *limit (near death)*
state: *physical and mental condition*

unnecessary: *of no use*
vouchsafe: *grant*

155

abated: *taken from*

160 top: *top;* young bones: *unborn*

165

tender-hefted nature: *womanly frame*

scant my sizes: *curtail my allowances*
oppose the bolt: *lock the door*
175 Thou better know'st: *you know better*

to th' purpose: *get to the point*

* 144–6   You should be ruled … you yourself: *as you are no longer able to understand nor rule yourself, you should allow yourself to be ruled discretely by the good sense of someone – such as Goneril – who understands your condition better.*

† 150   mark … house: *consider how to ask for her forgiveness would befit her power over the royal household.*

‡ 160   taking … lameness: *sharing pernicious airs, with such depravity.*

LEAR	Who put my man i' th' stocks?	180
CORNWALL	What trumpet's that?	
REGAN	I know't – my sister's. This approves her letter,	approves: *gives prove to*
	That she would soon be here.	

Enter OSWALD the Steward.

	Is your lady come?	185
LEAR	This is a slave, whose easy-borrowed pride	easy-borrowed: *easily assumed*
	Dwells in the fickle grace of her he follows.	fickle grace: *changeable favour*
	Out, varlet, from my sight!	varlet: *rogue*
CORNWALL	What means your Grace?	
LEAR	Who stock'd my servant? Regan, I have good hope	
	Thou didst not know on't. – Who comes here? *[Enter Goneril]*	on't: *of it*
	O heavens!	
	If you do love old men, if your sweet sway	sway: *power*
	Allow obedience – if yourselves are old,	
	Make it your cause! Send down, and take my part!	190 it: *the obligations due to parents*
	[To Goneril] Art not asham'd to look upon this beard? –	this beard: *sign of his status and age*
	O Regan, wilt thou take her by the hand?	
GONERIL	Why not by th' hand, sir? How have I offended?	
	All's not offence that indiscretion finds	indiscretion: *rashness*
	And dotage terms so.	dotage: *old age*
LEAR	O sides, you are too tough!	195
	Will you yet hold? How came my man i' th' stocks?	
CORNWALL	I set him there, sir; but his own disorders	disorders: *wrongdoing*
	Deserv'd much less advancement.	advancement: *promotion (sarcastic tone)*
LEAR	You? Did you?	
REGAN	I pray you, father, being weak, seem so.	
	If, till the expiration of your month,	200 expiration: *end*
	You will return and sojourn with my sister,	sojourn: *stay*
	Dismissing half your train, come then to me.	
	I am now from home, and out of that provision	
	Which shall be needful for your entertainment.	
LEAR	Return to her, and fifty men dismiss'd?	205
	No, rather I abjure all roofs, and choose	abjure: *renounce*
	To wage against the enmity o' th' air,	wage: *struggle*
	To be a comrade with the wolf and owl –	
	Necessity's sharp pinch! Return with her?	
	Why, the hot-blooded France, that dowerless took	210 hot-blooded: *passionate*
	Our youngest born, I could as well be brought	
	To knee his throne, and, squire-like, pension beg	knee: *kneel before*; pension: *payment*
	To keep base life afoot. Return with her?	
	Persuade me rather to be slave and sumpter	sumpter: *pack-horse*
	To this detested groom. *[Points at Oswald]*	215
GONERIL	At your choice, sir. (cold)	
LEAR	I prithee, daughter, do not make me mad.	
	I will not trouble thee, my child; farewell.	
	We'll no more meet, no more see one another.	
	But yet thou art my flesh, my blood, my daughter;	
	Or rather a disease that's in my flesh,	220
	Which I must needs call mine. Thou art a boil,	needs: *of necessity*
	A plague sore, an embossed carbuncle	embossed carbuncle: *swollen boil*
	In my corrupted blood. But I'll not chide thee.	corrupted: *diseased*
	Let shame come when it will, I do not call it.	
	I do not bid the Thunder-bearer shoot ·	225 Thunder-bearer: *Jupiter*
	Nor tell tales of thee to high-judging Jove.	Jove: *Roman god*

....

* 195   **O sides:** *sides of his chest, under pressure and strain from the passions of his heart;*

† 199   **being weak, seem so:** *as you are weak, submit to it.*

	Mend when thou canst; be better at thy leisure;	
	I can be patient, I can stay with Regan,	
	I and my hundred knights.	
REGAN	Not altogether so.	
	I look'd not for you yet, nor am provided	230
	For your fit welcome. Give ear, sir, to my sister;	
	For those that mingle reason with your passion	
	Must be content to think you old, and so – †	
	But she knows what she does.	
LEAR	Is this well spoken?	235
REGAN	I dare avouch it, sir. What, fifty followers?	
	Is it not well? What should you need of more?	
	Yea, or so many, sith that both charge and danger	
	Speak 'gainst so great a number? How in one house	
	Should many people, under two commands,	
	Hold amity? 'Tis hard; almost impossible.	240
GONERIL	Why might not you, my lord, receive attendance	
	From those that she calls servants, or from mine?	
REGAN	Why not, my lord? If then they chanc'd to slack ye,	
	We could control them. If you will come to me	
	(For now I spy a danger), I entreat you	245
	To bring but five-and-twenty. To no more	
	Will I give place or notice.	
LEAR	I gave you all –	
REGAN	And in good time you gave it!	
LEAR	Made you my guardians, my depositaries;	
	But kept a reservation to be followed	250
	With such a number. What, must I come to you	
	With five-and-twenty, Regan? Said you so?	
REGAN	And speak't again my lord. No more with me.	
LEAR	Those wicked creatures yet do look well-favour'd	
	When others are more wicked; not being the worst	255
	Stands in some rank of praise. [To Goneril] I'll go with thee.	
	Thy fifty yet doth double five-and-twenty,	
	And thou art twice her love.	
GONERIL	Hear, me, my lord.	
	What need you five-and-twenty, ten, or five,	
	To follow in a house where twice so many	260
	Have a command to tend you?	
REGAN	What need one?	
LEAR	O, reason not the need! Our basest beggars	
	Are in the poorest thing superfluous.	
	Allow not nature more than nature needs,	265
	Man's life is cheap as beast's. Thou art a lady:	
	If only to go warm were gorgeous,	
	Why, nature needs not what thou gorgeous wear'st ➤	

Glossary (right margin):

Give ear: *listen*

Avouch it: *confirm it to be true*

sith: *since;* charge: *expense*

amity: *peace*

slack: *disrespect*

spy: *see*

notice: *recognition*

depositaries: *trustees*
kept a reservation: *retained a right*
such a number: *of one hundred retainers*

Those wicked creatures: *ref. to Goneril*
more wicked: *ref. to Regan*

reason not: *do not argue about*

---

* 232   For those that mingle reason with your passion: *for those that respond with calm rationality to your passion, thus tempering it with reason;*

† 233   and so – : *Regan does not complete this train of thought, perhaps thinking it better to hold back at this point.*

[Handwritten notes:]

* Lear (storm) *

Disoder of Lears mind reflected in storm & d

Goneril + regan betray their lack of basic human instints when they tell Gloucester not to offer the shelter of his castle to their father but to let him fall the wild elements outdoors to endure the fury of the storm while they enjoy the comfort + safety of the castle

Which scarcely keeps thee warm. But, for true need –
You heavens, give me that patience, patience I need!
You see me here, you gods, a poor old man,
As full of grief as age; wretched in both.
If it be you that stirs these daughters' hearts
Against their father, fool me not so much†
To bear it tamely; touch me with noble anger,
And let not women's weapons, water drops,
Stain my man's cheeks! No, you unnatural hags!
I will have such revenges on you both
That all the world shall – I will do such things –
What they are yet, I know not; but they shall be
The terrors of the earth! You think I'll weep.
No, I'll not weep.
I have full cause of weeping, but this heart
Shall break into a hundred thousand flaws
Or ere I'll weep. O fool, I shall go mad!

Exeunt LEAR, GLOUCESTER, KENT, and FOOL.

Storm and tempest.

CORNWALL   Let us withdraw; 'twill be a storm.
REGAN   This house is little; the old man and's people
Cannot be well bestow'd.
GONERIL   'Tis his own blame; hath put himself from rest
And must needs taste his folly.
REGAN   For his particular, I'll receive him gladly,
But not one follower.
GONERIL   So am I purpos'd.
Where is my Lord of Gloucester?
CORNWALL   Followed the old man forth.

Enter GLOUCESTER.

                        He is return'd.
GLOUCESTER   The King is in high rage. (concern)
CORNWALL   Whither is he going?
GLOUCESTER   He calls to horse, but will I know not whither.
CORNWALL   'Tis best to give him way; he leads himself.
GONERIL   My lord, entreat him by no means to stay.
GLOUCESTER   Alack, the night comes on, and the bleak winds
Do sorely ruffle. For many miles about
There's scarce a bush.
REGAN   O, sir, to wilful men
The injuries that they themselves procure
Must be their schoolmasters. Shut up your doors.
He is attended with a desperate train,
And what they may incense him to, being apt
To have his ear abus'd, wisdom bids fear.
CORNWALL   Shut up your doors, my lord; 'tis a wild night.
My Regan counsels well. Come out o' th' storm.

Exeunt.

Glosses (right column):

true need: *higher than material need*

you: *you gods*

women's weapons, water drops: *tears*
you unnatural hags: *Goneril and Regan*

flaws: *fragments*
Or ere: *before*

bestow'd: *lodged*
blame: *fault*
taste: *experience*

he leads himself: *he will not be ruled*
entreat … means: *do not beg him*

ruffle: *rage*
bush: *for shelter*
wilful: *stubborn*

desperate: *reckless*
incense: *incite; apt: ready*

* 262–8 **Our basest beggars … keeps thee warm:** *even the very poorest of beggars have something more than what is strictly necessary for bare existence. If humankind's nature is allowed no more than what is strictly needed to survive then human life is reduced to that of animal life. Moreover, as Lear observes in a direct address to Regan, if warmth were the only measure of elegance, then Regan would not the scanty fashionable clothes she wears, which don't even meet the basic function of keeping her warm.*

† 273 **fool me not so much:** *do not make me such a fool.*

LEAR

Lear arrives at Gloucester's castle and is shocked to find his servant (Kent) in the stocks. He cannot believe that his own daughter would insult him in this manner. He attempts to meet with Cornwall and Regan, but they make excuses and refuse to see him.

When Cornwall and Regan eventually emerge from the castle to greet Lear, the king pleads with his daughter for compassion, but Regan remains cold and echoes her sister's complaints about her father and his knights.

When Goneril arrives, Regan sides with her, and together they strip Lear of his retinue. Lear is crushed and humiliated. He curses his daughters and once again fears he is going mad. He walks away from the castle just as a storm is brewing. Gloucester expresses concern for the king, but Regan and Goneril stand firm. They lock the doors of Gloucester's castle, thereby shutting Lear out.

ACTION

🔊 LINES 1–44: LEAR ARRIVES AT GLOUCESTER'S CASTLE

After his falling out with Goneril, Lear went to stay with Regan. However, when he reached Regan's castle, he found she was not at home, but had gone to visit Gloucester. Lear has now followed her to Gloucester's castle. Lear is puzzled that Regan and Cornwall should have left their castle without waiting to greet him: ''Tis strange that they should so depart from home,/ And not send back my messenger'. (1–2)

When he arrives at Gloucester's castle. Lear is shocked to find his servant Kent in the stocks. (7) To lock up the king's servant is to insult the king himself. Lear

assumes, therefore, that there has been some sort of mistake: 'What's he that hath so much thy place mistook/ To set thee here?' (11–12)

🔊 KENT TELLS LEAR WHY HE WAS PUT IN THE STOCKS

Kent tells Lear that Cornwall and Regan put him in the stocks even though they knew he was Lear's servant: 'It is both he and she,/ Your son and daughter'. (13–14) He explains how this came about.

He delivered the king's letter to Regan, as per Lear's instructions in Act 1, Scene 5. When Regan decided to leave her castle and visit Gloucester she ordered Kent to accompany her. Kent tells how he argued with Oswald and was put in the stocks as a result. (36–44)

Lear is overcome with grief and sorrow:
· He cannot believe that his children have disrespected him by putting his servant in the stocks: 'O! How this mother swells up toward my heart'. (54)
· He refuses to accept the truth of Kent's story, and denies it four times, in spite of Kent's confirmation. (15–21)
· Lear cannot fathom that his daughters would act in such a disrespectful manner: 'They durst not do't;/ They could not, would not do't; 'tis worse than murder'. (22–3)

A KEY MOMENT

This is a climactic scene in the play. Lear is finally confronted with the cruel betrayal of his daughters and the shattering of his world. He realises now that his daughters' declarations of love for him in the opening scene were false and insincere. Power was their only interest, and now that they possess it they have no further use for their father. Without the power that defined his life and position, Lear is stripped bare and reduced to a helpless old man, dependent on the charity and goodwill of others. The incredible trauma of this revelation means that further suffering awaits Lear on his path to self-knowledge.

Lear still thinks and acts like he is the most powerful man in the kingdom. In reality, however, he lost all his power when he gave away his land. In this scene, he is finally beginning to realise how powerless he actually is. He goes into the castle to find Regan.

⚓ THE FOOL'S VIEW OF LOYALTY

Kent wonders why the king has so small a retinue. (51) The Fool tells him that even loyal servants will desert a man whose fortunes begin to fade. He criticises Kent for following a man whose luck is so obviously on the wane: 'Let go thy hold when a great wheel runs down a hill, lest it break thy neck with following it'. (69–70) However, the Fool does not follow his own advice and declares that he will remain loyal to Lear:

LEAR

BLIND TO REALITY

Lear comes across as someone who is unable and unwilling to deal with reality. He is extremely slow to realise that he is no longer the all-powerful monarch, but a weak old man who is at his daughters' mercy. His blindness to this new reality is evident in the shock he feels at his daughters' treatment of him. He is horrified that Cornwall and Regan left their castle before he got there, put his servant in the stocks and refused to meet him.

Lear also deludes himself when it comes to Regan, clinging to the hope that she will help him even after she has treated him coldly and badly. His blindness to reality is also evident when his daughters strip him of his retinue. Only at this moment does he fully grasp that they and not he have the power of the kingdom.

Lear has been made to face reality in the most cruel and brutal manner. He has been emotionally tortured and humiliated, and does not know where to turn. The world of power and unconditional loyalty that he has lived in all of his life has vanished, and he is now at the bottom of the scheme of things. The man who was once an all-powerful king now accepts what he has been reduced to: 'You see me here, you gods, a poor old man,/ As full of grief and as age; wretched in both!' (270–1)

PROUD AND DEFIANT

Lear's pride and anger are still intact, however. He begs the gods to grant him the strength not to cry and the power to take revenge. Although he has been humiliated, he will not bow before his daughters: 'I have full cause of weeping, but this heart/ Shall break into a hundred thousand flaws/ Or ere I'll weep'. (282–4) The king has begun his journey to self-knowledge, but he has yet to be completely broken.

EMOTIONAL INSTABILITY

We have already seen that Lear is prone to radical mood swings. We witnessed this is Act 1, Scene 1 when he turned on both Cordelia and Kent. In this scene, Lear veers wildly between hope and desperation, anger and defiance. When Reagan tells him that he should return to Goneril, Lear falls to his knees and begs pathetically for her charity. (152–3) But when Regan repeats her suggestion that he should go back to his eldest daughter, the king's anger returns with even more vehemence. (164–6)

DESCENT INTO MADNESS

The emotional strain of his trial threatens to overwhelm him: 'O, me! My heart, my rising heart! But, down!' (118) The dawning realisation of his own foolishness in surrendering power is almost too much to bear for such a proud and wilful man. By the end of the scene, Lear fears that he will go mad. His last words in this scene are a fearful premonition of the horrors that still await him: 'O fool! I shall go mad'. (284)

But I will tarry; the fool will stay,
And let the wise man fly:
The knave turns fool that runs away;
The fool no knave, perdy (79–82)

Kent asks where the Fool learnt such wisdom. His answer is cutting: 'Not i' the stocks, fool'. (84)

LINES 85–123: LEAR IS ANGRY BECAUSE REGAN REFUSES TO SEE HIM

Lear emerges from Gloucester's castle in a rage. Regan and Cornwall have refused to meet with him, saying they are sick and tired having travelled hard through the night:

Deny to speak with me! They are sick! They are
*   weary.*
They have travell'd hard to-night! Mere fetches,
The images of a revolt and flying off. (85–7)

As king, Lear expects to be seen immediately: 'Inform'd them! Dost thou understand me, man?' (96) He still hasn't realised that he is yesterday's man.

Gloucester attempts to placate Lear by reminding him how stubborn Cornwall is: 'You know the fiery quality of the duke;/ How unremovable and fix'd he is/ In his own course'. (89–91) The king is scornful of Gloucester's excuses, and once again demands to speak with Cornwall and his daughter. (94)

Lear's tone softens briefly. He considers the possibility that Cornwall really is sick, and makes allowances for his discourteous behaviour: 'we are not ourselves/ When nature, being oppress'd,/ commands the mind/ To suffer with the body'. (104–6) He regrets being so hasty in his condemnation: 'I'll forbear;/ And am fallen out with my more headier will,/ To take the indispos'd and sickly fit/ For the sound man'. (105–8)

However, the sight of Kent in the stocks rekindles his anger and suspicion. He again suggests that Regan and Cornwall are deceiving him: 'This act persuades me/ That this remotion of the duke and her/ Is practice only'. (110–12) Lear is overcome by grief at this disrespectful treatment, and struggles to retain self-control: 'O, me! My heart, my rising heart! But, down!' (118)

CHARACTER DEVELOPMENT

REGAN

COLD AND PATRONISING

Regan's behaviour toward her father in this scene is clinical and heartless. Her initial greeting ('I am glad to see your highness') fills Lear with false hope, and she appears to derive pleasure from disillusioning the king. Her language is cold and patronising. She addresses Lear as 'sir', and is quick to tell him that Goneril is blameless in their quarrel: 'I cannot think my sister in the least/ Would fail her obligation'. (138–9) Her calm insistence that he should return to Goneril only serves to incite the king's rage.

It is difficult to know whether her apparently horrified reaction to Lear's tirade against Goneril is sincere or not: 'O the blest gods! So you will wish on me,/ When the rash mood is on'. (167–8) It is interesting to bear in mind the fact of Goneril's lack of complete faith in her sister's willingness to remove Lear. We might ask ourselves if there is anything in Regan's words at this point that indicate that she is still less than wholly committed to Goneril's plan.

TAUNTING AND CRUEL

If there are any doubts about Regan's selfishness, they are quickly removed when her sister arrives. Her taking of Goneril's hand is a symbolic display of their alliance and joint purpose. It is a public declaration that their father is of no significance now that he has renounced his power.

After Lear departs, Regan is quick to justify her cruelty by saying that her castle is too small for Lear and his followers: 'the old man and his people/ Cannot be well bestow'd'. (286–7) Her insincerity is obvious. Perhaps in an attempt to placate her conscience, she declares that her real problem lies with the king's retinue. She states that she would gladly take in Lear alone: 'I'll receive him gladly,/ But not one follower'. (290–1)

As if to prove the Fool's statement that by giving away his power Lear has made his daughters his mothers, Regan patronisingly suggests that her father needs to be taught a lesson: 'O! sir, to wilful men,/ The injuries that they themselves procure/ Must be their schoolmasters'. (301–3) It is she who issues the fatal command: 'Shut up your doors'. (303) It is possible that Regan is determined to prove her commitment to Goneril's scheme by emphasising her determination to see Lear suffer. Either way, she has now publicly displayed her hostility to her father.

REGAN & LEAR

✍ LINES 124–87: REGAN AND CORNWALL FINALLY FACE LEAR

Cornwall and Regan finally emerge to greet the king. Much to Lear's relief, Regan appears to be friendly. He tells her of his mistreatment at Goneril's hands: 'Thy sister's naught: O Regan! She hath tied/ Sharp-tooth'd unkindness, like a vulture, here'. (131–2) Regan's response is cold:

· She tells Lear that he is old and confused. (145–8)
· She says that Goneril has done nothing wrong: 'I cannot think my sister in the least/ Would fail her obligation'. (138–9)
· She echoes Goneril's complaints about Lear's rowdy knights.
· She chides her father for cursing Goneril, fearing that he will one day curse her in the same way. (166–7)
· She suggests that Lear should return to Goneril and apologise: 'Say you have wrong'd her, sir'. (132–48)

Lear clings to the hope that Regan is still on his side: 'Thy tender-hefted nature shall not give/ Thee o'er to harshness. (169–70) He kneels and begs for shelter and food. (151–3) Regan is unmoved and again tells him to go back to Goneril: 'Good sire, no more; these are unsightly tricks:/ Return you to my sister'. (154–5)

Lear gets up off his knees and demands to know who ordered Kent to be put in the stocks. (187) At this moment, however, Goneril and Oswald arrive. Lear is disgusted to see the servant who openly insulted him, and attempts to dismiss him: 'Out, varlet, from my sight!' (186) He is even more shocked to see Goneril.

✍ LINES 187–260: GONERIL AND REGAN JOIN AGAINST THEIR FATHER

Lear is horrified when Regan takes Goneril by the hand. He cannot believe that Regan can do this after Goneril treated him so badly: 'O Regan! Wilt thou take her by the hand?' (192) He is barely able to retain self-control: 'O sides! You are too tough;/ Will you yet hold?' (196–7)

Goneril feigns ignorance as to why her father is upset, suggesting that he is over-reacting due to his old age: 'All's not offence that indiscretion finds/ And dotage terms so'. (194–5)

Regan says that she hasn't got the means to accommodate Lear, and yet again asks that he return with Goneril. (203–4, 229–30)

> Fetch me a better answer
>
> *Lear (88)*

> No, rather I abjure all roofs, and choose
> To wage against the enmity o' the air;
> To be a comrade with the wolf and owl
>
> *Lear (206–8)*

> Those wicked creatures yet do look well-favor'd,
> When others are more wicked; not being the
>   worst
> Stands in some rank of praise
>
> *Lear (254–6)*

SOME LINES TO LEARN

CHARACTER DEVELOPMENT

Lear says that he would rather sleep outdoors than reside with Goneril. (206–8) He claims he would rather bow before France or even serve Oswald before returning with her. (210–15) He insults Goneril and declares that he is finished with her forever: 'I will not trouble thee, my child; farewell./ We'll no more meet, no more see one another'. (218–19) Goneril, however, remains coldly indifferent to Lear's anger: 'At your choice, sir'. (216)

LINES 230–60: GONERIL AND REGAN STRIP LEAR OF HIS KNIGHTS

Lear still clings to the slightest hope that Regan will help him: 'I can stay with Regan,/ I and my hundred knights'. (228–9) However, this hope is shattered as the two sisters strip him of his retinue.

Goneril and Regan discuss how many knights Lear should retain. Goneril persistently says that Lear does not need any knights of his own, saying that her and Regan's servants will look after him: 'Why might not you, my lord, receive attendance/ From those that she calls servants, or from mine?' (241–2) Regan says that fifty knights is enough for Lear, then twenty-five. Finally, she agrees with Goneril that he needs no knights at all: 'What need you five-and-twenty, ten, or five,/ To follow in a house, where twice so many/ have a command to follow you?' (261–3)

Regan and Goneril have several reasons for wanting to eliminate Lear's followers:

GONERIL & REGAN

A DESIRE TO DESTROY LEAR

Though Goneril does not say a lot in this scene, she has a powerful influence on events. In the early part of the scene, Regan is cold to Lear, but it is only when her sister arrives that she begins to treat him with real cruelty.

From the beginning, Goneril has been pushing for Lear to be eliminated. Regan has seemed less committed to this goal. She tries to avoid choosing between her sister and her father by telling Lear to return to Goneril's castle. However, Goneril's arrival forces her to make this choice. She takes her sister's hand and Lear is doomed.

CRUEL AND HEARTLESS

Throughout the scene, Goneril displays cruelty in different ways. She is the first to suggest that Lear should be left with no knights at all, saying that the sisters' own servants will look after him. When Lear turns to her in desperation after being rejected by Regan, she cruelly hurts him by repeating that he should dispense with his retinue. (240–1) When Lear is locked out, she says that it is no more than he deserves and tells Gloucester not to ask Lear to stay.

Regan too displays cruelty throughout the scene. She patronises Lear by calling him an old man. She cruelly refuses to accommodate Lear, saying that she is unprepared for his arrival. She begins the cruel game of slashing Lear's retinue, telling him to return to Goneril with only 'half your train'. (202) It is she who issues the fatal command to shut the doors and lock Lear out. (302)

SELF-JUSTIFICATION

There can be little doubt in this scene that Goneril comes across as the crueller of the two sisters. After Lear has been thrown out, Regan feels a need to justify her actions, saying that her house is too small for Lear, that his knights are too much of a problem and that the old man needs to be taught a lesson anyway. Goneril feels little or need for any such justification.

CORNWALL

A DOCILE HUSBAND

Cornwall plays a passive role in this scene. He supports his wife completely in her humiliation of Lear and makes no attempt to intervene. In fact, he objects to Lear's angry tirade against Goneril. (162) He makes his own small contribution to Lear's torment by informing him that it was he who put Kent in the stocks. (198–9)

After Lear exits in a rage, Cornwall shows no interest in persuading him to stay: ''Tis best to give him way; he leads himself'. (298) He echoes his wife's order to shut her father out and thereby displays his own subservience to her will. (307–8)

1. They claim that the knights are a rowdy and disruptive group of men.

2. Goneril and Regan know that Lear can turn on someone in the blink of an eye, just as he turned on Cordelia in Act 1, Scene 1. They worry that in the future he will turn against them and use his knights to attack them.

3. Having a hundred knights allows Lear to retain some power, status and influence. Goneril and Regan don't want this. Now that Lear has given up his lands, they want him to fade quietly into the background so that they might rule the country between them.

4. There is also a sense in which Goneril and Regan want to publicly crush Lear, emphasising that they, not he, have power over the land.

LINES 265–84: LEAR'S PRIDE AND GRIEF

The king has been publicly crushed and humiliated by his daughters. His illusions have been shattered. He realises that his daughters have turned against him. He also realises that he is no longer king, but just a feeble old man – it has finally dawned on him that when he gave away his land, he gave away his power, too.

Lear is devastated. He is thrown into a state of confusion and emotional turmoil.

· He pleads with his daughters not to ask why he needs a retinue of knights. It is simply fitting to his status to have one: 'O! Reason not the need'. (265)

· He calls on the gods for help, asking them to grant him patience and to pity him: 'You see me here, you gods, a poor old man,/ As full of grief as age; wretched in both!' (270–1)

· He says that his daughters are reducing him to the status of a beggar or an animal: 'Allow not nature more than nature needs,/ Man's life is as cheap as beast's'. (266)

· He swears he will have vengeance on his daughters: 'No, you unnatural hags,/ I will have such revenges on you both'. (276–7) Yet, with his power gone, he doesn't know what action he can possibly now take: 'I will do such things,/ What they are yet I know not, – but they shall be/ The terrors of the earth'. (278–80)

· Lear once more fears that he will lose his reason: 'O fool! I shall go mad'. (284)

Lear exits with Gloucester, Kent and the Fool.

GLOUCESTER

CONCERNED FOR LEAR

Gloucester wins our respect in this scene by his display of continuing concern for Lear. He attempts to calm Lear when Cornwall and Regan refuse to see him. He asks the sisters to let their father stay in the castle as it is a rough night: 'Alack! The night comes on, and the bleak winds/ Do sorely ruffle; for many miles about/ There's scarce a bush'. (298–300)

Gloucester obeys Goneril's command to shut his doors on Lear. We may find Gloucester's behaviour forgivable, as he must obey those who now hold power out of concern for his own safety. He remains loyal to Lear and intends to help him.

THE FOOL

WISE AND LOYAL

The Fool continues to display his wisdom in this scene. When Kent expresses puzzlement as to the small size of Lear's escort, the Fool recites a series of verses and tales that have a common message: servants are only loyal to their masters when times are good and prospects are bright. When things are bad, they desert out of concern for their own welfare.

In spite of this cynical wisdom, the Fool himself remains loyal to his master. He knows it will probably lead to his own destruction, but he will not abandon Lear: 'But I will tarry; the fool will stay'. (79)

KENT

LOYAL SERVANT

Kent does not play a very significant role in this scene. He delivers the first shock to Lear's system when he tells him that it was Regan and Cornwall who put him in the stocks, but does not feature afterwards. By the end of the scene, he and the Fool will be the only ones left to comfort Lear.

O! reason not the need; our basest beggars
Are in the poorest thing superfluous:
Allow not nature more than nature needs,
Man's life is cheap as beast's

Lear (265–8)

You see me here, you gods, a poor old man,
As full of grief as age; wretched in both!

Lear (270–1)

I have full cause of weeping, but this heart
Shall break into a hundred thousand flaws
Or ere I'll weep

Lear (282–4)

SOME LINES TO LEARN

LINES 285–8: LEAR IS SHUT OUT

Gloucester returns, expressing his concern for the king: 'The king is in high rage'. (295) He points out that a storm is brewing and that there is no shelter in the surrounding countryside: 'Alack! The night comes on, and the bleak winds/ Do sorely ruffle; for many miles about/ There's scarce a bush'. (298–300)

Regan and Goneril ruthlessly order the doors to be shut, leaving Lear outside. (303) Cornwall echoes this command. Goneril suggests that it is Lear's own fault he has been locked out: ''Tis his own blame; hath put himself from rest,/ And must needs taste his folly'. (288–9) Regan says that he must learn from his mistakes: 'to wilful men,/ The injuries that they themselves procure/ Must be their schoolmasters'. (301–3)

Regan says that she would be willing to take in Lear himself, but none of his retinue: 'For his particular, I'll receive him gladly,/ But not one follower'. (290–1) Goneril agrees with this: 'So am I purpos'd'. (292)

Cornwall suggests they withdraw indoors as a storm is brewing. (285) Regan shows her heartlessness again by saying that her small castle cannot accommodate Lear: 'This house is little: the old man and his people/ Cannot be well bestow'd'. (286–7) Goneril says Lear's misfortune is entirely is his own fault:

Regan, however, is merciless. She says that Lear will learn from his mistakes: She orders the doors to be shut on Lear: 'Shut up your doors'. (303) She returns to her fear of Lear's knights, saying it is wise to fear what they might provoke her father to do: 'He is attended with a desperate train,/ And what they may incense him to, being apt/ To have his ear abus'd, wisdom bids fear'. (304–6) Cornwall echoes his wife's command: 'Shut up your doors, my lord'. (307)

The emotional strain of his trial threatens to overwhelm him: 'O, me! My heart, my rising heart! But, down!' (118) The dawning realisation of his own foolishness in surrendering power is almost too much to bear for such a proud and wilful man. By the end of the scene, Lear fears that he will go mad. His last words in this scene are a fearful premonition of the horrors that still await him: 'O fool! I shall go mad'. (284)

Storm still. Enter KENT and a GENTLEMAN at several doors.

KENT	Who's there, besides foul weather?
GENTLEMAN	One minded like the weather, most unquietly.
KENT	I know you. Where's the King?
GENTLEMAN	Contending with the fretful elements;

Bids the wind blow the earth into the sea,   5
Or swell the curled waters 'bove the main,
That things might change or cease; tears his white hair,
Which the impetuous blasts, with eyeless rage,
Catch in their fury and make nothing of;
Strives in his little world of man to outscorn*   10
The to-and-fro-conflicting wind and rain.
This night, wherein the cub-drawn bear would couch,
The lion and the belly-pinched wolf
Keep their fur dry, unbonneted he runs,
And bids what will take all.

KENT	But who is with him? 15
GENTLEMAN	None but the fool, who labours to outjest

His heart-struck injuries.

KENT	Sir, I do know you,

And dare upon the warrant of my note
Commend a dear thing to you. There is division,
Although as yet the face of it be covered   20
With mutual cunning) 'twixt Albany and Cornwall;
Who have – as who have not, that their great stars
Thron'd and set high? – servants, who seem no less,
Which are to France the spies and speculations
Intelligent of our state. What hath been seen,   25
Either in snuffs and packings of the Dukes,
Or the hard rein which both of them have borne
Against the old kind King, or something deeper,
Whereof, perchance, these are but furnishings –
But, true it is, from France there comes a power   30
Into this scattered kingdom, who already,
Wise in our negligence, have secret feet
In some of our best ports and are at point
To show their open banner. Now to you:
If on my credit you dare build so far   35
To make your speed to Dover, you shall find
Some that will thank you, making just report
Of how unnatural and bemadding sorrow
The King hath cause to plain.
I am a gentleman of blood and breeding,   40
And from some knowledge and assurance offer
This office to you.

GENTLEMAN	I will talk further with you.

---

main: *mainland*
things: *the situation*
eyeless: *blind*

cub-drawn: *sucked dry by her cubs*
belly-pinched: *ravenous*
unbonneted: *without covering*
Bids … all: *as a gambler's last throw*

outjest: *drive out by jesting*

warrant … note: *strength … observation*
Commend: *entrust*
covered: *hidden*

seem no less: *seem to be servants*
speculations: *givers of unconfirmed report*
Intelligent: *information*
snuffs … packings: *huffs … plots*
hard rein: *inflexible attitude*

furnishings: *incidentals, trimmings*

scattered: *divided*
Wise in: *aware of;* feet: *landing, foothold*
at point: *of readiness*

credit: *credibility*

bemadding: *maddening*
Plain: *complain*

office: *service*

* 10   his little world of man: *man as microcosm, reflecting in miniature the entire macrocosm or universe.*

KENT   No, do not.
For confirmation that I am much more
Than my out-wall, open this purse and take
What it contains. If you shall see Cordelia
(As fear not but you shall), show her this ring,
And she will tell you who your fellow is
That yet you do not know. Fie on this storm!
I will go seek the King.   50

GENTLEMAN   Give me your hand. Have you no more to say?

KENT   Few words, but, to effect, more than all yet:
That, when we have found the King (in which your pain
That way, I'll this), he that first lights on him
Holla the other.

Exeunt severally.

out-wall: *outward show, exterior*

to effect: *in importance*
your pain: *your efforts*

As the storm rages out on the heath, Kent meets a gentleman who describes Lear's madness. Kent tells the gentleman that there is trouble brewing between Cornwall and Albany, and that Cordelia and French forces have landed at Dover. He instructs the gentleman to deliver a message to Cordelia informing her of Lear's predicament.

ACTION

LINES 1–17: THE GENTLEMAN DESCRIBES LEAR'S MADNESS

A storm is raging. Kent meets an unnamed gentleman on a heath. Lear's decline has brought this gentleman great distress. He says his mind is as unsettled and 'unquiet' as the weather: 'One minded like the weather, most unquietly'. (2) He provides Kent with a graphic description of Lear's madness:

> The weather is so bad that even bears, lions and wolves would stay sheltered. (12–14) Yet the King is running around in the storm with his head uncovered: 'unbonneted he runs'. (14)

The king is arguing with the wind and rain: 'Contending with the fretful elements'. (4)

He orders the wind to drown the world. He wants it to sweep the land into the sea or drive a tidal wave of water over the whole of mainland Britain: 'Bids the wind blow the earth into the sea, / Or swell the curled waters 'bove the main'. (5–6)

He tears his hair out: 'tears his white hair'. The locks he tears from his head are blown away the 'eyeless rage' of this violent storm. (8–9)

He is accompanied only by the fool who attempts to ease his grief with jokes and wisecracks. (16–17)

This is a devastating portrayal of madness. According to the gentleman, Lear's sanity has been consumed by grief and rage. His despair is so great that he wants the world to end, and longs for Britain itself to be consumed by the storm's rage. (5–9)

LINES 18–55: KENT CONFIDES IN THE GENTLEMAN

Kent knows this gentleman and decides to trust him with important or 'dear' information: 'Commend a dear thing to you'. (19) Firstly, he tells him that trouble is brewing between Albany and Cornwall: 'There is division … 'twixt Albany and Cornwall'. (19–21) On the surface, Albany and Cornwall seem to be working together in 'mutual cunning'. (21) Secretly, however, they are plotting against one another.

Kent reveals that an army from France has arrived at some of Britain's 'best ports': 'from France there comes a power / into this scatter'd kingdom'. (30–1) This army has landed secretly (with 'secret feet'), being clever enough to take advantage of British careless-ness: 'wise in our negligence'. (32) Now, however, these French invaders are on the point of revealing them-selves: 'are at point to show their open banner'. (34–5) Kent is convinced that Cordelia is with this invading army. (46–7)

Kent has a task or 'office' for the gentleman. (41–2) He says that if the gentleman 'credits' or trusts him, he will go to the French invasion force at Dover: 'if on my credit you dare build so far / To make your way to Dover'. (35–6) Once there, he should tell the invaders how Lear has been driven mad by his daughters' 'unnatural' treatment of him. The gentleman's report should be 'just' or accurate:

> making just report
> Of how unnatural and bemadding sorrow.
> The king hath cause to plain (37–9)

The gentleman wants to discuss the matter further. (43) Perhaps he is unsure that he can really trust Kent in the climate of suspicion and treachery that has engulfed the country. Kent, however, declares that it is time for action, not words: 'Few words, but, to effect, more than all yet'. (52) He gives the gentleman a ring. (45–6) When the gentleman reaches the invasion force at Dover, he must show Cordelia this ring. (47) If he does so, Cordelia will know the gentleman has been sent by Kent and can be trusted.

KENT

DECISIVE ACTION

We see Kent initiating the first positive steps to save Lear in this scene. He asks the gentleman he encounters in the storm to go to Dover and tell Cordelia of the suffering her father is undergoing. Kent clearly hopes that she will increase the speed of the build-up of the French forces that have already landed in England.

LEAR

RAGE

Through the gentleman's report, we learn that Lear's rage against his daughters' ingratitude has reached new proportions. He runs bareheaded ('unbonneted') in the rain, calling on the forces of nature to destroy mankind: 'Bids the wind blow the earth into the sea,/ Or swell the curled waters 'bove the main,/ That things might change or cease'. (5–7) The force and violence of the storm mirror the king's inner rage and turmoil. It is as if nature itself is now trying to destroy the king in a battle of fury: 'tears his white/ hair,/ Which the impetuous blasts, with eyeless rage,/ Catch in their fury and make nothing of'. (7–9) The king seems indifferent to his own life and 'bids what will take all'. (15)

THE FOOL

TOUCHING DEVOTION

We learn that the Fool is doing his best to comfort his master in his great pain and distress. He 'labours to out-jest/ His heart-struck injuries'. (15–16) Although the Fool has been Lear's harshest critic, we now see how much he loves and cares for the king.

ALBANY & CORNWALL

TROUBLE BREWING?

Kent makes mention of the potential conflict between Albany and Cornwall, which was alluded to in Act 1. Although yet to show itself openly, 'there is division'. (19) This is the first sign of tension brewing between Lear's enemies.

CHARACTER DEVELOPMENT

Contending with the fretful elements;
Bids the wind blow the earth into the sea,
Or swell the curled waters 'bove the
        main,
That things might change or cease
                              Gentleman (4-7)

SOME LINES TO LEARN

Storm still. Enter LEAR and FOOL.

LEAR Blow, winds, and crack your cheeks! rage! blow!
You cataracts and hurricanoes. spout
Till you have drench'd our steeples, drowned the cocks!
You sulph'rous and thought-executing fires,
Vaunt-couriers to oak-cleaving thunderbolts,   5
Singe my white head! And thou, all-shaking thunder,
Strike flat the thick rotundity o' th' world
Crack Nature's moulds, all germens spill at once,
That makes ingrateful man!

FOOL O nuncle, court holy-water in a dry house is   10
better than this rain water out o' door.
Good nuncle, in, and ask thy daughters blessing!
Here's a night pities neither wise men nor fools.

LEAR Rumble thy bellyful! Spit, fire! spout, rain!
Nor rain, wind, thunder, fire are my daughters.   15
I tax not you, you elements, with unkindness.
I never gave you kingdom, called you children,
You owe me no subscription. Then let fall
Your horrible pleasure. Here I stand your slave,
A poor, infirm, weak, and despis'd old man.   20
But yet I call you servile ministers,
That will with two pernicious daughters join
Your high-engender'd battles 'gainst a head
So old and white as this! O! O! 'tis foul!

FOOL He that has a house to put's head in has a good head-piece.   25
.   The codpiece that will house
Before the head has any,
The head and he shall louse:
So beggars marry many.   30
The man that makes his toe
What he his heart should make
Shall of a corn cry woe,
And turn his sleep to wake.
For there was never yet fair woman but she made mouths   35
in a glass.

Enter KENT.

LEAR No, I will be the pattern of all patience;
I will say nothing.

KENT Who's there?

FOOL Marry, here's grace and a codpiece; that's a wise   40
man and a fool.

---

cataracts: *heaven's floodgates*
cocks: *weathercocks*
thought-executing fires: *lightening speed*
Vaunt-couriers: *forerunners*

germens spill: *seeds destroy*
ingrateful: *ungrateful*
holy-water: *ceremonies*

Rumble: *moan;* bellyful: *heart's content*

subscription: *allegiance*

high-engender'd: *created in the heavens*

codpiece: *worn by men, ref. to phallus*
has any: *has any house*
louse: *have lice*
many: *one wife plus her lice*

mouths: *faces*

grace: *the King*

* 7–8   rotundity ... moulds: *rotundity refers to the spherical shape of the globe, but could be suggestive also of the roundness associated with pregnancy, particularly within the context of Lear's mention of moulds, that is the moulds used by nature to form 'ingrateful man'.*

KENT	Alas, sir, are you here? Things that love night
	Love not such nights as these. The wrathful skies
	Gallow the very wanderers of the dark
	And make them keep their caves. Since I was man,
	Such sheets of fire, such bursts of horrid thunder,
	Such groans of roaring wind and rain, I never
	Remember to have heard. Man's nature cannot carry
	Th' affliction nor the fear.
LEAR	Let the great gods,
	That keep this dreadful pudder o'er our heads,
	Find out their enemies now. Tremble, thou wretch,
	That hast within thee undivulged crimes
	Unwhipp'd of justice. Hide thee, thou bloody hand;
	Thou perjur'd, and thou simular man of virtue
	That art incestuous. Caitiff, in pieces shake
	That under covert and convenient seeming
	Hast practis'd on man's life. Close pent-up guilts,
	Rive your concealing continents, and cry
	These dreadful summoners grace. I am a man
	More sinn'd against than sinning.
KENT	Alack, bareheaded?
	Gracious my lord, hard by here is a hovel;
	Some friendship will it lend you 'gainst the tempest.
	Repose you there, whilst I to this hard house
	(More harder than the stones whereof 'tis raised,
	Which even but now, démanding after you,
	Denied me to come in) return, and force
	Their scanted courtesy.
LEAR	My wits begin to turn.
	Come on, my boy. How dost, my boy? Art cold?
	I am cold myself. Where is this straw, my fellow?
	The art of our necessities is strange,
	That can make vile things precious. Come, your hovel.
	Poor fool and knave, I have one part in my heart
	That's sorry yet for thee.
FOOL	[sings] He that has and a little tiny wit –
	With hey, ho, the wind and the rain –
	Must make content with his fortunes fit,
	For the rain it raineth every day.
LEAR	True, my good boy. Come, bring us to this hovel.

Gallow: *frighten* — 45

carry: *bear, cope with*

pudder: *turmoil* — 50

Unwhipp'd of: *unpunished by*
perjur'd: *perjurer;* simular: *false*
Caitiff: *wretch* — 55
covert: *hidden;* seeming: *pretense*
practis'd on: *plotted against*
Rive: *slit open;* continents: *coverings*

— 60

lend: *give, afford*
Repose: *rest;* hard house: *cruel household*
More harder: *more unyielding than* — 65
demanding: *asking*

scanted: *scarce, negligible*
wits: *thoughts (becoming aware of others)*

— 70

vile things: *such as straw (for bedding)*

— 75

* 51   **Find out their enemies now:** *by the terror the enemies will show in the presence of such force*

† 57   **Close pent-up guilts:** *crimes hidden and kept secret;*

‡ 58-9   **cry … grace:** *beg for mercy and forgiveness from the terrible ministers of vengeance and justice. A 'summoner' was an official who summoned offenders to the ecclesiastical courts.*

§ 60   **I am a man … sinning:** *meditating on the sins of the murderers and hypocrites he describes in this speech, Lear finds himself to be more of a victim of sin than guilty of sinning.*

Exeunt LEAR and KENT.

FOOL This is a brave night to cool a courtesan.
I'll speak a prophecy ere I go: 80

> *When priests are more in word than matter;*
> *When brewers mar their malt with water;*
> *When nobles are their tailors' tutors,*
> *No heretics burn'd, but wenches' suitors;*
> *When every case in law is right,*   85
> *No squire in debt nor no poor knight;*
> *When slanders do not live in tongues,*
> *Nor cutpurses come not to throngs;*
> *When usurers tell their gold i' th' field,*
> *And bawds and whores do churches build:*   90
> *Then shall the realm of Albion*
> *Come to great confusion.*
> *Then comes the time, who lives to see't,*
> *That going shall be us'd with feet.*

This prophecy Merlin shall make, for I live before his time.

Exit.

---

brave: *daringly suitable*

more ... : *preach rather than practice*

are ... : *more fashion conscious than tailors*
wenches' suitors: *lovers*

cutpurses: *thieves*
usurers tell: *moneylenders count*

Albion: *old name for Britain*

---

* 94   That going shall be us'd with feet.:
*feet shall be used for walking, that
is to say, normality will return and
perversions end.*

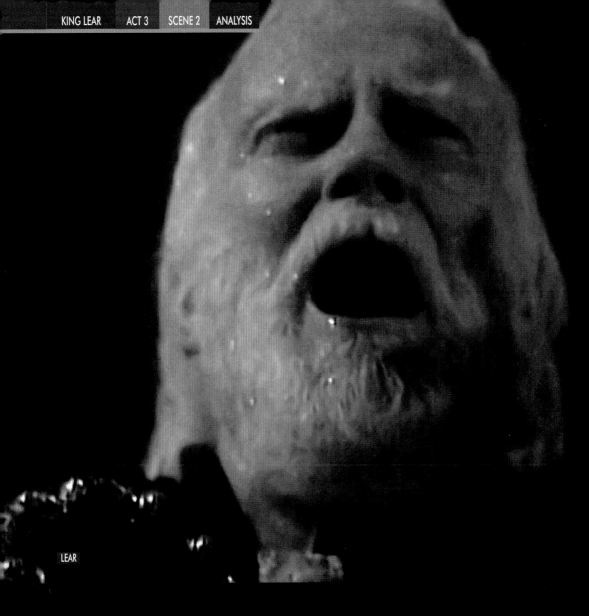

LEAR

Lear wanders through the heath in the storm, ranting and raving at the forces of nature. Kent arrives and is shocked to see the King, now accompanied by his fool, in this condition. He convinces Lear to take refuge from the storm in a hovel.

ACTION

⚘ LINES 1–36: LEAR RANTS AND RAVES

The demented Lear is wandering about the heath in the storm. He roars at the storm, urging it to wreak destruction on the world:

> *He calls on the gods of wind to blow until they have hurt or damaged their cheeks: 'Blow winds and crack your cheeks! Rage! Blow!'* (1)

He wants the rain to 'spout' from the heavens until floods ('cataracts') have covered the land, rising to the level of the steeples and weather cocks: 'spout / Till you have drenched our steeples, drown'd our cocks'. (2–3)

He calls on bolts of lightning to blast the earth, 'singing' his hair. (4–6) According to Lear, the lightning bolts smell of sulphur and are faster than thought ('thought-executing').

He wants the thunder to squash the world, making the round globe flat: 'And thou, all shaking thunder, / Strike flat the thick rotundity of the world'. (6–7)

He offers himself up to the storm like a sacrifice, letting it destroy him at its leisure: 'let fall / Your horrible pleasure, here I stand, your slave'. (17–19)

89

LEAR & THE FOOL

He says the elements have 'join'd' forces with his daughters to 'battle' against him: 'That have with two pernicious daughters join'd / Your high-engenered battles 'gainst ahead / So old and white as this'. (22–4) Yet he does not accuse ('tax') the elements of 'unkindness' for assaulting him: 'I tax not you, you elements, with unkindness'. (16) After all, he has given the elements nothing and they owe him no 'subscription' or loyalty. (17–18)

The fool attempts to talk Lear out of his crazed behaviour, urging him to return to the castle and ask his daughters to let him in. (12) He says that this ferocious weather will 'pity' no one. He sings a typically nonsensical verse which is presumably an attempt to lighten Lear's mood with laughter.

LINES 37–8: KENT ARRIVES
Kent arrives and seems saddened to see Lear running around in the storm like a madman. He says that even creatures of the night have stayed in their caves on this terrible evening: 'Things that love night / Love not nights such as these'. (42–5) He cannot remember ever seeing a storm this violent: 'Such groans of roaring wind and rain, I never / Remember to have heard'. (47–8) He seems horrified that Lear is wandering around without proper protection from the elements: 'Alack! Bare-headed!' (60) Kent urges Lear to come with him to a 'hovel' he has seen nearby. The occupants of the hovel didn't invite Kent out of the

CHARACTER DEVELOPMENT

LEAR

ANGRY FRENZY
In this scene, we witness the king's frenzied rage that the gentleman reported in the previous scene. Lear wishes for Nature to destroy all of human-kind, so enraged is he after being humiliated by his daughters:

And thou, all-shaking thunder
Strike flat the thick rotundity o' the world!
Crack nature's moulds, all germens spill at once
That make ingrateful man! (6–9)

In his delirious anger, Lear personifies Nature, viewing it as being allied to Goneril and Regan in their quest to destroy him. The elements have 'with two pernicious daughters join'd/ Your high-engender'd battles 'gainst a head/ So old and white as this'. (22–4)

SELF-AWARENESS
Stripped of his power and exposed to nature's fury, Lear finally realises what he is in essence: 'A poor, infirm, weak, and despis'd old man'. (20) He can no longer act like the all-powerful autocrat he has been for most of his life. The king has only begun his journey toward humility, however. He is still convinced that 'I am a man/ More sinn'd against than sinning'. (60)

SOCIAL CONSCIENCE
Lear's sufferings appear to have brought the first signs of a social conscience. He calls on the elements to strike down the man 'That hast within thee undivulged crimes,/ Unwhipp'd of justice'. (52–3) The king wishes revenge on all those 'That under covert and convenient seeming/ Hast practis'd on man's life'. (57–8)

After long years of power and a temperamental inability to see beyond himself, the king is finally realising some of the realities of life. This is made clearest by the compassion he shows for the Fool. He asks him if he is cold, and declares that 'I have one part in my heart/ That's sorry yet for thee'. (72–3) For the first time, Lear expresses concern for someone other than himself.

MADNESS LOOMS
The king is aware that he is running the risk of going mad. He knows that his ranting could lead him to the brink of reason, and tries to calm himself: 'No, I will be the pattern of all patience; I will say/ nothing'. (37–8) In spite of his efforts, he knows that insanity is not far off: 'My wits begin to turn'. (67) The prospect terrifies him.

Crack nature's moulds, all germens spill at once
That make ingrateful man!

Lear (8–9)

here I stand, your slave,
A poor, infirm, weak, and despis'd old man

Lear (19–20)

Man's nature cannot carry
The affliction nor the fear

Kent (48)

I am a man
More sinn'd against than sinning

Lear (60)

The art of our necessities is strange,
That can make vile things precious

Lear (70–1)

SOME LINES TO LEARN

CHARACTER DEVELOPMENT

rain, but now he suggests that they return and demand entry. (61–7)

Lear seems to sense that he's losing his mind, declaring that 'My wits begin to turn'. (67) Yet, for the first time, he expresses concern for others. He asks the fool how he is, and says he's sorry to see him out in such bad weather: 'How dost my boy? Art cold? … I have one part in my heart / That's sorry yet for thee'. (67, 72–3) Lear declares that he is cold, and agrees to go with Kent to the hovel: 'I am cold myself … Come, your hovel'. (68, 71) They depart, leaving the Fool behind to sing what he describes as a prophecy.

THE FOOL

CONCERNED FOR HIS MASTER
The Fool shows his love for his master in this scene. He attempts to persuade the king to take shelter from the furious storm, even suggesting that Lear should ask his daughters' forgiveness in order to gain shelter. (12–13) He will not abandon the king, and is desperate to protect him from the elements.

PROPHESYING THE WORST
The Fool's rather cryptic prophecy at the end of the scene appears to be referring to the general hypocrisy and falsity that governs the land. Every line suggests the triumph of appearance over reality: 'When priests are more in word than matter;/ When brewers mar their malt with water'. (81–2) Again, the Fool shows that he is well of aware of the realities of life.

KENT

SEEKING SHELTER FOR THE KING
Like the Fool, Kent also displays great love and care for Lear in this scene. He is horrified that the king is exposed bareheaded to the most furious storm he has seen in his life. He knows that it is too much for anyone to endure: 'man's nature cannot carry/ the affliction nor the fear'. (47–8) He tells the king and the Fool to stay where there are while he investigates a hovel he knows to be nearby.

KENT, LEAR & THE FOOL

Enter GLOUCESTER and EDMUND.

GLOUCESTER Alack, alack, Edmund, I like not this unnatural dealing!
When I desired their leave that I might pity him, they
took from me the use of mine own house, charged me on
pain of perpetual displeasure neither to speak of him,
entreat for him, nor any way sustain him.   5

EDMUND Most savage and unnatural!

GLOUCESTER Go to; say you nothing. There is division betwixt the
dukes, and a worse matter than that. I have received a
letter this night; 'tis dangerous to be spoken; I have locked
the letter in my closet. These injuries the king now bears   10
will be revenged home; there's part of a power
already footed; we must incline to the King.
I will seek him and privily relieve him. Go you and
maintain talk with the duke, that my charity be not of him
perceived. If he ask for me, I am ill and gone to   15
bed. Though I die for it, as no less is threatened me, the
king, my old master, must be relieved. There is some
strange thing toward, Edmund. Pray you be careful.

Exit.

EDMUND This courtesy, forbid thee, shall the duke
Instantly know, and of that letter too.   20
This seems a fair deserving, and must draw me
That which my father loses – no less than all.
The younger rises when the old doth fall.

Exit.

---

pity: *help, show kindness*

betwixt: *between*

revenged home: *brought to justice*
footed: *landed*
privily relieve: *privately help*
of: *by*

toward: *about to happen*

courtesy: *kindness;* **forbid:** *denied*

deserving: *of a reward;* **draw:** *earn*

GLOUCESTER & EDMUND

Gloucester is outraged at the behaviour of Cornwall and Regan. He confides in Edmund his feelings, telling him of a letter he has received describing the arrival of forces favourable to Lear's cause. Edmund decides to betray his father, and reveal all he has heard to Cornwall and Regan.

ACTION

⊛ GLOUCESTER CONFIDES IN EDMUND

Gloucester confides in Edmund his outrage at Cornwall, Goneril and Regan's treatment of Lear. He tells how Cornwall and Regan have taken charge of his house and forbidden him to show any kindness to Lear, threatening him with violence if he should attempt to assist the king: 'When I desired their leave that I might pity him, they took from me the use of my own house'. (2–3) Edmund pretends to sympathise with his father's predicament, telling him that Cornwall and Regan have acted in a most 'savage, and unnatural' way. (7)

Gloucester tells Edmund of trouble brewing between Albany and Cornwall: 'There is a division between the dukes'. He also confides in him that he has received a letter stating that forces are gathering to avenge the mistreatment of Lear and that he has locked this letter in his closet. He tells Edmund how he intends to help the king, and asks that a cover story be given should anybody ask his whereabouts: 'If he ask for me, I am ill and gone to bed'. (16)

When Gloucester leaves, Edmund reveals how he intends to tell Cornwall everything he has just heard. He hopes that such treacherous action will earn him a noble title: 'This seems a fair deserving, and must draw me/ That which my father loses'. (22–3) He knows that his father will suffer if it is discovered that he intends to aid the king, but Edmund cares little for this, saying that it is natural for the old to fall and the young to take their place: 'The younger rise when the old doth fall'. (24)

GLOUCESTER

MORAL COURAGE

In this scene, Gloucester finally decides where his true loyalties lie. In spite of the threat to his own life, he decides that he can no longer stand idly by and watch the king suffer. His conscience tells him that the 'unnatural dealing' of Goneril, Regan and Cornwall is excessive and cruel. We cannot but admire his bravery. He is willing to take the ultimate risk to see Lear rescued: 'If I die for it, as no less is threatened me, the/ king, my old master, must be relieved'. (17–18) Unfortunately for Gloucester, he has no way of knowing that Edmund is ready to betray him.

EDMUND

TREACHEROUS

Edmund displays total selfishness and heartlessness in this scene. He intends to betray his father, although he must surely know that there is a fair chance that Gloucester will be executed if he does so. He shows complete cynicism with his feigned agreement to Gloucester's condemnation of what has befallen the king: 'Most savage, and unnatural!' (7)

Edmund also makes clear the fact that he has no belief whatsoever in ties of family loyalty. He thinks it is perfectly natural for the young to take what he believes to be their rightful place at the top: 'This seems a fair deserving, and must draw me/ That which my father loses; no less than all:/ the younger rises when the old doth fall'. (22–4) He has no morality whatsoever.

The younger rises when the old doth fall
Edmund's view of the natural order (24)

SOME LINES TO LEARN

Storm still. Enter LEAR, KENT, and FOOL.

KENT   Here is the place, my lord. Good my lord, enter.
The tyranny of the open night's too rough
For nature to endure.

LEAR   Let me alone.

KENT   Good my lord, enter here.

LEAR   Wilt break my heart?

KENT   I had rather break mine own. Good my lord, enter.   5

LEAR   Thou think'st 'tis much that this contentious storm
Invades us to the skin. So 'tis to thee;
But where the greater malady is fix'd,
The lesser is scarce felt. Thou'dst shun a bear;
But if thy flight lay toward the raging sea,   10
Thou'dst meet the bear i' th' mouth. When the mind's free,
The body's delicate. The tempest in my mind
Doth from my senses take all feeling else
Save what beats there. Filial ingratitude!
Is it not as this mouth should tear this hand   15
For lifting food to't? But I will punish home!
No, I will weep no more. In such a night
'To shut me out! Pour on; I will endure.
In such a night as this! O Regan, Goneril!
Your old kind father, whose frank heart gave all!   20
O, that way madness lies; let me shun that!
No more of that.

KENT   Good my lord, enter here.

LEAR   Prithee go in thyself; seek thine own case.
This tempest will not give me leave to ponder
On things would hurt me more. But I'll go in.   25
[To the Fool] In, boy; go first, –
You houseless poverty –
Nay, get thee in. I'll pray, and then I'll sleep.

Exit FOOL.

Poor naked wretches, wheresoe'er you are,
That bide the pelting of this pitiless storm,
How shall your houseless heads and unfed sides,   30
Your looped and windowed raggedness, defend you   ＞

Wilt: *will thou*

Invades: *penetrates*
greater malady: *i.e. the mind's torment*
lesser: *i.e. bodily pains*

i' th' mouth: *face to face*
delicate: *prone to hurt*
senses: *physical senses*

punish home: *punish fully*

thine own case: *your own needs*

would: *that would*

bide: *endure*

defend: *protect*

....

* 15–6   **Is it not as this mouth … food
to't?:** *Is it not as if one part of the
body rebels against another part that
nourishes it. Lear conceives of himself
and his children as making up one
complete body, or organic whole.*

† 21   **O, that way madness lies:** *dwelling
on the injustice of his daughters'
ingratitude will lead him towards
madness.*

‡ 31   **Your loop'd and window'd raggedness:** *your ragged clothes, full of loops
and holes.*

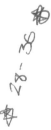

	From seasons such as these? O, I have ta'en	
	Too little care of this! Take physic, pomp;*	
	Expose thyself to feel what wretches feel,	
	That thou mayst shake the superflux to them	35
	And show the heavens more just.	
EDGAR	[Within] Fathom and half, fathom and half! Poor Tom!	

Enter FOOL from the hovel.

FOOL	Come not in here, nuncle, here's a spirit. Help me, help me!	
KENT	Give me thy hand. Who's there?	40
FOOL	A spirit, a spirit! He says his name's poor Tom.	
KENT	What art thou that dost grumble there i' th' straw?	
	Come forth.	

Enter EDGAR disguised as a madman.

EDGAR	Away! the foul fiend follows me!	
	Through the sharp hawthorn blow the winds.	
	Humh! go to thy cold bed, and warm thee.	45
LEAR	Hast thou given all to thy two daughters, and art thou come†	
	to this?	
EDGAR	Who gives anything to poor Tom, whom the foul fiend	
	hath led through fire and through flame, through ford	
	and whirlpool, o'er bog and quagmire; that hath laid	50
	knives under his pillow and halters in his pew,	
	set ratsbane by his porridge, made him proud of heart,	
	to ride on a bay trotting horse over four-inched	
	bridges, to course his own shadow for a traitor.	
	Bless thy five wits! Tom's a-cold. O, do de, do de,	
	do de. Bless thee from whirlwinds, star-blasting, and	55
	taking! Do poor Tom some charity, whom the foul fiend†	
	vexes. There could I have him now – and there	
	– and there again – and there!	

Storm still.

LEAR	What, have his daughters brought him to this pass?	60
	Couldst thou save nothing? Didst thou give 'em all?	
FOOL	Nay, he reserved a blanket, else we had been all shamed.	
LEAR	Now all the plagues that in the pendulous air	
	Hang fated o'er men's faults light on thy daughters!	
KENT	He hath no daughters, sir.	65
LEAR	Death, traitor! nothing could have subdued nature	
	To such a lowness but his unkind daughters.	
	Is it the fashion that discarded fathers	
	Should have thus little mercy on their flesh?	
	Judicious punishment! 'Twas this flesh begot	70
	Those pelican daughters.§	

[handwritten margin note: animal imagery]

care of: *consideration of, responsibility for*

superflux: *excess;* **them:** *the poor*
more just: *more egalitarian*
Fathom and half: *ref. to rain storm*

spirit: *demon*

foul fiend: *devil*

foul fiend: *devil*

ratsbane: *poison*

course: *to follow*
wits: *senses*
star-blasting: *fate*
taking: *infection, death*

blanket: *to cover himself*
pendulous: *threatening*
light: *descend*

subdued: *reduced*

Judicious: *fair, fitting*

* 33   **Take physic, pomp:** *take medical treatment, treat or purge thyself of luxurious, rich living*

† 47   **Hast thou given all to thy two daughters ... this?:** *Lear identifies himself with the disguised Edgar, assuming that he also must have been reduced to this beggared state because of his foolish generosity to his daughters.*

‡ 48–56   **foul fiend ... taking:** *the devil places temptations everywhere to lure him into taking his own life.*

§ 71   **pelican daughters:** *young pelicans were thought to feed from the flesh and blood they pecked from their parent's breast.*

EDGAR	Pillicock sat on Pillicock's Hill.
	'Allow, 'allow, loo, loo!
FOOL	This cold night will turn us all to fools and madmen.
EDGAR	Take heed o' th' foul fiend; obey thy parents: keep
	thy word justly; swear not; commit not with man's
	sworn spouse; set not thy sweet heart on proud array.
	Tom's a-cold.
LEAR	What hast thou been?
EDGAR	A servingman, proud in heart and mind; that curled
	my hair, wore gloves in my cap; served the lust of my
	mistress' heart and did the act of darkness with her;
	swore as many oaths as I spake words, and broke them
	in the sweet face of heaven; one that slept in the contriving
	of lust, and wak'd to do it. Wine lov'd I deeply,
	dice dearly; and in woman out-paramoured
	the Turk. False of heart, light of ear, bloody of hand;
	hog in sloth, fox in stealth, wolf in greediness, dog in
	madness, lion in prey. Let not the creaking of shoes
	nor the rustling of silks betray thy poor heart to woman.
	Keep thy foot out of brothel, thy hand out
	of placket, thy pen from lender's book, and defy
	the foul fiend. Still through the hawthorn blows the
	cold wind; says suum, mun, hey, no, nonny. Dolphin
	my boy, my boy, sessa! Let him trot by.

Storm still.

LEAR	Why, thou wert better in thy grave than to answer with
	thy uncovered body this extremity of the skies. Is
	man no more than this? Consider him well.
	Thou ow'st the worm no silk, the beast no hide, the sheep
	no wool, the cat no perfume. Ha! Here's three on's
	are sophisticated! Thou art the thing itself;
	unaccommodated man is no more but such a poor,
	bare, forked animal as thou art. Off, off, you
	lendings! Collie, unbutton here. *[Tears at his clothes]*
FOOL	Prithee, nuncle, be contented! 'Tis a naughty night to
	swim in. Now a little fire in a wild field were like an old
	lecher's heart-a small spark, all the rest on's body
	cold. Look, here comes a walking fire.

Enter GLOUCESTER with a torch.

EDGAR	This is the foul fiend Flibbertigibbet. He begins at
	curfew, and walks till the first cock. He gives the web
	and the pin, squints the eye, and makes the
	harelip; mildews the white wheat, and hurts the poor
	creature of earth.
	Swithold footed thrice the 'old;
	He met the nightmare, and her nine fold;
	Bid her alight
	And her troth plight,
	And aroint thee, witch, aroint thee!
KENT	How fares your Grace?
LEAR	What's he?
KENT	Who's there? What is't you seek?

clothing imagery

stealth: *craftiness*
prey: *preying*

placket: *opening in petticoat*

uncovered: *unclothed, unprotected*
him: *poor Tom*

on's: *ones (ref. to Fool, Kent & Gloucester)*
sophisticated: *cultured;* **thing:** *nature*
unaccommodated: *natural, without trappings*

lendings: *borrowed items (clothes*
naughty: *wicked*

lecher:????
walking fire: *sees torch*

Flibbertigibbet: *dancing devil*
the first cock: *dawn;* **web … pin:** *cataract*

Swithold … : *a charm*

aroint: *be gone*

What's he?: *who are you?*

---

* 86-7   **out-paramoured /** **the Turk:** *had*
more lovers than the Turkish Sultan
had in his harem;

† 87   **light of ear:** *ready to listen to the*
most malicious gossip;

‡ 88-9   **hog … lion:** *animals often served to*
represent the Seven Deadly Sins.

GLOUCESTER   What are you there? Your names?

EDGAR   Poor Tom, that eats the swimming frog, the toad, the
tadpole, the wall-newt and the water; that in the fury
of his heart, when the foul fiend rages' eats cow-dung   125
for sallets, swallows the old rat and the ditch-dog,
drinks the green mantle of the standing pool; who is
whipped from tithing to tithing, and stock-punished
and imprisoned; who hath had three suits to his
back, six shirts to his body, horse to ride, and weapons to   130
wear;
         But mice and rats, and such small deer,
         Have been Tom's food for seven long year.
Beware my follower. Peace, Smulkin! peace, thou
fiend!

GLOUCESTER   What, hath your Grace no better company?   135

EDGAR   The prince of darkness is a gentleman!
Modo he's call'd, and Mahu.

GLOUCESTER   Our flesh and blood is grown so vile, my lord,
That it doth hate what gets it.   140

EDGAR   Poor Tom's a-cold.

GLOUCESTER   Go in with me. My duty cannot suffer
T' obey in all your daughters' hard commands.
Though their injunction be to bar my doors
And let this tyrannous night take hold upon you,   145
Yet have I ventured to come seek you out
And bring you where both fire and food is ready.

LEAR   First let me talk with this philosopher.
What is the cause of thunder?

KENT   Good my lord, take his offer; go into th' house.   150

LEAR   I'll talk a word with this same learned Theban.
What is your study?

EDGAR   How to prevent the fiend and to kill vermin.

LEAR   Let me ask you one word in private.

KENT   Importune him once more to go, my lord.   155
His wits begin t' unsettle.

GLOUCESTER   Canst thou blame him?

Storm still.

His daughters seek his death. Ah, that good Kent!
He said it would be thus – poor banished man!
Thou say'st the King grows mad: I'll tell thee, friend,
I am almost mad myself. I had a son,   160
Now outlaw'd from my blood. He sought my life
But lately, very late. I lov'd him, friend –
No father his son dearer. True to tell thee,
The grief hath crazed my wits. What a night's this!
I do beseech your Grace –

LEAR   O, cry you mercy, sir.   165
Noble philosopher, your company.

EDGAR   Tom's a-cold.

GLOUCESTER   In, fellow, there, into th' hovel; keep thee warm.

LEAR   Come, let's in all.

KENT   This way, my lord.   170

LEAR   With him!
I will keep still with my philosopher.

KENT   Good my lord, soothe him; let him take the fellow.

GLOUCESTER   Take him you on.

---

sallets: *salads*
green mantle: *mildew*
tithing: *small parish (of ten families)*

follower: *fiend (that follows him)*

Modo … Mahu: *names for the devil*
Our flesh and blood: *our offspring*

this philosopher: *poor Tom*

Importune: *demand*

lately: *recently*

soothe: *mollify*

....

 * 133   **Smulkin:** *a devil taking the form of a
          mouse*

KENT   Sirrah, come on; go along with us.
LEAR   Come, good Athenian.   175
GLOUCESTER   No words, no words! hush.
EDGAR   Child Rowland to the dark tower came;
                         His word was still
                         Fie, foh, and fum!
                         I smell the blood of a British man.   180

Exeunt.

* 175   **good Athenian:** *refers to poor Tom*
         as if he was an ancient Greek philoso-
         pher

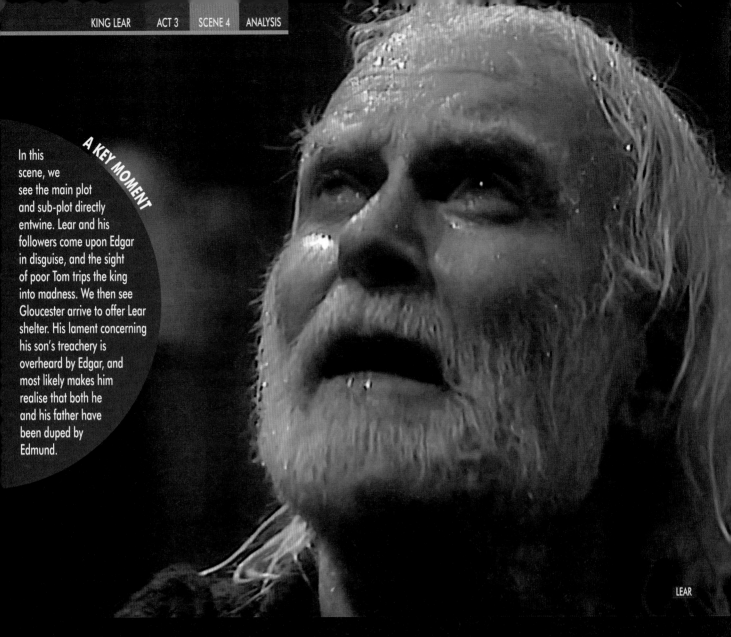

A KEY MOMENT

In this scene, we see the main plot and sub-plot directly entwine. Lear and his followers come upon Edgar in disguise, and the sight of poor Tom trips the king into madness. We then see Gloucester arrive to offer Lear shelter. His lament concerning his son's treachery is overheard by Edgar, and most likely makes him realise that both he and his father have been duped by Edmund.

LEAR

Lear, Kent and the Fool take refuge from the storm in a hovel. They are startled to find 'poor Tom' (Edgar in disguise) already in the hovel. Lear is drawn to poor Tom, moved by his naked, helpless state, and finding meaning in his ranting. Gloucester arrives at the hovel, saying that he has come to help Lear.

ACTION

LINES 1–40: LEAR, KENT AND THE FOOL REACH THE HOVEL

Lear, Kent and the Fool arrive at the hovel. Kent urges Lear to get in out of the storm. (1–3) Lear, however, refuses to go inside, telling Kent to 'Let me alone'. (3) He is so preoccupied with the 'great malady' of his mental torment that he 'scarcely' feels the 'lesser' malady of the storm raging around him. (8–9) His inner torment, the 'tempest in my mind', is all that he can focus on. (12–14)

He continues to obsess about his daughters' treatment of him. He has fed and clothed them and now they have turned on him: 'Filial ingratitude! Is it not at this

mouth / Should tear at this hand / For lifting food to't?' (14–16) He still seems shocked that Regan and Goneril have thrown him out of the castle: 'In such a night / To shut me out … O Regan, Goneril! / Your old, kind father'. (17–20) He vows to punish them. but then decides to avoid thinking about them altogether: 'let me shun that; / No more of that'. (21–2)

Lear recovered some of his sanity in Act 3, Scene 4, but he knows that if he thinks too much about his daughters misdeeds, he will go completely insane once more: 'O that way madness lies!' (21) His agitated mental state is evident in the way he repeatedly changes his mind about taking shelter in the hovel. (23–7) Finally, he agrees to spend the night there, saying that he will 'pray, and then I'll sleep'. (27) He sends the fool in first to check the place out: 'In, boy, go first'. (26)

LINES 41–108: THEY MEET 'POOR TOM'

Edgar is in the hovel disguised as a madman called 'poor Tom'. He startles the fool who runs out claiming the place is haunted: 'here's a spirit / Help me! Help me!' (38–9) Edgar follows the fool out of the hovel. He fakes madness, advising Lear and the others to flee because a 'fiend' or devil is pursuing him: 'Away! The foul fiend follows me!' (43) Edgar plays the part of a crazy person with great gusto:

· He is almost naked, wearing only a blanket. (62)
· He speaks a great deal of 'nursery rhyme' type gibberish, for example: 'Pillicock sat on Pillicock-hill: / Halloo, halloo, loo, loo!' (72-73) and 'Heigh no nonny. Dolphin, my boy, my boy!' (94–5)
· He says the he is being tormented by a devil, who has 'led' him through the wilds of the countryside: 'through fire and through ford and whirlpool, o'er bog and quagmire'. (48–50)
· He says that the devil constantly tempts him to commit suicide, leaving knives under his pillow, nooses ('halters') in his pew and poison ('wolfsbane') next to his porridge. (48–54)
· He says that he used to be a 'serving-man proud of heart and mind'. (80) However, his addiction to gambling drink and prostitution brought him to his current pitiful condition: 'Wine loved I deeply, dice dearly and in woman out-paramoured the Turk'. (86–8) He urges Lear and the others not to sin like he did lest they too fall under the devil's power. (93–4)

Lear suggests that Tom, like him, must have gone insane when he gave everything

LEAR

GRIEF-STRICKEN

At the beginning of this scene, Lear's anger appears to have calmed and he seems to be sunk in grief. When Kent asks him to take refuge in the hovel, he refuses, saying that the violence of the storm prevents him from dwelling on his daughters' cruelty: 'This tempest will not give me leave to ponder/ On things would hurt me more'. (23–4) The king has been crying ('I will weep no more') and still cannot come to terms with what has happened: 'Your old kind father, whose frank heart gave all'. (20)

SOCIAL CONSCIENCE AND COMPASSION

The king's social conscience continues to grow in this scene. Before he enters the hovel, he wonders how the poor outcasts of society will survive the ferocity of the storm: 'How shall your houseless heads and unfed sides/ Your loop'd and window'd raggedness, defend you/ From seasons such as these?' (30–2)

Lear realises that he showed great negligence over the plight of the disadvantaged when he was king:

> O! I have ta'en
> Too little care of this. Take physic, pomp;
> Expose thyself to feel what wretches feel,
> That thou mayst shake the superflux to them,
> And show the heavens more just (32–6)

Lear sees in poor Tom man reduced to his bare natural essence: 'thou art the thing itself;/ Unaccommodated man is no more but such a poor,/ bare forked animal as thou art'. (108–10) In his new-found solidarity with society's outcasts, the king decides to remove his clothing: 'Off, off, you/ lendings! Come; unbutton here'. (110–11)

Lear's realisation of the plight of others is also reflected by the fact that he urges the Fool to enter the hovel first: 'In, boy; go first. You houseless/ poverty'. (26)

MADNESS

It is in this scene that we see Lear slip into insanity. Outside of the hovel, he knows madness is very close: 'O! that way madness lies; let me shun that;/ No more of that'. (21–2)

It appears to be the sight of poor Tom that drives the king over the edge. The first sign that he has lost his reason is when he asks if Tom was reduced to poverty on account of having selfish daughters: 'Didst thou give all to thy two daughters?/ And art thou come to this?' (47–8) He harps on this theme, and when Kent gently tries to dissuade him, Lear grows very angry: 'Death, traitor! Nothing could have subdued nature/ To such a lowness, but his unkind daughters'. (69–70)

Lear refers to Tom as a 'learned Theban' and a 'philosopher', and refuses to leave the hovel without him. As Kent puts it, 'his wits begin to unsettle'. (165)

CHARACTER DEVELOPMENT

to his daughters: 'Couldst thou save nothing? Didst thou give them all?' (46–7, 60-61) He wonders if poor Tom's 'daughters brought him to this pass'. (60) Kent tells Lear that Tom has no daughters, but Lear ignores this, insisting that only 'unkind daughters' could bring someone to 'such a lowness'. (66–7)

Lear's mind continues its plunge into insanity. He begins to take off his clothes. He says that we 'borrow' clothes from other animals to conceal our nakedness. Lear seems to admire the fact that poor Tom doesn't bother with these 'lendings', but goes around more or less naked: 'Thou owest the worm no silk, the beast no hide, the sheep no wool'. (98–9) According to Lear, poor Tom does not attempt to disguise the fact that as a human being he is weak and vulnerable: 'a poor, bare, forked animal'. (104)

The king is so impressed with Tom's lack of attire that he starts to strip off himself: 'Off, off, you lendings! Come; unbutton here'. (103–4) The fool responds to this in a typically witty fashion, telling Lear that it is a 'naughty', or nasty, night for swimming: 'Prithee, nuncle, be contented, 'tis a naughty night to swim in'. (105–6) At that moment the fool sees Gloucester arriving with a torch: 'Look! Here comes a walking fire'. (108)

LINES 109–47: GLOUCESTER ARRIVES

Gloucester has come looking for Lear. In the storm and darkness, he doesn't recognise Kent. Nor does he realise that 'poor Tom' is really his son Edgar: 'What are you there? Your names?' (122) He seems shocked that Lear has only what seem to be beggars and mad men for company: 'What! Hath your grace no better company?' (135)

Gloucester laments the fact that both he and Lear have been turned on by their children. (139–40) (Lear has been turned on by Goneril and Regan, while Gloucester believes he has turned on by his son Edgar). Gloucester says that his sense of loyalty or 'duty' prevented him from following the sisters' orders. He couldn't just 'bar his doors' and leave Lear at the mercy of this 'tyrranous' storm:

> My duty cannot suffer
> To obey in all your daughters' hard commands:
> Though their injunction be to bar my doors
> And let this tyrranous night take hold upon you. (142–5)

Instead, Gloucester has decided to venture out into the storm, find Lear and bring him to a nearby house where food and shelter has been arranged: 'Yet have I ventur'd to come seek you out / And bring you where both food and fire is ready'. (146–7)

CHARACTER DEVELOPMENT

EDGAR

POOR TOM
We see Edgar in his new role as poor Tom in this scene. What is most striking and impressive is the apparent ease with which he acts out his new identity. He completely fools Lear, Kent and the Fool, and even Gloucester shows no sign of recognising his son.

The character of Tom is a raving, pauperised madman, possessed by demons, who makes constant reference to 'the foul fiend' that haunts him. According to his story, he was once a serving-man who was seduced by his mistress and became an outcast as a result.

His warnings to beware of the guiles of women obviously strike a chord with Lear: 'Let not the creaking of shoes/ nor the rustling of silks betray thy poor heart to/ woman'. (95–6) The king refers to him as a 'learned Theban' and 'philosopher'. We suspect that Tom's advice is Edgar giving voice to his own honourable moral code: 'Obey thy parents; keep/ thy word justly; swear not; commit not with man's/ sworn spouse; set not thy sweet heart on proud array'. (79–81)

GLOUCESTER

ACTING NOBLY
Gloucester puts his intention to help Lear into action in this scene: 'My duty cannot suffer/ To obey in all your daughter's hard commands'. (152–3) He intends to rescue the king and bring him to 'where both fire and food are ready'. (157) Gloucester also reveals the disturbing information that Goneril and Regan are now set on having Lear murdered: 'His daughters seek his death'. (167)

SORROWFUL
Further parallels are established between Gloucester and Lear in this scene. Like the king, he is grief-stricken at what he thinks is Edgar's betrayal: 'he sought my life,/ But lately, very late; I lov'd him, friend,/ No father his son dearer'. (171–3) He has no idea that the son he thinks betrayed him is in front of his very eyes.

> But where the greater malady is fix'd,
> The lesser is scarce felt
>
> *Lear (8-9)*

> Expose thyself to feel what wretches feel,
> That thou mayst shake the superflux to them,
> And show the heavens more just
>
> *Lear (34-6)*

> Thou art the thing itself;
> unaccommodated man is no more but such a poor,
> bare, forked animal as thou art
>
> *Lear (108-10)*

SOME LINES TO LEARN

LINES 148–80: LEAR REGARDS POOR TOM AS A WISE MAN

We see Lear's crazed state of mind when he describes poor Tom as a 'philosopher': 'First let me talk with this philosopher'. (148) He refers to Tom as an 'Athenian' and a 'Theban' because the Greek cities of Athens and Thebes were famous for their wisdom. (151, 177) He seems convinced that poor Tom is a wise and 'learned' man. He asks him what his specialist area of study is, and quizzes him on the origins of thunder. (149, 152)

He is more interested in talking to this 'noble philosopher' than he is in taking up Gloucester's offer of shelter 'Let me ask you one word in private … Noble philosopher your company'. (154, 176) Kent laments the fact that Lear's mind, having recovered somewhat (in Act 3, Scene 2) has once again been gripped by insanity: 'His wits begin to unsettle'. (156) He and Gloucester repeatedly urge the king to take shelter from the storm. (155, 165, 170)

Finally, Lear agrees to take shelter in the hovel, but only on condition that poor Tom can stay with him: 'Come let's all in … I will keep still with my philosopher'. (160–71) Kent and Gloucester agree to this: 'Sirrah, come on; go along with us'. (175) The little group will shelter briefly in the hovel before going on to the house that Gloucester has prepared for them. As they enter the hovel, poor Tom utters a final nonsense rhyme, this time mixing lines from Jack and the Beanstalk with lines from an old poem called 'Childe Roland'. (178–80)

KENT

PROTECTING THE KING

Kent acts his typical self in this scene. He urges the king to take shelter in the hovel, and also advises him to accept Gloucester's offer of food and protection. His loyalty is well summed up by his response when Lear asks him if is trying to break his heart: 'I'd rather break mine own'. (7)

THE FOOL

WORRIED FOR HIS MASTER

Like Kent, the Fool also seeks to protect his master. He tells the king to keep his clothes on when the latter tries to pull them off in his show of solidarity with Edgar. It is also noticeable, however, that he is quieter in this scene than before. The suffering he is enduring, and that of the king, appear to be wearing him down: 'This cold night will turn us all to fools and madmen'. (78)

CHARACTER DEVELOPMENT

LEAR & EDGAR

Enter CORNWALL and EDMUND.

CORNWALL   I will have my revenge ere I depart his house.

EDMUND   How, my lord, I may be censured, that nature thus
gives way to loyalty, something fears me to think of.

CORNWALL   I now perceive it was not altogether your brother's evil
disposition made him seek his death; but a provoking   5
merit, set a-work by a reproveable badness in himself.

EDMUND   How malicious is my fortune that I must repent to
be just! This is the letter he spoke of, which approves
him an intelligent party to the advantages of France.
O heavens! That this treason were not – or not I the   10
detector!

CORNWALL   Go with me to the Duchess.

EDMUND   If the matter of this paper be certain, you have mighty
business in hand.

CORNWALL   True or false, it hath made thee Earl of Gloucester.   15
Seek out where thy father is, that he may be ready for our
apprehension.

EDMUND   *[Aside]* If I find him comforting the King, it will stuff
his suspicion more fully. I will persever in my course of
loyalty, though the conflict be sore between that and my   20
blood.

CORNWALL   I will lay trust upon thee, and thou shalt find a dearer
father in my love.

Exeunt.

---

ere: *before*

censured: *judged;* **nature:** *bond of kinship*

something fears: *somewhat frightens*

disposition: *character*

reproveable: *reprehensible*

apprehension: *arrest*

stuff: *support*

persever: *persevere*

loyalty: *to the duke*

---

* 4–6   **I now perceive … badness in
himself:** *I see now that it was not just
an innate evil in your brother, but
Gloucester's deserving nature coupled
with your brother's reprehensible badness, that incited him to kill his father.*

† 7–8   **How malicious is my fortune that
I must repent to be just :** *what poor
fortune I have that in order to do the
right thing by my country I must,
with regret, betray my father.*

CORNWALL

EDMUND

Edmund tells Cornwall that Gloucester is trying to help Lear, and gives him the letter Gloucester received from France as proof. Cornwall tells Edmund that he will be rewarded with his father's title for his loyalty. He instructs Edmund to find his father so that he might be punished for his treachery.

ACTION

EDMUND MEETS WITH CORNWALL

Edmund has told Cornwall that Gloucester is still loyal to King Lear. He gives Cornwall the letter Gloucester received from France. He says that this letter proves ('approves') that Gloucester is in league with the French invaders: 'This is the letter he spoke of, which approves him an intelligent party to the advantages of France'. (8–9) Cornwall, he says, must handle the 'mighty business' of punishing his father: 'If the matter of this paper be true you have mighty business in hand'. (13–14)

Edmund pretends to be saddened and shocked that his father has sided against Goneril and Regan, and stayed loyal to King Lear: 'Oh heavens! that this treason were not'. (10) He pretends that he has only reluctantly told Cornwall about his father's dealings with the French. (2–3) He says that he is torn between loyalty to his father ('blood') on one hand and loyalty to his country on the other: 'I will persevere in my course of loyalty, though the conflict be sore between that and my blood'. (20–1) In reality, however, he is

delighted at how things have worked out. He hopes that Gloucester will be found 'comforting' King Lear because this will confirm Cornwall's suspicions about him. (18–19)

Cornwall declares that Gloucester's earldom will be taken from him and given to Edmund. (15) He says that from now on he will be a father figure to Edmund, claiming he will be a better 'father' to Edmund that Gloucester ever was: 'I will lay trust upon thee; and thou shalt find a dearer father in my love'. (22–3)

Cornwall claims that Gloucester is an evil man, filled with 'reprovable badness'. (6) He regards Gloucester as a traitor because he has stayed loyal to King Lear and has been in contact with the French invaders. He vows to avenge this 'treachery', and sends Edmund to find Gloucester so that he can be arrested: 'Seek out where thy father is, that he may be ready for our apprehension'. (1, 16–17)

EDMUND

CYNICAL TRAITOR

Edmund shows the depths of his ambition and heartlessness in this scene. He betrays Gloucester to Cornwall, knowing full well that his father may lose his life as a result. Edmund's only interest lies in attaining power, and by removing Gloucester he takes another step nearer that goal.

Edmund's cynicism is on full display here. He acts as if he is struggling with his soul in doing his duty to Cornwall: 'O heavens! That this treason were not, or not I the/ detector!' (13–14) He is either an excellent actor, or else Cornwall is very gullible and an easy target for his wiles.

CORNWALL

CRUEL

We see in this scene a hint of the cruelty in Cornwall's soul that will be on full display shortly. He is determined to extract revenge for Gloucester's 'betrayal': 'I will have my revenge ere I depart his house'. (1) He is determined to paint his host in as black a way as possible, claiming it was no surprise that Edgar betrayed him. (4–6)

Like Gloucester and Edgar before him, Cornwall also shows no suspicion of Edmund's deeper motives. Instead, he rewards him by making him the new Earl of Gloucester. (18) He is also eager to adopt Edmund: 'I will lay my trust upon thee: and thou shalt find a dearer/ father in my love'. (26) Edmund's scheming appears to be progressing according to plan.

> How malicious is my fortune that I must repent to be just!
> *Edmund (10)*

SOME LINES TO LEARN

A farmhouse near Gloucester's castle

Mock trial

Enter GLOUCESTER, LEAR, KENT, FOOL, and EDGAR.

GLOUCESTER Here is better than the open air; take it thankfully. I will piece out the comfort with what addition I can. I will not be long from you.

KENT All the power of his wits have given way to his impatience. The gods reward your kindness! 5

Exit GLOUCESTER.

EDGAR Frateretto calls me, and tells me Nero is an angler in the lake of darkness. Pray, innocent, and beware the foul fiend.

FOOL Prithee, nuncle, tell me whether a madman be a gentleman or a yeoman. 10

LEAR A king, a king!

FOOL No, he's a yeoman that has a gentleman to his son; for he's a mad yeoman that sees his son a gentleman before him.

LEAR To have a thousand with red burning spits
Come hizzing in upon 'em – 15

EDGAR The foul fiend bites my back.

FOOL He's mad that trusts in the tameness of a wolf, a horse's health, a boy's love, or a whore's oath.

LEAR It shall be done; I will arraign them straight. 20
[To Edgar] Come, sit thou here, most learned justicer.
[To the Fool] Thou, sapient sir, sit here. Now, you she-foxes!

EDGAR Look, where he stands and glares! Want'st thou eyes at trial, madam?

    Come o'er the bourn, Bessy, to me. 25

FOOL   Her boat hath a leak,
    And she must not speak
    Why she dares not come over to thee. 30

EDGAR The foul fiend haunts poor Tom in the voice of a nightingale. Hoppedance cries in Tom's belly for two white herring. Croak not, black angel; I have no food for thee.

KENT How do you, sir? Stand you not so amazed. 35
Will you lie down and rest upon the cushions?

LEAR I'll see their trial first. Bring in their evidence.
[To Edgar] Thou, robed man of justice, take thy place.
[To the Fool] And thou, his yokefellow of equity,‡
Bench by his side. *[To Kent]* You are 40
o' th' commission,
Sit you too.

---

piece: *augment*

impatience: *passion*

Frateretto: *a demon*

yeoman: *farmer*

to: *as*

a thousand: *i.e a thousand devils*

arraign: *accuse, put (his daughters) on trial*

sapient: *wise;* **she-foxes:** *Goneril and Regan*
eyes: *witnesses, spectators*

bourn: *river*

nightingale: *ref. to Fool's singing*

bench: *judges' bench*
o' th' commission: *one of the commissioned*

....
* 6   **Nero is an angler:** *reference to Chaucer's 'Monk's Tale'.*

† 32   **Hoppedance:** *devil*

‡ 39   **yokefellow of equity:** *partner in fairness, judge in court*

EDGAR   Let us deal justly.

             Sleepest or wakest thou, jolly shepherd?
             Thy sheep be in the corn;   45
             And for one blast of thy minikin mouth
             Thy sheep shall take no harm.
    Purr! the cat is gray.

LEAR   Arraign her first. 'Tis Goneril. I here take my oath
before this honourable assembly, she kicked the   50
poor King her father.

FOOL   Come hither, mistress. Is your name Goneril?

LEAR   She cannot deny it.

FOOL   Cry you mercy, I took you for a joint-stool.†

LEAR   And here's another, whose warped looks proclaim   55
What store her heart is made on. Stop her there!
Arms, arms! sword! fire! Corruption in the place!
False justicer, why hast thou let her scape?

EDGAR   Bless thy five wits!

KENT   O pity! Sir, where is the patience now   60
That you so oft have boasted to retain?

EDGAR   [Aside] My tears begin to take his part so much
They'll mar my counterfeiting.

LEAR   The little dogs and all,
Tray, Blanch, and Sweetheart, see, they bark at me.‡   65

EDGAR   Tom will throw his head at them.
Avaunt, you curs!

             Be thy mouth or black or white,
             Tooth that poisons if it bite;
             Mastiff, greyhound, mongrel grim,   70
             Hound or spaniel, brach or lym,
             Bobtail tyke or trundle-tail – §
             Tom will make them weep and wail;
             For, with throwing thus my head,
             Dogs leap the hatch, and all are fled.   75
Do de, de, de. Sessa! Come, march to wakes and
fairs and market-towns. Poor Tom, thy horn is dry.

LEAR   Then let them anatomize Regan. See what breeds
about her heart. Is there any cause in nature that
makes these hard hearts? [To Edgar] You, sir – I   80
entertain you for one of my hundred; only I do not
like the fashion of your garments. You'll
say they are Persian attire; but let them be changed.

KENT   Now, good my lord, lie here and rest awhile.

LEAR   Make no noise, make no noise; draw the curtains.   85
So, so, so. We'll go to supper i' th' morning. So, so, so.

FOOL   And I'll go to bed at noon.

Enter GLOUCESTER.

GLOUCESTER   Come hither, friend. Where is the king my master?

KENT   Here, sir; but trouble him not; his wits are gone.

---

minikin: *little*

Arraign: *accuse*

another: *Regan;* warped: *proclaim*
store: *stock*

scape: *escape*
wits: *senses*

mar … counterfeiting: *damage my disguise*

Avaunt: *go away*

brach: *hound (bitch);* lym: *bloodhound*
trundle: *long and curly*

horn is dry: *thirsty, empty*
anatomize: *dissect, examine*

my hundred: *his hundred knights*

- *   48   the cat is gray: *evil spirits were often thought to appear as cats*
- †   54   Cry you mercy, I took you for a joint-stool: *commonly used as an excuse for overlooking someone*
- ‡   64–5   The little dogs … bark at me: *Lear imagines that even his lapdogs have turned against him.*
- §   72   Bobtail tyke: *small dog with its tail cut short*

GLOUCESTER   Good friend, I prithee take him in thy arms.
              I have o'erheard a plot of death upon him.   90
              There is a litter ready; lay him in't   **litter:** *vehicle*
              And drive towards Dover, friend, where thou shalt meet
              Both welcome and protection. Take up thy master.
              If thou shouldst dally half an hour, his life,   95
              With thine, and all that offer to defend him,
              Stand in assured loss. Take up, take up!   **assured:** *certain*
              And follow me, that will to some provision
              Give thee quick conduct.   **quick conduct:** *act quickly*
KENT   Oppressed nature sleeps.
              This rest might yet have balmed thy broken sinews,   100   **balmed:** *soothed;* **sinews:** *nerves*
              Which, if convenience will not allow,   **convenience:** *circumstance;* **allow:** *fix*
              Stand in hard cure. *[To the Fool]* Come, help to bear
                                  thy master.
              Thou must not stay behind.
GLOUCESTER   Come, come, away!
Exeunt all but EDGAR.
EDGAR   When we our betters see bearing our woes,
              We scarcely think our miseries our foes.   105
              Who alone suffers suffers most i' th' mind,
              Leaving free things and happy shows behind;   **free:** *carefree*
              But then the mind much sufferance doth o'erskip   **o'erskip:** *lessen*
              When grief hath mates, and bearing fellowship.   **hath mates:** *is shared;* **bearing:** *suffering*
              How light and portable my pain seems now,   110   **portable:** *endurable*
              When that which makes me bend makes the King bow,†
              He childed as I fathered! Tom, away!‡
              Mark the high noises, and thyself bewray   **thyself bewray:** *reveal your true self*
              When false opinion, whose wrong thought defiles thee,   **defiles:** *slanders*
              In thy just proof repeals and reconciles thee.   115   **just proof:** *of his integrity*
              What will hap more to-night, safe scape the King!   **What … more:** *whatever else will happen*
              Lurk, lurk.
Exit.

---

*   100   **broken sinews:** *shattered nerves*

†   111   **that which makes me bend makes the King bow:** *that which weighs so heavily on me, making me bend, bows the king down*

‡   112   **He childed as I fathered:** *he is turned into a child by his suffering, I a father; or perhaps it may be read as, his treatment by his children is similar to my treatment by my father.*

THE FOOL, LEAR & EDGAR

Gloucester brings Lear and the others to a farmhouse and goes to find provisions. Lear conducts a mock-trial of Goneril and Regan, assisted by Edgar and the Fool. Gloucester returns with news that a plot is afoot against the king's life, and says that Lear must be brought to Dover, where Cordelia waits with the French troops. Edgar is left behind and makes a speech about suffering.

ACTION

✒ LINES 1–19: SHELTER

Gloucester has brought Lear and the others to a farmhouse where they can take shelter from the storm: 'Here is better than the open air, take it thankfully'. (1) Gloucester goes to find provisions, much to the relief of Kent: 'The gods reward your kindness!' (5)

Edgar continues to play the role of madman with great gusto, ranting about the demons that are pursuing him: 'the foul fiend bites my back'. (17) He says that the fiend is looking at him: 'Look, where he stands and glares!' (25) Bizarrely, he says that demons are singing in his 'belly' with the voice of a nightingale. (31–2) As usual he misses no opportunity to burst in to song. (43, 68)

✒ LINES 19–87: THE MOCK TRIAL

Lear declares that he will put his daughters on trial for their misdeeds right now ('arraign' them): 'it shall be done; I will arraign them straight'. (20) The crazed Lear isn't about to let the fact that his daughters aren't actually present get in the way of this plan. He ignores Kent's suggestion that he should rest, declaring that Kent, Edgar and the Fool will play the part of judges at this imaginary trial. (37–40) Poor Tom, he says, is a judge or 'robed man of justice', and the fool and Kent must join him on the magistrate's bench.

Lear, in his demented state, declares that Goneril and Regan have come before this 'honourable assembly' for trial: 'Arraign her first; 'tis Goneril … And here's another'. (49) He accuses her of kicking him, and says that Regan's face reveals the hardness of her heart. (50–5)

Lear becomes increasingly agitated. Firstly, he accuses the three 'judges' of letting Goneril and Regan escape the trial: 'Corruption in the place! / False justicer, why hast thou let her 'scape?' (38–9) He begins to hallucinate, claiming that he sees three imaginary little dogs called Tray, Blanch and Sweet-heart. (65) (It has been suggested that these represent his three daughters). He then attempts to employ poor Tom as one of his hundred knights, on the condition that he changes his style of dress. Finally, he collapses in what seems to be a state of nervous exhaustion, saying 'Make no noise, make no noise; draw the curtains'. (86)

Edgar, the fool and Kent are all deeply moved by this display of complete and total insanity. Edgar fears that he'll burst into tears, ruining his disguise: My tears begin to take his part so much, / They'll mar my counterfeiting'. (61–2) Kent, too, is moved by Lear's decline: 'O Pity!' (60) The Fool's declaration that he will 'go to bed at noon' is generally taken as a statement of his complete despair at Lear's situation. As Kent puts it, Lear's 'wits are gone'. (89)

LINES 88–116: LEAR IS CARRIED TO SAFETY

Gloucester returns with news that a plot is afoot against the king's life: 'I have o'erheard a plot of death upon him'. (91) Gloucester has arranged a litter, or carriage, into which they must place Lear and carry him to Dover, where they will find safety and Cordelia:

> There is a litter ready; lay him in't,
> And drive toward Dover, friend, where thou
>   shalt meet
> Both welcome and protection (92–4)

Gloucester stresses that there is no time to waste – if they delay even half an hour, they will be found and killed. (95–100) Kent says that Lear must be allowed to sleep, in order that his shattered mind might heal. (99–102) Kent, Gloucester and the Fool carry the unconscious Lear to the waiting litter.

CHARACTER DEVELOPMENT

LEAR

MADNESS

Throughout this scene, we see that Lear's madness has totally enveloped him. Whatever shreds of reason he clung to in the storm and in the hovel have finally disappeared under the weight of his suffering.

The king seems possessed by notions of revenge and justice. He dreams of vengeance: 'To have a thousand with red burning spits/ Come hizzing in upon 'em'. (17–18) He then proceeds to stage a mock-trial of Goneril and Regan, with pieces of furniture representing his daughters. If he cannot take revenge in reality, he will try and exact it in the world of madness.

The depths of the pain caused by their cruelty is made evident by the fact that Lear is obsessed with finding an explanation for their actions: 'Is there any cause in nature that/ makes these hard hearts?' (81–2) The king is by now a completely helpless figure, dependent on the loyalty of his followers.

EDGAR

A COMPANION IN MADNESS

Edgar continues his role as poor Tom, again with great ease and skill. Like before, he makes continuous reference to 'the foul fiend' that haunts him. Edgar appears to be doing his best to comfort the king by being his mad friend. By engaging with Lear, and entering into his world of insanity, he is making the king feel less alone.

COMPASSIONATE

Edgar shows his compassionate side in this scene. When Lear imagines that he is being attacked by a pack of wild dogs, Edgar pretends to frighten them off. He is obviously distressed by the depths of misery that Lear has sunk to: 'My tears begin to take his part so much,/ They'll mar my counterfeiting'. (63–4)

Edgar is able to derive some consolation from the king's misery, however. He sees that Lear is undergoing much greater pain and suffering than he is, and this helps him bear his own lot more easily: 'How light and portable my pain seems now,/ When that which makes me bend makes the king/ bow'. (117–18) Edgar wants deeply to see the king brought to safety: 'What will hap more to-night, safe 'scape the king!' (123)

GLOUCESTER & KENT

GLOUCESTER

LOYAL TO THE KING

Gloucester continues to exhibit his new found bravery by showing great care for the king. He is determined to rescue Lear from the storm: 'Here is better than the open air'. (1) When he returns, he confirms the rumours of a plot against Lear's life made mention of in the previous scene. Gloucester has prepared a litter in order that the king can be brought with all speed to Dover. His courage, and the risk he runs to his own life, win him our admiration.

KENT

THE KING'S MINDER

Like Gloucester, Kent continues to show his unconditional loyalty to Lear. He tries to make his master comfortable in the shelter ('Will you lie down and rest upon the cushions?') and regrets that the king must be moved to Dover when he desperately needs rest: 'Oppress'd nature sleeps:/ This rest might yet have balm'd thy broken sinews'. (107)

Kent is obviously greatly distressed by the pain his master is going through: 'O pity! Sir, where is the patience now/ That you so oft have boasted to retain?' (61–2)

THE FOOL

HEARTBROKEN

This scene marks the final appearance of the Fool in the play. He continues to do his best to cheer up his master with jokes and riddles, and plays along with the mock-trial. Unfortunately, the sight of Lear's insanity seems to finally break the Fool's spirit. His last words are 'And I'll go to bed at noon' (91) which seem to indicate either a death-wish or else his weary resignation. We hear no more of him.

❧ EDGAR'S SPEECH

Edgar is left behind, and makes a speech about suffering. He says that there are similarities between his own situation and that of Lear. Just as he has been banished by his father, so Lear was cast out by his children: 'He childed as I fathered!' (112) Yet Edgar declares that his own suffering is nothing compared to that of Lear: 'How light and portable my pain seems now / When that which makes me break makes the king bow'. (110–11) He says that it is easier to bear our troubles when others are suffering, too, especially when we see our elders and betters suffering. (104–5) Edgar vows to continue playing the role of poor Tom until he has been proved innocent of the accusations against him, and he is reconciled with his father. (104–5) He concludes with the hope that whatever else happens on this dreadful night, the king will be brought to safety in Dover: 'What will hap more to-night, safe 'scape the king!' (116)

CHARACTER DEVELOPMENT

SOME LINES TO LEARN

Is there any cause in nature that makes these hard hearts?

Lear (81)

When we our betters see bearing our woes,
We scarcely think our miseries our foes

Edgar (112–13)

Enter CORNWALL, REGAN, GONERIL, EDMUND the Bastard, and SERVANTS.

CORNWALL *[to Goneril]* Post speedily to my lord your husband, show him
this letter. The army of France is landed. Seek out the traitor
Gloucester.

Exeunt some of the Servants.

REGAN Hang him instantly.

GONERIL Pluck out his eyes.   5

CORNWALL Leave him to my displeasure. Edmund, keep you our
sister company. The revenges we are bound to take
upon your traitorous father are not fit for your
beholding. Advise the Duke where you
are going, to a most festinate preparation. We are bound to the   10
like. Our posts shall be swift and intelligent betwixt us.
Farewell, dear sister; farewell, my Lord of Gloucester.

Enter OSWALD the Steward.

How now? Where's the King?

OSWALD My Lord of Gloucester hath conveyed him hence:
Some five or six and thirty of his knights,   15
Hot questrists after him, met him at gate;
Who, with some other of the lord's dependants,
Are gone with him towards Dover, where they boast
To have well-armed friends.

CORNWALL Get horses for your mistress.

GONERIL Farewell, sweet lord, and sister.   20

CORNWALL Edmund, farewell.

Exeunt GONERIL, EDMUND, and OSWALD.

Go seek the traitor Gloucester,
Pinion him like a thief, bring him before us.

Exeunt other Servants.

Though well we may not pass upon his life
Without the form of justice, yet our power   25
Shall do a courtesy to our wrath, which men
May blame, but not control.

Enter GLOUCESTER, brought in by two or three.

Who's there? the traitor?

REGAN Ingrateful fox! 'Tis he.

CORNWALL Bind fast his corky arms.

GLOUCESTER What mean, your Graces? Good my friends, consider
You are my guests. Do me no foul play, friends.   30

CORNWALL Bind him, I say.

Servants bind him.

REGAN   Hard, hard. O filthy traitor!

GLOUCESTER Unmerciful lady as you are, I am none.

CORNWALL To this chair bind him. Villain, thou shalt find –

REGAN plucks his beard.

---

him: *Gloucester*

traitorous: *against the new regime*
Duke: *Duke of Albany (Goneril's husband)*
festinate: *speedy;* preparation: *for war*
intelligent: *well-informed*

Hot questrists: *quick searchers*

Pinion: *bind*

not pass … life: *sentence him to death*

do a courtesy: *yield;* wrath: *anger*

Ingrateful: *ungrateful*
corky: *withered*

filthy: *foul*

GLOUCESTER	By the kind gods, 'tis most ignobly done	
	To pluck me by the beard.	35
REGAN	So white, and such a traitor!	
GLOUCESTER	Naughty lady,	
	These hairs which thou dost ravish from my chin	
	Will quicken, and accuse thee. I am your host.	
	With robber's hands my hospitable favours	
	You should not ruffle thus. What will you do?	40
CORNWALL	Come, sir, what letters had you late from France?	
REGAN	Be simple-answered, for we know the truth.	
CORNWALL	And what confederacy have you with the traitors	
	Late footed in the kingdom?	
REGAN	To whose hands have you sent the lunatic king?	
	Speak.	45
GLOUCESTER	I have a letter guessingly set down,	
	Which came from one that's of a neutral heart,	
	And not from one opposed.	
CORNWALL	Cunning.	
REGAN	And false.	
CORNWALL	Where hast thou sent the King?	
GLOUCESTER	To Dover.	
REGAN	Wherefore to Dover? Wast thou not charged at peril –	50
CORNWALL	Wherefore to Dover? Let him first answer that.	
GLOUCESTER	I am tied to th' stake, and I must stand the course.	
REGAN	Wherefore to Dover, sir?	
GLOUCESTER	Because I would not see thy cruel nails	
	Pluck out his poor old eyes; nor thy fierce sister	55
	In his anointed flesh stick boarish fangs.	
	The sea, with such a storm as his bare head	
	In hell-black night endured, would have buoyed up	
	And quenched the stellèd fires.	
	Yet, poor old heart, he holp the heavens to rain.	60
	If wolves had at thy gate howled that dearn time,	
	Thou shouldst have said, 'Good porter, turn the key.'	
	All cruels I'll subscribe. But I shall see	
	The winged vengeance overtake such children.	
CORNWALL	See't shalt thou never. Fellows, hold the chair.	65
	Upon these eyes of thine I'll set my foot.	
GLOUCESTER	He that will think to live till he be old,	
	Give me some help! – O cruel! O ye gods!	
REGAN	One side will mock another. Th' other too!	
CORNWALL	If you see vengeance –	70
FIRST SERVANT	Hold your hand, my lord!	
	I have served you ever since I was a child;	
	But better service have I never done you	

white: *his hair is white from age*
Naughty: *wicked*
ravish: *pluck*
quicken: *take on life*

ruffle: *violently treat*

simple-answered: *direct*
confederacy: *conspiracy*
Late footed: *recently landed*

neutral: *fair, unbiased*

peril: *at risk of your life*

buoyed: *risen*
stellèd fires: *stars*
holp: *helped*
dearn: *dreary*

winged: *divine*

---

* 34–5 Regan plucks his beard: *this pluck-ing of his beard is a major, contemptu-ous insult.*

† 46 guessingly set down: *written without certainty;*

‡ 52 I am tied to th' stake, and I must stand the course: *the image is of a bear tied to a post and baited. There is a similar image in Macbeth: 'They have tied me to a stake. I cannot fly, / But bear-like I must fight the course'* (5. 7. 1–2).

§ 56 anointed flesh: *at his coronation, the king was anointed with holy oil.*

¶ 61–3 if wolves … subscribe: *on such a night, even cruel wolves howling outside Regan's gates would have been pitied and allowed shelter.*

Regan
Even the intense physical suffering inflicted on Glouster does not satisfy Regan appitet for revenge on those who would help her father. She must also torment gloucester with revalation that it was his fav son edmund that betrayed him.

	Than now to bid you hold.	
REGAN	How now, you dog?	75
FIRST SERVANT	If you did wear a beard upon your chin,	
	I'd shake it on this quarrel.	
REGAN	What do you mean?	
CORNWALL	My villain! [Draw and fight]	
FIRST SERVANT	Nay, then, come on, and take the chance of anger.	
REGAN	Give me thy sword. A peasant stand up thus?	

She takes a sword and runs at him behind.

FIRST SERVANT	O, I am slain! My lord, you have one eye left	
	To see some mischief on him. O! [He dies]	80
CORNWALL	Lest it see more, prevent it. Out, vile jelly!	
	Where is thy lustre now?	
GLOUCESTER	All dark and comfortless! Where's my son Edmund?	
	Edmund, enkindle all the sparks of nature	
	To quit this horrid act.	85
REGAN	Out, treacherous villain!	
	Thou call'st on him that hates thee. It was he	
	That made the overture of thy treasons to us;	
	Who is too good to pity thee.	
GLOUCESTER	O my follies! Then Edgar was abused.	
	Kind gods, forgive me that, and prosper him!	90
REGAN	Go thrust him out at gates, and let him smell	
	His way to Dover.	

Exit one with GLOUCESTER.

	How is't, my lord? How look you?	
CORNWALL	I have received a hurt. Follow me, lady.	
	Turn out that eyeless villain. Throw this slave	95
	Upon the dunghill. Regan, I bleed apace.	
	Untimely comes this hurt. Give me your arm.	

Exit CORNWALL, led by REGAN.

SECOND SERVANT	I'll never care what wickedness I do,	
	If this man come to good.	
THIRD SERVANT	If she live long,	
	And in the end meet the old course of death,	
	Women will all turn monsters.	100
SECOND SERVANT	Let's follow the old Earl, and get the bedlam	
	To lead him where he would. His roguish madness	
	Allows itself to anything.	
THIRD SERVANT	Go thou. I'll fetch some flax and whites of eggs	
	To apply to his bleeding face. Now heaven help him!	

Exeunt.

chance of anger: *risk of my anger*
stand up: *confront*

jelly: *eye*
lustre: *sparkle, sight*

quit: *requite, avenge*

he: *Edmund*
overture: *disclosure*

Abused: *wronged, falsely accused*
that: *believing in Edgar's guilt*

this slave: *the corpse of the servant*
apace: *profusely*

meet … death: *die naturally of old age*

bedlam: *Edgar as poor Tom*

Allows itself: *will agree*
flax … eggs: *traditional remedy*

handwritten note:
* Gloucester *
Displays courage + tremendous
bravery not simply passive victim
Reacts with anger + indignation
Refuses to

-----

* 92   **How is't, my lord? How look you?:**
*Cornwall has been injured in his fight
with the servant.*

† 100   **Women will all turn monsters:**
*because, with Regan as their example,
they will never fear divine punishment, no matter what they do.*

CORNWALL, REGAN, EDMUND & GONERIL

Oswald informs Goneril, Regan and Cornwall that Gloucester has helped Lear escape to Dover.
Gloucester is captured and brought before Cornwall and Regan. Cornwall tears out Gloucester's
eyes and is subsequently slain by a servant. Regan has her servants throw the blind Gloucester
out of the castle.

ACTION

LINES 1–27: CORNWALL VOWS VENGEANCE ON GLOUCESTER

In Act 3, Scene 5, Cornwall learned that Gloucester
has been in contact with the French invasion force and
still supports King Lear. Cornwall wants to punish
him for this, and sends servants to track him down:
'Seek out the traitor Gloucester'. (2–3) Goneril and
Regan also want to see Gloucester punished, and tell
Cornwall to hang him or 'Pluck out his eyes'. (4–5)

Their desire for revenge is increased once Oswald
enters and tells them that Gloucester has helped Lear
escape to the French army at Dover. Around thirty-five
of Gloucester's men are 'gone with him toward Dover,
where they boast / To have well armed friends'. (17–18)

Goneril is returning to her husband Albany. Cornwall
sends Edmund away with her so that he won't have
to see his father's punishment. (6–9) Edmund, he
says, must advise Albany to prepare for battle with
the invading French army. (10) Cornwall promises
Edmund that he will keep in touch by letter: 'Our
posts shall be swift and intelligent between us'. (11)

LINES 28–64: GLOUCESTER IS QUESTIONED

No sooner are Goneril, Oswald and Edmund out
of the way than Cornwall's servants return with the
captive Gloucester. Cornwall orders the servants to tie
him to a chair. (28, 33) Gloucester is horrified at this
rough treatment. He says that Cornwall and Regan
are under his roof and must do him no harm: 'You are
my guests: do me no foul play, friends'. (30) To injure
him is to go against all the laws of hospitality. (38–40)
He denies that he is a traitor. (32)

Cornwall and Regan quiz him about the letter he received
from France. They ask him if he is in league with the
French invasion force: 'what confederacy have you with
the traitors / Late footed in the kingdom?' (43–4) They
also ask him where he has sent King Lear. (17) They warn
Gloucester not to lie, telling him that they already know
the answers to these questions: 'Be simple-answer'd for
we know the truth'. (42)

Initially Gloucester attempts to talk his way out of
trouble, saying that the letter he received from France
was written by a 'neutral heart', not by an opponent
of Regan and Goneril. (45–6) Yet he quickly realises

I would not see thy cruel nails
Pluck out his poor old eyes
Gloucester (56–7)

I shall see
The winged vengeance overtake
such children
Gloucester (65–6)

Out, vile jelly!
Cornwall (83)

All dark and comfortless
Gloucester (85)

SOME LINES TO LEARN

CHARACTER DEVELOPMENT

that there is nothing to be gained by lying. He must take whatever treatment Cornwall and Regan have in store for him: 'I am tied to the stake, and I must stand the course'. (52) He defiantly tells Regan that he sent Lear to Dover in order to escape her and Goneril's cruelty. (54–6) He vows that he will live to see the sisters' treatment of their father avenged. (64)

LINES 65– c.105: GLOUCESTER IS BLINDED

At that, Cornwall plucks out one of Gloucester's eyes. He is about to pluck out the other eye when one of his servants intervenes, telling him to stop. The servant says he has served Cornwall loyally since he was a child. He claims to be doing Cornwall a great service by preventing him from carrying out this gruesome act. (70–3) Cornwall attacks this rebellious servant and is wounded. Regan, however, kills the servant, taking another servant's sword and stabbing him in the back. (78–81)

The wounded Cornwall is free to pluck out Gloucester's remaining eye: 'Out, vile jelly!' (81) The blind Gloucester laments the fact that he is 'All dark and comfortless', and calls out for his son Edmund to help him and avenge, or 'quit', this terrible wrong that has been done him. (83–5)

GLOUCESTER

GREAT BRAVERY

Gloucester displays tremendous bravery and courage in this scene. He is completely defiant in the face of his cruel captors, knowing that the longer he can defy them, the greater the chance of Lear reaching safety in Dover.

Gloucester is not simply a passive victim of torture. He reacts with anger and indignation when Cornwall and Regan set to work on him: 'By the kind gods, 'tis most ignobly done/ To pluck me by the beard'. (34–5) He also does his best to deceive his captors, and even earns Cornwall's admiration for his defiance ('Cunning'). Gloucester knows he must hold out as long as he can: 'I am tied to the stake, and I must stand the course'. (54)

MORAL INTEGRITY

Gloucester refuses to be cowed by the cruelty and violence of his captors. He has no problem in telling Regan and Cornwall why he acted to save the king: 'Because I would not see thy cruel nails,/ Pluck out his poor old eyes; nor thy fierce sister/ In his anointed flesh stick boarish fangs'. (56–8) He fervently hopes for justice to be done: 'I shall see/ The winged vengeance overtake such children'. (65–6)

REALISES THE TRUTH

Gloucester receives two cruel blows in this scene. As well as being blinded, he learns that it was Edmund who betrayed him. His reaction is not one of self-pity, but instead one of regret for the wrong he did Edgar: 'O my follies! Then Edgar was abus'd./ Kind gods, forgive me that, and prosper him!' (91–2) Whatever doubts we may have had about Gloucester's character up until now are totally removed by the courage and integrity he shows throughout this scene.

CORNWALL

SAVAGE CRUELTY

Cornwall's cruelty and sadism is on full show in this scene. As before, he is determined to assert his authority by commanding everyone present. It is as if he feels the need to prove himself a man in front of the wife who usually cows him.

He advertises his intention to torture Gloucester before the latter is brought in, using the pretext that men cannot control their anger as an excuse for the savagery that follows: 'yet our power/ Shall do a courtesy to our wrath, which men,/ May blame but not control'. (26–7)

It is Cornwall who decides to blind Gloucester: 'See't shalt thou never. Fellows, hold the chair,/ Upon those eyes of thine I'll set my foot'. (67–8) One eye is not enough for him, and in his rage after being attacked by his servant, he finishes the job: 'Out, vile jelly!/ Where is thy lustre now?' (83–4) Even when he knows he is wounded, his cruelty does not let up. He orders the servant to be thrown 'upon the dunghill', and for the 'eyeless villain' Gloucester to be sent into the wild. (95–6)

We can only take a certain grim satisfaction in seeing him being fatally wounded. For once in the play, there is a hint that evil is repaid on the characters that perpetrate it.

REGAN & GLOUCESTER

Regan cruelly tells Gloucester that Edmund hates him and has betrayed him. Edmund, she says, revealed to her and Cornwall that Gloucester was collaborating with the French invaders: 'it was he that made the overture of thy treasons to us'. (86–7)

Gloucester now regrets his foolishness or folly in trusting Edmund: 'O my follies!' (89) He also regrets treating Edgar so badly, realising that Edmund was deliberately attempting to get his brother in trouble: 'Then Edgar was abus'd'. (89–90) Regan has her servants throw the blind Gloucester out of the castle: 'Go thrust him out at gates, and let him smell / His way to Dover'. (91–2)

Cornwall's wound seems to be bad ('I bleed apace'), and Regan leads him away for treatment. (92–6) Cornwall's remaining servants are horrified at the cruelty they have witnessed, and resolve to help the blinded Gloucester: 'I'll fetch some flax, and whites of eggs, / To apply to his bleeding face'. (104–5) They decide to entrust Gloucester to poor Tom, the 'bedlam', or madman, who's been hanging around: 'Let's follow the old earl, and get the Bedlam / To lead him where he would'. (101–2) (In reality, of course, poor Tom is Gloucester's son Edgar in disguise.)

CHARACTER DEVELOPMENT

REGAN

VICIOUS

Regan's savagery and heartlessness matches that of her husband. She has no interest in sparing Gloucester, and wants him executed immediately: 'Hang him instantly'. (4) She orders her servants to bind Gloucester's arms as tightly as they can and then plucks his beard. She clearly revels in being able to torture her helpless host, and has no hesitation in murdering the rebellious servant from behind.

Her sadism is on further display when she takes great relish in informing Gloucester that it was Edmund who betrayed him: 'Thou call'st on him that hates thee; it was he/ That made the overture of thy treasons to us/ Who is too good to pity thee'. (88–90) She is completely callous: 'Go thrust him out at gates, and let him smell/ His way to Dover'. (93–4) Regan's cruelty is frightening in its intensity.

CORNWALL'S SERVANTS

DECENCY AND COMPASSION

The one glimmer of light in this scene dominated by savage cruelty is the compassion and moral decency shown by Cornwall's servants. One of them feels obliged to intervene and try and stop Gloucester's torture, regardless of the risk to himself: 'I have served you ever since I was a child,/ But better service have I never done you/ Than now to bid you hold'. (74–6) He even insults Regan: 'If you did wear a beard upon your chin,/ I'd shake it on this quarrel'. (76–7) Although he is killed, we cannot help be satisfied knowing that he has fatally wounded Cornwall.

The other two servants also show decency. They both fear the worse if Regan and Cornwall should escape punishment for their cruelty, and decide to get poor Tom to lead Gloucester to Dover, as well as easing the latter's pain by applying egg-white to his eyes. In a world apparently dominated by evil and selfishness, their compassion is one of the few manifestations of ordinary decency.

EDMUND

TOTALLY UNFEELING

Although Edmund does not actually say anything in this scene, it is worth noting that he does not make any attempt to intervene on his father's behalf by asking for mercy, or requesting that he not be punished too severely for his crimes. All Edmund cares for is his own advancement.

Sad, moving scene

Enter EDGAR.

EDGAR Yet better thus, and known to be contemned,
Than still contemned and flattered. To be worst,
The lowest and most dejected thing of fortune,
Stands still in esperance, lives not in fear.
The lamentable change is from the best;
The worst returns to laughter. Welcome then,
Thou unsubstantial air that I embrace!
The wretch that thou hast blown unto the worst
Owes nothing to thy blasts.

Enter GLOUCESTER, led by an OLD MAN.

But who comes here?
My father, poorly led? World, world, O world!
But that thy strange mutations make us hate thee,
Life would not yield to age.

OLD MAN   O my good lord,
I have been your tenant, and your father's tenant,
These fourscore years.

GLOUCESTER Away, get thee away! Good friend, be gone.
Thy comforts can do me no good at all;
Thee they may hurt.

OLD MAN   You cannot see your way.

GLOUCESTER I have no way, and therefore want no eyes;
I stumbled when I saw. Full oft 'tis seen
Our means secure us, and our mere defects
Prove our commodities. Ah dear son Edgar,
The food of thy abused father's wrath!
Might I but live to see thee in my touch,
I'd say I had eyes again!

OLD MAN   How now? Who's there?

EDGAR *[Aside]* O gods! Who is't can say 'I am at the worst'?
I am worse than ever I was.

Glossary (right margin):

5
esperance: *hope*
lamentable: *regrettable*
laughter: *good times*
unsubstantial air: *fortune*

Owes nothing: *has paid all, so owes nothing*

10
mutations: *vicissitudes, changes*
yield: *submit*

15

20

25

Handwritten notes:

Edgar

Noble (edmund), holds no grudges against his father + brother affectionate, oblinging nature shines through, forgiving + gentle with is father. Symbolise's pure love almost abondens his disguse. (Cordelia).

Footnotes:

* 1–2 **Yet better thus … flattered:** *if you are condemned, it is better to know it than to suffer it unawares and under false flattery.*

† 2–4 **To be worst … lives not in fear:** *if one is at the very bottom of fortune's wheel, there is no fear of falling further, but one may still hope for better.*

‡ 20–1 **Our means … commodities:** *our belongings and securities often prove to be our downfall, whilst our disadvantages may serve us.*

§ 22 **food … wrath:** *fed his father's anger.*

‖ 25–6 **worst … worst:** *as long as we have breath to say 'This is the worst', we may yet experience and suffer worse.*

Sad, moving [handwritten, top margin]

OLD MAN	'Tis poor mad Tom.
EDGAR	[Aside] And worse I may be yet. The worst is not
	So long as we can say 'This is the worst.'
OLD MAN	Fellow, where goest?
GLOUCESTER	Is it a beggarman?
OLD MAN	Madman and beggar too. 30
GLOUCESTER	He has some reason, else he could not beg.
	I' th' last night's storm I such a fellow saw,
	Which made me think a man a worm. My son
	Came then into my mind, and yet my mind
	Was then scarce friends with him. I have heard more 35
	since.
	As flies to wanton boys are we to th' gods.
	They kill us for their sport.
EDGAR	[Aside] How should this be?
	Bad is the trade that must play fool to sorrow,
	Ang'ring itself and others. [To Gloucester] Bless thee, master!
GLOUCESTER	Is that the naked fellow? 40
OLD MAN	Ay, my lord.
GLOUCESTER	Then prithee get thee gone. If for my sake
	Thou wilt overtake us hence a mile or twain
	I' th' way toward Dover, do it for ancient love;
	And bring some covering for this naked soul,
	Who I'll entreat to lead me. 45
OLD MAN	Alack, sir, he is mad!
GLOUCESTER	'Tis the time's plague when madmen lead the blind.
	Do as I bid thee, or rather do thy pleasure.
	Above the rest, be gone.
OLD MAN	I'll bring him the best 'parel that I have,
	Come on't what will. [Exit] 50
GLOUCESTER	Sirrah naked fellow –
EDGAR	Poor Tom's a-cold. [Aside] I cannot daub it further.
GLOUCESTER	Come hither, fellow.
EDGAR	[Aside] And yet I must. Bless thy sweet eyes, they bleed.
GLOUCESTER	Know'st thou the way to Dover?
EDGAR	Both stile and gate, horse-way and footpath. Poor 55
	Tom hath been scared out of his good wits. Bless
	thee, good man's son, from the foul fiend! Five fiends
	have been in poor Tom at once: of lust, as Obidicut;
	Hobbididence, prince of dumbness; Mahu, of
	stealing; Modo, of murder; Flibbertigibbet, of 60
	mopping and mowing, who since possesses
	chambermaids and waiting women. So, bless thee, master!

Glossary (right margin):

man … worm: *biblical idea of man*

twain: *two*
I' th' way: *on the way;* ancient: *old*

time's plague: *curse of our time*

the rest: *all else*
'parel: *apparel, clothes*
on't: *of it, whatever the consequence*

daub it: *maintain the pretence*

mopping … mowing: *making faces, grimacing*

Handwritten note (bottom):

＊Gloucester＊

His insight through blindness echoes Lear's knowledge through madness + thus highlights the intensity of Lear's tragedy. He has grown through his suffering. humbly admits his errors, longs for edgar's love, understands better plight of the poor + exploited yet has decided to end his life by suicide

Footnotes (bottom right):

* 35–6   **flies … sport:** expresses a despairing and cynical view of life, suggesting that human life is of no more importance or value to the gods than are flies to playful children who kill them for enjoyment.

† 38   **Bad … sorrow:** Edgar regrets having to play the part of poor Tom (the fool) instead of being able to comfort his father.

GLOUCESTER	Here, take this Purse, thou whom the heavens' plagues
	Have humbled to all strokes. That I am wretched
	Makes thee the happier. Heavens, deal so still
	Let the superfluous and lust-dieted man,
	That slaves your ordinance, that will not see
	Because he does not feel, feel your power quickly;
	So distribution should undo excess,
	And each man have enough. Dost thou know Dover?
EDGAR	Ay, master.
GLOUCESTER	There is a cliff, whose high and bending head
	Looks fearfully in the confined deep.
	Bring me but to the very brim of it,
	And I'll repair the misery thou dost bear
	With something rich about me. From that place
	I shall no leading need.
EDGAR	Give me thy arm.
	Poor Tom shall lead thee.

Exeunt.

65

70

75

plagues: *curses*
strokes: *of fortune*
the happier: *the more fortunate*
lust-dieted: *man who satisfies his lusts*

quickly: *sharply, or soon*
distribution: *redistribution of goods*

* Irony *

Edgar's moraliseings about the power of good to over come evil are horribly shattered by the brute fact of Gloucester's apperence. Irony's multiply throughout this scene the disgused Edgar will not revel his identy to his father his must endure the painful ordeal of withholding comfort + reckatration from a father who despeartly needs both. Gloucester unwittingly plays upon his son's feelings by mawling his changed attidude towards him. even more powering for edgar is Gloucester expression of longing for his presence

* 67   That slaves your ordinance: *submits your rights to his desire;*
† 68   feel, feel: *empathise, experience*

GLOUCESTER & EDGAR

Edgar tries to remain positive, though his life has fallen apart. Gloucester laments the cruelty of life. Edgar meets Gloucester and despairs at what has become of his father. Still disguised as poor Tom, he agrees to lead Gloucester to the Cliffs of Dover where the old man plans to plunge to his death and end his suffering.

ACTION

⤳ LINES 1–9: EDGAR SPEAKS ABOUT HIS MISFORTUNE

Edgar is alone out on the heath. He tries to be positive about his circumstances, saying that it is better to be a beggar and know what people think of you than to be falsely flattered. (1–2) For those who have nothing, things can only get better. The poorest, therefore, are the most hopeful. It is the people who have everything, he says, that live in greatest fear of misfortune:

> *To be worst,*
> *The lowest and most dejected thing of fortune,*
> *Stands in esperance, lives not in fear.*
> *The lamentable change is from the best* (2–5)

However, just as Edgar says this, he catches sight of his father being led by an Old Man through the heath. Seeing the eyeless Gloucester makes Edgar despair at the world. It is the terrible changes of fortune throughout our lives, Edgar says, that make

us hate the world and not fear old age and death: 'But that thy strange mutations make us hate thee/ Life would not yield to age'. (11–12) He now realises that he was wrong to think only moments before that he was at his lowest and worst: 'I am worse than e'er I was'. (26)

⤳ LINES 10–40: GLOUCESTER LAMENTS THE CRUELTY OF LIFE

The Old Man trying to help Gloucester tells the blinded man that he has been a tenant of his all his life. Gloucester tells the Old Man to 'be gone', as his life could be in danger if he stays: 'Thy comforts can do me no good at all;/ Thee they may hurt'. (16–17) When the Old Man points out that Gloucester cannot see where he is going, Gloucester says that he has lost his path through life and no longer has need of sight. He says that when he could see, he made many errors: 'I stumbled when I saw'. (19) Being deprived of things, Gloucester says, can sometimes be

EDGAR

FACING THE WORST
Edgar shows us in this scene that he is determined to accept whatever fate throws at him. He tries to find consolation in his plight by thinking that he is at the lowest possible state, and can sink no further:

> *To be worst,*
> *The lowest and most dejected thing of fortune,*
> *Stands still in esperance, lives not in fear* (2–4)

Unfortunately for him, the gods seem to mock his courage by presenting him immediately afterwards with the sight of his blind father. Edgar realises that he can suffer more than he has already:

> *And worse I may be yet; the worst is not,*
> *So long as we can say, 'This is the worst'* (26–7)

COMPASSION
In spite of the wrong inflicted on him by Gloucester, Edgar shows nothing but compassion for his blind and helpless father. He is so overwhelmed by pity, that his ability to act as poor Tom is momentarily threatened: 'I cannot daub it further'. (52) Edgar is horrified by the injuries that have been inflicted on Gloucester: 'Bless thy sweet eyes, they/ bleed'. (54) He bears his father no grudge, and sees in him another helpless victim of fate. As a loyal and loving son, he will lead Gloucester to Dover and protect him from further suffering as best he can.

GLOUCESTER

WISDOM THROUGH SUFFERING
Like Lear, Gloucester has begun a journey toward wisdom as a result of the suffering inflicted upon him. He realises now that he saw nothing for what it really was when he had his sight: 'I stumbled when I saw'. (19) He knows that he committed a great wrong against Edgar, and the only thing he wishes for is to meet his son and beg his forgiveness:

> *Ah! Dear son Edgar,*
> *The food of thy abus'd father's wrath;*
> *Might I but live to see thee in my touch,*
> *I'd say I had eyes again* (21–4)

COMPASSION FOR OTHERS
Again like Lear, Gloucester's plight leads him to show great compassion for the sufferings of others. He worries that the old man who leads him may be punished for his kindness: 'good friend, be gone;/ Thy comforts can do me no good at all;/ Thee they may hurt'. (16–18) When departing with Edgar for Dover, he tells the old man to try and fetch some clothes for his new guide: 'bring some covering for this naked soul/ Who'll entreat to lead me'. (45–6) He gives Edgar his purse, feeling an urge to help the poor and wretched: 'So distribution should undo excess,/ And each man have enough'. (71–2) Although he has been reduced to nothing, Gloucester realises that he is not the only one at the bottom of fortune's ladder.

IN DESPAIR
Although he has gained insight, the suffering he has undergone makes Gloucester believe that men are only play-things for the cruel gods that rule above:

> *As flies to wanton boys, are we to the gods;*
> *They kill us for their sport* (34–5)

He says that the sight of poor Tom in the hovel the previous night 'made me think a man a worm'. (33) Gloucester feels he cannot bear his misery for very much longer and wishes to be led to the cliffs at Dover. It is obvious that he intends to commit suicide: 'from that place/ I shall no leading need'. (78–9)

best for us as we become over-confident when we have every-thing: 'Our means secure us, and our mere defects/ rove our commodities'. (20–1) He laments the way he treated Edgar, and prays that he might live to meet once again the son he now knows he wronged: 'Might I live to see thee in my touch/ I'd say I had eyes again'. (23–4)

The Old Man sees Edgar and asks him where he is going. Edgar is still reluctant to reveal his true identity, and so continues to act as 'poor Tom'. Gloucester asks the Old Man if Edgar is 'a beggar-man', saying that he met such a man during the storm of the previous night. He says that meeting poor Tom made him think that man is a 'worm', and that human beings are mere playthings of the cruel and capricious gods. The gods treat us like mischievous boys do flies: 'They kill us for their sport'. (37) Gloucester tells the Old Man to leave him alone with Edgar. The Old Man departs, promising to return with some clothes for Edgar. (49)

LINES 40–62: GLOUCESTER ASKS EDGAR TO BRING HIM TO DOVER

Hearing Gloucester speak so pessimistically about life causes Edgar to wonder how his father could have changed so dramat-ically: 'How should this be?' (37) He finds it difficult, given the circumstances, to keep up the act of being poor Tom ('I cannot daub it further') but feels that he must. He tells Gloucester that for 'poor Tom', the countryside is a scary place where the devil ('the foul fiend') has appeared in many guises. (57–62)

Gloucester is beginning to understand that there is great social imbalance in the world. He hands Edgar a purse, telling him that great wealth should be distributed amongst the poor and needy: 'dis-tribution should undo excess/ And each man have enough'. (69–70) He tells Edgar that there is a cliff in Dover that he wishes to be brought to. If Edgar leads him to the edge of that cliff, he will be given more money.

CHARACTER DEVELOPMENT

THE OLD MAN

COMPASSIONATE

The old man who leads Gloucester is an example of the kind of common decency and compassion that survives in the universe of the play, despite the prepon-derance of evil and selfishness. When Gloucester tells him to be gone for his own sake, he says 'You cannot see your way' (17) and refuses to leave. He also promises to bring Edgar some clothes: 'I'll bring him the best 'parel that I have'. (49) The old man is willing to risk his life in order to help those worse off than himself. His humanity stands in stark contrast to the selfishness that domin-ates life at court.

CONSIDER THIS

Critics have often wondered why Edgar does not reveal his true identity to his father at this point. There does not seem to be any need for him to maintain his disguise as poor Tom once they are left alone, but Edgar chooses to carry on the pretence. He must know that his father's pain would be greatly eased by the knowledge that the son he thought lost to him was by his side, but he decides that he will continue in the guise of a madman. Does he fear being recognised by Cornwall's men? Does he believe his father needs to gain more insight through further suffering?

SOME LINES TO LEARN

To be worst,
The lowest and most dejected thing of fortune,
Stands still in esperance, lives not in fear:
The lamentable change is from the best;
The worst returns to laughter

Edgar (2–6)

World, world, O world!
But that thy strange mutations make us hate thee,
Life would not yield to age

Edgar (10–12)

I have no way, and therefore want no eyes;
I stumbled when I saw

Gloucester (18–19)

The worst is not,
So long as we can say, 'This is the worst.'

Edgar (26–7)

As flies to wanton boys, are we to the gods;
They kill us for their sport

Gloucester (34–5)

So distribution should undo excess,
And each man have enough

Gloucester (71–2)

Enter GONERIL and EDMUND the Bastard.

GONERIL	Welcome, my lord. I marvel our mild husband
	Not met us on the way.

Enter OSWALD the Steward.

	Now, where's your master?
OSWALD	Madam, within, but never man so changed.
	I told him of the army that was landed:
	He smiled at it. I told him you were coming:
	His answer was, 'The worse.' Of Gloucester's treachery
	And of the loyal service of his son
	When I informed him, then he call'd me sot
	And told me I had turned the wrong side out.
	What most he should dislike seems pleasant to him;
	What like, offensive.
GONERIL	*[to Edmund]* Then shall you go no further.
	It is the cowish terror of his spirit,
	That dares not undertake. He'll not feel wrongs
	Which tie him to an answer. Our wishes on the way
	May prove effects. Back, Edmund, to my brother.
	Hasten his musters and conduct his powers.
	I must change arms at home and give the distaff
	Into my husband's hands. This trusty servant
	Shall pass between us. Ere long you are like to hear
	(If you dare venture in your own behalf)
	A mistress's command. Wear this. *[Gives a favour]*
	Spare speech.
	Decline your head. This kiss, if it durst speak,
	Would stretch thy spirits up into the air.
	Conceive, and fare thee well.
EDMUND	Yours in the ranks of death! *[Exit]*
GONERIL	My most dear Gloucester!
	O, the difference of man and man!
	To thee a woman's services are due;
	My fool usurps my body.
OSWALD	Madam, here comes my lord. *[Exit]*

5

10

15

20

25

Not met: *did not meet*

the army: *the French forces*

sot: *fool*

What like: *what he should like*

cowish: *cowardly*

undertake: *take action;* **wrongs:** *injuries*

tie: *commit;* **answer:** *response*

musters: *troops;* **conduct:** *escort*

change: *exchange*

trusty servant: *Oswald*

Ere: *before*

Conceive: *understand (my meaning)*

of man … : *between Albany and Edmund*

My fool: *her husband;* **usurps:** *takes*

....

* 9   **turned … out:** *clothing metaphor, suggesting that Oswald has an inverse understanding of who is treacherous, who loyal.*

† 14–15   **Our wishes … prove effects:** *our desires may yet be fulfilled.*

‡ 17   **distaff:** *stick on which wax or wool was wound, symbol of woman's work. Goneril is saying that she must change gender roles with her 'mild' husband and go fight the French while her husband keeps house.*

§ 22   **Decline your head:** *she asks him to bring his head towards hers do that she can kiss him.*

Enter ALBANY.

GONERIL	I have been worth the whistle.	
ALBANY	O Goneril,	
	You are not worth the dust which the rude wind	30
	Blows in your face! I fear your disposition.	
	That nature which contemns it origin	
	Cannot be bordered certain in itself.	
	She that herself will sliver and disbranch	
	From her material sap, perforce must wither	35
	And come to deadly use.	
GONERIL	No more! The text is foolish.	
ALBANY	Wisdom and goodness to the vile seem vile;	
	Filths savour but themselves. What have you done?	
	Tigers, not daughters, what have you performed?	40
	A father, and a gracious aged man,	
	Whose reverence even the head-lugged bear would lick,	
	Most barbarous, most degenerate, have you madded.	
	Could my good brother stiffer you to do it?	
	A man, a prince, by him so benefited!	45
	If that the heavens do not their visible spirits	
	Send quickly down to tame these vile offences,	
	It will come,	
	Humanity must perforce prey on itself,	
	Like monsters of the deep –	50
GONERIL	Milk-liver'd man!	
	That bear'st a cheek for blows, a head for wrongs;	
	Who hast not in thy brows an eye discerning	
	Thine honour from thy suffering; that not know'st	
	Fools do those villains pity who are punished	
	Ere they have done their mischief. Where's thy drum?	55
	France spreads his banners in our noiseless land,	
	With plumed helm thy slayer begins to threat,	
	Whiles thou, a moral fool, sit'st still, and criest	
	'Alack, why does he so?'	
ALBANY	See thyself, devil!	
	Proper deformity seems not in the fiend	60
	So horrid as in woman.	
GONERIL	O vain fool!	
ALBANY	Thou changed and self-cover'd thing, for shame!	
	Bemonster not thy feature! Were't my fitness	
	To let these hands obey my blood,	65
	They are apt enough to dislocate and tear	
	Thy flesh and bones. Howe'er thou art a fiend,	
	A woman's shape doth shield thee.	

(right-margin glosses)

the whistle: *the seeking out*

disposition: *character, mood*

sliver … disbranch: *sever*
material sap: *from her female (bodily) nature*

The text: *what you're saying*

savour: *enjoy*

head-lugged: *baited, angry*
madded: *gone mad*
good brother: *Cornwall*

visible spirits: *manifest angels*

prey on: *devour, destroy*
monsters: *predatory fish; deep: sea*

bear'st: *makes defenseless*

drum: *symbol of preparation for war*
noiseless: *peaceful*

moral: *moralizing*

deformity: *monstrosity*
… woman: *because it transgresses nature*

self-cover'd: *transformed*
feature: *appearance*
blood: *passion*

....

* 32–3   nature … itself: *despising its own origins, nature cannot be contained by that which should define it.*

† 51   Milk-liver'd man: *milk is associated with the female and with maternal gentleness. By saying that Albany has milk rather than blood in his liver (which was considered at this time to house the passions) she is calling him both cowardly and womanly.*

‡ 54   discerning … suffering: *Goneril maintains that Albany lacks the ability to see the difference between that which honours him and that which harms him.*

§ 55–6   Fools … mischief: *only fools take pity on villains who are punished before they get a chance to commit their crimes (Goneril's justification for their ill-treatment of Lear and Gloucester).*

(handwritten annotations)

N.B

Goneril Devouring Rivalry. (unfaithful).

Hoping to win love of Edmund if Albany cast aside. On hearing of Cornwall's death filled with jealousy (Regan widow). This nigling rivalry may be her own undoing + we begin to hope that the evil in the Kingdom will help to bring its own retribution. Gourneil's thrust for power is upper most in her mind + her evil influence is strong still.

GONERIL	Marry, your manhood, mew!	

Enter a GENTLEMAN.

ALBANY	What news?	
GENTLEMAN	O, my good lord, the Duke of Cornwall is dead,	70
	Slain by his servant, going to put out	
	The other eye of Gloucester.	
ALBANY	Gloucester's eyes?	
GENTLEMAN	A servant that he bred, thrilled with remorse,	
	Opposed against the act, bending his sword	75
	To his great master; who, thereat enraged,	
	Flew on him, and amongst them fell'd him dead;	
	But not without that harmful stroke which since	
	Hath plucked him after.	
ALBANY	This shows you are above,	
	You justicers, that these our nether crimes	
	So speedily can venge! But O poor Gloucester!	80
GENTLEMAN	Both, both, my lord.	
	This letter, madam, craves a speedy answer.	
	'Tis from your sister.	
GONERIL	*[Aside]* One way I like this well;	
	But being widow, and my ~~Gloucester~~ Edmund; with her,	85
	May all the building in my fancy pluck	
	Upon my hateful life. Another way	
	The news is not so tart. – I'll read, and answer.	

Exit.

ALBANY	Where was his son when they did take his eyes?	
GENTLEMAN	Come with my lady hither.	90
ALBANY	He is not here.	
GENTLEMAN	No, my good lord; I met him back again.	
ALBANY	Knows he the wickedness?	
GENTLEMAN	Ay, my good lord. 'Twas he informed against him,	
	And quit the house on purpose, that their punishment	95
	Might have the freer course.	
ALBANY	Gloucester, I live	
	To thank thee for the love thou show'dst the King,	
	And to revenge thine eyes. Come hither, friend.	
	Tell me what more thou know'st.	100

Exeunt.

he bred: *Gloucester brought up*

great master: *Cornwall*

without: *before receiving*
plucked: *killed*

justicers: *judges*
venge: *avenge*

my Gloucester: *my beloved Edgar*

tart: *bitter*

Albany Justice + Goodness.
Denounces the inhuman cruelty of Goneril + Regan to their father. abhors the barbarity of Gloucester's blinding + swears to punish Edmunds gross treasury to Gloucester. Declares Goneril unfit to be in charge + he is taking command. Believes justice will be done. more assertive + manly we sympatise in his delimma + admire the spirit he shows against Goneril.

* 85–6   **May all the building … life:** *Goneril is expressing her jealous fear that this new situation (the newly widowed Regan alone with Edgar) may destroy the life that she has amorously imagined for herself, thus making her life hateful to her.*

GONERIL & EDMUND

Goneril and Edmund arrive at Goneril's castle and are surprised when Albany does not come to meet them. Oswald tells Goneril that her husband no longer supports her cause. Goneril tells Edmund to go back to Cornwall and speed up the enlistment of soldiers. She hints at an affair that is blossoming between herself and Edmund.

When Albany emerges from the castle, Goneril calls him a coward. He tells her that her actions are despicable. News is brought of Cornwall's death. Goneril now fears that Regan might interfere with her plans to be with Edmund.

ACTION

Goneril and Edmund arrive at Goneril's castle. Goneril is surprised that her husband has not come forward to greet them, and asks her steward, Oswald, where Albany is.

✍ LINES 1–9: OSWALD TELLS GONERIL HOW ALBANY HAS CHANGED

Oswald tells her that Albany is inside the castle, but that he has changed dramatically: 'but never man so changed'. (3) News that would have once upset Albany now pleases him and he no longer seems to favour his wife and her actions:

· When he was told of the French forces landing at Dover, '[Albany] smiled at [the news]'. (5)
· He replied 'The worse' when he heard that Goneril was on her way.
· He called Oswald a 'sot' when the steward told him about 'Gloucester's treachery' and of Edmund's 'loyal service'.
· Albany said to Oswald that they were wrong to turn Gloucester out of his castle and favour Edmund.
· Goneril is disgusted when she hears that her husband has acted like this. She says that Albany is cowardly and afraid of commitment: 'It is the cowish terror of his spirit/ That dares not undertake'. She instructs Edmund to go back to Cornwall and speed up his enlistment of soldiers, saying that

she will remain behind to take control of her house-hold. A 'trusty servant' will be sent with news of any developments.

GONERIL SPEAKS TO EDMUND ABOUT THEM BEING TOGETHER

Goneril tells Edmund that what they spoke about on the way, the possibility of them being together, might now come about: 'Our wishes on the way/ May prove effects'. Just before he departs for Cornwall's castle, Goneril kisses him and hints at future sexual favours: 'To thee a woman's services are due'. Edmund, she says, is a proper man while her husband is a 'fool'.

LINES 10–70: ALBANY CRITICISES GONERIL

When Edmund has departed, Albany appears. He tells Goneril that she is worthless and that he fears her destructive character. Someone who coldly distances themselves from their parent, he says, will come to no good: 'She that herself will sliver and disbranch/ From her material sap perforce must wither/ And come to deadly use'. (34–6) He tells Goneril that the way she treated her father was 'barbarous', and that her actions have resulted in Lear going mad.

Albany wonders how his brother-in-law, Cornwall, having 'benefited' so greatly from the King's recent gen-erosity, could stand idly by and watch Goneril act this way: 'Could my good brother suffer you to do it?' (44) He tells his wife that heaven will surely intervene when mankind starts to lose all sense of morality and starts to act monstrously: 'Humanity must perforce prey on itself/ Like monsters of the deep'. (49–50) Albany tells Goneril that she is the devil disguised as a woman and that if he were so disposed he would 'tear' her apart.

Goneril considers her husband's moral concerns to be a result of his cowardice. She tells him that female milk rather than manly blood flows through his liver, and that he is foolish to not see the wisdom of her preventative actions when the country is under threat from a foreign force: 'With plumed helm thy state begins to threat,/ Whilst thou, a moral fool, sits still and cries/ 'Alack, why does he so?' (57–9)

LINES 70–100: NEWS OF CORNWALL'S DEATH

When a messenger arrives with news of Cornwall's death and the gouging of Gloucester's eyes, Albany is completely horrified at what is happening. He says that heaven must not care to play a role in Man's affairs if such despicable acts of vengeance can be permitted to take place: 'This shows you are above,/ You justicers, that these our nether crimes/ So speedily can venge'. (79–80)

ALBANY

A CRISIS OF CONSCIENCE

We see Albany's moral conscience assert itself in this scene. He has decided that he can no longer stand idly by and be a passive witness to the cruelty of his wife and her sister. He condemns her in no uncertain terms: 'You are not worth the dust which the rude wind/ Blows in your face'. (40–1)

Albany views Goneril's behaviour as deeply unnatural, and sees her character as being funda-mentally perverse and dangerous: 'That nature, which contemns its origin,/ Cannot be border'd certain'. (42–3) He fears that she may self-destruct ('perforce must whither/ And come to deadly use').

With his awakened sense of right and wrong, he can no longer stand alongside the evil perpetrated by his wife and her associates: 'Wisdom and goodness to the vile seem vile;/ Filths savour but themselves'. (38–9) He views the treatment meted out to Lear as gross and unnatural: 'Tigers, not daughters, what have you perform'd?' (40)

ASSERTIVE

If Albany previously appeared as a weak and passive husband, his behaviour in this scene represents a dramatic turnaround. He shows no hesitation or fear in standing up to his domineering wife, and threatens her with violence: 'Were't my fitness/ To let these hands obey my blood,/ They are apt enough to dislocate and tear/ Thy flesh and bones'. (64–7) He now seems determined to take command.

BELIEF IN COSMIC JUSTICE

Albany's firm belief in right and wrong is mirrored in his belief in the justice of the gods. He fears the worse if the heavens do not punish Goneril's cruelty: 'Humanity must perforce prey on itself,/ Like monsters of the deep'. (49–50)

When news is brought of Cornwall's death, Albany sees this as a sign of the gods' existence, and their wish to punish evil:

This shows you are above,
You justicers, that these our nether crimes
So speedily can venge! (77–9)

He is grateful for Gloucester's moral courage, and determined to avenge him: 'Gloucester, I live/ To thank thee for the love thou show'dst the king,/ And to revenge thine eyes'. (95–7) Albany has discovered a deep sense of morality within himself.

A KEY MOMENT

Albany's crisis of conscience and his determination to stand up to the behaviour of the sisters and Edmund represents the first real setback to the forces of selfishness and evil in the play so far. Albany's morality also puts him in a difficult position, however, as he is forced to choose between fighting against the French, and therefore aiding his wife and her associates, or else standing back and letting the country be overrun by an invader. He has a difficult choice to make.

ALBANY & GONERIL

GONERIL

TREACHEROUS AND CONTEMPTUOUS

Goneril's contempt for Albany is shown by her insulting remarks about his behaviour to Edmund. She decides to take it upon herself to lead the army against the French forces, believing her husband to be too soft and cowardly for the task: 'I must change arms at home, and give the distaff/ Into my husband's hands'. (17–18)

Goneril believes that, as a strong woman, she merits an equally strong husband, and is willing to betray Albany in order to gain Edmund's affections: 'O! the difference of man and man!/ To thee a woman's services are due:/ My fool usurps my bed'. (27–9)

Her self-assuredness does not appear shaken in the face of Albany's new-found moral courage. She views him as weak and insufficient to the task of fighting the French. She will soon learn that she has underestimated her husband.

SUSPICIOUS

The news of Cornwall's death shows once again Goneril's tendencies toward paranoia, as well as her lack of complete trust in her sister. She fears that Regan may now make a move on Edmund: 'But being widow, and my Gloucester with her,/ May all the building in my fancy pluck'. (85–6) The seeds of the sisters' downfall are beginning to sprout at this point in the play.

CHARACTER DEVELOPMENT

Goneril has mixed feelings about the news of Cornwall's death. She is pleased because she knows that this brings her closer to having power over the entire land. However, she is concerned by the fact that her sister is now a widow and in the company of Edmund. She fears that Regan might interfere with her dreams to be with Edmund: 'But being widow, and my Gloucester with her,/ May all the building in my fancy pluck/ Upon my hateful life'. (84–6)

The messenger hands Goneril a letter from her sister, and tells her that Regan wishes to receive a speedy response. Goneril leaves to read the letter, and Albany asks the messenger where Edmund was when his father's eyes were been gouged out. The messenger tells Albany that Edmund was accompanying Goneril to the castle at the time, and that it was Edmund who betrayed Gloucester in the first place. Albany vows to avenge the brutal punishment meted out to Gloucester, a loyal supporter of the king, and he asks the messenger to tell him all he knows.

EDMUND

OBJECT OF DESIRE

Although Edmund only speaks one line in this scene, it is clear that he is now moving ever closer toward his goal of supreme power. Goneril has fallen for his charms, and he is put in a position to exploit her desire for him. Given his treacherous behaviour toward his father, we can doubt the sincerity of his pledge to Goneril: 'Yours in the ranks of death'. (25)

SOME LINES TO LEARN

Wisdom and goodness to the vile seem vile;
Filths savour but themselves

Albany (38–9)

Tigers, not daughters, what have you perform'd?

Albany (40)

Proper deformity seems not in the fiend
So horrid as in woman

Albany (60–1)

This shows that you are above,
You justicers, that these our nether crimes
So speedily can venge

Albany (77–9)

ACT 4 · SCENE 3

The French camp near Dover

Enter KENT and a GENTLEMAN.

KENT	Why the King of France is so suddenly gone back know you the reason?
GENTLEMAN	Something he left imperfect in the state, which since his coming forth is thought of, which imports to the kingdom so much fear and danger that his personal return was most required and necessary.
KENT	Who hath he left behind him general?
GENTLEMAN	The Marshal of France, Monsieur La Far.
KENT	Did your letters pierce the Queen to any demonstration of grief?
GENTLEMAN	Ay, sir. She took them, read them in my presence, And now and then an ample tear trilled down Her delicate cheek. It seemed she was a queen Over her passion, who, most rebel-like, Sought to be king o'er her.
KENT	O, then it moved her?
GENTLEMAN	Not to a rage. Patience and sorrow strove Who should express her goodliest. You have seen Sunshine and rain at once: her smiles and tears Were like a better way. Those happy smilets That played on her ripe lip seemed not to know What guests were in her eyes, which parted thence As pearls from diamonds dropped. In brief, Sorrow would be a rarity most beloved, If all could so become it.
KENT	Made she no verbal question?
GENTLEMAN	Faith, once or twice she heaved the name of 'father' Pantingly forth, as if it pressed her heart; Cried 'Sisters, sisters! Shame of ladies! Sisters! Kent! father! sisters! What, i' th' storm? i' th' night? Let pity not be believed!' There she shook The holy water from her heavenly eyes, And clamour moistened. Then away she started To deal with grief alone.
KENT	It is the stars, The stars above us, govern our conditions; Else one self mate and make could not beget Such different issues. You spoke not with her since?
GENTLEMAN	No.
KENT	Was this before the King returned?
GENTLEMAN	No, since.

imperfect: *unfinished*
imports: *portends*

Queen: *Cordelia*

trilled: *trickled*

be king: *take command*

goodliest: *best, most fittingly*

smilets: *little smiles*

guests: *tears*

heaved: *sighed*

holy water: *her tears*

....

* 31   **clamour moistened:** *her verbal outpouring of grief was moistened (softened) by her tears.*

† 33–5   **stars … issues:** *the influence of the stars determine our lives and our character, for how else could the same parents give birth to such different offspring.*

131

KENT	Well, sir, the poor distressed Lear's i' th' town;
	Who sometime, in his better tune, remembers
	What we are come about, and by no means
	Will yield to see his daughter.
GENTLEMAN	Why, good sir?
KENT	A sovereign shame so elbows him; his own unkindness,
	That stripped her from his benediction, turned her
	To foreign casualties, gave her dear rights
	To his dog-hearted daughters – these things sting
	His mind so venomously that burning shame
	Detains him from Cordelia.
GENTLEMAN	Alack, poor gentleman!
KENT	Of Albany's and Cornwall's powers you heard not?
GENTLEMAN	'Tis so; they are afoot.
KENT	Well, sir, I'll bring you to our master Lear
	And leave you to attend him. Some dear cause
	Will in concealment wrap me up awhile.
	When I am known aright, you shall not grieve
	Lending me this acquaintance. I pray you go
	Along with me.

Exeunt.

40

sovereign: *overwhelming;* **elbows:** *moves*

45   **foreign casualties:** *to life overseas*

powers: *army*

50

dear cause: *important business*

55

* 53   **When I am known aright:** *when my true identity is known*

*It is the stars,
The stars above us, govern our
conditions*
Kent (35–6)

SOME LINES TO LEARN

Kent hears from a Gentleman how the King of France has landed troops in Britain but has had to return to France. The Gentleman tells Kent how Cordelia responded emotionally to news of her father's ill treatment and vowed to help.

ACTION

having just arrived in Britain with his forces, has suddenly gone back home. The Gentleman tells Kent that the king had urgent business to attend to back in France, and has left his general, the Marshal of France, in charge of the French force in Britain.

LINES 1–6: KENT SPEAKS OF THE LATEST DEVELOPMENTS

Kent speaks with a Gentleman about the King of France. The King of France,

LINES 7–38: KENT HEARS HOW CORDELIA REACTED TO HIS LETTER

Kent asks the Gentleman if the letters he sent to the Queen, Cordelia, telling her of Lear's recent ill-treatment and insanity, moved her when she read them. The Gentleman says that Cordelia tried to control her emotions, but could not stop the occasional tear falling. She did not fly into a rage, but, rather, remained composed. However, her deep sorrow at her father's suffering could not be contained and hidden. Though she smiled, tears dropped from her eyes.

The Gentleman says that Cordelia's passions and her power of control appeared like competitors in her face, each seeming to make her more lovely than the other: 'patience and sorrow strove/ Who should express her goodliest'. (16–17) Once or twice she spoke her father's name, and expressed her disbelief at the cruelty of her sisters, sending their father out into the storm: 'What, i' th' storm? i' th' night?/ Let pity not be believed!' (28–9)

Kent says that people's characters must be governed by the stars because it is surely impossible for a couple to create siblings that are so different to one another, as is the case with Cordelia and her sisters:

> *It is the stars,*
> *The stars above us govern our conditions.*
> *Else one self mate and make could not beget*
> *Such different issues.* (32–5)

LINES 38–55: KENT SPEAKS OF LEAR

Kent says that Lear, in moments of lucidity, is aware of what is happening, but does not wish to see Cordelia. The king is full of shame and remorse for the heartless way he treated his daughter: 'these things sting/ His mind so venomously that burning shame/ Detains him from Cordelia'. (45–7)

Kent asks the Gentleman if he is aware that Albany and Cornwall have amassed forces to deal with the French. He says that he will take him to Lear and leave him there while he takes care of other business. Still disguised as Caius, he tells the Gentleman that he will reveal his true identity very soon: 'Some dear cause/ Will in concealment wrap me up awhile./ When I am known you shall not grieve'. (51–3)

CHARACTER DEVELOPMENT

CORDELIA

AN ALL-FORGIVING DAUGHTER

In this scene, we learn through the gentleman's reports that Cordelia bears no grudge against her father for the treatment she suffered at his hands. The information she received concerning her father's plight moved her deeply: 'now and then an ample tear trill'd down/ Her delicate cheek'. (13–14)

Cordelia was shocked to learn of her sisters' behaviour: ''Sisters! Sisters! Shame of ladies! Sisters!/ Kent! Father! Sisters! What, i' th' storm? 'i th'/ night?' (28–30) She is presented as being almost an angelic figure, soon to rescue Lear in his hour of need: 'There she shook/ The holy water from her heavenly eyes,/ And clamour-moisten'd'. (31–3) It seems as if Lear is about to be rescued from his misery.

LEAR

ASHAMED

We learn from Kent that Lear is close to Dover. His reason apparently returns in flashes, as he sometimes knows why he has been brought there: 'Who sometime, in his better tune, remembers/ What we are come about'. (41–2)

Lear is deeply ashamed of his behaviour toward his youngest daughter and, as a result, refuses to meet her: 'burning shame/ Detains him from Cordelia'. (47–8) We can see from this that Lear, through his great suffering, has become an entirely different individual from the unforgiving autocrat we saw on stage at the beginning of the play.

KENT

THE GO-BETWEEN

As always, Kent continues to act as the dutiful servant. He acts as the vital strategic link between Lear and Cordelia, relaying information and trying to bring the two together.

We also see Kent display his belief in astrological determinism, which is not altogether unlike Gloucester's. Learning of Cordelia's forgiveness toward Lear, he simply cannot believe that the same man raised such different daughters: 'The stars above us, govern our conditions;/ Else one self mate and make could not beget/ Such different issues'. (36–8)

ACT 4 SCENE 4

The French camp

Enter, with Drum and Colours, CORDELIA, DOCTOR, and Soldiers.

CORDELIA   Alack, 'tis he! Why, he was met even now
As mad as the racked sea, singing aloud,
Crowned with rank fumiter and furrow weeds,
With hardocks, hemlock, nettles, cuckoo flow'rs,
Darnel, and all the idle weeds that grow   5
In our sustaining corn. A century send forth.
Search every acre in the high-grown field
And bring him to our eye. *[Exit an Officer]* What can man's wisdom
In the restoring his bereaved sense?
He that helps him take all my outward worth.   10

DOCTOR   There is means, madam.
Our foster-nurse of nature is repose,
The which he lacks. That to provoke in him
Are many simples operative, whose power
Will close the eye of anguish.   15

CORDELIA   All blest secrets,
All you unpublished virtues of the earth,
Spring with my tears! be aidant and remediate
In the good man's distress! Seek, seek for him!
Lest his ungoverned rage dissolve the life
That wants the means to lead it.   20

Enter Messenger.

MESS   News, madam.
The British powers are marching hitherward.

CORDELIA   'Tis known before. Our preparation stands
In expectation of them. O dear father,
It is thy business that I go about.   25
Therefore great France
My mourning and important tears hath pitied.
No blown ambition doth our arms incite,
But love, dear love, and our aged father's right.
Soon may I hear and see him!

Exeunt.

---

racked: *tormented*

idle: *useless*
sustaining: *nourishing*

wisdom: *knowledge, science*
bereaved: *robbed*
helps: *cures;* take: *may take*
means: *a way*
repose: *rest*
That to provoke: *to induce that (rest)*
simples: *medicinal herbs*

unpublished virtues: *unknown cures*
aidant and remediate: *helpfully remedial*

ungoverned: *uncontrolled*
the means: *i.e. reason*

blown: *inflated, false*

---

* 2–6   **Crowned ... corn:** *wearing the most luxurious of herbs known to nourish and to treat madness, that yet are useless in Lear's case:* 'rank fumiter': *vigorous green weed;* 'furrow-weeds': *weed that grows on the furrows of ploughed lands;* 'burdocks': *weed that produces burrs;* 'hemlock': *used as a sedative;* 'Darnel': *weed with narcotic powers.*

† 6   **A century send forth:** *send out one hundred men.*

Cordelia has landed in Britain with the French troops. She speaks to a doctor about her father's condition, and says that she will do everything in her power to help Lear. She instructs a group to go and look for the king.

ACTION

CORDELIA INSTRUCTS HER MEN TO FIND LEAR

Cordelia is somewhere in the vicinity of Dover with the French forces and a doctor. She is distressed at a report of a recent sighting of her father in a field, dressed in flowers and weeds and 'singing aloud'. She instructs a hundred soldiers to search the 'high-grown field' and find Lear. She asks the doctor if there is hope of her father recovering his senses. The doctor tells her that the king needs rest ('repose'), and that certain herds ('simples') might be effective in aiding his recovery. Cordelia calls on the hidden or unknown recuperative powers of herbs to spring out of the earth, nourished by her tears: 'All blest secrets,/ All you unpublished virtues of the earth,/ Spring with my tears!' (15–17)

A messenger arrives with reports of the British forces advancing towards Dover. Cordelia says that she knew of this already and that they are prepared to meet them. She says that it not personal political ambition that now drives her, but the restoration of her father: 'No blown ambition doth our arms incite/ But love, dear love, and our aged father's right'. (27–8)

SOME LINES TO LEARN

No blown ambition doth our arms incite,
But love, dear love, and our aged father's right
Cordelia (28–9)

CHARACTER DEVELOPMENT

CORDELIA

COMPASSIONATE

Cordelia's love for her father is made manifest in this scene. She has heard that the mad Lear is wandering the fields near Dover, and is deeply concerned that he be found and brought to safety. She offers everything she has to anyone who can cure him: 'He that helps him takes all my outward worth'. (10) Cordelia is fearful that Lear's anguish may drive him to suicide: 'Seek, seek for him,/ Lest his ungoverned rage dissolve the life/ That wants the means to lead it'. (18–20)

Cordelia's fear and compassion reveal the limitless love she has for her father. Through the use of language and imagery, she is portrayed as being akin to a Nature goddess: 'All bless'd secrets,/ All you unpublish'd virtues of the earth,/ Spring with my tears! Be aidant and remediate/ In the good man's distress!' (15–18)

There is not a hint that she is even slightly resentful toward Lear for the humiliation he inflicted on her in the opening scene. Everything she does is for his sake. This is made clear by the fact that she insists she is not invading England for political reasons, but purely in order to rescue her father: 'No blown ambition doth our arms incite,/ But love, dear love, and our aged father's right'. (28–9) Nevertheless, she is firm and resolute, and prepared to meet the English forces in battle.

LEAR

MAD AGAIN

We learn from Cordelia's description of her father that he has lapsed back into madness. Although Kent spoke in the previous scene of the king's lucid episodes, insanity appears to have taken hold of him again. He wanders the fields crowned with plants and flowers, his appearance like that of a god of nature. The fact that he is 'crown'd with rank fumiter, and furrow weeds' makes a mockery of his previous status as lord of the realm.

ACT 4 SCENE 5

Gloucester's castle

Enter REGAN and OSWALD the Steward.

REGAN	But are my brother's powers set forth?	powers: *forces*
OSWALD	Ay, madam.	
REGAN	Himself in person there?	
OSWALD	Madam, with much ado.	ado: *protest*
	Your sister is the better soldier.	5
REGAN	Lord Edmund spake not with your lord at home?	your lord: *Albany*
OSWALD	No, madam.	
REGAN	What might import my sister's letter to him?	might import: *meaning might it bear*
OSWALD	I know not, lady –	
REGAN	Faith, he is posted hence on serious matter.	
	It was great ignorance, Gloucester's eyes being out,	ignorance: *folly*
	To let him live. Where he arrives he moves	10
	All hearts against us. Edmund, I think, is gone,	
	In pity of his misery, to dispatch	misery: *suffering;* dispatch: *end*
	His nighted life; moreover, to descry	nighted: *darkened, despairing*
	The strength o' th' enemy.	
OSWALD	I must needs after him, madam, with my letter.	15
REGAN	Our troops set forth to-morrow. Stay with us.	
	The ways are dangerous.	
OSWALD	I may not, madam.	
	My lady charged my duty in this business.	charged: *emphasised*
REGAN	Why should she write to Edmund? Might not you	
	Transport her purposes by word? Belike,	20 Transport: *deliver;* Belike: *it's likely*
	Something – I know not what – I'll love thee much –	Something: *of importance;* love: *give*
	Let me unseal the letter.	
OSWALD	Madam, I had rather –	
REGAN	I know your lady does not love her husband;	
	I am sure of that; and at her late being here	25
	She gave strange oeilliads and most speaking looks	oeilliads: *loving glances*
	To noble Edmund. I know you are of her bosom.	of her bosom: *in her trust*
OSWALD	I, madam?	
REGAN	I speak in understanding. Y'are! I know't.	understanding: *full knowledge*
	Therefore I do advise you take this note.	
	My lord is dead; Edmund and I have talked,	30
	And more convenient is he for my hand	for my hand: *in marriage*
	Than for your lady's. You may gather more.	
	If you do find him, pray you give him this;	
	And when your mistress hears thus much from you,	
	I pray desire her call her wisdom to her.	35 wisdom: *senses*
	So farewell.	
	If you do chance to hear of that blind traitor,	blind traitor: *Gloucester*
	Preferment falls on him that cuts him off.	Preferment: *promotion*
OSWALD	Would I could meet him, madam! I should show	
	What party I do follow.	40
REGAN	Fare thee well.	

Exeunt.

(Goneril comanding Albany's army)

REGAN & OSWALD

Oswald delivers Goneril's letter to Regan, and tells her that her sister now commands Albany's troops. Regan is suspicious and jealous about her sister's involvement with Edmund, and tries to convince Oswald to give her the letter that Goneril is sending to Edmund. Oswald refuses to give her the letter, but agrees to convey news of Cornwall's death to Goneril. Regan tells him that there will be a reward given to whomever finds and kills Gloucester.

A KEY MOMENT This scene brings ever closer the inevitable showdown between Goneril and Regan over Edmund's affections. Regan's desire that Oswald should warn his mistress to see sense and let Edmund go is more or less a declaration of open hostility. Their lust for Edmund threatens to destroy their uneasy alliance.

ACTION

✏ LINES 1–9: OSWALD DELIVERS GONERIL'S LETTER TO REGAN

Oswald has delivered the letter that Goneril promised to send to Regan in Act 4, Scene 2. Regan questions Oswald about Albany's forces. He tells her that Albany's army is on the move but that it is Goneril who now commands it: 'Your sister is the better solider'. (3) Regan is surprised that Edmund did not speak with Albany when he went to Goneril's castle. She also wonders why Oswald is carrying with him a letter from Goneril to Edmund: 'What might import my sister's letter to him?' (6) Oswald tells her that he does not know what the letter is about: 'I know not, lady'. (7)

✏ LINES 10–46: REGAN IS JEALOUS OF GONERIL AND EDMUND

Regan is concerned that her sister is now competing with her for Edmund's affections. Anxious that this is the case, she looks to delay Oswald reaching Edmund with Goneril's letter. She suggests that Edmund has become remorseful over the cruel punishment of his father, and wishes to kill himself ('to dispatch/ His nighted life') and has gone over to the enemy. When Oswald says that he must go to Edmund with Goneril's letter, Regan gets desperate and pleads with him to stay where he is: 'stay with us./ The ways are dangerous'. (16–17)

In her panic to overcome her sister's advantage with Edmund, Regan tries to convince Oswald that something improper is happening, but she ends up sounding confused. She suggests it is strange that Goneril should send a letter to Edmund, but she cannot come up with a plausible, concrete reason to convince Oswald that her sister is acting inappropriately: 'Why should she write to Edmund? Might not you/ Transport her purposes by word? Belike – / Some things – I know not what –'. (19–21) In her desperation to find out what is going on, she begs Oswald to let her open her sister's letter: 'I'll love thee much – / Let me unseal the letter'. (21–2)

Finally, Regan looks to convince Oswald that it is more fitting that Edmund should marry her and not Goneril: 'My lord is dead; Edmund and I have talked,/ And more convenient is he for my hand/ Than for your lady's'. (30–2) She asks Oswald to speak to Goneril and make her see reason: 'I pray desire call her wisdom to her'. Regan bids Oswald farewell, and tells him that if he should hear of Gloucester's whereabouts, let it be known that the one who kills him will be rewarded: 'If you do chance to hear of that blind traitor,/ Preferment falls on him that cuts him off'. (37–8)

CHARACTER DEVELOPMENT

REGAN

SUSPICIOUS

We see in this scene that Regan's suspicion of Goneril is rapidly consuming her. She is paranoid as to her sister's intentions toward Edmund and wonders what her letter to him could mean: 'What might import my sister's letter to him!' (6) She is desperate to know its contents, and even tries to bribe Oswald with her favours if he will let her open it: 'I'll love thee much,/ Let me unseal the letter'. (21–2)

Regan is firmly convinced that Edmund is hers. She tells Oswald that the two of them have talked and are pledged to each other. (32–3) She decides that the latent hostility between the two sisters should become open by having Oswald tell Goneril to keep away from Edmund: 'I pray desire her call her wisdom to her'. (36) Her desperation to have Edmund is becoming more pronounced.

BLOODTHIRSTY

Even in the midst of her jealousy, Regan does not neglect her murderous instincts. She now believes that it was a tactical error to let Gloucester go alive, as he can stir up animosity against the new regime. She offers Oswald a bounty if he is able to find and kill him: 'If you do chance to hear of that blind traitor,/ Preferment falls on him that cuts him off'. (37–9) She is completely without mercy.

OSWALD

A DISLOYAL SERVANT

Oswald is easily persuaded by Regan to serve her as well as her sister. The thought of Regan's favour is too much for him to refuse. He has no difficulty in accepting her offer of bounty to kill Gloucester: 'Would I could meet him, madam: I would show/ What party I do follow'. (40–1) He comes across as base and despicable.

EDMUND

DEVIOUS

Although he does not appear in the scene, we learn through Regan's words that he has promised himself to her as well as to Goneril. Clearly he is manipulating both sisters in order to be in a position where he can seize total power when the circumstances are right. Again we see that Edmund views people as being only pawns in his game of power politics.

ACT 4 · SCENE 6

The country near Dover

Enter GLOUCESTER, and EDGAR, like a Peasant.

GLOUCESTER	When shall I come to th' top of that same hill?
EDGAR	You do climb up it now. Look how we labour.
GLOUCESTER	Methinks the ground is even.
EDGAR	Horrible steep.
	Hark, do you hear the sea?
GLOUCESTER	No, truly.
EDGAR	Why, then, your other senses grow imperfect
	By your eyes' anguish.
GLOUCESTER	So may it be indeed.
	Methinks thy voice is altered, and thou speak'st
	In better phrase and matter than thou didst.
EDGAR	Y'are much deceived. In nothing am I changed
	But in my garments.
GLOUCESTER	Methinks y'are better spoken.
EDGAR	Come on, sir; here's the place. Stand still. How fearful
	And dizzy 'tis to cast one's eyes so low!
	The crows and choughs that wing the midway air
	Show scarce so gross as beetles. Halfway down
	Hangs one that gathers sampire – dreadful trade!
	Methinks he seems no bigger than his head.
	The fishermen that walk upon the beach
	Appear like mice; and yond tall anchoring bark,
	Diminished to her cock; her cock, a buoy
	Almost too small for sight. The murmuring surge
	That on th' unnumbered idle pebbles chafes
	Cannot be heard so high. I'll look no more,
	Lest my brain turn, and the deficient sight
	Topple down headlong.
GLOUCESTER	Set me where you stand.
EDGAR	Give me your hand. You are now within a foot
	Of th' extreme verge. For all beneath the moon
	Would I not leap upright.
GLOUCESTER	Let go my hand.
	Here, friend, is another purse; in it a jewel
	Well worth a poor man's taking. Fairies and gods
	Prosper it with thee! Go thou further off;
	Bid me farewell, and let me hear thee going.
EDGAR	Now fare ye well, good sir.
GLOUCESTER	With all my heart.
EDGAR	*[Aside]* Why I do trifle thus with his despair
	Is done to cure it.

5

10

15

20

25

30

35

Horrible: *awfully*

anguish: *pain*

didst: *used to*

choughs: *jackdaws*
gross: *large*

anchoring bark: *anchored ship*
cock: *cockboat*

unnumbered: *innumerable;* **chafes:** *scrape*

turn: *spin, become dizzy*

---

* 15   **Hangs one that gathers sampire:** *A herb-gatherer is balancing half-way down the cliff, picking sampire (an aromatic plant).*

† 19   **Diminished to her cock:** *appears as undersized as the ship's small boat.*

‡ 34–5   **Why … cure it:** *Edgar is only deceiving Gloucester in order that he might help him.*

GLOUCESTER	O you mighty gods! *He kneels.*
	This world I do renounce, and, in your sights,
	Shake patiently my great affliction off.
	If I could bear it longer and not fall
	To quarrel with your great opposeless wills,
	My snuff and loathed part of nature should
	Burn itself out. If Edgar live, O, bless him!
	Now, fellow, fare thee well.

He falls forward and swoons.

EDGAR	Gone, sir, farewell.
	And yet I know not how conceit may rob
	The treasury of life when life itself
	Yields to the theft. Had he been where he thought,
	By this had thought been past. – Alive or dead?
	Ho you, sir! friend! Hear you, sir? Speak! –
	Thus might he pass indeed. Yet he revives.
	What are you, sir?
GLOUCESTER	Away, and let me die.
EDGAR	Hadst thou been aught but gossamer feathers, air,
	So many fathom down precipitating,
	Thou'dst shivered like an egg; but thou dost breathe;
	Hast heavy substance; bleed'st not; speak'st; art sound.
	Ten masts at each make not the altitude
	Which thou hast perpendicularly fell.
	Thy life is a miracle. Speak yet again.
GLOUCESTER	But have I fall'n, or no?
EDGAR	From the dread summit of this chalky bourn.
	Look up a-height. The shrill-gorg'd lark so far
	Cannot be seen or heard. Do but look up.
GLOUCESTER	Alack, I have no eyes!
	Is wretchedness deprived that benefit
	To end itself by death? 'Twas yet some comfort
	When misery could beguile the tyrant's rage
	And frustrate his proud will.
EDGAR	Give me your arm.
	Up – so. How is't? Feel you your legs? You stand.
GLOUCESTER	Too well, too well.
EDGAR	This is above all strangeness.
	Upon the crown o' th' cliff what thing was that
	Which parted from you?
GLOUCESTER	A poor unfortunate beggar.
EDGAR	As I stood here below, methought his eyes
	Were two full moon; he had a thousand noses,
	Horns whelk'd and waved like the enridged sea.
	It was some fiend. Therefore, thou happy father,
	Think that the clearest gods, who make them honours
	Of men's impossibility, have preserved thee.
GLOUCESTER	I do remember now. Henceforth I'll bear
	Affliction till it do cry out itself
	'Enough, enough,' and die. That thing you speak of,
	I took it for a man. Often 'twould say
	'The fiend, the fiend' – he led me to that place.

Glossary (right margin):

it: *life*
quarrel with: *rebel against;* your: *the gods'*
snuff: *smouldering wick (old age)*
40 Burn itself out: *die naturally*

conceit: *imagination*

45 Had he been: *at the cliff's edge*
By this: *his fall;* thought: *life*

What: *who*

gossamer: *flimsy*
50 precipitating: *falling headlong*
shivered: *into pieces*
art sound: *you're fine*
at each: *placed together, end to end*
fell: *fallen*

55

Bourn: *boundary between land and sea*
shrill-gorg'd: *throaty*

60

beguile: *cheat*
frustrate: *by suicide*

65

70

whelk'd: *twisted*
father: *old man*
clearest: *purest*

75

* 73–4 honours … ./Of men's impossibil-
ity: *the gods acquire reverence by
performing that which is impossible
for humans to do.*

EDGAR	Bear free and patient thoughts.	80

Enter LEAR, mad, fantastically dressed with weeds.

	But who comes here?	
	The safer sense will ne'er accommodate	
	His master thus.	
LEAR	No, they cannot touch me for coming;	
	I am the King himself.	85
EDGAR	O thou side-piercing sight!	
LEAR	Nature is above art in that respect. There's your press-	
	money. That fellow handles his bow like a crow-	
	keeper. Draw me a clothier's yard. Look, look, a	
	mouse! Peace, peace; this piece of toasted cheese	
	will do't. There's my gauntlet; I'll prove it	90
	on a giant. Bring up the brown bills. O, well flown, bird! i'	
	th' clout, i' th' clout! Hewgh! Give the word.	
EDGAR	Sweet marjoram.	
LEAR	Pass.	
GLOUCESTER	I know that voice.	95
LEAR	Ha! Goneril with a white beard? They flattered me	
	like a dog, and told me I had white hairs in my beard	
	ere the black ones were there. To say 'ay' and 'no' to	
	everything I said! 'Ay' and 'no' too was no good	
	divinity. When the rain came to wet me once, and the	100
	wind to make me chatter; when the thunder would	
	not peace at my bidding; there I found 'em, there I smelt 'em	
	out. Go to, they are not men o' their words! They told	
	me I was everything. 'Tis a lie – I am not ague-proof	
GLOUCESTER	The trick of that voice I do well remember.	105
	Is't not the King?	
LEAR	Ay, every inch a king!	
	When I do stare, see how the subject quakes.	
	I pardon that man's life. What was thy cause?	
	Adultery?	110
	Thou shalt not die. Die for adultery? No.	
	The wren goes to't, and the small gilded fly	
	Does lecher in my sight.	
	Let copulation thrive; for Gloucester's bastard son	
	Was kinder to his father than my daughters	115
	Got 'tween the lawful sheets.	
	To't, luxury, pell-mell! for I lack soldiers.	
	Behold yond simpering dame,	
	Whose face between her forks presageth snow,	
	That minces virtue, and does shake the head	
	To hear of pleasure's name.	120
	The fitchew nor the soiled horse goes to't ➤	

free: *guiltless*

safer sense: *saner sense, right mind*

side-piercing: *heart-rending*

That fellow: *imagined soldier*
crow-keeper: *scarecrow*

do't: *catch the mouse;* **gauntlet:** *challenge*
giant: *prove myself even against a giant*
i' th' clout: *center of target*
marjoram: *remedial herb*

divinity: *theology, wisdom*

ague: *disease*
trick: *distinctive tone*

cause: *crime*

lecher: *fornicate*

Got: *conceived*
luxury: *lust;* **pell-mell:** *headlong*

forks: *thighs*

fitchew: *pole-cat (prostitute)*

*   86   **press-money:** *payment for enlisting in the king's army. Lear distributes his imaginary coins to Edgar and Gloucester, and perhaps also to imaginary soldiers.*

†   91   **brown bills:** *rustic soldiers carrying weapons;*

‡   91   **O, well flown, bird:** *imagines a hawk swooping on its prey;*

§   97–8   **I had white hairs … black ones:** *that I was wise before my time,*

₵   102   **there I found 'em:** *It was in my suffering that I saw their true nature;*

**   118–9   **face … virtue:** *whose facial expression suggests chastity that mimics virtue.*

	With a more riotous appetite.	
	Down from the waist they are centaurs,	centaurs: *mythological beasts*
	Though women all above.	
	But to the girdle do the gods inherit,	to the girdle: *only to the waist*
	Beneath is all the fiend's. There's hell, there's darkness,	
	there's the sulphurous pit; burning, scalding,	
	stench, consumption. Fie, fie, fie! pah, pah!	consumption: *death*
	Give me an ounce of civet, good apothecary,	civet: *used to cure melancholy*
	to sweeten my imagination.	
	There's money for thee.	

GLOUCESTER   O, let me kiss that hand!

LEAR   Let me wipe it first; it smells of mortality.

GLOUCESTER   O ruin'd piece of nature! This great world   piece of nature: *man; once masterpiece, now ruin*
              Shall so wear out to naught. Dost thou know me?   wear out to: *disintegrate into*

LEAR   I remember thine eyes well enough. Dost thou squiny   squiny: *squint, make eyes*
                                              at me?
              No, do thy worst, blind Cupid! I'll not love. Read thou this
              challenge; mark but the penning of it.   penning: *style*

GLOUCESTER   Were all the letters suns, I could not see.

EDGAR   *[Aside]* I would not take this from report. It is,   take: *believe*
              And my heart breaks at it.

LEAR   Read.

GLOUCESTER   What, with the case of eyes?   case of eyes: *empty sockets*

LEAR   O, ho, are you there with me? No eyes in your head,
              nor no money in your purse? Your eyes are in a heavy   heavy case: *sad situation (pun on case)*
              case, your purse in a light. Yet you see how this world
                                              goes.

GLOUCESTER   I see it feelingly.   Feelingly: *with (and by) feeling*

LEAR   What, art mad? A man may see how the world goes
              with no eyes. Look with thine ears. See how yond
              justice rails upon yond simple thief. Hark in thine ear.   Simple: *ordinary*
              Change places and, handy-dandy, which is the justice,   handy-dandy: *take your choice*
              which is the thief? Thou hast seen a
              farmer's dog bark at a beggar?

GLOUCESTER   Ay, sir.

LEAR   And the creature run from the cur? There thou mightst behold
              the great image of authority: a dog's obeyed in office.
              Thou rascal beadle, hold thy bloody hand!   beadle: *constable*
              Why dost thou lash that whore? Strip thine own back.
              Thou hotly lusts to use her in that kind
              For which thou whip'st her. The usurer hangs the cozener.*
              Through tattered clothes small vices do appear;
              Robes and furred gowns hide all. Plate sin with gold,   Robes and furred gowns: *as judges wear*
              And the strong lance of justice hurtless breaks;   hurtless: *without power*
              Arm it in rags, a pygmy's straw does pierce it.
              None does offend, none – I say none! I'll able 'em.   able: *vouch for*
              Take that of me, my friend, who have the power   that: *pardon*
              To seal th' accuser's lips. Get thee glass eyes   glass eyes: *spectacles*
              And, like a scurvy politician, seem   scurvy: *diseased, worthless*
              To see the things thou dost not. Now, now, now, now!
              Pull off my boots. Harder, harder! So.

Line numbers: 125, 130, 135, 140, 145, 150, 155, 160, 165

* 159   **The usurer hangs the cozener:** *a judge, guilty of the crime of usury (money-lending), passes sentence on one guilty of a lesser crime of trickery*

EDGAR   *[Aside]* O, matter and impertinency mixed!
        Reason, in madness!

LEAR   If thou wilt weep my fortunes, take my eyes.
        I know thee well enough; thy name is Gloucester.
        Thou must be patient. We came crying bother;
        Thou know'st, the first time that we smell 'the air
        We wail and cry. I will preach to thee. Mark.

GLOUCESTER   Alack, alack the day!

LEAR   When we are born, we cry that we are come
        To this great stage of fools. This' a good block.
        It were a delicate stratagem to shoe
        A troop of horse with felt. I'll put't in proof,
        And when I have stol'n upon these sons-in-law,
        Then kill, kill, kill, kill, kill, kill!

Enter a GENTLEMAN with Attendants.

GENTLEMAN   O, here he is! Lay hand upon him. – Sir,
            Your most dear daughter –

LEAR   No rescue? What, a prisoner? I am even
        The natural fool of fortune. Use me well;
        You shall have ransom. Let me have a surgeon;
        I am cut to th' brains.

GENTLEMAN   You shall have anything.

LEAR   No seconds? All myself?
        Why, this would make a man a man of salt,
        To use his eyes for garden waterpots,
        Ay, and laying autumn's dust.

GENTLEMAN   Good sir –

LEAR   I will die bravely, like a smug bridegroom. What!
        I will be jovial. Come, come, I am a king;
        My masters, know you that?

GENTLEMAN   You are a royal one, and we obey you.

LEAR   Then there's life in't. Nay, an you get it, you shall get it
        by running. Sa, sa, sa, sa!

Exit running. Attendants follow.

GENTLEMAN   A sight most pitiful in the meanest wretch,
            Past speaking of in a king! Thou hast one daughter
            Who redeems nature from the general curse
            Which twain have brought her to.

EDGAR   Hail, gentle sir.

GENTLEMAN   Sir, speed you. What's your will?

EDGAR   Do you hear aught, sir, of a battle toward?

GENTLEMAN   Most sure and vulgar. Every one hears that
            Which can distinguish sound.

EDGAR   But, by your favour,
        How near's the other army?

GENTLEMAN   Near and on speedy foot, the main;
            descriers
            Stands on the hourly thought.†

EDGAR   I thank you sir. That's all.

---

170   matter … impertinency: *sense … nonsense*

      weep: *cry over*

      came: *were born*
175   we … air: *arrive into this world*

      block: *template, mould*
180   delicate stratagem: *resourceful trick*
      put't in proof: *put it to the test*

185

190   seconds: *supporters*
      salt: *tears*
      waterpots: *perforated containers*
      Laying … dust: *causing the dust to settle*

195

200

205

      toward: *on the way*
      vulgar: *loud*

210   main: *main part of the army*

. . . .

* 203   **Who redeems … brought her to:**
         *who converts the curse that her two
         sisters have brought on her into a
         virtue.*

† 211   **descriers … hourly thought:** *their
         spies demand our hourly attention;*

GENTLEMAN	Though that the Queen on special cause is here,		Though that: *although*; Queen: *Cordelia*
	Her army is moved on.	215	
EDGAR	I thank you, sir		

Exit GENTLEMAN.

GLOUCESTER	You ever-gentle gods, take my breath from me;		breath: *passion*
	Let not my worser spirit tempt me again		worser spirit: *my melancholy*
	To die before you please!		
EDGAR	Well pray you, father.		
GLOUCESTER	Now, good sir, what are you?		what: *who*
EDGAR	A most poor man, made tame to fortune's blows,		
	Who, by the art of known and feeling sorrows,		
	Am pregnant to good pity. Give me your hand;	220	pregnant: *receptive*
	I'll lead you to some biding.		
GLOUCESTER	Hearty thanks.		
	The bounty and the benison of heaven		benison: *blessing*
	To boot, and boot!		

Enter OSWALD the Steward.

OSWALD	A proclaim'd prize! Most happy!		
	That eyeless head of thine was first framed flesh		fram'd flesh: *created*
	To raise my fortunes. Thou old unhappy traitor,	225	
	Briefly thyself remember. The sword is out		Briefly … remember: *say your last prayer*
	That must destroy thee.		
GLOUCESTER	Now let thy friendly hand		
	Put strength enough to't.		

EDGAR interposes.

OSWALD	Wherefore, bold peasant,		
	Dar'st thou support a published traitor? Hence!		published: *outlawed*
	Lest that th' infection of his fortune take	230	
	Like hold on thee. Let go his arm.		
EDGAR	Chill not let go, zir, without vurther 'cagion.[†]		Chill: *I will*; vurther 'cagion: *further reason*
OSWALD	Let go, slave, or thou diest!		
EDGAR	Good gentleman, go your gait, and let poor voke pass. An chud	235	go your gait: *walk away*; An chud: *if I could*
	ha' bin zwagger'd out of my life, 'twould not ha' bin zo long as		
	'tis by a vortnight. Nay, come not near th' old man. Keep out,[‡]		
	che vore ye, or Ise try whether your costard or my ballow be the		
	harder. Chill be plain with you.[§]		
OSWALD	Out, dunghill!	240	
EDGAR	Chill pick your teeth, zir. Come! No matter vor your		
	foins.		foins: *thrusts*

They fight. OSWALD falls.

* Gloucester's Salvation *

Edgar Rises to the occasion twice
+ saves his father first from
suicide + then from murder (oswald), he
parallels the loyalty + goodness of cordelia (Act 4 scene 4)

* King Lear *

Pathetic figure wavers between dignity +
idiocy. He manners + speech sometimes
reflect his majesty "every inch a king".
Sometimes he speaks sense "… to the
great stage of fools"! Sometimes he reveals
his true self "… ague-proof" +
sometimes he acts on utter nonsense.

---

* 223   **A proclaim'd prize:** *Regan has offered a reward to whoever will kill Gloucester, which Oswald now sets out to proclaim as his;*

† 232   **Chill not let go, zir, without vurther 'cagion:** *Edgar assumes another disguise, adopting the dialect of a rustic;*

‡ 236–7   **bin zwagger'd … vortnight:** *If I could have been killed by such swaggering talk, I would not have lasted a fortnight;*

§ 238–9   **che vore … harder:** *I warn you to keep out, or else try whether your head or my cudgel be the harder.*

OSWALD   Slave, thou hast slain me. Villain, take my purse.
If ever thou wilt thrive, bury my body,
And give the letters which thou find'st about me
To Edmund Earl of Gloucester. Seek him out   245
Upon the British party. O, untimely death! Death! *[He dies]*

EDGAR   I know thee well. A serviceable villain,
As duteous to the vices of thy mistress
As badness would desire.   250

GLOUCESTER   What, is he dead?

EDGAR   Sit you down, father; rest you.
Let's see his pockets; these letters that he speaks of
May be my friends. He's dead. I am only sorry
He had no other deathsman. Let us see.   255   deathsman: *executioner*
Leave, gentle wax; and, manners, blame us not.'
To know our enemies' minds, we'd rip their hearts;
Their papers, is more lawful.

Reads the letter.

'Let our reciprocal vows be remembered. You have
many opportunities to cut him off. If your will want
not, time and place be fruitfully offer's. There is   him: *Albany, her husband*
nothing done, if he return the conqueror. Then am I the   260
prisoner, and his bed my jail; from
the loathed warmth whereof deliver me, and supply the   supply: *take*
place for your labour.   place: *the marriage bed*
            'Your (wife, so I would say) affectionate servant,
                                        'Goneril.'   265

O indistinguish'd space of woman's will!   indistinguish'd space: *imponderable depth*
A plot upon her virtuous husband's life,
And the exchange my brother! Here in the sands
Thee I'll rake up, the post unsanctified   270   rake up: *bury; post: ground*
Of murtherous lechers; and in the mature time   mature: *ripe, right*
With this ungracious paper strike the sight   ungracious paper: *disgraceful letter*
Of the death-practis'd duke, For him 'tis well   death-practis'd duke: *Albany*
That of thy death and business I can tell.   thy: *Oswald's*

GLOUCESTER   The king is mad. How stiff is my vile sense,   275   stiff: *stubborn*
That I stand up, and have ingenious feeling   ingenious: *conscious*
Of my huge sorrows! Better I were distract.   distract: *mad*
So should my thoughts be severed from my griefs,   severed: *separate, distinct*
And woes by wrong imaginations lose†
The knowledge of themselves.   280

A drum afar off.

EDGAR   Give me your hand.
Far off methinks I hear the beaten drum.
Come, father, I'll bestow you with a friend.

Exeunt.

Handwritten notes:

Pg 148 Key
Moment

* Goneril *
Although absent shows the depths to which
she has stooped to gain her desires Her
plot is reaveled to kill Albany + marry
Edmund, her villiany is sworded + despecable
       * Paradox of Insight *
The wronged fathers console eachother + par
eachothers' insights in misfortunes of ma
+ blindness.

---

* 255-6   **Leave, gentle wax ... lawful:** to break
the wax seal of the letter will not of-
fend, for it is more lawful to learn the
enemies's mind by the breaking open
of their letter than by the ripping open
of their heart.

† 279   **wrong imaginations:** *false delusions*

EDGAR & GLOUCESTER

Edgar pretends to bring his father to the edge of a cliff. Gloucester is duped into believing that he has plunged to the bottom of the cliff and been miraculously saved from death.

Lear appears, crowned with flowers, and delivers a speech of mad moral eloquence, railing against human corruption and hypocrisy. Cordelia's men appear and try to take hold of Lear, but the king runs away.

Edgar hears how the English forces are drawing near. Oswald appears and tries to kill Gloucester but is slain by Edgar. Edgar reads the letter that Oswald was carrying from Goneril to Edmund. He despairs at Goneril's wicked plans to have her husband killed so she could marry Edmund. The battle drums are sounded and Edgar looks to bring his father to a safe place.

ACTION

LINES 1–80: EDGAR PRETENDS TO BRING GLOUCESTER TO THE EDGE OF A CLIFF

Edgar, still disguised as poor Tom, leads his blind father, Gloucester, to what the old man thinks are the Cliffs of Dover. Edgar tricks Gloucester into thinking they are approaching the cliffs by means of verbal deception:

· He tells Gloucester that the ground they walk on is steeply inclined ('Horrible steep') though it is actually flat.

· He asks Gloucester if he can hear the sea, and when the old man says he cannot, Edgar suggests that the his other senses have become deficient with his blindness: 'Why then your other senses grow imperfect/ By your eyes' anguish'. (5–6)

· He feigns vertigo in order to convince Gloucester that they have reached the edge of the cliff: 'How fearful/ And dizzy 'tis to cast one's eyes so low!' (11–12)

· He paints a vivid picture of what he can see from the cliff's edge, describing how everything appears so small from such a great height: 'The fishermen that walk upon the beach/ Appear like mice'. (17–18)

Gloucester is convinced that he has been led to the edge of a cliff and prepares to jump to his death. He hands Edgar a purse containing a valuable jewel, and asks to be left alone: 'Bid me farewell; and let me hear thee going'. (31)

When he thinks that Edgar has gone, Gloucester kneels down at what he supposes to be the edge of a cliff and prays to the 'mighty gods'. He tells them that he is giving up on life ('This world I do renounce') and that he wishes to end his painful existence without passionate despair: 'Shake patiently my great affliction off'. (36) He tells the 'gods' that if his suffering was bearable, he would continue to live and expire of old age ('My snuff and loathed part of nature should/ Burn itself out'. (39–40) He knows that by taking his own life, he is going against the will of the gods, but he says that he can no longer continue living. He throws himself forward.

Edgar tells Gloucester that his life has been miraculously saved. Edgar wishes his father

CHARACTER DEVELOPMENT

GLOUCESTER

READY FOR DEATH

We see in this scene that Gloucester's sufferings have brought him to a point where he wishes to die. He has lost his sight and his two sons, and can see no reason to continue living. Although on one level he believes that suicide is an affront to the gods, and he would go on if he could, he feels he does not have the strength to endure any more of their cruelty:

If I could bear it longer, and not fall
To quarrel with you great opposeless wills,
My snuff and loathed part of nature should
Burn itself out (38–41)

THINKING OF OTHERS

Although Gloucester wishes to die, he still shows compassion and thought for others. He gives the disguised Edgar a purse with a jewel in it as a reward for being guided to Dover, and it is quite touching that his last thought before he throws himself from the 'cliff' is of his son: 'If Edgar live, O, bless him!' (41)

RESCUED FROM DESPAIR?

Gloucester is initially distraught after surviving his 'fall'. He laments the fact that the gods will not even give men the option of suicide as a means of escaping the pain of life:

Is wretchedness depriv'd that benefit
To end itself by death? 'Twas yet some comfort,
When misery could beguile the tyrant's rage,
And frustrate his proud will (62–5)

However, Edgar's words of encouragement and the fact that he apparently survived such a great fall appear to restore Gloucester's strength. He feels he can go on: 'henceforth I'll bear/ Affliction till it do cry out itself/ "Enough, enough", and die'. (76–8)

After his encounter with the mad Lear, Gloucester's will to live seems even more invigorated. The sight of a man who has suffered even more gives him the impetus to bear his own pain:

You ever-gentle gods, take my breath from me;
Let not my worser spirit tempt me again
To die before you please (223–5)

However, Gloucester is still prone to anguish and despair. Not long after he utters those words, Oswald appears and declares that he is going to kill him in order to claim the bounty on his head. Gloucester's reaction seems to show that he wishes for death again:

Now let thy friendly hand
Put strength enough to 't (235–6)

Although Edgar saves him, Gloucester does not appear that overjoyed. In fact, he now envies Lear for the fact that he is mad, and so therefore distracted from his pain:

*   How stiff is my vile sense,*
That I stand up, and have ingenious feeling
Of my huge sorrows! Better I were distract (287–9)

We should not be surprised that, after all he has undergone, Gloucester's mood swings wildly between wishing to die and desiring to go on.

to think that he has actually fallen from a great height, and that he has been saved from death by a miracle. He approaches Gloucester, pretending to be someone on the beach at the foot of the cliff who witnessed the old man falling. He tells him that nothing could have survived such a fall, and that it is incredible that he is not only alive, but unscathed: 'Thy life's a miracle'. (55)

Gloucester despairs at being alive. The thought that he could take his own life was the one comfort left him: "Twas yet some comfort/ When misery could beguile the tyrant's rage/ And frustrate his proud will'. (62–4) In a further effort to convince his father that he is blessed, Edgar tells him that he was sure he saw an evil demon stand with Gloucester at the top of the cliff: 'As I stood here below methought his eyes/ Were two full moons; he had a thousand noses,/ Horns welked and waved like the enridged sea'. (69–71) He suggests to Gloucester that he ought to think the pure gods have intervened to save him from the hands of a devil, preserving his life with a miraculous deed: 'Therefore, thou happy father,/ Think that the clearest gods, who make them honours/ Of men's impossibilities, have preserved thee'. (72–4)

Gloucester is convinced that the man he thought to be a beggar (Edgar, disguised as 'poor Tom') might well have been some evil fiend, and vows to carry on living and endure the pains of life until those very pains tire of paining him: 'Henceforth I'll bear/ Affliction till it do cry out itself/ "Enough, enough", and die'. (75–7)

A KEY MOMENT

The main plot and the sub-plot meet in this scene. We see two old men, each laid low by fortune and their own misjudgement, come together. Each has been betrayed by ungrateful children, and each has suffered and gained knowledge as a result. Lear has found wisdom in insanity and Gloucester has found insight in blindness. The question now remains as to what fate has in store for them.

EDGAR

A LOVING SON

We see the true depths of Edgar's love for his father in this scene. His only concern is to save his father from despair, and to give him renewed strength and courage. Again, Edgar displays great skill and cunning in convincing Gloucester that he stands on top of a mighty cliff. All of this is done with the ultimate aim of pulling his father back from death:

Why I do trifle thus with his despair
Is done to cure it (35–6)

Edgar appears to be successful in his aim. After Gloucester's 'fall', Edgar adopts a new role as a peasant who saw him survive the jump. He cunningly tells his father that he must be favoured by the gods in order to have survived such a drop:

Think that the clearest gods, who make them
*   honours*
Of men's impossibilities, have preserv'd thee (74–5)

Edgar's clever ruse works, for a time at least, and Gloucester is filled with determination to go on.

COMPASSION FOR THE KING

Edgar is also seized with compassion and pity when confronted by the sight of the mad Lear. His initial reaction is one of terrible sadness at seeing a once-great man reduced to insanity: 'O thou side-piercing sight!' (86) As Lear raves, Edgar cannot believe the spectacle before him: 'I would not take this from report; it is,/ And my heart breaks at it'. (145–6) The sight of his blind father and the mad king in conversation is overwhelming to him.

SAVING GLOUCESTER AGAIN

Edgar once again exhibits his unconditional love and absolute determination to protect his father, when Oswald appears, looking to murder his father. He puts on yet another accent and warns Goneril's servant to keep away. When the latter refuses, Edgar has no choice but to kill him.

This turn of events leads to Edgar discovering Goneril's treacherous letter to Edmund. Edgar now has proof of his brother's betrayal and intends to show no mercy. He will inform Albany of the plot against his life, and see his brother brought to justice. After all he has endured, it appears that Edgar may rewarded for his courage.

CHARACTER DEVELOPMENT

LEAR

⚘ LINES 80–110: LEAR APPEARS

At this point, Lear enters, dressed in wild flowers, and speaking in a disjointed and irrational manner. He seems hardly aware of Edgar and Gloucester at first, but when he notices them, he challenges them to reveal the secret word that will tell him if they are friend or foe. Edgar says 'Sweet marjoram', and this satisfies Lear.

The king's voice seems familiar to Gloucester, and he drops to his knees respectfully. Lear seems to think that Gloucester is trying to flatter him, and this causes the king to speak bitterly about Goneril and Regan, saying that they treated him no better than a dog with their false words of flattery and fawning behaviour. Lear says that it was when he was exposed to the storm and found himself powerless and vulnerable that he realised his daughters were false: 'They told me I was everything. 'Tis a lie: I am not ague-proof'. (104)

When Gloucester recognises Lear's voice and asks if it is 'the King', Lear replies sardonically that he is 'every inch a king'. (107) He imagines Gloucester is some form of culprit seeking to be pardoned for his crimes. Lear pardons Gloucester and guesses that his crime was 'adultery'. (109–10) The king then makes a speech in which he suggests that the notion of 'adultery' being something sinful is ridiculous.

⚘ LINES 111–83: LEAR SPEAKS OF HUMAN HYPOCRISY AND CORRUPTION

Sexual copulation, Lear says, occurs everywhere in nature: 'The wren goes to't, and the small guilded fly/ Does lecher in my sight'. (112–13) The notion of sexual morality and virtue, therefore, is a farce. Men and women are part-animal. and it is futile to

CHARACTER DEVELOPMENT

LEAR

WISDOM IN MADNESS

When Lear first appears in this scene, it seems as if he has once again slid into total madness. He is dressed in flowers, and raves incomprehensibly.

However, we quickly see that the king has gained great insight in the midst of his insanity. He now realises how hypocritical his former life was. Lear sees that he was flattered relentlessly by others in order to gain favour: 'To say "ay" and "no" to/ everything I said! "Ay" and "no" too was no good divinity'. (99–101) In his exile and madness, the king acknowledges that he is just a man:

Go to, they are not men o' their words: they
told me I was everything; 'tis a lie, I am not ague
proof (104–6)

Lear also returns to the theme of social justice that struck him first when he was exposed to the great storm. He now sees how hypocrisy and selfishness dominate the lives of those at the top of the social order:

A dog's obey'd in office
Thou rascal beadle, hold thy bloody hand!
Why dost thou lash that whore? Strip thine own
   back;
Thou hotly lust'st to use her in that kind
For which thou whipp'st her (163–7)

The king sees that behind the glitz and pomp of court life, deceit and immorality can easily be hidden:

Through tatter'd clothes small vices do appear;
Robes and furr'd gowns hide all. Plate sin with gold,
And the strong lance of justice hurtles breaks;
Arm it in rags, a pigmy's straw doth pierce it (169–72)

He has lost all faith in the word of those that wield power: 'Get thee glass eyes;/ And, like a scurvy politician, seem/ To see the things thou dost not'. (175–7)

THE ABSURDITY OF LIFE

As a result of his suffering and the wisdom he has gained, Lear now sees life as an absurd journey full of pain and suffering. He tells Gloucester that he must endure his suffering, as it is man's natural state:

Thou must be patient; we came crying hither:
Thou know'st the first time that we smell the air
We waul and cry (183–5)

continued over

149

repress and seek to control by law what is natural. Lear compares men to 'centaurs', saying that they are bestial, like horses below the waist. He says that men and women's bodies are controlled by both gods and 'fiends'. The top half of our bodies belong to the gods, the part below the waist to the devils: 'But to the girdle do the gods inherit,/ Beneath is all the fiends'. (126–7) Lear's speech climaxes in hysterical disgust at female sexuality: 'There's hell, there's darkness, there is the sulphorous/ pit – burning, scalding, stench, consumption! Fie, fie,/ fie! Pah, pah!' (128–30)

The world, according to Lear, is a place of hypocrisy and injustice:

· A whisper in the ear of a judge can bribe him to reverse his decision.
· Social status is an accident of fortune, and authority has nothing to do with intrinsic worth: 'a dog's obeyed in office'. (159–60)
· Those who administer punishment are hypocrites. The man who whips the whore 'hotly lusts' to use her for the very crime she is being punished. (162–4)
· The rich are immune to justice while the poor must suffer the full force of the law. (161–3)

Lear hands Gloucester flowers as though they were coins, pretending to bribe him. He tells Gloucester to fit himself with glass eyes and be like the corrupt politicians who have the art of seeming to see what they cannot actually see. Eventually exhausted by his speech, Lear sinks down and gives the command to have his boots removed.

LEAR & GLOUCESTER

Gloucester despairs at the king's behaviour, and considers him to be a 'ruined piece of nature'. He asks Lear if he recognises him, and the king initially answers in a strange fashion, calling Gloucester 'blind Cupid'. He tells Gloucester that he sees him as a kindred spirit, someone who has also lost direction and wealth. Though blind, Gloucester is

The king sees the world as being filled with people deluding themselves as to their own importance. The wise man knows better:

> When we are born, we cry
>   that we are come
> To this great stage of fools
> (187–8)

All of the false trappings and pomp that marked his old existence are gone. The king now sees life for what it is.

DISGUST AT FEMALE SEXUALITY

We see also in this scene that Lear is still obsessed with the cruelty of his daughters:

> Let copulation thrive; for
>   Gloucester's bastard son
> Was kinder to his father than
>   my daughters
> Got 'tween the lawful sheets
> (117–19)

Lear's fixation leads him to condemn women and their sexuality. He views them all as being treacherous and untrustworthy:

> Down from the waist they are
>   Centaurs,
> Though women all above;
> But to the girdle do the gods
>   inherit, Beneath is all
> the fiends' (127–30)

The act of sexual intercourse is viewed by Lear with horror, as it leads only to the creation of creatures like Goneril and Regan: 'There's hell, there's darkness, there is the sulphurous/ pit, Burning, scalding, stench, consumption'. (131–2) Lear is disgusted with the human condition. When Gloucester asks for his hand, he replies: 'Let me wipe it first; it smells of mortality'. (137)

If I could bear it longer, and not fall
To quarrel with you great opposeless wills,
My snuff and loathed part of nature should
Burn itself out

Gloucester (38–41)

O ruin'd piece of nature! This great world
Shall so wear out to nought

Gloucester (138-9)

Through tatter'd clothes small vices do appear;
Robes and furr'd gowns hide all

Lear (169-70)

Thou must be patient; we came crying hither:
Thou know'st the first time that we smell the air
We waul and cry

Lear (183-5)

When we are born, we cry that we are come
To this great stage of fools

Lear (187-8)

SOME LINES TO LEARN

someone who sees how the world works: 'Your eyes are in a heavy case, your purse in a light: yet you see how this world goes'. (143–5)

Lear seems to be aware of who Gloucester is. He tells him that he knows him 'well enough' and that his 'name is Gloucester'. (173) He looks to console the distraught Gloucester, telling him to have patience and endure his suffering. The world, Lear tells him, is a place where humans suffer from the moment they are born: 'we came crying hither'. (174) Lear begins to preach about human suffering, but is quickly distracted by a hat he is holding: 'This' a good block!' (179) Contemplating the material of the hat gets Lear to thinking about shoeing a 'troop of horses with felt'. (180) With their hoofs so clad, Lear imagines how he could sneak quietly up on Cornwall and Albany and 'kill, kill, kill, kill, kill, kill!' (183)

CHARACTER DEVELOPMENT

LEAR & CORDELIA'S MEN

🔊 LINES 184– 200: CORDELIA'S MEN FIND LEAR

At this moment, the men Cordelia sent to find her father enter. A Gentleman instructs the other men to get a hold of Lear. He tries to explain to Lear that he is acting on behalf of Cordelia and is looking out for the king's best interests, but Lear is paranoid and thinks that he is being captured: 'No rescue? What, a prisoner?' (186) He tells the men to

OSWALD

MURDEROUS
Oswald meets his end in this scene. When he sees Gloucester, he has no hesitation in drawing his sword to kill him, seeing a great opportunity for his own advancement: 'That eyeless head of thine was first fram'd flesh/ To raise my fortunes'. (233–4) He has no mercy whatsoever for the helpless blind man before him.

Oswald's overconfidence is his undoing, however. He takes Edgar for a powerless peasant and pays the price. Although he is generally a slimy and despicable character, there is something almost oddly touching about his dying words. He wishes to be buried properly, and is desperate that the task he was charged with is carried out: 'If ever thou wilt thrive, bury my body;/ And give the letters which thou find'st about me/ To Edmund Earl of Gloucester'. (253-5) Ironically, his words lead to Edgar's discovery of his brother's treachery.

GONERIL

TREACHEROUS
Although Goneril does not appear in the scene, we learn through her letter that she is hoping that Edmund will kill Albany and take her as his wife. Clearly, she has been rattled by her husband's new-found strength and moral integrity, and is willing to have Albany murdered in order to be free of him.

EDGAR & OSWALD

handle him carefully and that they will receive their required ransom in due course. (187–8) He calls out for 'surgeons', saying that he is wounded mentally: 'I am cut to the brains'. (189)

The Gentleman looks to ease Lear's concerns, acknowledging the fact that he is king and that he will be obeyed. (198) When Lear gets a sense that the men he presumes are his captors are not as threatening as he thought, he decides to make a run for it. He tells them that if they want him they will have to chase him: 'Nay, an you get it, you shall get it by running'. (199–200) He exits, pursued by Cordelia's men.

LINES 200–210: EDGAR ASKS THE GENTLEMAN FOR INFORMATION OF THE COMING BATTLE

Edgar asks Cordelia's attendant if he knows anything about an imminent battle between the French (Cordelia's forces) and English (Goneril and Regan's forces). The Gentleman tells him that the English forces are very close and are moving quickly. He says that a sighting of the main force of their army is expected very soon. (210)

LINES 210– 225: EDGAR KILLS OSWALD

Gloucester is left alone with Edgar and is moved to hear of Cordelia's arrival and intention to right the wrongs inflicted on her father. He prays to the 'ever-gentle gods' that he may never desire to end his own life again: 'Let not my worser spirit tempt me again/ To die before you please!' (215–16) He asks Edgar who he is, and Edgar, still reluctant to reveal his true identity, tells him that he is a 'poor man' who has been humbled and filled with pity by recent events. He takes

Gloucester by the hand and offers to take him to a place where he can stay. Gloucester is most gracious for the help.

Oswald appears and recognises Gloucester as a wanted man with a price on his head. He knows that if he kills Gloucester he will be rewarded by Goneril and Regan: 'that eyeless head of thine was first fram'd flesh/ To raise my fortunes. (224–5) He tells Gloucester to say his last prayers and draws his sword. Gloucester greets the prospect of death happily, but Edgar steps in to save his father. Oswald and Edgar fight, and Oswald is slain.

LINES 226–83: EDGAR READS GONERIL'S LETTER TO EDMUND

As he lies dying, Oswald asks Edgar to take the letter he is carrying and deliver it to Edmund. Edgar takes the letter and, when Oswald has died, opens it and reads. The letter is from Goneril and it reveals her plot to have Edmund kill Albany and marry her. Edgar is horrified by Goneril's terrible wishes: 'A plot upon her virtuous husband's life,/ And the exchange my brother!' (268–9) He says that he cannot apprehend the range of woman's lust: 'O undistinguished space of woman's will'. (267)

Edgar looks to bury Oswald's corpse in 'the sands'. (269–70) Gloucester wishes he were mad so that he would not have to be aware of all the terrible things that are happening: 'Better I were distract./ So should my thoughts be severed from my griefs'. (277–8) The drums of battle are heard in the distance. Edgar takes his father by the hand and promises to bring him to a safe place.

ACT 4 SCENE 7

A tent in the French camp

Enter CORDELIA, KENT, Doctor, and GENTLEMAN.

CORDELIA O thou good Kent, how shall I live and work
To match thy goodness? My life will be too short
And every measure fail me.

KENT To be acknowledged, madam, is o'erpaid. 5
All my reports go with the modest truth;
Nor more nor clipped, but so.

CORDELIA Be better suited.
These weeds are memories of those worser hours.
I prithee put them off.

KENT Pardon, dear madam.
Yet to be known shortens my made intent.
My boon I make it that you know me not 10
Till time and I think meet.

CORDELIA Then be't so, my good lord. *[To the Doctor]* How, does the King?

DOCTOR Madam, sleeps still.

CORDELIA   O you kind gods,
Cure this great breach in his abused nature!
Th' untun'd and jarring senses, O, wind up 15
Of this child-changed father!

DOCTOR So please your Majesty
That we may wake the King? He hath slept long.

CORDELIA Be governed by your knowledge, and proceed
I' th' sway of your own will. Is he arrayed? 20

Enter LEAR in a chair carried by Servants.

GENTLEMAN Ay, madam. In the heaviness of sleep
We put fresh garments on him.

DOCTOR Be by, good madam, when we do awake him.
I doubt not of his temperance.

CORDELIA Very well, 25

Music.

DOCTOR Please you draw near. Louder the music there!

CORDELIA O my dear father, restoration hang
Thy medicine on my lips, and let this kiss
Repair those violent harms that my two sisters
Have in thy reverence made!

KENT Kind and dear princess!

CORDELIA Had you not been their father, these white flakes 30
Had challenged pity of them. Was this a face
To be opposed against the warring winds?
To stand against the deep dread-bolted thunder?
In the most terrible and nimble stroke
Of quick cross lightning? to watch – poor perdu! – ➤ 35

---

clipped: *made less*

weeds: *ragged clothes*

breach: *wound*
untun'd: *out of harmony;* **wind up:** *tune*
child-changed: *changed into a child*

temperance: *mood, self-control*

restoration: *restoration personified*

white flakes: *white wispy hair*
challenged: *demanded*

dread-bolted: *hurling, dreadful*

perdu: *a sentry*

* **9–11** **shortens my made intent … I think meet:** *to lose my disguise at this stage would spoil my plans, as a favour, act as if you don't known me until the time and circumstances are right to reveal myself.*

	With this thin helm? Mine enemy's dog,	
	Though he had bit me, should have stood that night	
	Against my fire; and wast thou fain, poor father,	
	To hovel thee with swine and rogues forlorn,	
	In short and musty straw? Alack, alack!	40
	'Tis wonder that thy life and wits at once	
	Had not concluded all. – He wakes. Speak to him.	
DOCTOR	Madam, do you; 'tis fittest.	
CORDELIA	How does my royal lord? How fares your Majesty?	
LEAR	You do me wrong to take me out o' th' grave.	45
	Thou art a soul in bliss; but I am bound	
	Upon a wheel of fire, that mine own tears	
	Do scald like molten lead.	
CORDELIA	Sir, do you know me?	
LEAR	You are a spirit, I know. When did you die?	
CORDELIA	Still, still, far wide!	50
DOCTOR	He's scarce awake. Let him alone awhile.	
LEAR	Where have I been? Where am I? Fair daylight,	
	I am mightily abused. I should e'en die with pity,	
	To see another thus. I know not what to say.	
	I will not swear these are my hands. Let's see.	55
	I feel this pin prick. Would I were assured	
	Of my condition!	
CORDELIA	O, look upon me, sir,	
	And hold your hands in benediction o'er me.	
	No, sir, you must not kneel.	
LEAR	Pray, do not mock me.	
	I am a very foolish fond old man,	60
	Fourscore and upward, not an hour more nor less;	
	And, to deal plainly,	
	I fear I am not in my perfect mind.	
	Methinks I should know you, and know this man;	
	Yet I am doubtful; for I am mainly ignorant	65
	What place this is; and all the skill I have	
	Remembers not these garments; nor I know not	
	Where I did lodge last night. Do not laugh at me;	
	For (as I am a man) I think this lady	
	To be my child Cordelia.	70
CORDELIA	And so I am! I am!	
LEAR	Be your tears wet? Yes, faith. I pray weep not.	
	If you have poison for me, I will drink it.	
	I know you do not love me; for your sisters	
	Have, as I do remember, done me wrong.	75
	You have some cause, they have not.	
CORDELIA	No cause, no cause.	
LEAR	Am I in France?	
KENT	In your own kingdom, sir.	
LEAR	Do not abuse me.	
DOCTOR	Be comforted, good madam. The great rage	
	You see is killed in him; and yet it is danger	
	To make him even o'er the time he has lost.	80
	Desire him to go in. Trouble him no more	
	Till further settling.	
CORDELIA	Will't please your Highness walk?	

helm: *covering (of hair)*

concluded all: *ended (in death)*

wheel of fire: *image of hell*

wide: *wide of the mark, rambling*

abused: *two senses: ill treated, deluded*

benediction: *blessing*

fond: *in his dotage*

abuse: *deceive*
rage: *mad passion*

even o'er: *fill in, recollect*

further settling: *calmer*

LEAR	You must bear with me.	
	Pray you now, forget and forgive. I am old and foolish.	85

Exeunt all but KENT and Gentleman.

GENTLEMAN	Holds it true, sir, that the Duke of Cornwall was so slain?	
KENT	Most certain, sir.	
GENTLEMAN	Who is conductor of his people?	
KENT	As 'tis said, the bastard son of Gloucester.	
GENTLEMAN	They say Edgar, his banished son, is with the Earl of	90
	Kent in Germany.	
KENT	Report is changeable. 'Tis time to look about; the powers of	
	he kingdom approach apace.	
GENTLEMAN	The arbitrement is like to be bloody.	
	Fare you well, sir. *[Exit]*	95
KENT	My point and period will be throughly wrought,	
	Or well or ill, as this day's battle's fought. *[Exit]*	

conductor: *leader*

Report: *news, rumour*

arbitrement: *outcome of the encounter*

---

* 87   **Holds it true:** *is it still true;*

† 96–7   **My point and period will be throughly wrought, / Or well or ill, as this day's battle's fought:** *This day's battle will determine my life's purpose and length, for good or for bad.*

CORDELIA

Cordelia and Kent are at the French camp where the king has been brought to recover. Cordelia thanks Kent for all he has done. She prays for the recovery of her father. Lear is brought in, and the doctor instructs that he should be woken. When the king wakes, he is confused and disorientated. He recognises Cordelia, and begs her forgiveness. The British forces are fast approaching the French camp.

ACTION

✒ LINES 1–11: CORDELIA THANKS KENT

Kent and Cordelia meet in the French camp. Cordelia expresses her gratitude to Kent for all he has done for her father. Kent tells her that he never wanted any reward other than her kind words for what he did: 'To be acknowledged, madam, is o'er-paid'. (4) Cordelia tells Kent that he should drop his disguise now that things are improving, but Kent says that he has need still to keep his identity concealed.

✒ LINES 12–44: LEAR IS BROUGHT IN

Cordelia asks the doctor how Lear is doing, and is told that the king still sleeps. She prays to the gods to make right the wrongs inflicted upon her father. The doctor tells her it is time to wake Lear, and the king is brought in on a chair.

Cordelia kisses Lear and asks that he be restored to health. Looking upon her father, so old and fragile, she cannot believe that her sisters could treat him so cruelly. Even if he wasn't their father, she says, his old age should have made them pity him. Cordelia says that she would not have sent her enemy's dog out into such a storm: 'Mine enemy's dog,/ Though he had bit me, should have stood that night/ Against my fire'. (36–8) She is amazed that her father even survived the harsh elements of the night: ''Tis wonder that thy life and wits at once/ Had not concluded all. (41–2)

✒ LINES 45–85: LEAR WAKES UP

The king wakes, and the doctor tells Cordelia to speak to him. She addresses her father formally, and asks how he is. At first, Lear is disorientated and confused. He imagines that he is experiencing some form of life after death: 'You do me wrong to take me out o'the

I am bound
on a wheel of fire, that mine own tears
scald like molten lead

Lear (46-8)

y you now, forget and forgive: I am old and foolish

Lear (85)

SOME LINES TO LEARN

grave'. (45) He takes it that Cordelia is in heaven and that he is in hell:

> *Thou art a soul in bliss; but I am bound*
> *Upon a wheel of fire, that mine own tears*
> *Do scald like molten lead.* (46–8)

Lear recognises his daughter, and falls to his knees looking for forgiveness. He tells her that he is nothing but a 'very foolish fond old man', and that he fears he might not yet be completely sane. He is unsure of where he is and what has happened: 'I am mainly ignorant/ What place this is'. (65) He tells Cordelia that, if she wishes, he will drink poison for the wrongs he did to her. He says that she has good reason to hate him while her sisters, who did him such harm, had no cause. (72–5)

Cordelia weeps with happiness to see her father so restored. She assures her father that she bears no anger towards him: 'No cause, no cause'. (75) The doctor tells her that her father is over the worst of it, but that it would be best not to relive the events of the recent past as this might only cause the king distress. They go in to the tent, Lear leaning on Cordelia for support.

🐾 LINES 86–97: KENT SPEAKS TO THE GENTLEMAN ABOUT THE LATEST EVENTS

When the others have left, Kent speaks with the Gentleman about the latest developments. Kent confirms that Cornwall has been killed and that it is Edmund who now leads his people. The Gentleman says that there are rumours going around that Edgar is with Kent in Germany. Kent, still in disguise, tells the Gentleman that such reports can change. He advises the Gentleman that it is time to take stock of what is happening, as the English forces are advancing. The Gentleman says that the outcome of the pending battle is likely to be 'bloody'. They bid each other farewell, and Kent says that his life will find its purpose and end, for good or bad, in the coming battle.

LEAR

RESTORED TO CORDELIA

In this scene, Lear is finally reunited with Cordelia. At first, he believes he has died and awoken in the afterlife: 'You do me wrong to take me out of the grave'. (45) Lear thinks that Cordelia is an angel, whereas he is still in torment: 'I am bound/ Upon a wheel of fire, that mine own tears/ Do scald like molten lead'. (46-8) The king is in a state of great confusion.

TOTALLY CONTRITE

Once Lear realises that he still lives and that Cordelia is real, he is absolutely contrite and humble. He is willing to accept the ultimate punishment for his actions:

> *If you have poison for me, I will drink it.*
> *I know you do not love me; for your sisters*
> *Have, as I do remember, done me wrong:*
> *You have some cause, they have not* (73–6)

There is no more trace of the arrogant king we saw at the beginning of the play. Instead, we see – as he tries to kneel and beg for his daughter's forgiveness – a tired old man, aware of his faults and hoping to be forgiven. His language, in contrast to the stately rhetoric he once held forth with, is simple and affecting: 'Pray you now, forget and forgive: I am old and foolish'. (85)

CORDELIA

A LOVING DAUGHTER

Once again, we see Cordelia's total love for her father on display. She is absolutely desperate to see her father cured and restored: 'O my dear father! Restoration, hang/ Thy medicine on thy lips'. (25-6) She is still incredulous as to the cruelty shown to Lear by her sisters: 'Mine enemy's dog,/ Though he had bit me, should have stood that night/ Against my fire'. (36-8)

When Lear does awake, she shows no sign of bearing a grudge against him. Instead, she kneels and asks for his blessing. (56-8) When he says that she has plenty of cause for wanting him dead, her reply is simple and moving: 'No cause, no cause'. (77) Her only wish is to see her father safe and restored to health. Cordelia's pure love is absolutely unconditional. Everything she does is done purely for Lear's sake.

KENT

NOBLE DUTY

As ever, Kent serves his master with complete loyalty and devotion. He refuses to accept Cordelia's offer of a reward for his actions, saying that even for his duty to be recognised is too much: 'To be acknowledg'd madam, is o'er-paid'. (4) He is still active at the end of the scene, working toward protecting the king.

CHARACTER DEVELOPMENT

ACT 5 SCENE 1

The British camp near Dover

Enter, with Drum and Colours, EDMUND, REGAN, Gentleman, and Soldiers.

EDMUND	Know of the duke if his last purpose hold,*
	Or whether since he is advised by aught
	To change the course. He's full of alteration
	And self-reproving; bring his constant pleasure.

Exit an Officer.

REGAN	Our sister's man is certainly miscarried.
EDMUND	'Tis to be doubted, madam.
REGAN	Now, sweet lord,
	You know the goodness I intend upon you.
	Tell me – but truly – but then speak the truth –
	Do you not love my sister
EDMUND	In honour'd love.
REGAN	But have you never found my brother's way
	To the forfended place?
EDMUND	That thought abuses you.
REGAN	I am doubtful that you have been conjunct
	And bosomed with her, as far as we call hers.
EDMUND	No, by mine honour, madam.
REGAN	I never shall endure her. Dear my lord,
	Be not familiar with her.
EDMUND	Fear me not.
	She and the duke her husband!

Enter, with Drum and Colours, ALBANY, GONERIL, Soldiers.

GONERIL	*[Aside]* I had rather lose the battle than that sister
	Should loosen him and me.
ALBANY	Our very loving sister, well bemet.
	Sir, this I hear: the King is come to his daughter.
	With others whom the rigour of our state
	Forced to cry out. Where I could not be honest,
	I never yet was valiant. For this business,†
	It toucheth us as France invades our land,
	Not bolds the king, with others whom, I fear,
	Most just and heavy causes make oppose.
EDMUND	Sir, you speak nobly.
REGAN	Why is this reasoned?
GONERIL	Combine together 'gainst the enemy;
	For these domestic and particular broils
	Are not the question here.
ALBANY	Let's then determine
	With th' ancient of war on our proceeding.
EDMUND	I shall attend you presently at your tent.

Line numbers: 5, 10, 15, 20, 25, 30

aught: *anything*

constant pleasure: *final decision*

miscarried: *brought to an early end*

honour'd: *honourable*

brother: *Albany, Goneril's husband*
forfended: *forbidden*

doubtful: *fearful;* conjunct: *united together*
bosomed: *close, as lovers*

loosen: *break the bond between*
bemet: *met*

rigour: *harshness*
cry out: *leave, reluctantly rebel*
For: *as for*
toucheth: *deeply concerns*
Not bolds: *not encouraged by;* with: *but with*

reasoned: *argued*
the enemy: *France*
broils: *fights*

th' ancient: *experienced warriors*

* [1]   Know of the duke if his last purpose hold: *do you know if Albany's latest intention to go to war still holds?*

† [23–4]   honest ... valiant: *in a case where as I could not admit the truth (such as the case of the harshness of the state), I could not act bravely.*

REGAN	Sister, you'll go with us?	35
GONERIL	No.	
REGAN	'Tis most convenient. Pray you go with us.	
GONERIL	*[Aside]* O, ho, I know the riddle. – I will go.	

As they are going out, enter EDGAR disguised

EDGAR	If e'er your Grace had speech with man so poor,	
	Hear me one word.	
ALBANY	I'll overtake you. – Speak.	

Exeunt all but ALBANY and EDGAR.

EDGAR	Before you fight the battle, ope this letter.	40
	If you have victory, let the trumpet sound	
	For him that brought it. Wretched though I seem,	
	I can produce a champion that will prove	
	What is avouched there. If you miscarry,	45
	Your business of the world hath so an end,	
	And machination ceases. Fortune love you!	
ALBANY	Stay till I have read the letter.	
EDGAR	I was forbid it.	
	When time shall serve, let but the herald cry,	
	And I'll appear again.	
ALBANY	why, fare thee well. I will o'erlook thy paper.	50

Exit EDGAR.
Enter EDMUND

EDMUND	The enemy's in view; draw up your powers.	
	Here is the guess of their true strength and forces	
	By diligent discovery; but your haste*	
	Is now urged on you.	
ALBANY	We will greet the time. *[Exit]*	55
EDMUND	To both these sisters have I sworn my love;	
	Each jealous of the other, as the stung	
	Are of the adder. Which of them shall I take?	
	Both? one? or neither? Neither can be enjoyed,	
	If both remain alive. To take the widow	
	Exasperates, makes mad her sister Goneril;	60
	And hardly shall I carry out my side,	
	Her husband being alive. Now then, we'll use	
	His countenance for the battle, which being done,	
	Let her who would be rid of him devise	
	His speedy taking off. As for the mercy	65
	Which he intends to Lear and to Cordelia –	
	The battle done, and they within our power,	
	Shall never see his pardon; for my state	
	Stands on me to defend, not to debate. *[Exit]*	

Glossary (right column):

riddle: *game*

overtake: *catch-up*

ope: *open, read*

avouched: *asserted; miscarry: lose the battle*
business of the world: *life*
machination: *plot, intrique*

o'erlook: *look over*

powers: *troops*
guess: *estimate*

greet the time: *be ready on time*

side: *preference, plan*

countenance: *authority*
her: *Goneril*
taking off: *death*

state: *position*

* [53] **By diligent discovery:** *obtained by careful monitoring*

REGAN

EDMUND

The British forces under Albany and Edmund are preparing for battle against Cordelia and the French invaders. Regan expresses her concern that Edmund might be having a relationship with Goneril. The two begin to quarrel over Edmund's love. Before they leave for a council of war, 'Poor Tom' gives Albany the letter detailing Edmund and Goneril's plot to kill him. Edmund declares that if Lear and Cordelia fall into this power, he will have them executed.

ACTION

➳ LINES 1–4: EDMUND DOUBTS ALBANY

Edmund, Reagan, and a group of soldiers are in the British camp near Dover. Edmund is worried that Albany will not join him in the coming battle. He knows that Albany is full of uncertainty: 'he's full of alteration/ And self-reproving'. (3–4) He sends an officer to discover Albany's intentions.

➳ LINES 5–19: REGAN'S INSECURITY

Regan is anxious and insecure. She wishes to know if Edmund is in love with Goneril: 'Tell me, but truly, but then speak the truth,/ Do you not love my sister?' (8) She asks him if he has slept with her: 'But have you never found my brother's way/ To the forefended palce?' (10–11) She pleads with Edmund not to become intimate with Goneril: 'I never shall endure her: dear my lord,/ Be not familiar with her'. (15–16)

Edmund repeatedly reassures Regan that there is nothing between himself and Goneril. He says that his love for Goneril is honourable and dutiful, and that Regan's blunt questions about possible sexual relations does her no credit: 'That thought abuses you'. (12)

➳ LINES 20–37: TENSION AMONGST LEAR'S ENEMIES

Albany, Goneril and their military forces arrive. Albany tells Edmund he has learnt that Lear has been reunited with Cordelia. He says that Lear and Cordelia have been joined by others who have suffered under the new regime: 'the king is come to his daughter,/ With others; whom the rigour of our state/ Forc'd to cry out'. (21–3)

Albany is unsure if he is on the right side in the

EDMUND

CLOSE TO COMPLETE VICTORY

This scene shows Edmund at the high point of his success. As far as he is aware, Gloucester and Edgar are no longer threats to his ambition, and he has Goneril and Regan competing for his love. All that apparently stands between him and total victory is the threat of the French army. If the invader is defeated, then he plans to take complete control.

TENSION WITH ALBANY

Apart from the French, the only other obstacle facing Edmund is Albany. Edmund has learnt something of Albany's troubled conscience, and appears worried that he may have to face the invader without his help. He is concerned that Albany may be suffering from a sense of guilt: 'he's full of alteration/ and self-reproving'. (3–4) For a ruthless pragmatist like Edmund, such doubts are inconceivable.

MANIPULATIVE

Edmund clearly enjoys being the focus of the two sisters' attention. He appears to take pleasure in delaying giving Regan a direct answer to her questions about his relationship with Goneril ('That thought abuses you'). From being a social outcast on account of his illegitimacy, Edmund is now revelling in being at the centre of events.

SELFISH AND HEARTLESS

Edmund's speech at the end of this scene reveals the utter depths of his amorality and selfishness. He derives great narcissistic pleasure from being able to play the two sisters off against each other, while he himself appears not too bothered about either: 'Which of them shall I take?/ Both? One? or neither?' (48)

For Edmund, their love for him is only a tool that he can manipulate in his quest for complete power. He intends to use Goneril's desire for him as a means by which he can have Albany eliminated: 'Let her who would be rid of him devise/ His speedy taking off'. (64) His attitude toward Albany himself is similarly ruthless: 'we'll use/ His countenance for the battle'. (62) Edmund views people purely as a means by which to further his selfish ambitions.

In similar fashion, he intends to show no mercy to Lear and Cordelia if he captures them. He knows that the king could serve as a rallying-point for those opposed to his rule, and so must not be allowed remain alive: 'for my state/ Stands on me to defend, not to debate'. (68–9) Edmund does not think twice about using murder as a tool to ensure his own position.

ALBANY, GONERIL, EDMUND & REGAN

coming conflict: 'Where I could not be honest/ I never yet was valiant'. (23–4) He says he views the coming battle as a fight against the French, not Lear. Edmund hypocritically agrees with Albany: 'Sir, you speak nobly'. (28)

Regan and Goneril impatiently ask why they are discussing such matters when the French are so close: 'For these domestic and particular broils/ Are not the question here'. (30–1) Albany agrees and suggests they hold a council of war. (32) Edmund says he will join him shortly.

Goneril tries to stay behind so that she can talk to Edmund alone. She, too, is jealous of Edmund, and fears that Regan may come between her and him: 'I had rather lose the battle than that sister/ Should loosen him and me'. (19) Regan realises what Goneril is up to, and insists they both head to Albany's tent for the council of war: ''Tis most convenient; pray you, go with us'. (36)

LINES 38–50: EDGAR DELIVERS GONERIL'S LETTER

Edgar enters in disguise and asks to speak with Albany. Albany agrees, and sends the others on ahead of him. Edgar hands him Goneril's treacherous letter to Edmund and asks him to read it (this was the letter he took from Oswald's corpse). He says that if Albany is successful in the coming battle, he should sound the trumpet. At the sound of this trumpet, Edgar will come and prove Edmund's guilt in a trial by combat. Edgar wishes Albany luck for the fight.

LINES 51–69: EDMUND'S RUTHLESSNESS

Edmund returns, tells Albany that the French forces are in sight, and asks him to draw up his army. By responding calmly, Albany shows that he will not be ordered around by Edmund: 'We will greet the time'. (54) He exits.

Edmund is now alone, and expresses the true depths of his callousness:

- He enjoys being the object of the sisters' attention and revels in their jealousy: 'To both these sisters I sworn my love;/ Each jealous of the other, as the stung/ Are of the adder'. (55–7)
- He is indifferent to both of them. and intends to use them for his own advancement and amusement: 'Which of them shall I take?/ Both? One? or neither? (57–8)

CHARACTER DEVELOPMENT

ALBANY

A TROUBLED CONSCIENCE

Albany's revulsion at the treatment meted out to Lear and Gloucester has clearly had a major impact. We learn from Edmund that he is wavering in his resolution to fight the French ('he's full of alteration/ And self-reproving'), and is clearly troubled by the prospect of being allied to his wife, Edmund and Regan.

When Albany arrives on the battlefield, he is open about the consequences of the harsh rule of the new order. He describes how Lear and Cordelia have been joined by 'others; whom the rigour of our state/ Forc'd to cry out'. (22–3) He knows he cannot fight specifically against the king and his daughter, as 'Where I could not be honest/ I never yet was valiant'. (23–4)

Albany justifies his decision to fight by claiming that it is purely against the foreign invader that he takes arms. Albany's guilty conscience demands that he employs a kind of moral weighing-scale in order to join battle. His morality allows us to think that there is hope for Lear and Cordelia.

IN COMMAND

Although Albany's conscience is troubled, he also appears quite assured and certain of his authority. He delivers his speech about the necessity of fighting the French without allowing interruption or dissent. When Edmund urges him to the frontline, his response is calm and unruffled. He clearly wishes to show that he will not be ordered about by Edmund: 'We will greet the time'. (55) He also shows dignity and consideration by agreeing to speak with Edgar at a time when he has quite a lot to be worried about. Albany shows that he possesses the qualities to be a just and fair king.

REGAN

INSECURE AND PARANOID

Regan betrays her total insecurity about Edmund's feelings for her in this scene. She is paranoid that Edmund has slept with Goneril: 'But have you never found my brother's way/ To the forefended place?' (10–11) She is desperate to prevent Goneril from having any time alone with Edmund, and is insistent that she accompany them to the war council: ''Tis most convenient; pray you, go with us'. (36)

She is desperate to believe that he belongs entirely to her: 'I am doubtful that you have been conjunct/ And bosom'd with her'. (13) Her jealousy only feeds her hostility toward her sister: 'I never shall endure her'. (15)

I had rather loose the battle than that sister
Should loosen him and me

Goneril (18–19)

Where I could not be honest
I never yet was valiant

Albany (23)

Which of them shall I take?
Both? One? or neither?

Edmund (57–8)

SOME LINES TO LEARN

- Edmund says that he cannot properly have either of them if the other lives: 'Neither can be enjoy'd/ If both remain alive'. (58) To take Regan would drive Goneril mad with jealousy, and vice versa.
- He needs Albany dead in order to take full control of the kingdom: 'And hardly shall I carry out my side,/ Her husband being alive'. (61–2)
- He will use Albany by letting him defeat the French in battle, and then have Goneril orchestrate his demise: 'we'll use/ His countenance for the battle; which being done/ Let her who would be rid of him devise/ His speedy taking off'. (62–5)
- Edmund declares that he intends to show no mercy to Lear and Cordelia if they are captured in the battle. (65–7) They are too much of a threat to his plans for complete domination: 'for my state/ Stands on me to defend, not to debate'. (68–9)

CHARACTER DEVELOPMENT

GONERIL

OBSESSIVE DESIRE FOR EDMUND
Goneril's desire for Edmund has completely overtaken her. She states she would rather lose the battle to the French than see Regan with Edmund: 'I had rather lose the battle than that sister/ Should loosen him and me.'(19) When the others leave to pursue the war, she tries to remain behind with him.

PRAGMATIC
Goneril and Regan are only interested in their own power. Albany worries about whether their cause is just. The sisters see this as a waste of time. All that matters to them is that their enemies are crushed and their power secured. They are untroubled by these moral questions: 'Why is this reason'd?'

EDGAR

DETERMINATION
Edgar shows in this scene that he is absolutely determined to seek justice against Edmund. He is prepared to fight his brother in single combat to gain retribution for the suffering inflicted on him and Gloucester: 'I can produce a champion that will prove/ What is avouched here'. (43–4) We cannot but be impressed by his determination.

A BLEAK VIEW OF LIFE
Edgar's experiences as an outcast and his witnessing of the great suffering endured by both his father and Lear have clearly solidified his fatalism. As he leaves Albany, he cannot help remarking on how, if he loses the battle, his personal quest will become irrelevant: 'If you miscarry,/ Your business of the world hath so an end,/ And your machination ceases'. (44–6) Edgar has been deeply marked by all that he has endured.

163

Alarum within. Enter, with Drum and Colours, the Powers of France over the stage,
CORDELIA with her Father in her hand, and exeunt.

Enter EDGAR and GLOUCESTER.

EDGAR	Here, father, take the shadow of this tree	
	For your good host. Pray that the right may thrive.	
	If ever I return to you again,	
	I'll bring you comfort.	
GLOUCESTER	Grace go with you, sir!	5

Exit EDGAR.

Alarum and retreat within. Enter EDGAR,

EDGAR	Away, old man! give me thy hand! away!	
	King Lear hath lost, he and his daughter ta'en.	
	Give me thy hand! come on!	
GLOUCESTER	No further, sir. A man may rot even here.	
EDGAR	What, in ill thoughts again? Men must endure	10
	Their going hence, even as their coming hither;	
	Ripeness is all. Come on.	
GLOUCESTER	And that's true too.	

Exeunt.

good host: *shelterer*

ta'en: *captured*

Ripeness: *readiness*

> No further, sir; a man may rot even here
> *Gloucester (8)*
>
> Men must endure
> Their going hence, even as their coming hither:
> Ripeness is all
> *Edgar (9–11)*

SOME LINES TO LEARN

A KEY MOMENT

The defeat of Cordelia's army would appear to indicate the complete victory of the forces of evil and selfishness in the play. Lear and Cordelia have been captured, and given what we know of Edmund's intentions, there seems to be little chance for them. Only Albany's decency and Edgar's determination to punish his brother leave any grounds for hope.

EDGAR & GLOUCESTER

The French and British armies march into battle. Gloucester shelters under a tree near the battlefield while Edgar goes to check on the progress of the battle. He returns with terrible news: Lear and Cordelia have been defeated and taken prisoner. Gloucester is filled with despair and yearns for death.

ACTION

LINES 1–12: LEAR AND CORDELIA DEFEATED IN BATTLE

The scene is set in a field between the two armies. Cordelia, Lear and their army pass through as they march into battle.

Edgar and Gloucester enter. Edgar seeks a safe place to hide his father while the battle rages and leaves him sitting under a tree. He promises to return with good news: 'If ever I return to you again,/ I'll bring you comfort'. (3–4)

Edgar returns with bad news. The French forces have been defeated and Lear and Cordelia have been captured. He tries to lead Gloucester away. (6–8) Gloucester has had enough of suffering, however, and refuses to move. He is resigned to death: 'No further, sir; a man may rot even here'. (8)

Edgar will not accept his father's death wish. He tells Gloucester that men must endure everything that life throws at them: 'Men must endure/ Their going hence, even as their coming hither:/ Ripeness is all'. (9–11) Gloucester accepts his son's words ('And that's true too'), and they exit.

CHARACTER DEVELOPMENT

GLOUCESTER

RESIGNED
Gloucester's reaction to the news of Cordelia's defeat is one of total resignation. He initially refuses to flee with Edgar: 'No further, sir; a man may rot even here'. (8) The immense suffering he has endured and witnessed has left him only with a desire to die. He appears to be temporarily revived by Edgar's exhortations, however, and leaves with his son.

EDGAR

DETERMINATION
In spite of everything he has seen and suffered personally, Edgar shows amazing resilience and strength, even though Cordelia's army has been defeated, and she and her father taken prisoner. He refuses to accept his father's wish to die, and leads him to safety. Clearly, Edgar intends to take his revenge upon Edmund. The trials he has been put through in the course of the drama have filled him with a stoical determination to accept everything that life brings: 'Men must endure/ Their going hence, even as their coming hither:/ Ripeness is all'. (9–11)

165

Enter, in conquest, with Drum and Colours, EDMUND;
LEAR and CORDELIA as prisoners; Soldiers, CAPTAIN.

EDMUND	Some officers take them away. Good guard
	Until their greater pleasures first be known
	That are to censure them.
CORDELIA	We are not the first
	Who with best meaning have incurred the worst.
	For thee, oppressed king, am I cast down;
	Myself could else outfrown false Fortune's frown.
	Shall we not see these daughters and these sisters?
LEAR	No, no, no, no! Come, let's away to prison.
	We two alone will sing like birds i' th' cage.
	When thou dost ask me blessing, I'll kneel down
	And ask of thee forgiveness. So we'll live,
	And pray, and sing, and tell old tales, and laugh
	At gilded butterflies, and hear poor rogues
	Talk of court news; and we'll talk with them too –
	Who loses and who wins; who's in, who's out –
	And take upon's the mystery of things,
	As if we were God's spies; and we'll wear out,
	In a walled prison, packs and sects of great ones
	That ebb and flow by th' moon.
EDMUND	Take them away.
LEAR	Upon such sacrifices, my Cordelia,
	The gods themselves throw incense. Have I caught thee?
	He that parts us shall bring a brand from heaven
	And fire us hence like foxes. Wipe thine eyes.
	The good-years shall devour 'em, flesh and fell,
	Ere they shall make us weep! We'll see 'em starved first.
	Come.

Exeunt LEAR and CORDELIA, guarded.

EDMUND	Come hither, Captain; hark.
	Take thou this note [*gives a paper*]. Go follow them to prison.
	One step I have advanced thee. If thou dost
	As this instructs thee, thou dost make thy way
	To noble fortunes. Know thou this, that men
	Are as the time is. To be tender-minded
	Does not become a sword. Thy great employment
	Will not bear question. Either say thou'lt do't,
	Or thrive by other means.
CAPTAIN	I'll do't, my lord.
EDMUND	About it! and write happy when th' hast done.
	Mark – I say, instantly; and carry it so
	As I have set it down.

Handwritten note in left margin: – Thinks about Lear the whole way through

Line numbers (right): 5, 10, 15, 20, 25, 30, 35

Glossary (right margin):

Good: *careful*

their: *those in command*

censure: *judge*

cast down: *disheartened*

outfrown: *out do in frowning*

cage: *prison*

poor rogues: *wretched creatures*

mystery: *divine truth*

wear out: *outlive*

packs and sects: *cliques and parties*

moon: *associated with changeability*

such sacrifices: *renunciation of the world*

throw incense: *priestly ritual*

flesh and fell: *altogether; fell: skin*

sword: *soldier; employment: order (in note)*

question: *discussion, query*

Mark: *attend to it*

* [22–3] **He that parts us ... like foxes:** *it is only through divine intervention that we will ever suffer to be parted again*

† [28] **note:** *this turns out to be the death warrant for Lear and Cordelia*

CAPTAIN	I cannot draw a cart, nor eat dried oats;
	If it be man's work, I'll do't. *[Exit]*

Flourish. Enter ALBANY, GONERIL, REGAN, Soldiers.

ALBANY	Sir, you have showed to-day your valiant strain,
	And fortune led you well. You have the captives
	Who were the opposites of this day's strife.
	We do require them of you, so to use them
	As we shall find their merits and our safety
	May equally determine.
EDMUND	Sir, I thought it fit
	To send the old and miserable king
	To some retention and a pointed guard;
	Whose age has charms in it, whose title more,
	To pluck the common bosom on his side
	And turn our impressed lances in our eyes
	Which do command them. With him I sent the queen,
	My reason all the same; and they are ready
	To-morrow, or at further space, t' appear
	Where you shall hold your session. At this time
	We sweat and bleed: the friend hath lost his friend;
	And the best quarrels, in the heat, are curs'd
	By those that feel their sharpness.
	The question of Cordelia and her father
	Requires a fitter place.
ALBANY	Sir, by your patience,
	I hold you but a subject of this war,
	Not as a brother.
REGAN	That's as we list to grace him.
	Methinks our pleasure might have been demanded
	Ere you had spoke so far. He led our powers,
	Bore the commission of my place and person,
	The which immediacy may well stand up
	And call itself your brother.
GONERIL	Not so hot!
	In his own grace he doth exalt himself
	More than in your addition.
REGAN	In my rights
	By me invested, he compeers the best.
GONERIL	That were the most if he should husband you.
REGAN	Jesters do oft prove prophets.
GONERIL	Holla, holla!
	That eye that told you so looked but asquint.
REGAN	Lady, I am not well; else I should answer
	From a full-flowing stomach. General,
	Take thou my soldiers, prisoners, patrimony;
	Dispose of them, of me; the walls are thine.
	Witness the world that I create thee here
	My lord and master.

40

captives: *Lear and Cordelia*

45

retention: *imprisonment*
Whose age: *ref. to king*
50 **common bosom:** *the people's hearts*
impressed lances: *i.e. soldiers*

55 **at further space:** *at a future date*
session: *court of justice*

60

by your patience: *pardon me*
but a subject: *subordinate*
a brother: *an equal*
list to grace: *wish to honour*
65 **pleasure:** *wishes, authority*
spoke so far: *said so much*

grace: *merit*
your addition: *the rights you bestow*

70 **compeers:** *equals*

75

full-flowing …: *flood of anger*

walls: *walls of my heart*

---

* [66]   **The which immediacy … your brother:** *Regan seems to be making the argument that the close relationship Edmund shares with her as her immediate representative entitles him to consider himself Albany's brother (and thus his equal).*

† [72]   **Jesters do oft prove prophets:** *There is many a true word spoken in jest.*

‡ [78]   **My lord and master:** *traditional way to address one's husband in such a deeply patriarchal society as Shakespeare's.*

	Mean you to enjoy him?	enjoy: *marry*
ALBANY	The let-alone lies not in your good will.	80 let-alone: *power to control*
EDMUND	Nor in thine, lord.	
ALBANY	Half-blooded fellow, yes.	half-blooded: *illegitimate*
REGAN	[*to Edmund*] Let the drum strike, and prove my title thine.	
ALBANY	Stay yet; hear reason. Edmund, I arrest thee	
	On capital treason; and, in thine attaint,	85 attaint: *impeachment*
	This gilded serpent [*points to Goneril*]. For your claim, fair	gilded: *of superficial worth*
	sister,	
	I bar it in the interest of my wife.	bar: *forbid*
	'Tis she is subcontracted to this lord,	subcontracted: *promised in marriage*
	And I, her husband, contradict your banns.	banns: *marriage banns (declaration)*
	If you will marry, make your loves to me;	make: *direct*
	My lady is bespoke.	90 bespoke: *spoken for*
GONERIL	An interlude!	interlude: *farce*
ALBANY	Thou art armed, Gloucester. Let the trumpet sound.	armed: *carrying a weapon*
	If none appear to prove upon thy person	
	Thy heinous, manifest, and many treasons,	
	There's my pledge [*throws down a glove*]! I'll prove it on thy	95 pledge: *challenge*
	heart,	
	Ere I taste bread, thou art in nothing less	nothing: *no way*
	Than I have here proclaimed thee.	
REGAN	Sick, O, sick!	
GONERIL	[*Aside*] If not, I'll ne'er trust medicine.	medicine: *used as poison*
EDMUND	There's my exchange [*throws down a glove*]. What	What: *whoever*
	in the world he is	
	That names me traitor, villain-like he lies.	
	Call by thy trumpet. He that dares approach,	
	On him, on you, who not? I will maintain	100
	My truth and honour firmly.	
ALBANY	A herald, ho!	
EDMUND	A herald, ho, a herald!	
ALBANY	Trust to thy single virtue; for thy soldiers,	105 single virtue: *own valour*
	All levied in my name, have in my name	
	Took their discharge.	Took: *taken*
REGAN	My sickness grows upon me.	
ALBANY	She is not well. Convey her to my tent.	

Exit REGAN, led.

Enter a Herald.

	Come hither, herald. Let the trumpet sound,	
	And read out this.	110
CAPTAIN	Sound, trumpet!	

A trumpet sounds.

HERALD	[*reads*] 'If any man of quality or degree within the lists of	
	the army will maintain upon Edmund, supposed Earl	
	of Gloucester, that he is a manifold traitor, let him	
	appear by the third sound of the trumpet.	115
	He is bold in his defence.'	
EDMUND	Sound!	

First trumpet.

HERALD	Again!

Second trumpet.

HERALD	Again!

Third trumpet.

Trumpet answers within.
Enter EDGAR, armed, at the third sound, a Trumpet before him.

ALBANY	Ask him his purposes, why he appears
	Upon this call o' th' trumpet.
HERALD	What are you?
	Your name, your quality? and why you answer
	This present summons?
EDGAR	Know my name is lost;
	By treason's tooth bare-gnawn and canker-bit.
	Yet am I noble as the adversary
	I come to cope.
ALBANY	Which is that adversary?
EDGAR	What's he that speaks for Edmund Earl of Gloucester?
EDMUND	Himself. What say'st thou to him?
EDGAR	Draw thy sword,
	That, if my speech offend a noble heart,
	Thy arm may do thee justice. Here is mine.
	Behold, it is the privilege of mine honours,
	My oath, and my profession. I protest,
	Maugre thy strength, youth, place, and eminence,
	Despite thy victor sword and fire-new fortune,
	Thy valour and thy heart – thou art a traitor;
	False to thy gods, thy brother, and thy father;
	Conspirant 'gainst this high illustrious prince;
	And from th' extremest upward of thy head
	To the descent and dust beneath thy foot,
	A most toad-spotted traitor. Say thou 'no,'
	This sword, this arm, and my best spirits are bent
	To prove upon thy heart, whereto I speak,
	Thou liest.
EDMUND	In wisdom I should ask thy name;
	But since thy outside looks so fair and warlike,
	And that thy tongue some say of breeding breathes,
	What safe and nicely I might well delay
	By rule of knighthood, I disdain and spurn.
	Back do I toss those treasons to thy head;
	With the hell-hated lie o'erwhelm thy heart;
	Which – for they yet glance by and scarcely bruise –
	This sword of mine shall give them instant way
	Where they shall rest for ever. Trumpets, speak!

Alarums. Fight. EDMUND falls.

ALBANY	Save him, save him!
GONERIL	This is mere practice, Gloucester.
	By th' law of arms thou wast not bound to answer
	An unknown opposite. Thou art not vanquished,
	But cozened and beguiled.
ALBANY	Shut your mouth, dame,
	Or with this paper shall I stop it. *[Shows her letter to*
	Edmund] – *[To Edmund]* Hold, sir.
	[To Goneril] Thou worse than any name, read thine own evil.
	No tearing, lady! I perceive you know it.

120

125

130

135

140

145

150

155

What: *who*
quality: *rank*

gnawn: *gnaw, bite*
      adversary: *opponent*

What's: *it is*

mine: *my sword*

Maugre: *regardless of*
victor: *victorious; fire-new: brand new*
heart: *courage*

high illustrious prince: *Albany*

Say thou 'no': *if you deny it*

fair: *noble*
say: *evidence*

instant way: *direct access (to your heart)*

practice: *treachery*

cozened ... beguiled: *tricked ... deceived*

···

* [124]   canker-bit: *eaten by worms*

† [131]   My oath, and my profession: *my sword is symbol of both the oath I swore when I was made a Knight and the profession itself.*

‡ [140]   To prove upon thy heart, whereto I speak: *To prove, by a duel, that what I say is true, and that you are lying.*

§ [142]   In wisdom ... : *he would not be bound by honour to fight a man of lower rank.*

¶ [147–8] Back do I toss ... o'erwhelm thy heart: *it is you that have committed the treasons of which you speak, and along with the lies that you tell, may they overwhelm your heart.*

I ♥ Kevin

GONERIL   Say if I do – the laws are mine, not thine.
          Who can arraign me for't?   160   arraign: *charge*
ALBANY   Most monstrous!
          Know'st thou this paper?
GONERIL   Ask me not what I know. *[Exit]*
ALBANY   Go after her. She's desperate; govern her.   desperate: *capable of suicide*

Exit an Officer.

EDMUND   What, you have charged me with, that have I done,   165
          And more, much more. The time will bring it out.
          'Tis past, and so am I. – But what art thou   what: *who*
          That hast this fortune on me? If thou'rt noble,   fortune: *victory*
          I do forgive thee.
EDGAR   Let's exchange charity.   charity: *forgiveness, honesty*
          I am no less in blood than thou art, Edmund;
          If more, the more thou hast wrong'd me.   If more: *because legitimate*
          My name is Edgar and thy father's son.   170
          The gods are just, and of our pleasant vices   pleasant vices: *lust*
          Make instruments to scourge us.   instruments: *offspring*
          The dark and vicious place where thee he got   got: *begot*
          Cost him his eyes.
EDMUND   Th' hast spoken right; 'tis true.   175
          The wheel is come full circle; I am here.   here: *at the bottom of fortune's wheel*
ALBANY   Methought thy very gait did prophesy   gait: *bearing*
          A royal nobleness. I must embrace thee.
          Let sorrow split my heart if ever I
          Did hate thee, or thy father!
EDGAR   Worthy prince, I know't.
ALBANY   Where have you hid yourself?   180
          How have you known the miseries of your father?
EDGAR   By nursing them, my lord. List a brief tale;   List: *listen to*
          And when 'tis told, O that my heart would burst!
          The bloody proclamation to escape   bloody proclamation: *death sentence*
          That followed me so near (O, our lives' sweetness!   185
          That with the pain of death would hourly die
          Rather than die at once!) taught me to shift†
          Into a madman's rags, t' assume a semblance   semblance: *outward appearance*
          That very dogs disdained; and in this habit   habit: *disguise*
          Met I my father with his bleeding rings,   190   rings: *eye sockets*
          Their precious stones new lost; became his guide,   stones: *eyes*
          Led him, begged for him, saved him from despair;
          Never (O fault!) revealed myself unto him
          Until some half hour past, when I was armed,   armed: *ready with my sword*
          Not sure, though hoping of this good success,   195
          I asked his blessing, and from first to last
          Told him my pilgrimage. But his flawed heart   pilgrimage: *suffering, journey*
          (Alack, too weak the conflict to support!)
          'Twixt two extremes of passion, joy and grief,
          Burst smilingly.   200
EDMUND   This speech of yours hath moved me,
          And shall perchance do good; but speak you on;   do good: *by my repentance*
          You look as you had something more to say.
ALBANY   If there be more, more woeful, hold it in;
          For I am almost ready to dissolve,   205   dissolve: *into tears*
          Hearing of this.

. . . .

† [185–7] **O, our lives' sweetness! / That with
          the pain of death would hourly die
          / Rather than die at once!):** *our lives
          are so precious to us that we would
          rather suffer the pains of death hour
          after hour than to die once.*

handwritten notes:

started at the bottom, rose to the top, then went down to the bottom again.

NB

Gloucester died – Edgar revealed his true self. N.B

EDGAR	This would have seemed a period
	To such as love not sorrow; but another,
	To amplify too much, would make much more,
	And top extremity.
	Whilst I was big in clamour, came there a man,
	Who, having seen me in my worst estate,
	Shunned my abhorred society; but then, finding
	Who 'twas that so endured, with his strong arms
	He fastened on my neck, and bellowed out
	As he'd burst heaven; threw him on my father;
	Told the most piteous tale of Lear and him
	That ever ear received; which in recounting
	His grief grew puissant, and the strings of life
	Began to crack. Twice then the trumpets sounded,
	And there I left him tranc'd.
ALBANY	But who was this?
EDGAR	Kent, sir, the banished Kent; who in disguise
	Followed his enemy king and did him service
	Improper for a slave.

Enter a GENTLEMAN with a bloody knife.

GENTLEMAN	Help, help! O, help!
EDGAR	What kind of help?
ALBANY	Speak, man.
EDGAR	What means that bloody knife?
GENTLEMAN	'Tis hot, it smokes.
	It came even from the heart of – O! she's dead!
ALBANY	Who dead? Speak, man.
GENTLEMAN	Your lady, sir, your lady! and her sister
	By her is poisoned; she hath confessed it.
EDMUND	I was contracted to them both. All three
	Now marry in an instant.

Enter KENT.

EDGAR	Here comes Kent.
ALBANY	Produce their bodies, be they alive or dead.

Exit GENTLEMAN.

	This judgement of the heavens, that makes us tremble
	Touches us not with pity. O, is this he?
	The time will not allow the compliment
	That very manners urges.
KENT	I am come
	To bid my king and master aye good night.
	Is he not here?
ALBANY	Great thing of us forgot!
	Speak, Edmund, where's the King? and where's Cordelia?

The bodies of GONERIL and REGAN are brought in.

	Seest thou this object, Kent?
KENT	Alack, why thus?
EDMUND	Yet Edmund was beloved.
	The one the other poisoned for my sake,
	And after slew herself.
ALBANY	Even so. Cover their faces.

Margin glosses:

a period: *an end, limit*
such as: *those who;* another: *tale of woe*
amplify: *tell, detail;* more: *sorrow*
top extremity: *outdo the limits of endurance*
clamour: *expression of grief*

210

endured: *suffered*

he'd: *if he'd*
215   him: *himself*

puissant: *powerful*

tranc'd: *coma-like*

220

225

Your lady: *Goneril*

230   marry: *united in death*

235   compliment: *ceremonious greeting*
That ... urges: *that courtesy demands*

240

Handwritten annotation:
Regan pois[oned]
by Goneril
the Goneril
committed
suicide.

[233]   This judgement of the heavens, that makes us tremble / Touches us not with pity: this divine retribution is fearful in its swiftness, but as they deserved their fate, we do not feel pity for them.

EDMUND	I pant for life. Some good I mean to do,	245
	Despite of mine own nature. Quickly send	
	(Be brief in't) to the castle; for my writ	
	Is on the life of Lear and on Cordelia.	
	Nay, send in time.	
ALBANY	Run, run, O, run!	
EDGAR	To who, my lord? Who has the office? Send	
	Thy token of reprieve.	250
EDMUND	Well thought on. Take my sword;	
	Give it the Captain.	
ALBANY	Haste thee for thy life. *[Exit Edgar]*	
EDMUND	He hath commission from thy wife and me	
	To hang Cordelia in the prison and	255
	To lay the blame upon her own despair	
	That she fordid herself.	
ALBANY	The gods defend her! Bear him hence awhile.	

EDMUND is borne off.

Enter LEAR, with CORDELIA dead in his arms; EDGAR, CAPTAIN,

and others following.

LEAR	Howl, howl, howl, howl! O, you are men of stone.	
	Had I your tongues and eyes, I'd use them so	
	That heaven's vault should crack. She's gone for ever!	260
	I know when one is dead, and when one lives.	
	She's dead as earth. Lend me a looking glass.	
	If that her breath will mist or stain the stone	
	Why, then she lives.	
KENT	Is this the promised end?	265
EDGAR	Or image of that horror?	
ALBANY	Fall and cease!	
LEAR	This feather stirs; she lives! If it be so,	
	It is a chance which does redeem all sorrows	
	That ever I have felt.	
KENT	O my good master!	
LEAR	Prithee away!	
EDGAR	'Tis noble Kent, your friend.	
LEAR	A plague upon you, murderers, traitors all!	270
	I might have saved her; now she's gone for ever!	
	Cordelia, Cordelia! stay a little. Ha!	
	What is't thou say'st, Her voice was ever soft,	
	Gentle, and low – an excellent thing in woman.	
	I killed the slave that was a-hanging thee.	275
CAPTAIN	'Tis true, my lords, he did.	
LEAR	Did I not, fellow?	
	I have seen the day, with my good biting falchion	
	I would have made them skip. I am old now,	
	And these same crosses spoil me. Who are you?	
	Mine eyes are not o' th' best. I'll tell you straight.	280
KENT	If fortune brag of two she loved and hated,	
	One of them we behold.	
LEAR	This' a dull sight. Are you not Kent?	
KENT	The same –	
	Your servant Kent. Where is your servant Caius?	285
LEAR	He's a good fellow, I can tell you that.	
	He'll strike, and quickly too. He's dead and rotten.	
KENT	No, my good lord; I am the very man –	

brief: *quick;* writ: *written command*

office: *task*

reprieve: *stay of execution*

fordid: *did away with*

her: *Goneril (but not Edmund)*

stone: *polished glass*

promised end: *the Last Day*

redeem: *make up for*

good biting: *keen;* falchion: *short sword*

crosses: *troubles;* spoil: *ruin*

straight: *honestly*

Caius: *probably Kent's disguise name*

* [263–4] promised end … horror: *the horror of the Last day as prophesied in the Book of Revelation*

† [265] Fall and cease: *let the heavens fall and everything come to an end.*

‡ [281] If fortune brag of two she loved and hated / One of them we behold: *Kent and Lear are presumably facing each other – they behold (see) each other. Thus, they are both looking at one that fortune, personified as a woman, has both loved (favoured) and hated (brought low).*

LEAR	I'll see that straight.	
KENT	That from your first of difference and decay	
	Have followed your sad steps	290
LEAR	You're welcome hither.	
KENT	Nor no man else! All's cheerless, dark, and deadly.	
	Your eldest daughters have fordone themselves,	
	And desperately are dead.	
LEAR	Ay, so I think.	295
ALBANY	He knows not what he says; and vain is it	
	That we present us to him.	
EDGAR	Very bootless.	

Enter a CAPTAIN.

CAPTAIN	Edmund is dead, my lord.	
ALBANY	That's but a trifle here.	
	You lords and noble friends, know our intent.	
	What comfort to this great decay may come	
	Shall be applied. For us, we will resign,	300
	During the life of this old Majesty,	
	To him our absolute power; *[to Edgar and Kent]* you to your	
	rights;	
	With boot, and such addition as your honours	
	Have more than merited. – All friends shall taste	
	The wages of their virtue, and all foes	305
	The cup of their deservings. – O, see, see!	
LEAR	And my poor fool is hanged! No, no, no life!	
	Why should a dog, a horse, a rat, have life,	
	And thou no breath at all? Thou'lt come no more,	
	Never, never, never, never, never!	310
	Pray you undo this button. Thank you, sir.	
	Do you see this? Look on her! look! her lips!	
	Look there, look there! *[He dies]*	
EDGAR	He faints! My lord, my lord!	
KENT	Break, heart; I prithee break!	315
EDGAR	Look up, my lord.	
KENT	Vex not his ghost. O, let him pass! He hates him	
	That would upon the rack of this tough world	
	Stretch him out longer.	
EDGAR	He is gone indeed.	
KENT	The wonder is, he hath endured so long.	
	He but usurped his life.	
ALBANY	Bear them from hence. Our present business	320
	Is general woe. *[To Kent and Edgar]* Friends of my soul, you	
	twain	
	Rule in this realm, and the gored state sustain.	
KENT	I have a journey, sir, shortly to go.	
	My master calls me; I must not say no.	
ALBANY	The weight of this sad time we must obey,	325
	Speak what we feel, not what we ought to say.	
	The oldest have borne most; we that are young	
	Shall never see so much, nor live so long.	
	The oldest have borne most; we that are young	
	Shall never see so much, nor live so long.	

Exeunt with a dead march.

---

difference: *change of fortune*

fordone: *killed*
Desperately: *in despair*

bootless: *useless*

great decay: *ref. to Lear*

rights: *proper titles*
boot: *something additional*

wages: *rewards*
see, see: *looks to Lear*

this: *Cordelia's corpse*

ghost: *departing spirit*

Usurped: *appropriated*

gored: *brutally divided, bleeding*

weight: *heavy burden*
we feel: *from our heart*

....

* [288] **I'll see that straight:** *I'll look into that in a moment. Lear doesn't want to be distracted from Cordelia.*

† [307] **And my poor fool is hanged:** *recalls Lear's Fool (last seen in Act 3), but may be a ref. to Cordelia: 'fool' was a common term of endearment.*

‡ [315–6] **That would upon the rack of this tough world / Stretch him out longer:** *Kent is visualizing the world as an instrument of torture (rack) on which the body is bound and slowly stretched. In this conceit, the stretching of the racked body equates with the extending of Lear's life, which has become a torment.*

SOME LINES TO LEARN

We are not the first,
Who, with best meaning, have incurr'd the worst
Cordelia (4–5)

Come, let's away to prison;
We two alone will sing like birds i' the cage
Lear (8–9)

Know thou this, that men
Are as the time is
Edmund (30–1)

LEAR, EDMUND & CORDELIA

Lear and Cordelia are brought in as Edmund's prisoners. Lear declares that he will be happy to spend the rest of his life in prison as long as Cordelia is at his side. Edmund instructs one of his officers to take them away and hang them.

Albany wants Lear and Cordelia treated well, and is angry because Edmund had them taken away without consulting him. Regan declares that Edmund is now her husband, the new Duke of Cornwall, and is therefore Albany's equal. She complains of feeling sick, and is taken away. We learn later that Goneril has poisoned her so she can have Edmund to herself. Albany wittily remarks that Edmund cannot legally be made Regan's husband because he is also promised to Goneril.

Albany accuses Edmund and Goneril of conspiring to kill him and take over the kingdom. He challenges Edmund to prove his innocence in single combat. A trumpet will be sounded to summon challengers. If no one comes forward, Albany will fight Edmund himself. Edgar, with his face hidden, arrives to answer the challenge. He fights Edmund, mortally wounds him and reveals his true identity. Albany produces the treasonous letter, and the dying Edmund confesses his guilt. Goenril, with her dreams of power broken, leaves in despair and stabs herself to death.

Edgar tells his story, revealing that Gloucester died of a broken heart after learning of Lear's defeat in battle.

Edmund, in what seems a last-minute bid to redeem himself, reveals that he has arranged for Lear and Cordelia to be hanged. Albany sends men to stop the execution but they are too late. A distraught Lear enters with the dead Cordelia. He reveals that he killed the hangman but was too late to save her. He rants and raves before dying of a broken heart, desperately trying to convince himself that his beloved daughter is still alive.

Albany promises to restore order and justice to the kingdom. He declares that Edgar and Kent will serve with him as joint rulers. Kent, however, refuses this honour. He says that he is not long for this world but will soon follow his master into death.

✎ LINES 1–27: LEAR AND CORDELIA

The scene takes place in the British camp. Edmund and his forces enter in triumph with Lear and Cordelia as their prisoners. Edmund orders them to be taken away until their fate is decided. (1–3)

Cordelia is deeply depressed by the defeat of her forces, and laments their misfortune: 'We are not the first/ Who, with best meaning, have incurr'd the worst'. (4–5) She says that it is for Lear's sake, and not her own, that she is despondent: 'For thee, oppressed king, am I cast down'. (6)

Lear views imprisonment with Cordelia as a form of liberation, where he can spend the remainder of his life with his beloved daughter: 'Come, let's away to prison;/ We two alone will sing like birds i' the cage'. (8–9) He dreams of a paradise of love and forgiveness with the child he wronged:

When thou dost ask me blessing, I'll kneel down,
And ask of thee forgiveness: so we'll live,
And pray, and sing, and tell old tales, and laugh
At gilded butterflies (10–13)

Lear no longer cares for worldly events or the affairs of state. He and Cordelia will watch it all with amused indifference: 'and we'll wear out,/ In a wall'd prison, packs and sets of great ones/ That ebb and flow by the moon'. (17–19)

As they are taken away, Lear continues to try and reassure Cordelia that they are protected by heaven: 'Upon such sacrifices, my Cordelia,/ The gods themselves throw incense'. (20–1) The king has convinced himself that he and his daughter are safe from harm: 'Wipe thine eyes;/ The goujeres shall devour them, flesh and fell,/ Ere they shall make us weep'. (23–5)

SOME LINES TO LEARN

The wheel is come full circle; I am here
                   Edmund (177)

I pant for life: some good I mean to do
Despite of mine own nature
                   Edmund (246–7)

LEAR & CORDELIA

LEAR

EUPHORIC

At the beginning of this scene, King Lear is in a state of blissful euphoria. He regards being imprisoned with his daughter to be a wonderful prospect. The only person who exists for him now is Cordelia, and to spend the remainder of his life alone with her is his deepest wish.

We two alone will sing like birds i' the cage:
When thou dost ask me blessing, I'll kneel down,
And ask of thee forgiveness (8–11)

The greater world of politics and power no longer means anything to the king. His experiences as an outcast have made him realise how fundamentally unimportant such things are:

We'll wear out,
In a wall'd prison, packs and sets of great ones
That ebb and flow by the moon (17–19)

Lear is living now in a fantastic imaginary world. He tries to convince Cordelia that they are beyond harm: 'He that parts us shall bring a brand from heaven,/ And fire us hence like foxes'. (23) Unfortunately for the king, reality will shatter his fantasies.

DEVASTATION

Edmund's evil ambitions destroy Lear's dreams of a blissful end to his life. The stage direction '*Enter Lear, with Cordelia dead in his arms*' is considered to be possibly the most tragic in all drama. The grief that engulfs Lear is overwhelming:

Howl, howl, howl, howl! O! you are men
of stones:
Had I your tongues and eyes, I'd
use them so
That heaven's vaults should
crack (258–60)

The shock to the king of seeing his daughter hanged is indicated by his desperate wish that she may still live: 'Lend me a looking-glass;/ If that her breath will mist or stain the stone,/ Why, then she lives'. (262–4) We can only feel total sympathy and pity for the old man as he refuses to accept Cordelia's death.

RAGE

The final trauma inflicted on Lear induces a return of his violent temper and rage. He curses all those around him, holding everyone equally responsible for Cordelia's fate: 'A plague upon you, murderers, traitors, all!/ I might have sav'd her; now, she's gone for ever!' (272–3)

Surprisingly for an old man who has suffered so much, the king was able to summon up the strength to kill Cordelia's murderer: 'I kill'd the slave that was a hanging thee'. (276) In his desperation, Lear wishes he still had his youthful strength: 'I have seen day, with my good biting falchion/ I would have made them skip'. (280–1) At this moment of ultimate tragedy, it is as if we see flashes of the powerful leader Lear once must have been.

DEATH

Ultimately, the experience of his daughter's death is too much for Lear. The cruel nature of Fate is impossible for the king to accept:

Why should a dog, a horse, a rat, have life,
And thou no breath at all! Thou'lt come no more,
Never, never, never, never, never! (308–10)

The king dies, having been savagely punished for his initial foolishness and vanity. After a journey of overwhelming suffering, the king's acceptance of humility and love is not to be rewarded. We are left with the sense that he suffered out of all proportion to his crimes. It is difficult not to agree with Albany that 'The oldest hath borne most'. (327)

A KEY MOMENT

The ending of the play leaves most readers filled with a sense of tragedy and loss. In spite of Albany's noble intentions to establish just rule, the merciless fate that befalls Lear and Cordelia leaves any thoughts for a bright future seem somewhat hollow. Most critics regard *King Lear* as the darkest of Shakespeare's tragedies, and we are left to ask if there is any glimmer of light left at the play's conclusion.

LINES 27–40: A DEATH SENTENCE

Lear's fantasies are not to be. Edmund summons a captain and hands him a note. He tells him to follow Lear and Cordelia to the prison and to obey the written instructions. It is clear that Edmund intends to have the captives murdered: 'know thou this, that men/ Are as the time is; to be tender-minded/ Does not become a sword'. (31–3)

Edmund sends the captain away with urgency. He obviously fears that his instructions will be discovered and countermanded by Albany. The captain feels he has no choice but to obey Edmund's orders as he needs to make a living. He cannot live like a beast: 'I cannot draw a cart nor eat dried oats;/ If it be man's work I will do it'. (39–40)

LINES 40–62: TENSION BETWEEN ALBANY AND EDMUND

Albany, Goneril, Regan and their attendants enter. Albany congratulates Edmund on his conduct during the battle. (41–2) He asks him to hand over Lear and Cordelia so they can be fairly judged: 'so as to use them/ As we shall find their merits and our safety/ May equally determine'. (45)

Edmund attempts to dissuade Albany from the necessity of judging them immediately. Edmund says that Lear and Cordelia should be locked up for now. If Lear and Cordelia are free, the common folk might rally to them and oppose Edmund and Albany. The king may 'pluck the common bosom on his side,/ And turn our impress'd lances in our eyes/ Which do command them'. (50–2) Edmund says that they may be sent for tomorrow or at a later date.

Edmund attempts to distract Albany from his purpose by focusing on the casualties the British forces suffered during the battle. He claims that the matter of the prisoners is of secondary importance: 'The question of Cordelia and her father/ Requires a fitter place'. (58–9) Albany, however, has no intention of being taken in by Edmund. He will not take orders from him, and puts Edmund in his place by reminding him of his lower rank: 'I hold you but a subject of this war,/ Not as a brother'. (61–2)

CHARACTER DEVELOPMENT

EDMUND

Edmund's ruthlessness is evident in the way he has Cordelia executed. He tells the captain he entrusts with the job that any moral qualms he may have are a sign of weakness in such brutal times: 'know thou this, that men/ Are as the time is; to be tender-minded/ Does not become a sword'. (31-3)

In this scene, Edmund is flushed with victory and full of self-confidence. He treats Albany as an equal even though Albany is a duke and he is technically nothing. Nor does he betray any fear at fighting a duel to defend his honour. Edmund is confident enough that he can defeat any challengers and prove that the lies against him are false: 'This sword of mine shall give them instant way,/ Where they shall rest for ever'. (151-2) He will pay for his over-confidence with his life.

REPENTANT?

Once Edmund has been defeated by Edgar, he appears to undergo something of a change of heart:

* He confesses to the charges of treachery: 'that have I done,/ And more, much more'. (165)
* He says he is prepared to forgive his killer if that man is of good breeding: 'If thou'rt noble/ I do forgive thee'. (167-8)
* He is moved by the news of Gloucester's death: 'This speech of yours hath mov'd me,/ And shall perchance do good'. (202-3)

He confesses that he ordered the execution of Lear and Cordelia, and urges Albany to stop this taking place: 'some good I mean to do/ Despite of mine own nature'. (246)

Is Edmund's repentance genuine, or is it just a final attempt to hog the limelight? It is difficult not to suspect that he revels in being at the centre of events at the very climax of the play. When the bodies of Regan and Goneril are brought in, he cannot help but announce how they both died for his love: 'Yet Edmund was belov'd:/ The one the other poison'd for my sake,/ And after slew herself'. (242-4)

We might also wonder why he did not try to prevent Cordelia's execution earlier. Ultimately, we must ask ourselves whether we believe in his repentance, or, like Albany, view his death as a just reward for his crimes: 'That's but a trifle here'. (297)

LINES 63–106: LEAR'S ENEMIES TURN ON EACH OTHER

Albany's tone displeases Regan. She says that she has the power to make Edmund a duke by marrying him: 'That's as we list to grace him'. (63) Regan points out that Edmund was her representative in battle: 'He led our powers,/ Bore the commission of my place and person'. (66–7)

Goneril jealously interrupts, saying that Edmund has earned the right to be a duke by his own courage and not Regan's approval: 'In his own grace he doth exalt himself/ More than in your addition'. (70–1)

After some more barbs are exchanged, Regan suddenly announces that she feels ill: 'Lady, I am not well; else I should answer/ From a full-flowing stomach'. (74–5) Despite Goneril's protests, she hands her power and forces over to Edmund, and announces that she is making him her husband: 'Witness the world, that I create thee here/ My lord and master'. (78–9)

The hostility between Albany and Edmund now becomes more open. Albany makes an insulting reference to Edmund's illegitimacy, calling him a 'Half-blooded fellow'. (82) He reveals his knowledge of the plotting between Edmund and Goneril. He says that they are both under arrest but that Edmund will have a chance to prove his innocence in a trial by combat.

A trumpet will be sounded and anyone willing to fight Edmund can step forward. If no one comes forward, Albany himself will fight Edmund. (93–5) Edmund declares that he is ready to fight, and dares anyone to challenge him. His lying hypocrisy is still completely intact: 'I will maintain/ My truth and honour firmly'. (101–2)

Regan tells Edmund to prepare for battle against Albany: 'Let the drum strike, and prove my title/ thine'. (83) Her sickness grows worse, and Albany orders her to be conveyed to his tent. (106) Goneril's aside confirms our suspicion that she has poisoned her sister: 'If not, I'll ne'er trust medicine'. (97)

LINES 107–65: EDGAR AND EDMUND DUEL

A herald calls upon anyone who can prove Edmund's treachery to do so by defeating him in combat. (111–14) Edgar appears, ready for combat and with his face covered. The herald asks him to identify himself. (121–3) Edgar expresses the loss of identity his sufferings have forced on him: 'Know, my name is lost;/ By treason's tooth bare-gnawn and canker-bit'. (122–3) He is ready to fight though: 'Yet I am as noble as the adversary/ I come to cope'. (124)

Edgar declares that Edmund is guilty of treachery and is conspiring against Albany: 'thou art a traitor,/ False to thy gods, thy brother, and thy father,/ Conspirant 'gainst this high illustrious prince'. (135–7) He is openly insulting: 'And, from the extremest upward of thy head/ To the descent and dust below thy foot,/

EDGAR & EDMUND

A most toad-spotted traitor'. (138–40) Edgar says that he will prove Edmund's guilt by defeating him in combat. (140–3)

Edmund responds by saying that although he should ask for his adversary's name, his attire and learned manner of speech have impressed him enough to fight. (145–7) He says that he will prove his challenger's accusations false by defeating him in battle: 'This sword of mine shall give them instant way,/ Where

they shall rest for ever'. (151–2) The brothers fight and Edmund is defeated.

Albany orders Edmund to be saved. He produces the letter Goneril wrote to Edmund and orders him to read it: 'Thou worse than any name, read thine own evil'. (158) He also threatens to stuff the letter down Goneril's throat. (156) Despite this evidence, Edmund refuses to admit his guilt. 'Ask me not what I know'. (164)

CHARACTER DEVELOPMENT

ALBANY

ASSERTIVE

Albany makes a very commanding and powerful impression in the final scene.

He takes no nonsense from Edmund and immediately asserts his rank and authority once the latter tries to deceive him: 'I hold you but a subject of this war,/ Not as a brother'. (61–62)

He puts Goneril in her place when she protests at the prospect of Regan marrying Edmund: 'The let-alone lies not in your good will'. (80)

He knows his wife would gladly see him dead and has no hesitation in arresting her along with Edmund, referring to her as a 'gilded serpent'. (85) When his wife attempts to destroy the incriminating letter, Albany threatens to ram it down her throat. (158)

At the end of the scene he takes charge of the situation, rewarding Kent and Edgar for their loyalty and establishing a new government.

BRAVE

Albany displays no fear in his willingness to fight Edmund in a duel: 'I'll prove it on thy heart,/ Ere I taste bread, thou art in nothing less/ Than I have here proclaim'd thee'. (95–97)

A SENSE OF JUSTICE

Albany displays a keen sense of justice throughout the scene. He believes that people should be punished or rewarded for their actions:

All friends shall taste
The wages of their virtue, and all foes
The cup of their deservings. (305–6)

He feels no pity over the deaths of Regan and Goneril,

believing that they got what they deserved: 'This judgement of the heavens, that makes us tremble,/ Touches us not with pity'. (234) As we noted above, he is equally unmoved by Edmund's death. (297)

He declares that Kent and Edgar should be rewarded for staying loyal to Lear and doing the right thing. He says they will be raised to a higher rank of nobility. After Lear's death he offers to let rule jointly with him.

He can also be capable of mercy. He orders Edmund to be kept alive after his defeat at the hands of Edgar: 'Save him, save him'. (153) In spite of her treachery, he also orders Goneril to be watched over: 'Go after her: she's desperate; govern her'. (165)

SYMPATHETIC TO SUFFERING

Albany sensitivity is evident in his reaction to Edgar's heartrending depiction of Gloucester's death. He finds it almost overwhelming: 'If there be more, more woeful, hold it in;/ For I am almost ready to dissolve,/ Hearing of this'. (205–207) Likewise, he is moved to deep pity by the spectacle of Lear carrying Cordelia: 'Fall and cease?' (267)

RESTORER OF LAW AND ORDER

Albany's role is to restore law and order following the chaos that has recently engulfed the kingdom. Initially he promises to hand back power to King Lear. But when Lear dies he decides to rule jointly with Edgar and Kent, promoting a new regime of stability and justice. His last words include a pledge to begin a rule that will be characterised by honesty and openness:

The weight of this sad time we must obey;
Speak what we feel, not what we ought to say (325–6)

His promise allows us to feel a faint sense of hope for the future, in spite of the appalling tragedy that we have just witnessed.

Goneril's reaction is one of despair and anger. She tells Edmund that he was tricked, as there was no legal obligation on him to fight an opponent who would not identify himself: 'thou art not vanquish'd,/ But cozen'd and beguil'd'. (155) She then makes one last effort to assert her power: 'Say, if I do, the laws are mine, not thine:/ Who can arraign me for't?' (160–1) She exits in a rage. Albany orders an officer to follow Goneril, as he fears she may do something rash in her desperation. (165)

LINES 166–81: EDGAR REVEALS HIMSELF

Edmund – realising that he is dying – sees no further need to lie. He says that he is guilty of treachery and more besides: 'And more, much more; the time will bring it out'. (167) He asks his killer to identify himself, saying he will forgive him if he is of noble breeding: 'If thou'rt noble,/ I do forgive thee'. (169)

Edgar is in a forgiving mood now that he has taken his revenge: 'Let's exchange charity'. (168) He reveals his identity: 'My name is Edgar, and thy father's son'. (171) He says that Gloucester's punished for having sex outside marriage was to have an evil child like Edmund.

The gods are just, and of our pleasant vices
Make instruments to plague us:
The dark and vicious place where thee he got
Cost him his eyes (172–5)

Edmund is resigned to his fate, and agrees with his brother: 'Thou hast spoken right, 'tis true;/ The wheel is come full circle; I am here'. (176–7)

Albany wishes to be reconciled with Edgar. He expresses his deep sorrow for any wrong he inflicted on him or his father: 'I must embrace thee:/ Let sorrow split my heart, if ever I/ Did hate thee or thy father'. (178–9) Edgar accepts Albany's apology: 'Worthy prince, I know't'. (180) Albany asks Edgar to explain where he has been since he went on the run.

LINES 183–23: EDGAR TELLS HIS STORY

Edgar tells Albany how he disguised himself as a madman and in this guise met his blind father, protected him and saved him from despair. (189–93) He says that he only revealed his true identity to his father within the last half-hour. (194–8) The

CHARACTER DEVELOPMENT

EDGAR

DETERMINED
Edgar is determined to seek justice for his father and punish Edmund for his crimes. In spite of all the trials he has endured, he will let nothing stand in his way: 'This sword, this arm, and my best spirits are bent/ To prove upon thy heart, whereto I speak,/ Thou liest'. (141–3) We can only admire his unshakeable strength of character.

CHARITABLE
Like Albany, Edgar believes in right and wrong. Edgar's experience as poor Tom has taught him the necessity for compassion and forgiveness. Although he has every reason to hate Edmund, once he has won the duel, he is ready to forgive his brother: 'Let's exchange charity'. (168)

Edgar's good nature is also indicated by his attempt to make Lear recognise Kent ("Tis noble Kent, your friend'), and by his desperate attempt to revive the king ('Look up, my lord'). We can only believe that he will prove to be a just and strong ruler.

A BLEAK VIEW OF LIFE
Edgar's trial of endurance has left him with a bleak view of life. He almost laments the way we cling to life in spite of its sorrow: 'O! our lives' sweetness,/ That we the pain of death would hourly die/ Rather than die at once!' (186–7) His sentiments become more understandable when we learn that Gloucester died in his arms and that he had to endure the spectacle of Kent's grief. He displays a certain grim acceptance of fate: 'The gods are just, and of our pleasant vices/ Make instruments to plague us'. (172–3)

KENT

LOYAL TO THE END
Kent's loyalty is evident when he comes to the British camp in an effort to see King Lear before he dies. It is he who reminds Albany about Lear and Cordelia when they have been temporarily forgotten. (236–7)

His final meeting with his master is like the end of the world for him: 'Is this the promis'd end?' (265) He desperately tries to make himself known to Lear, but the king is too confused to recognise him. We can only feel pity for Kent, as he strives to help the man he has followed with unquestioning loyalty for all of his life.

With Lear dead, Kent's world no longer has meaning. He ignores Albany's promise to make him a ruler of the kingdom, and announces that he must follow Lear to the grave: 'I have a journey, sir, shortly to go;/ My master calls me, I must not say no'. (323–4) Even in death, Kent will continue to serve his king.

emotional trauma caused by this was too much for Gloucester, who died overcome by a mixture of happiness and sorrow:

But his flaw'd heart –
Alack! Too weak the conflict to support;
'Twixt two extremes of passion, joy and grief,
Burst smilingly (198–201)

As Edgar was mourning his father's death, he was joined by another man who revealed himself as Kent. Gloucester's death, added to the trauma of recent events, caused Kent to collapse with grief: 'His grief grew puissant, and the strings of life/ Began to crack'. (216–18) Edgar left him there and came to find Edmund.

Edmund responds to the news of his father's death by saying that he is deeply moved. Albany says he can hardly bear to hear anymore, as he finds the grief overwhelming: 'For I am almost ready to dissolve,/ Hearing of this'. (206–7)

LINES 223–5: THE DEATHS OF GONERIL AND REGAN
Edgar's tale is dramatically interrupted when a gentleman enters holding a blooded knife and calling for help. He reveals that Goneril has committed suicide and that Regan has died as a result of being poisoned by her: 'Your lady, sir, your lady: and her sister/ By her is poison'd, she confesses it'. (228–2)

Edmund's response to the news is typically self-centred. He says that he will soon be united with the two sisters in a bond of death: 'I was contracted to them both: all three/ Now marry in an instant'. (230–1) Edmund in his death-throes appears amazed by the fact that two women loved him: 'Yet Edmund was belov'd:/ The one the other poison'd for my sake,/ And after slew herself'. (242–4) Albany orders the bodies to be produced. He says that the heavens are terrible in their decrees, but that the sisters deserve no pity: 'This judgement of the heavens, that makes us tremble,/ Touches us not with pity'. (234–5)

LINES 236–58: A DESPERATE ATTEMPT TO SAVE LEAR AND CORDELIA
Kent enters and says he has come to say farewell to Lear. (Presumably he thinks that the king will be executed by the triumphant British forces.) Albany has forgotten Lear amidst all of the drama ('Great thing of us forgot!'). He demands Edmund to tell him where Lear and Cordelia are. (239)

Edmund decides to redeem himself at the very end of his life: 'some good I mean to do/ Despite of mine own nature'. (245) He reveals that he has ordered Lear and Cordelia to be executed, and urges Albany to save them. (246–2)

Albany orders Edgar to run and try to prevent the murders. Edmund tells Edgar to take his sword to the captain as a sign that he wants his orders countermanded, and Edgar exits. Albany prays for the gods to protect Cordelia, and orders Edmund to be carried away. (257)

LINES 258–95: LEAR RETURNS WITH CORDELIA
Albany's hope that Lear and Cordelia may be saved is shattered dramatically. The king enters, carrying his daughter in his arms. He is in total despair:

Howl, howl, howl, howl! O! you are men of stones:
Had I your tongues and eyes, I'd use them so
That heaven's vaults should crack. (258–60)

Lear is in complete turmoil:

· He declares that Cordelia is dead: 'She's gone/ for ever./ I know when one is dead, and when one loves;/ She's as dead as earth'. (260–2)
· Such is the king's anguish that he immediately contradicts himself and tries desperately to believe that his daughter may still be alive: 'Lend me a looking-glass;/ If that her breath will mist or stain the stone,/ Why, then she lives'. (262–4)
· Lear thinks that Cordelia may still be breathing. He says that if she lives, it will compensate him for every suffering he has ever endured: 'if it be so,/ It is a chance which does redeem all sorrows/ That ever I have felt'. (268)
· In his despairing rage, he condemns everyone present: 'A plague upon you, murderers, traitors, all!/ I might have sav'd her; now, she's gone for ever!' (272–3)
· He begs his daughter to live and thinks he hears her speak: 'What is't thou sayst!' (275)
· He says he murdered the captain who hanged Cordelia: 'I kill'd the slave that was a hanging thee'. (277) One of the officers confirms Lear's story.
· The king in his grief laments his age: 'I have seen the day, with my good fighting falchion/ I would have made them skip'. (279)

The onlookers are seized with horror. Kent asks if the day of judgement has come, and he laments the

LEAR & CORDELIA

CHARACTER DEVELOPMENT

merciless fate that has befallen his master: 'If fortune brag of two she lov'd and hated,/ One of them we behold'. (282) He despairs at the horror of the situation: 'all's cheerless, dark, and deadly'. (292) He feels obliged to tell Lear that his other daughters have killed themselves and have no hope of salvation in the afterlife ('And desperately are dead'). (293)

After some confusion, Lear recognises Kent, but he does not realise that Kent and his servant Caius are the same person. Albany thinks the king is lost to them: 'He knows not what he says, and vain it is/ That we present us to him'. (295)

GLOUCESTER

A COMFORTING DEATH

Although Gloucester does not appear in the final scene, we learn of his fate through Edgar. Once his son revealed his identity, Gloucester was so overcome by conflicting emotions of happiness and sorrow that his heart broke:

But his flaw'd heart,
Alack! Too weak the conflict to support;
'Twixt two extremes of passion, joy and grief,
Burst smilingly (198–201)

Like Lear, Gloucester's sufferings finally prove too much for him. Our only consolation is that he died knowing that his son had proven to be loyal and unwavering in his unconditional love. Like the king, death for Gloucester comes as a release from further pain and grief.

REGAN

DETERMINED TO HAVE EDMUND

Regan is completely determined to have Edmund for herself, and is jealous of her sister's interest in him. She declares that she is the one who made him what he is: 'In my rights,/ By me invested, he compeers the best'. (69–70) She hands over her estate in its entirety to Edmund and publicly announces that he will be her husband: 'Witness the world, that I create thee here/ My lord and master'. (78–9) There is a certain grim irony in the fact that she is completely unaware of Edmund's lack of real feeling for her.

GONERIL

A JEALOUS MURDERER

Goneril will not tolerate the possibility of Regan winning Edmund. She is determined to assert that Edmund is a self-made man who owes nothing to her sister: 'In his own grace he doth exalt himself/ More than in your addition'. (69–70) She is willing to commit the ultimate crime of murder in order to get her man, and the fact that her rival is her sister means nothing to her. As with Regan, she is also unaware that Edmund views her only as a plaything for his own amusement.

CORDELIA

MARTYRED TO LEAR

Cordelia is made distraught by her defeat in battle. She wished only to avenge her father and to comfort him in his old age. She cares nothing for herself: 'For thee, oppressed king, am I cast down;/ Myself could else out-frown false Fortune's frown'. (6–7) Her silence in response to Lear's fantasies about their life together in prison suggests that she knows she is doomed.

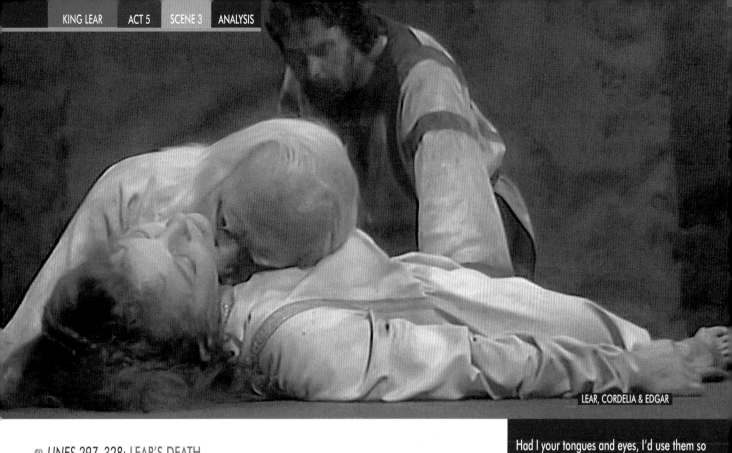

LEAR, CORDELIA & EDGAR

✑ LINES 297–328: LEAR'S DEATH

Lear appears to have acknowledged that Cordelia is dead, and is completely overwhelmed by grief: 'And my poor fool is hang'd! No, no, no life!' (307) The injustice of her death is incomprehensible to him:

Why should a dog, a horse, a rat, have life
And thou no breath at all! Thou'lt come no more,
Never, never, never, never, never! (308–10)

The sorrow is finally too much for Lear, and he collapses dead. Edgar thinks the king has only fainted and tries to revive him. Kent tells him to stop, and prays for his master to be released from his suffering:

Vex not his ghost: O! let him pass; he hates him
That would upon the rack of this tough world
Stretch him out longer (316–17)

Edgar confirms that the king is dead. (318) Kent is amazed that he lived so long at all, given what he had to endure: 'The wonder is he hath endured so long:/ He but usurp'd his life'. (319)

✑ RESTORING ORDER

An officer enters and declares that Edmund has died of his wounds. (297) Albany is unmoved: 'That's but a trifle here'. (298) He declares his determination to rescue something from this dreadful situation and restore the rule of law: 'All friends shall taste/ The wages of their virtue, and all foes/ The cup of their deservings'. (303)

He orders the bodies to be removed, and announces that Kent and Edgar will rule with him. (321)

Kent, however, has no wish to go on living now that Lear is dead: 'I have a journey, sir, shortly to go;/ My master calls me, I must not say no'. (323–4) Albany ends the play by declaring that from now on people must express their true feelings, and not what convention demands. He says that Lear suffered more than anyone, and that the young who live will neither live as long as the king or have to endure what he did:

The weight of this sad time we must obey;
Speak what we feel, not what we ought to say.
The oldest hath borne most: we that are young,
Shall never see so much, nor live so long (325–8)

The corpses are carried away to the accompaniment of funeral music.

Had I your tongues and eyes, I'd use them so
That heaven's vaults should crack
                                    Lear (259-60)

All's cheerless, dark, and deadly
                                    Kent (293)

He hates him
That would upon the rack of this tough world
Stretch him out longer
                                    Kent (314-16)

The oldest hath borne most: we that are young
Shall never see so much, nor live so long
                                    Albany (327-8)

SOME LINES TO LEARN

CHARACTERS

LEAR

LEAR AT THE BEGINNING OF THE PLAY

At the beginning of the play, Lear comes across as a powerful and well-respected king. He speaks in way that is stately, powerful and commanding. We can guess immediately that this is a man who is used to power and secure in his identity as the head of his kingdom. Yet this great and noble king has several negative characteristics. He is vain, unwilling to listen to others, wrathful and a poor judge of character.

Perhaps Lear's most negative characteristic at the start of the play is his vanity. He desires to be worshipped and flattered in public. We see this when he demands that his daughters proclaim their love for him in the most lavish and flattering terms they can manage: 'Which of you shall we say doth love us most?' (51) When Cordelia refuses to play this game, the blow to his ego is too much, and he reacts impulsively by completely disowning her. (1.1.177–9)

Like many egotistical rulers, Lear is not great at listening to others, especially when they tell him things he does not want to hear. When Kent tells him that he is making a mistake, Lear banishes him and threatens to kill him if he doesn't leave the kingdom within ten days. (1.1.177–9)

The most striking feature of Lear in the opening scene is his volcanic temper. He is enraged when Cordelia refuses to flatter him in public. His ferocious reaction to her stance seems out of all proportion to her 'crime'. He describes her as 'that little-seeming substance', 'a wretch', and so on. He is also enraged when Kent questions his judgement, warning him not to 'come between the dragon and his wrath'. (1.1.122)

Lear is also rash and impulsive. He acts on the spur of the moment, disowning his daughter and banishing Kent without really thinking things through. He turns against his most loyal servant and favourite daughter without a second thought. We learn from Goneril that Lear has always been prone to this kind of rash behaviour, and Regan points out that in his old age, these 'unconstant starts' have become more common. (1.1.300)

Although Goneril will prove to be a despicable figure, we cannot but agree with her when she condemns her father for having 'poor judgement'. After all, he has punished characters who really like him, such as Cordelia and Kent, and punished those who care nothing for him. Lear's lack of judgement extends to his own personality. He lacks all self-understanding and self-knowledge. As Regan puts it: 'he hath ever but slenderly known himself'. (1.1.292) Lear's journey through the play will prove to be a bitter path toward the self-knowledge that he so sadly lacks at the beginning.

LEAR'S BEHAVIOUR IN RETIREMENT

In his retirement, Lear continues to exhibit terrible judgement. He is blind to the fact that the balance of power in the kingdom has shifted: when he gave up his throne, he became little more than a powerless old man. Yet Lear lacks the judgement to see this, and continues to act as if he has absolute power.

This arrogant man is so used to being answerable to no one – to being the majestic king whose wrath is feared by all – that he cannot get his head around the fact that his daughters, not he, now wield power in the kingdom.

Throughout Acts 1 and 2, Lear continues to act as if he is king:

- He demands that his dinner be brought to him straightaway: 'Let me stay not a jot for dinner: go, get it ready'. (1.4.8)
- He is shocked when Oswald fails to treat him as if he is still the ruler: 'Why come not the slave back to me when I called him?' (1.4.49)
- He is equally shocked when Regan and Cornwall leave their castle when they know he is visiting.
- When he follows them to Gloucester's castle, he is horrified that they don't come out to greet him immediately.
- He is also horrified when he finds that Kent has

been placed in the stocks. An insult to the king's servant is an insult to the king himself.

· He and his servants treat Goneril's house with little respect, behaving in a disruptive and rowdy manner. Though he is Goneril's guest, he bombards her with complaints about her treatment of him. (1.3.3–7) We must bear in mind, however, that Goneril may be exaggerating the extent of Lear's misdeeds.

In his retirement, Lear also continues to be wrathful. His response to any negative situation is to fly into a rage.

· We learn from Goneril that Lear has struck one of her servants for 'chiding' his fool. (1.3.1)
· He beats Oswald when the latter insults him.
· He also flies into a rage with Goneril when she criticises the behaviour of him and his knights, calling her a 'Degenerate bastard'. (1.4.241) He calls on the gods of nature to make her womb barren: 'Into her womb convey sterility!/ Dry up her organs of increase'. (1.4.269–70)
· Lear also shows his anger when he arrives at Gloucester's castle, where Regan and Cornwall refuse to meet him: 'Are they informed of this? My breath and blood!/ 'Fiery'? The fiery duke, tell the hot Duke that …' (2.4.100–2)

In his retirement, Lear also continues to be rash and impulsive. He is casual enough when deciding whether to retain the disguised Kent: 'if I like thee no worse/ after dinner I will not part from thee yet'. (1.4.38)

THE SLOW REALISATION THAT THINGS HAVE CHANGED
Lear gradually comes to terms with the fact that he is no longer the most powerful person in the kingdom. Firstly, he notices that Goneril's servants are no longer treating him with the respect that they used to: 'I have perceived a most faint neglect of late'. (1.4.64)

When Goneril threatens to remove his knights, Lear cannot believe what is happening: 'Are you our daughter?' (1.4.203) He cannot deal with the fact that his daughters, not he, now wield power in the kingdom.

The self-identity that he has fashioned over the long years of absolute rule begins to crumble and he is left helpless and confused:

Does any here know me? This is not Lear:
Does Lear walk thus? Speak thus?
… Who is it that can tell me who I am? (1.4.210–14)

Lear begins to fear that the sudden loss of status will drive him mad:

O! let me not be mad, not mad, sweet heaven;
Keep me in temper; I would not be mad! (1.5.42–3)

It becomes more and more obvious to him that he is no longer a king but a powerless old man. Regan insults him by leaving home before his visit, by having his servant placed in the stocks, and by refusing to meet him when he arrives at Gloucester's castle. She repeatedly tells Lear to return to Goneril. In the face of these insults, it becomes more and more obvious to Lear that his status has vanished.

Lear's reaction to these insults, as we have seen, is to fly into a rage. Yet he is no longer the terrifying dragon of the first scene. He kneels before Regan and begs her to accommodate him and his knights. We now see the king as a vulnerable and physically weak old man whose ordeals induce a choking sensation. (2.4.54–5) Lear fears for his health at the shock of what he witnesses: 'O sides! You are too tough;/ Will you yet hold?' (2.4.196–7)

The final insult comes when Goneril arrives, joins hands with Regan, and together they strip him of his knights. (1.4.192) Once it has been made clear that both of his daughters are now his enemies, Lear finally realises how vulnerable and weak he is in the new scheme of things. He finally acknowledges that he is only …

a poor old man
As full of grief as age; wretched in both! (2.4.270–1)

LEAR'S REACTION TO THE STORM
Lear is so full of rage and despair that he wants the entire world to be destroyed. He calls on the tempest to accomplish this:

· He wants thunder to flatten the world with its force.
· He wants the rain to flood the world until the cocks are 'drowned' on the steeples of churches.
· He wants lightening to flare down upon the earth.
· He wants the winds to rage and blow.

Lear is in such despair that he wants the storm to extinguish the seeds of life itself so that no future generations will inhabit the earth.

Lear says that the storm battles against him, blasting him with its winds and lashing him with its rain. In a sense, therefore, the storm has joined his daughters in an effort to destroy him. However, Lear does not blame the storm for doing so. Unlike his daughters, the storm owes him no 'subscription' or allegiance. He blames his daughters for turning on him because he gave them everything, including his kingdom. But he doesn't blame the elements because he gave them nothing:

I tax not you, you elements, with unkindness.
I never gave you kingdom, called you children:
You owe me no subscription. (3.2.16–18)

Lear also believes that the gods will use the storm to seek out and destroy various wrongdoers for their crimes: 'Let the great gods/ That keep this dreadful pudder o'er our heads/ Find out their enemies now'. (3.2.49–51)

There is an importance sense in which Lear views the storm as a comfort because it distracts him and stops him obsessing about his daughters' misdeeds: 'This tempest will not give me leave to ponder/ On things that would hurt me more'. (3.4.24–5) Having to confront the storm outside means that he doesn't have to deal with the storm that in his mind, the rage and despair that he feels at his daughters' treachery. (3.4.6–14)

SOCIAL CONSCIENCE

Once he is ejected from Gloucester's castle and exposed to the elements, Lear finally begins to develop an awareness of the sufferings of others. Although suffering profoundly himself, he starts to show compassion for the plight of the men that have stayed loyal to him: 'Come on, my boy. How dost, my boy? Art cold? … Poor fool and knave, I have one part in my heart/ That's sorry yet for thee'. (3.2.72)

As he wanders through the heath, Lear comes to realise how vulnerable human beings really are. He finally understands that he is nothing but 'A poor, infirm weak, and despis'd old man'. (3.2.20) He realises all human beings are weak and vulnerable, but cover up their helplessness with the trappings of power.

Lear sees in poor Tom a figure that represents man reduced to his most basic animal level:

thou art the thing itself;
unaccomodated man is no more but such a poor,
bare, forked animal as thou art. (3.4.108–10)

He seems to feel that poor Tom is honest about

his vulnerability, that he doesn't look to cover up his weakness with cloth borrowed from animals and insects. In an attempt to follow Tom's example, Lear starts to tear off his own clothes: 'Off, off, you/ lendings! Come; unbutton here'. (3.4.110–11)

For the first time ever, Lear begins to think about the poor subjects of his kingdom. He laments the fact that he did little to help them when he was in power:

O! I have ta'en
Too little care of this. Take physic, pomp;
Expose thyself to feel what wretches feel,
That thou mayst shake the superflux to them,
And show the heavens more just. (3.4.33–6)

It is also possible that Lear's decision to strip off in the storm is an act of solidarity with these poor, naked wretches that he neglected to help.

DESCENT INTO MADNESS

It is obvious that Lear's sanity is in jeopardy from the moment he is shut out of Gloucester's castle. As the Gentleman tells Kent, he seems almost crazed with fury as he wanders around the heath shouting and roaring at the storm. (3.1.4–15) He seems to be completely obsessed with his daughters and their poor treatment of him: what he describes as their 'filial ingratitude'. (3.4.14)

Lear himself feels his sanity begin to slip: 'My wits begin to turn'. (3.2.67) He realises that continuing to obsess about his daughters will drive him insane: 'O! that way madness lies; let me shun that'. (3.4.21)

However, Lear cannot keep his mind off his daughter's misdeeds, and his sanity continues to give way. This is evident from his encounter with poor Tom at the hovel. He assumes that Tom's daughters reduced him to poverty: 'Didst thou give all to thy two daughters?' (3.4.47) He insists that only unkind daughters could do this to a man, and he threatens Kent with death when he disagrees. Although poor Tom only talks gibberish, Lear refers to him as a 'Noble philosopher', and asks him what is the cause of thunder. (3.4.148) He is anxious for the company and wisdom of this 'learned Theban'. (3.4.153)

The clearest illustration of the king's madness comes in the mock-trial scene. In his deluded state, Lear decides to try Goneril and Regan for their crimes. He seems convinced that two pieces of furniture are his daughters. He declares that poor Tom, the Fool and Kent will act as judges. (3.6.37–40)

Lear suffers a final mental collapse. He accuses the 'judges' of being corrupt and allowing his daughters to escape. He starts babbling incoherently and makes senseless remarks: 'The little dogs and all,/ Tray, Blanch, and Sweet-heart, see, they bark at me'. (3.6.65–6) He offers to make poor Tom one of his hundred knights on condition that Tom change his style of dress. Finally, he collapses in a state of exhaustion, losing consciousness:

Make no noise, make no noise; draw the curtains: so, so, so. We'll to supper in the morning: so, so, so. (3.6.85–6)

LEAR'S REDEMPTION

Kent and Gloucester's servants bring the unconscious Lear to Dover. Yet we learn from Cordelia that he ends up wandering the fields near the French camp wearing a crown made out of flowers and weeds. According to Kent, he is too ashamed to enter the camp and face the daughter he has wronged so badly. (4.2.42–6)

Though Lear is still quite mad, he has gained great insight in the midst of his insanity. Edgar sums up nicely Lear's state of mind at this point: 'O! matter and impertinency mix'd;/ Reason in madness!' (4.6.179–80) The king continues to spout what can only be described as gibberish. Yet he also seems to have gained powerful insights into both himself and society.

He now realises how hypocritical his former life was. Lear sees that he was flattered relentlessly by others in order to gain favour: 'To say "ay" and "no" to/ everything I said!' "Ay" and "no" too was no good divinity'. (4.6.99–1) In his exile and madness, the king acknowledges that he is just a man. (4.6.104–6)

Lear also returns to the theme of social justice that struck him first when he was exposed to the great storm. He now sees how hypocrisy and selfishness dominate the lives of those at the top of the social order:

A dog's obey'd in office
Thou rascal beadle, hold thy bloody hand!
Why dost thou lash that whore? Strip thine own back;
Thou hotly lust'st to use her in that kind
For which thou whipp'st her. (4.6.163–7)

The king sees that behind the glitz and pomp of court life, deceit and immorality can easily be hidden:

Through tatter'd clothes small vices do appear;
Robes and furr'd gowns hide all. Plate sin with gold,

And the strong lance of justice hurtles breaks;
Arm it in rags, a pigmy's straw doth pierce it. (4.6.169–72)

He has lost all faith in the word of those that wield power: 'Get thee glass eyes;/ And, like a scurvy politician, seem/ To see the things thou dost not'. (4.6.175–7)

As a result of his ordeal, Lear now sees life as an absurd journey full of pain and suffering. He tells Gloucester that he must endure his suffering, as it is man's natural state: 'Thou must be patient; we came crying hither:/ Thou know'st the first time that we smell the air/ We waul and cry'. (4.6.183–5)

When Lear is finally rescued by Cordelia's forces and reunited with his daughter, he is at first convinced that he has died: 'You do me wrong to take me out o' the grave;/ Thou art a soul in bliss; but I am bound/ Upon a wheel of fire'. (6.7.45–6)

When the king realises that he still lives, he expresses his total repentance for the wrongs he inflicted on Cordelia, and understands that he deserves nothing from her:

If you have poison for me, I will drink it
I know you do not love me; for your sisters
Have, as I do remember, done me wrong:
You have some cause, they have not. (4.7.73–6)

In sharp contrast to the regal and harsh language with which he disowned her at the beginning of the play, the king asks for forgiveness from his youngest daughter in very simple and moving words: 'Pray you now, forget and forgive: I am old and foolish'. (4.7.85)

So overwhelming is the king's joy at being reunited with Cordelia that even when her forces are defeated in battle, he is still blissfully happy. He imagines that imprisonment with his daughter will be a happy liberation from the cares of the wider world:

Come, let's away to prison;
We two alone will sing like birds i' the cage:
When thou dost ask me blessing, I'll kneel down,
And ask of thee forgiveness: so we'll live,
And pray, and sing, and tell old tales. (5.3.8–12)

Lear believes that the forces of politics and power can no longer touch them. We might wonder if the king properly understands what happened during the battle, or if his reason is too far gone to comprehend the danger he and Cordelia are in.

LEAR'S TRAGIC DEMISE

Lear's final appearance in the play is one of the most tragic in all of literature. He enters with Cordelia in his arms, his hopes of a happy future with his daughter shattered. The grief he feels is unbearable. He wants to howl in despair so much that the noise will crack the domes of the heavens:

Howl, howl, howl, howl! O! you are men of stones:
Had I your tongues and eyes, I'd use them so
That heaven's vaults should crack. (5.3.258–60)

Lear's trials have culminated in the horrific tragedy of his daughter's murder. Cordelia was the only person he cared about, but now she is gone and he has nothing.

The king is in a state of absolute turmoil and confusion. He declares Cordelia dead, only seconds later to start hoping she may yet live: 'She's as dead as earth. Lend me a looking-glass;/ If that her breath will mist or stain the stone,/ Why, then she lives'. (5.3.263–5) He meets and recognises Kent, but is unable to fathom that his servant Caius was actually Kent in disguise. (5.3.284–9)

The king's rage returns: 'A plague upon you, murderers, traitors, all!/ I might have sav'd her; now, she's gone for ever!' (5.3.272–3) We are reminded of Lear's former power and strength when he declares that he killed the man who hanged Cordelia. (5.3.276) It is as if the king momentarily returns to being the majestic and powerful ruler he was at the beginning of the play.

The brutal injustice of life and death is finally too much for the king. He is simply unable to accept the fact that his daughter is gone while life continues elsewhere:

And my poor fool is hang'd! No,no,no,life!
Why should a dog, a horse, a rat, have life,
And thou no breath at all! (5.3.308–10)

Lear dies desperately hoping that Cordelia may live after all: 'Do you see this! Look on her, look, her lips,/ Look there, look there!' (5.3.312–13) We can only attempt to derive some consolation from the fact that the king died in the grip of this comforting delusion.

LEAR: THE FINAL JUDGEMENT

There can be little doubt that Lear contributes to his own demise. He ignores the wise advice of Kent and gives his kingdom away. The vanity and arrogance he betrays during the 'love-test' is extraordinary. His judgement is also shockingly off the mark. He exiles and casts away those who want to help him – Cordelia and Kent – and rewards those who care nothing for him.

His behaviour in retirement also does little to elicit our sympathy. Lear behaves a little like a spoilt child, demanding his dinner straight away and flying into a rage at the slightest provocation. If Goneril is to be even half-believed, he is a terrible house guest, constantly complaining to his hosts about the littlest matters.

Yet we begin to feel sympathy for Lear as he comes to realise the consequences of giving his kingdom away. There is something terrible about seeing this poor man shaking with fear, confusion and helpless rage during his confrontations with Goneril and Regan. This sympathy grows when we see him on the heath, ranting and raving into the storm as his mental health decays.

Lear is no innocent, but compared to his daughters, his misdeeds are forgivable. He also has the ability to change and grow. Having been reduced to nothing, he gains new insights into himself, society and the nature of human existence. He becomes a wiser and humbler person, as evidenced by his moving reconciliation with Cordelia.

This makes his end all the more difficult to take. No sooner has Lear learned the error of his ways than life is snatched away from him in the most brutal manner. It is difficult not to conclude, therefore, that Lear is, as he puts it himself, 'more sinned against than sinning'.

GLOUCESTER

Our first impression of Gloucester is that of a typical 'hail fellow, well met' individual. He jokes shamelessly to Kent about Edmund's illegitimacy and the 'good sport at his making'. He displays a certain insensitivity by making these remarks in Edmund's presence, but we do not feel he is being deliberately cruel. Gloucester's deep belief in astrology also adds to the impression that he is not a particularly clever individual. This is further reinforced by the ease with which Edmund deceives him.

LOYAL

Whatever about his shortcomings, Gloucester does also possess some admirable features. He is a well-respected figure in the kingdom, as is proven by the fact that Regan comes to him to seek his 'needful counsel'. (2.1.127)

More importantly, he shows loyalty and respect toward Lear, even after the king loses power. He has the courage to openly challenge Cornwall's decision to put Kent in the stocks, viewing it as a terrible insult to the king's honour: 'the king must take it ill,/ That he, so slightly valu'd in his messenger,/ Should have him thus restrain'd'. (2.2.143–5) When his request is ignored, he apologises to Kent ('I am sorry for thee, friend').

Gloucester also attempts to act as the peacemaker in the climactic confrontation between Lear and his daughters. He is horrified by the treatment meted out to the king, and he also does his best to calm his rage by acting as a go-between: 'I would have all well betwixt you'. (2.4.117) Although he does not intervene directly in the exchanges, he does point out how terrible is the storm that Lear has disappeared into: 'Alack! The night comes on, and the bleak winds/ Do sorely ruffle; for many miles about/ There's scarce a bush'. (2.2.298–300)

BRAVERY

Gloucester possess a moral conscience that is triggered by his abhorrence at the treatment he sees meted out to Lear: 'I like not this unnatural dealing'. (3.3.1) Although some critics have commented negatively on what they perceive as Gloucester's 'cowardly' defiance, it is difficult to see how he could act otherwise given that Regan, Cornwall and Goneril hold power. It should be remembered that Gloucester takes his life into his hands by seeking out the king and offering shelter to him and his followers.

Gloucester also shows great fortitude and resilience, and earns our admiration in defying his capturers after being betrayed: 'I am tied to the stake, and I must stand the course'. (3.7.54) Even Cornwall admits that his attempts to deceive them are 'cunning'. He also displays moral courage in his open expression of disgust for Regan and Goneril's behaviour: 'I would not see thy cruel nails,/ Pluck out his poor old eyes; nor thy fierce sister/ In his anointed flesh stick boarish fangs'. (3.7.56–8) Like Edgar, he is determined to see justice done: 'I shall see/ The winged vengeance overtake such children'. (3.7.65–6)

Even when Gloucester learns that it was Edmund who betrayed him, he is not filled with self-pity, but instead expresses remorse for his treatment of Edgar and prays for forgiveness and his son's salvation: 'O my follies! Then Edgar was abus'd./ Kin gods, forgive me that, and prosper him!' (3.7.91–2)

INSIGHT & COMPASSION

One of Gloucester's main functions is to act as a parallel character to Lear. Like the king, he undergoes horrendous physical and mental sufferings, and attains a degree of wisdom and self-knowledge as a result.

Gloucester acknowledges that his blindness makes him realise the truth of things: 'I stumbled when I saw'. (4.1.18) He shows great compassion for those who try to help him in his distress, urging the old man who guides him on the heath to leave him for his own sake: 'Away, get thee away; good friend, be gone;/ Thy comforts can do me no good at all;/ Thee they may hurt'. (4.1.16–18)

Like Lear, Gloucester also develops a sense of social justice. When giving Edgar his purse, he declares 'So distribution should undo excess,/ And each man have enough'. (4.1.71–2) As with the king, Gloucester has to be reduced to the lowest level before he realises the privileged and pampered nature of his former existence.

DESPAIRING

Gloucester's suffering also leads to him a state of despair where he wishes to end his life. He sees recent events as proof that the gods are malevolent and torture men for their own amusement:

As flies to wanton boys, are we to the gods;
They kill us for their sport. (4.1.35–6)

The fact that he survives his suicide attempt only

adds to Gloucester's hopelessness. He is denied even the solace of choosing to end his own misery:

Is wretchedness depriv'd that benefit
To end itself by death? (1.1.62–3)

Edgar's encouraging words of consolation do seem to temporarily cure Gloucester of his death-wish ('henceforth I'll bear/ Affliction till it do cry out itself'), but once news is brought to him of Cordelia's defeat in battle, he hopes for the end once again: 'a man may rot even here'. (5.2.8) Although he does eventually flee with Edgar, we sense that Gloucester is near the end of his tether.

We can at least draw some consolation from the fact that Gloucester dies with his son beside him, and has the comfort of knowing that one of his sons loved him unconditionally. It is a more easy death to bear than that of Lear's.

EDMUND

REBEL WITH A CAUSE

Edmund is a cold-hearted and ambitious egotist. The central motive that drives him is his bitterness concerning his low status as a bastard son. He refuses to 'stand in the plague of custom', viewing his existence as being as legitimate as that of his brother Edgar:

Why bastard? Wherefore base?
When my dimensions are as well compact,
My mind as generous, and my shape as true,
As honest madam's issue? (1.2.6–9)

Edmund views himself as a representative of disenfranchised illegitimate children everywhere ('Now, gods, stand up for bastards!'). His most defining characteristic is his refusal to acknowledge any of the standard conventions and ties that generate family loyalty and love.

He is a ruthless pragmatist, who sole aim is complete power. Edmund scorns Gloucester's belief in astrology, as he views men as makers of their own destiny. At first, the apparent justice of his complaints and his verbal skill and wit tend to make us feel a certain amount of sympathy toward him.

MANIPULATIVE & TREACHEROUS

Edmund displays a great deal of intelligence and cunning in his manipulative scheming. He is a clever

psychologist, as is proven by the fact that he warns his father not to be too hasty in condemning Edgar after the latter's apparent plot has been revealed. (1.2.78–85) He also shows himself to be an excellent actor when telling Edgar that his life is in danger: 'Brother, I advise you to the best; go armed; I am no/ honest man if there be any good meaning toward/ you'. (1.2.169–71)

Like all clinical pragmatists, Edmund also seizes upon opportunities for advancement whenever he sees them. When Regan and Cornwall arrive at his father's castle, and the former tars Edgar by associating him with Lear's knights, Edmund endorses her claims: 'Yes, madam, he was of that consort'. (2.1.97) His ability to seize the moment is rewarded when Cornwall takes him into his service on account of his apparent loyalty to his father.

His opportunism is also made apparent in his dealings with Goneril and Regan. He is fundamentally indifferent to both of them. It is very noticeable that when Goneril makes her feelings for him explicit, he responds only with a formulaic answer: 'Yours in the ranks of death'. (4.2.25) He is perfectly content to let his suitors fight over him if it will serve his own ends.

When Regan expresses her fear that he has slept with Goneril, Edmund appears to enjoy torturing her by delaying in giving her a direct answer, and even then his language is still formal: 'No, by mine honour, madam'. (5.1.14) He views the two women merely as objects of amusement: 'Which of them shall I take?/ Both? One? or neither?' (5.1.57–8)

Edmund sees only the political consequences of their desire to have him as their husband. He believes that Goneril can be manipulated into killing Albany once the latter has served his purpose by defeating the French: 'we'll use/ His countenance for the battle; which being done/ Let her who would be rid of him devise/ His speedy taking off'. (5.1.62–5)

Of course, Edmund's most callous acts are his betrayals of Edgar and Gloucester. He is indifferent to the fact that both may lose their lives as the result of his actions. Family loyalty means nothing to him. In Edmund's eyes, people are only pawns in the ruthless game of power.

OVERCONFIDENT

Edmund's downfall comes largely as a result of his overconfidence. The success of his schemes and the fact that he meets very little opposition lead him to believe he is invulnerable. He appears to believe that his part in the defeat of the French has elevated him in status, and he talks to Albany as if he were his equal. Like Goneril, he is surprised and unable to deal with Albany's new-found strength of character and moral purpose. Nevertheless, this does not prevent Edmund from having absolute confidence in his ability to defeat either him or Edgar in single combat.

Edmund's success brings out the latent snobbery in his character. Like a lot of rebels in history, his real aim is to be part of that order which he protests so strongly about. He agrees to fight Edgar, although the latter refuses to identify himself on account of the fact that 'thy tongue some say of breeding breathes'. (5.3.146) Likewise, when he has been defeated, he declares that he will forgive his slayer if that man is of good birth: 'If thou'rt noble,/ I do forgive thee'. (5.3.167) For all of his earlier talk about standing up for the illegitimate, Edmund is eager to take his place in the old nobility.

REPENTANT OR ENJOYING THE LIMELIGHT?

Edmund's apparent change of character as he lies dying is not quite a simple moral conversion. There are good reasons to think he is enjoying playing his final part, and savours being the centre of attention. He is eager to tell his audience that his soul is being enhanced by Edgar's recounting of Gloucester's sufferings: 'This speech of yours hath mov'd me,/ And shall perchance do good'. (5.3.202–3)

In similar fashion, he cannot help but tell everyone that the two sisters died on account of their love for him: 'Yet Edmund was belov'd:/ The one the other poison'd for my sake,/ And after slew herself'. (5.2.242–4) The realisation that other people actually cared for him seems to prompt his revelation that he has ordered Lear and Cordelia to be executed, but by then it is too late to save them. We might ask why Edmund did not reveal their fate earlier if he was being sincere. We also need to ask if he is putting on a good performance of morality, or whether Shakespeare is telling us that even the most apparently selfish of people are capable of genuine repentance.

EDGAR

RESOURCEFUL & CLEVER

Critics have often commented on the inconsistencies in Edgar's character, remarking on how Edmund's naive dupe goes on to become a powerful avenging figure. Nowhere is this more apparent in Edgar's transformation into 'poor Tom'.

His radical disguise shows depths of cunning and resourcefulness that we could not have suspected after his initial betrayal by his brother. Edgar knows that as a pauperised madman he will attract very little attention whatsoever, and therefore will escape his pursuers: 'poor Tom!/ That's something yet; Edgar, I nothing am'. (2.3.20–1)

Edgar's ingenuity is further demonstrated when Lear and his companions come to his hovel. Edgar seemingly has no difficulty in acting the role of madman. His speeches and poetry match those of the Fool, who gradually fades into the background to let Tom take his place as Lear's mad companion.

COMPASSION

Edgar's exile and new role as a mad beggar gives him the same kind of insight into human suffering as comes to Lear and Gloucester. Although he can act the role of the lunatic with ease, his dealings with Lear fill him with immense pity and compassion: 'My tears begin to take his part so much,/ They'll mar my counterfeiting'. (3.6.63–4)

In spite of the fact that Edgar has been exiled by his father, he displays unquestioning love and devotion when Gloucester is delivered into his hands. It is a great testament to his fundamental decency and loyalty that he has not been embittered by his experiences. He escorts his father to Dover, determined to cure Gloucester of his despair. His trick with the suicide attempt again shows his resourcefulness and ingenuity, and he tries to console his father by telling him in his new guise as a peasant that the gods must love him if he survived such a fall: 'Think that the clearest gods, who make them/ honours/ Of men's impossibilities, have preserv'd thee'. (4.6.74–5)

He is determined not to let Gloucester succumb to his hopelessness, and tells him to 'Bear free and patient thoughts'. (4.6.81) He displays an even more direct form of protection when he kills Oswald when the latter tries to murder his father. (4.6.232–59) Even when the French are defeated and Gloucester wishes again to die, Edgar will not allow him to succumb to his hopelessness: 'Men must endure/ Their going hence, even as their coming hither:/ Ripeness is all'. (5.2.8–11) Like Cordelia, Edgar will do anything to save his father.

FAITH IN THE GODS

In spite of everything he suffers and has to undergo, Edgar is determined throughout the play not to give in to despair. He never loses faith in the gods, and tries to learn from his experiences. The sight of Lear's pain makes his own difficulties seem small in comparison:

When we our betters see bearing our woes,
We scarcely think our miseries our foes. (3.6.112–13)

Edgar's level-headedness is tested to the limit by his reunion with his blind father. He is reflecting on how fortune can bring him no lower, and that he has nothing to fear:

The lowest and most dejected thing of fortune,
Stands still in esperance, lives not in fear:
The lamentable change is from the best;
The worst returns to laughter. (4.1.3–6)

As if to mock his words, the next thing he sees is the blind Gloucester being led along by the old man. He is struck by the cruelty of fate: 'And worse I may be yet; the worst is not,/ So long as we can say, 'This is the worst'. (4.1.29–30) In spite of this, he never succumbs to hopelessness.

AN AGENT OF JUSTICE

Edgar has a very strong sense of right and wrong, and is determined to see justice done. His sufferings, and those of Gloucester and Lear, inspire him to seek his revenge against Edmund. He is a somewhat chilling avenging angel in his confrontation with his brother. He appears with his face hidden and speaks in grim, uncompromising terms of his determination to punish his brother: 'This sword, this arm, and my best spirits are bent/ To prove upon thy heart, whereto I speak,/ Thou liest'. (5.3.141–3)

It has to be said that Edgar's vision of justice is a grim one. Although he extends the hand of forgiveness to Edmund, he believes that his father suffered rightly on account of his original lust in begetting an illegitimate son:

The gods are just, and of our pleasant vices
Make instruments to plague us:
The dark and vicious place where thee he got
Cost him his eyes. (5.3.172–5)

The prospect of Edgar as a ruler is one of the few hopeful prospects at the play's end. We can imagine that the suffering he has undergone, and the insights he has acquired as a result, will mean that he will be a just and compassionate king.

ALBANY

A PASSIVE FIGURE?

In the play's early stages, Albany is often portrayed as a rather passive figure who remains very much in the background. He is present in the first scene but says nothing. He spends most of the first three acts in his castle, away from the dramatic events that unfold.

Goneril, it seems, leaves him in the dark about her plan to antagonise Lear. He enters midway through their confrontation, and seems genuinely confused as to what's going on: 'Now, gods that we adore, whereof comes this?' (1.4.279) He doesn't understand why Lear is so upset: 'My Lord, I am guiltless as I am ignorant/ Of what has moved you … What's the matter sir?' (1.4.259–60, 286)

Goneril and her servant Oswald view Albany as a rather pathetic and spineless figure. Goneril refers to him as her 'mild husband'. (4.2.1) Oswald, meanwhile, suggests that he is a weaker soldier than his wife. (4.4.3) These barbed comments, along with Albany's lack of stage time, lead many readers to regard him as something of a weakling when compared to his vicious and domineering wife.

Yet Albany is not completely passive. He criticises Goneril for her harsh treatment of Lear, saying that, though he loves her, he must upbraid her for her cruel behaviour : 'I cannot be so partial, Goneril, / To the great love I bear you …' (1.4.298–9) He suggests that Goneril's fear of Lear's knights is paranoid and exaggerated, and that her actions may well lead to harm. (1.4.317, 335–6) He also cuts her off, declaring that only time will tell the consequences of her actions: 'Well, well, the event'. (1.4.337)

Furthermore, in Act 2, Scene 1, we are made aware of 'likely wars' between Albany and Cornwall. (2.1.11) The exact cause of the conflict between the two is left unclear. Yet the fact that trouble is brewing between the two suggests that Albany is not a completely weak and passive figure.

MORAL CONSCIENCE & STRENGTH

By the time Goneril returns to his castle in Act 4, Scene 2, Albany is resolved to have nothing more to do with her. He is disgusted by her cruel actions, and voices his criticisms of her behaviour in no uncertain terms: 'O Goneril,/ You are not worth the dust which the rude wind/ Blows in your face'. (4.2.30–1) He describes her and Regan as 'tigers, not daughters'

Albany's performance from this moment on is both impressive and, perhaps, unexpected, as he emerges as a man of substance and strength. He threatens Goneril, claiming that he is capable of matching her in violence if necessary:

Were't my fitness
To let these hands obey my blood,
They are apt enough to dislocate and tear
Thy flesh and bones. (4.2.64–7)

His conscience puts him in a difficult position. He acknowledges the wrongs perpetrated against Lear, but he feels obliged to fight the French forces as a matter of national security. (5.1.23–7)

During this conflict, Albany emerges an assertive leader. In the final scene, he spots easily that Edmund is trying to distract him in regard to the fate of Lear and Cordelia. He is quick to put the upstart in his place: 'I hold you but a subject of this war,/ Not as a brother'. (5.3.61–2) He unceremoniously tells Goneril to be silent: 'Shut your mouth, dame,/ Or with this paper shall I stop it'. (5.2.155–6) He publicly accuses Edmund of treason. He declares that if no one comes forth to prove Edmund's guilt in trial by combat, he will do so himself. (5.3.92–5)

COMPASSIONATE

Albany also shows himself capable of compassion. After Edmund is defeated in battle, he orders him to be saved. (5.3.153) He is also deeply moved by the story of Gloucester's suffering: 'If there be more, more woeful, hold it in; / For I am almost ready to dissolve,/ Hearing of this'. (5.3.203–6)

A BELIEVER IN JUSTICE

Albany comes across as a great believer in divine justice. He seems to believe that the Gods inevitably punish the wicked for their crimes. Once he turns against his wife and condemns her cruelty, he declares that humanity will devour itself unless the heavens exact retribution. (4.2.46–50) He finds his faith in heavenly justice affirmed when news is brought that Cornwall has been killed by one of his servants:

This shows you are above,
You justicers, that these our nether crimes
So speedily can venge! (4.2.78–80)

Albany's belief in the gods' righteousness is, like Edgar's, somewhat clinical. When in Act 5 he orders the corpses of Goneril and Regan to be brought out, he declares solemnly that they got what they deserved: 'This judgement of the heavens, that makes us tremble,/ Touches us not with pity'. (5.3.235) Similarly, he describes Edmund's death as only a 'trifle', a matter of no importance. (5.3.296)

Throughout the play, Albany is determined to see justice served. In Act 4, he declares that he will avenge the blinding of Gloucester. (4.2.94–7) At the play's conclusion, he declares his determination to have the good rewarded and the wicked punished:

All friends shall taste
The wages of their virtue, and all foes
The cups of their deservings. (5.3.305–7)

Albany's determination to see justice done leads him to declare that Lear will have his power restored. (5.2.300–2) The final tragedy of Lear's death only strengthens this resolve. He intends to make Edgar and Kent co-rulers, and declares that a new rule will begin that will absorb the lessons of recent events and be characterised by honesty and fair dealing:

The weight of this sad time we must obey
Speak what we feel, not what we ought to say. (5.3.325–6)

Albany's impressive determination to begin a new era is one of the few positive signs in the play's general bleakness.

CORDELIA

HONEST & PROUD

Cordelia is generally seen as a good and virtuous person, a proud and loving daughter who is incapable of false flattery. Her inability to flatter Lear comes, it seems, from a need for total honesty. She finds it hard to put into words her love for the king, and so opts to say nothing: 'my love's/ More richer than my tongue'. (1.1.78) She is also repelled by the idea of massaging her father's ego in order to gain her inheritance: 'I love your majesty/ According to my bond; nor more nor less'. (1.1.92–3)

Cordelia also shows that she possesses the same kind of pride as her father. She refuses to back down in the face of Lear's gross insults, and is unapologetic for her stance:

But even for want of that for which I am richer,
A still-soliciting eye, and such a tongue
That I am glad I have not, though not to have it
Hath lost me in your liking. (1.1.231–4)

In spite of the fact that she has been disowned, Cordelia knows her own worth. She is eager to tell Burgundy that she has as little time for him as he has for her: 'Since that respects of fortune are his love,/ I shall not be his wife'. (1.1.249–50) Cordelia is by no means a meek, timid figure incapable of defending herself.

RESOURCEFUL & INSIGHTFUL

Cordelia appears to begin planning how best to safeguard her father from the very moment she is disowned. It is noticeable that she is eager to let France know that she has not lost Lear's favour on account of any 'vicious blot nor other foulness,/ No unchaste action, or dishonour'd step'. (1.1.228–9) She knows that she will be in a strong strategic position if France takes her as his wife and she is successful in her aim.

Cordelia also makes it perfectly clear that she is aware of her sisters' true colours: 'I know what you are;/ And like a sister am most loath to call/ Your faults as they are nam'd'. (1.1.270–2) She makes a thinly veiled reference to her intention to protect her father as she departs: 'Time shall unfold what plighted cunning hides;/ Who covers faults, at last shame them derides'. (1.1.281–2)

Although Cordelia is absent from the play for a long time, we see her influence at work throughout. Kent reveals in the stocks that he has received a letter from her, and he is hopeful that she 'shall find time/ From this enormous state, seeking to give/ Losses their remedies'. (2.2.166–7)

Cordelia appears to waste no time in mobilising her husband's forces against her sisters. Even before the storm scenes, Kent tells us that the French are in Dover. (3.1.30–40) It is clear that Cordelia began persuading her husband of the need to protect her father more or less from the moment she left with him for France.

Cordelia makes it clear that she is invading Britain not for any political reasons, but purely in order to protect Lear: 'O dear father!/ It is thy business that I go about.' (4.4.24–5) She acts only out of 'love, dear love, and our aged father's right'. (4.4.30)

TOTALLY FORGIVING

That Cordelia bears her father absolutely no bitterness is proven by her reaction to Kent's letters informing her of the cruelty of her sisters: 'now and then an ample tear trill'd down/ Her delicate cheek'. (4.3.12) When Cordelia is finally reunited with her father, she is overcome with emotion and refuses to accept his shouldering of the blame for what has happened:

And hold your hands in benediction o'er me.
No, sir, you must not kneel. (4.7.56–8)

Lear declares that she has ample reason to hate him, but Cordelia is adamant she does not: 'No cause, no cause'. (4.7.77) Her love for Lear is completely unconditional, and expresses itself in actions rather than words.

A TRAGIC VICTIM

Unfortunately for Cordelia and Lear, the French forces are defeated in battle. Cordelia is distraught, not for her own sake, but for Lear's:

For thee, oppresses king, am I cast down;
Myself could else out-frown false Fortune's frown.
(5.3.6–7)

It is quite noticeable that she is silent in response to her father's happy delusions about the future that awaits them in prison. Cordelia knows that she and Lear are too much of a threat to her sisters to be let live. Her forebodings are fulfilled in a brutal manner. Her death is one of the most tragic and poignant in all of Shakespeare's plays.

QUESTIONABLE DECISION ?

Some critics have pointed the finger of guilt at Cordelia for instigating the tragedy by her proud refusal to play along with her father's game. Certainly, her honesty can appear highly insensitive and misguided. Had she taken her share of the kingdom and remained in Britain, Lear would never have been so cruelly mistreated, and Goneril and Regan would have had greater difficulty asserting their authority.

GONERIL

AMBITIOUS & MANIPULATIVE

Goneril is Lear's eldest daughter. She is ambitious and willing to do what it takes to have power. When Lear uses a 'love-test' to determine how his kingdom will be divided, Goneril is the first to speak. Keenly aware of her father's egotism and vanity, she knows what she must do, and has no qualms about flattering the king. Her false words earn her a bountiful section of the kingdom:

Sir, I love you more than words can wield the matter;
Dearer than eye-sight, space, and liberty;
Beyond what can be valued, rich or rare;
No less than life, with grace, health, beauty, honour
(1.1.55–8)

The moment the king has departed, she speaks to Regan, looking to convince her of the need to treat Lear firmly: 'Sister, it is not little I have to say what most nearly/ appertains to us both'. (1.1.285) Goneril shows great skill in psychological manipulation, planting the seeds of fear in Regan's mind: 'we must look to receive form his age … the unruly waywardness that infirm/ and choleric years bring with them'. (1.1.297–9) And once she has convinced Regan of the need to manage and control Lear, Goneril wastes little time in taking direct action against the king, using the pretext of the riotous behaviour of Lear's knights to begin the process of his expulsion.

HEARTLESS & CRUEL

At no point in the play does Goneril display genuine love or affection for any character. She shows by her words that she has no respect whatsoever for her father. Her language is cold and rhetorical, and there is not a trace of filial love in the manner in which she speaks to him. She patronises the king by making constant reference to his old age:

Idle old man,
That still would manage those authorities
That he hath given away! Now, by my life,
Old fools are babes again (1.3.17–20)

Goneril shares Edmund's belief that the old should get out of the way and allow the rise and rule of the young. Once Lear has given away his land and power, he ceases to matter to Goneril. She sees him as a potential nuisance and a burden, a problem that needs to be dealt with. Having witnessed his violent, irrational outburst at Cordelia, and his hasty banishment of his loyal servant Kent, Goneril knows that Lear's erratic behaviour could potentially interfere with her ability to rule in peace.

Now that Lear is old and starting to weaken, Goneril no longer respects him as a man and a father. She treats him as a burden, a wayward child that needs to be tolerated and controlled. Her decisions regarding Lear are selfish and cold.

Goneril does not trust in anyone. She tells her husband nothing about her plans to diminish Lear, and feels no need to enlighten him: 'Never afflict yourself to know the cause'. (1.4.279) When Albany tells her that she is being paranoid about Lear, Goneril contradicts him immediately: 'Safer than trust too far'. (1.4.315) She is also suspicious of Regan's reliability. She fears that her sister may display the same 'weak' behaviour as her husband:

If she sustain him and his hundred knights,
When I have show'd the unfitness (1.4.319–20)

Goneril's savage and cruel nature is directly evident when Gloucester is brought before Cornwall for his 'treachery'. Regan suggests hanging him straightaway, but Goneril is keen to torture him: 'Pluck out his eyes'. (3.7.4) By doing so, she confirms Lear's description of her as a 'marble-hearted fiend'.

Goneril sees in Edmund a soulmate who possesses the same bloodthirsty and ruthless pragmatism that drives her. She comes to loathe Albany as a weakling: 'O! the difference of man and man!/ To thee a woman's services are due:/ My fool usurps my bed'. (4.2.27–9) When Albany expresses his disgust at her cruelty toward Lear, Goneril is completely unmoved. She is totally besotted with Edmund, and condemns her husband as being a 'Milk-liver'd man!', and goes on to speak to him in tones of complete disrespect and scorn.

Her total selfishness is further revealed when news is brought of Cornwall's death. She is pleased that Regan may now be more vulnerable, but also fears that she may prove to a rival for Edmund's affections: 'One way I like this well;/ But being widow, and my Gloucester with her, May all the building in my fancy pluck'. (4.2.84–6) Goneril is a coldly calculating individual, prepared to sacrifice anyone who stands in her way.

DOMINANT

Many critics have noted the dominating 'masculine' features of Goneril's character. One of the most striking examples of this is her behaviour toward her husband Albany. She seems to pity him, and is contemptuous of his kindness and sympathy, which she sees as a weakness:

This milky gentleness and course of yours
Though I condemn not, yet under pardon,
You are much more at task for want of wisdom
Than praised for harmful mildness (1.4.328–31)

It is Goneril who dominates Regan in the early stages of the play, controlling and directing the way they treat Lear. Her arrival at Gloucester's castle in Act 2, Scene 2 has a clear effect on Regan, instantly hardening her attitude toward the increasingly desperate Lear. Goneril's very presence strengthens Regan's resolve, and together they humiliate their father by stripping him of his knights and ejecting him from the castle. One wonders whether Regan would have had the nerve to treat Lear so cruelly had she been alone.

ENSLAVED TO HER LUST

For much of the play, Goneril comes across as a detached and ice-cold operator. However, when she falls for Edmund, she starts to lose control. There is a certain grim irony in watching Goneril become slowly enslaved to her passion for Edmund. At the beginning of the play, she treated her father with total contempt and manipulated his need for love, but now she is overcome by desire and a need for Edmund to requite her love.

So strong is her desire for Edmund, she would rather see Cordelia triumph in battle than lose him to Regan: 'I had rather lose the battle then that sister/ Should loosen him and me'. (5.1.19) Her calculating pragmatism has given way to irrational desire. The ultimate irony is that Edmund does not particularly care for either her or Regan.

The sisters' desire for Edmund breaks out into open quarrelling in the final scene. Regan's public attempt to claim Edmund as her representative is met with contempt by Goneril: 'Not so hot;/ In his own grace he doth exalt himself/ More than in your addition'. (5.3.69–71)

Goneril's jealousy finally drives her to murder her own sister. Goneril's reaction to Regan's pain shows that bonds of nature mean absolutely nothing to her: 'If not, I'll ne'er trust medicine'. (5.3.97) However, Goneril's heartless plans are finally foiled by Edmund's defeat in battle. Her reaction is one of fury and despair at her would-be lover's demise: 'thou art not vanquish'd,/ But cozen'd and beguiled'. (5.3.156–7) And once fate turns against her, and others begin to oppose her will, Goneril is unable to cope. The final straw for her is when Albany asserts his authority with unquestionable force: 'Shut your mouth, dame,/ Or with this paper shall I stop it'. (5.3.158–9)

Goneril simply cannot believe that the man she viewed with such contempt and disrespect has now become a leader. She makes one last defiant attempt to assert her primacy over him: 'the laws are mine, not thine: / Who can arraign me for't?' (5.3.160–1) She knows, however, that her efforts are in vain. With Edmund dying and Albany in control, she has nothing left to live for, and chooses suicide. Her scheming for total power ends in death.

REGAN

A WILLING OR RELUCTANT ACCOMPLICE TO GONERIL?

Early in the play, Regan appears more reluctant than Goneril to plot against her father. At the end of the first scene, it is Goneril who initiates the plot, outlining why even in retirement Lear will pose a threat to the sisters' power. Regan only listens and agrees. Goneril wishes to act against Lear immediately. Regan, however, wishes to 'further think on't'. (1.1.305) It is unsurprising, therefore, that Goneril doubts Regan. She questions Regan's willingness to join her in curbing Lear's remaining power.

In Act 2, Regan insults her father in various ways. She leaves her home even though she knows he is coming to visit. She allows his servant Kent to be placed in the stocks (an insult to the king's servant is an insult to the king himself). She refuses to see him when he follows her to Gloucester's castle. When she finally does meet Lear, she defends Goneril's behaviour toward him: 'I cannot think my sister in the least/ Would fail her obligation'. (2.4.138–9) She enrages the king by telling him to return to Goneril's castle and seek her forgiveness.

Yet it could be argued that, in Act 2, Regan attempts to avoid choosing between her father and her sister. Regan must choose either to turn the king away, which will incur his wrath, or help him, which will incur Goneril's wrath. She may be genuine when she claims that she has come to seek Gloucester's advice on this difficult dilemma. Regan, it could be argued, attempts to avoid this decision by leaving her castle before Lear arrives, and by refusing to see him when he follows her to Gloucester's, and by repeatedly telling him to return to Goneril's castle. It's as if by sending the old man away with his remaining fifty knights, she can avoid making the ultimate choice between her father and her sister. However, Goneril's arrival in Act 2, Scene 4 forces Regan to finally make this choice. She takes Goneril's hand and unites with her against Lear.

REGAN'S CRUELTY & THIRST FOR BLOOD
Regan, it must be said, is an exceptionally cruel character. Once she has finally turned against her father, she treats him with great callousness. Together, she and Goneril strip him of his remaining fifty knights, claiming that he has no need of such a retinue. While it could be argued that Goneril subtly leads this process, it is Regan who delivers the final crushing blow: 'What need you one?' When Lear protests that he gave her everything, she responds callously, saying that it was about time he did so: 'And in good time you gave it'. (2.4.248) After Lear exits in a rage, Regan urges Gloucester to shut the castle gates, leaving Lear locked out in the storm: 'Shut up your doors'. (2.4.303)

Unlike Goneril, Regan attempts to justify her cruel treatment of her father, suggesting that she has more of a conscience than her sister. She says she would be willing to accommodate Lear himself, but none of his followers. (2.5.290–1) She also reiterates her fear of Lear's knights, suggesting that this 'desperate' retinue are nothing but trouble: 'He is attended with a desperate train, / And what they may incense him to, being apt, / To have his ear abus'd, wisdom bids fear' (2.4.303–6). We can be fairly sure, however, that this is no more than an attempt at self-justification, a weak attempt to excuse her selfishness and cruelty.

Regan's cruelty and bloodlust are also evident when she is told that Edgar tried to kill Gloucester. She is eager for Edgar to be punished: 'If it be true, all

vengeance comes too short/ Which can pursue the offender'. (2.1.89–90) She also thinks that Cornwall is too lenient in his punishment of Kent, and extends his sentence in the stocks: 'Till noon! Till night, my lord; and all night too'. (2.2.133)

Her most extreme display of wanton cruelty comes when Gloucester is brought in as a traitor:

- She wants him executed immediately: 'Hang him instantly'. (3.7.4)
- When Cornwall decides to torture him instead, Regan relishes the opportunity to inflict pain. She orders him to be bound tight, and plucks at his beard.
- She also tells her husband to blind Gloucester completely: 'One side will mock another; the other too'. (3.2.71)
- She relishes the chance to tell Gloucester that it was Edmund who betrayed him and showed no mercy in doing so: 'it was he/ That made the overture of thy treasons to us,/ Who is too good to pity thee'. (3.7.88–90)
- Her final act of callousness in this scene is to exile the blind Gloucester: 'Go thrust him out at gates, and let him smell/ His way to Dover'. (3.7.93)

Regan's savagery in this scene is genuinely shocking. She even stoops to murder by stabbing the rebellious servant. (3.7.80) Her cruelty is also evident when she later regrets not having the blinded Gloucester put to death. (4.9–10) She instructs Oswald to kill him if he meets him on his travels: 'If you do chance to hear of that blind traitor,/ Preferment falls on him that cuts him off'. (4.5.38–9)

DECEITFUL & MANIPULATIVE
Not only is Regan cruel, she is also deceitful and manipulative. Like Goneril, she shamelessly flatters Lear in Act 1, Scene 1 in order to further her own ends: 'I am alone felicitate /In your dear highness' love'. (1.1.75–6) She also refers to Gloucester as our 'good old friend' when seeking his advice on her father.

Regan's talent for manipulation is also evident when she learns of Edgar's 'plot' against his father. She attempts to discredit Lear's knights by declaring that they are associates of Edgar: 'Was he not companion with the riotous knights/ That tend upon my father?' (2.1.94–5) She even declares straight out, without a shred of evidence, that the knights urged Edgar to kill his father: ''Tis they have put him on the old man's death,/ To have the expense and waste of his revenues'. (2.99–100)

A VICTIM OF DESIRE

Regan eventually begins to fall apart due to her desire for Edmund. She begins to display signs of insecurity and paranoia regarding his relationship with her sister. She tells Oswald that he is pledged to her, not Goneril: 'Edmund and I have talk'd,/ And more convenient is he for my hand/ Than your lady's'. (4.5.31–3) She is suspicious of the flirtatious glances Goneril gave Edmund during her last visit: 'She gave strange oeilliads and most speaking looks / To noble Edmund'. (4.5.24–5) She is desperate to see the letters that Goneril has written to him. (4.5.22)

Her insecurity regarding Edmund is also evident before the battle against the French. She asks him repeatedly if he has slept with Goneril: 'Have you never found my brother's way to the forfended place? (5.1.10–11) She almost begs Edmund not to sleep with Goneril, saying that she will not be able to endure it if he does: 'I never shall endure her: dear my lord,/ Be not familiar with her'. (5.1.15–16) We also see this paranoia and insecurity when she attempts to stop Goneril staying behind with Edmund while she and Albany attend the council of war. (5.1.38)

Regan's desire for Edmund is her undoing, leading her sister to poison her. She declares publicly that she will be taking Edmund as her husband: 'Witness the world that I create thee here / My lord and master'. (5.3.75–6) As she does so, however, she begins to feel the poison's effects, and has to be carried away to die. (5.3.104–5) Regan's cruelty and deceit are thus paid back fully as she falls victim to the same kind of plotting and lust for power that led her to destroy her father. It is one of the few indications in the play that the world is a just place.

KENT

LOYAL SERVANT

Kent is a loyal and devoted servant of Lear. However, he is not a lickspittle – someone who, like Oswald, serves unquestioningly. Kent is capable of disobedience when he thinks it is in the interest of his master. As such, he displays a higher standard of loyalty. In spite of Lear's warnings to hold his tongue, Kent will not stand idly by while the king gives away everything:

My life I never held but as a pawn
To wage against thine enemies; nor dear to lose it,
Thy safety being the motive (1.1.154–6)

Such is Kent's loyalty and overwhelming fear for the king's future that he risks his life to tell Lear the truth: 'Revoke thy gift;/ Or, whilst I can vent clamour from my throat,/ I'll tell thee thou dost evil'. (1.1.164–6) The absolute nature of Kent's devotion is proven by the fact he chooses to continue to serve Lear in spite of the death sentence passed on him:

If thou canst serve where thou dost stand condemn'd,
So may it come, thy master, whom thou lov'st,
Shall find thee full of labours (1.4.5–7)

It is Kent who protects Lear during the storm and afterwards. He finds poor Tom's hovel and makes the king take shelter there: 'The tyranny of the open night's too rough/ For nature to endure'. (3.4.2–3) He also urges Lear to accept Gloucester's offer of shelter: 'Good my lord, take his offer; go into the house'. (3.4.160)

One of Kent's vital functions within the drama is to act as a connecting link between Lear and Cordelia. It is Kent who acts as Cordelia's informant and ensures that she is made aware of the brutality inflicted on the king by Goneril and Regan. And when Gloucester tells him that there is a plot afoot to have the king murdered, it is Kent who immediately organises for him to be escorted to Dover to meet the French. (3.6.109–10)

Kent is absolutely selfless in his devotion to the king. He seeks no reward for his service, and when Cordelia is effusive in her praise for his loyalty, his reply is modest and self-effacing: 'To be acknowledg'd, madam, is o'er-paid'. (4.7.4)

KENT'S SUFFERING

It is worth noting that Kent also suffers during the play. He finds the sight of his beloved master's descent into insanity torturous to watch: 'O pity! Sir, where is the patience now/ That you so oft have boasted to retain?' (3.7.61–2)

Behind the front of his seemingly imperturbable cool-headedness, Kent is being buffeted by events. He finally cracks when he comes upon Edgar and Gloucester after the battle. As he recounts the suffering that has befallen Lear, 'his grief grew puissant, and the strings of life/ Began to crack'. (5.3.215–17)

He recovers himself in time to be able to remind Albany that Lear and Cordelia are in danger, but his loyal service is not rewarded. He is desperate for Lear to acknowledge him, but the king is too lost to madness and grief to do so.

Kent knows that Lear has had enough of life, and gently tells Edgar to give up trying to revive him: 'O! let him pass; he hates him/ That would upon the rack of this tough world/ Stretch him out longer'. (5.3.316–17)

With Lear dead, Kent has no reason to live. Even Albany's offer to give him power is not enough to hold him to life. He wishes to be reunited with his master:

I have a journey, sir, shortly to go;
My master calls me, I must not say no (5.3.323–4)

Along with Cordelia, Kent is the perfect embodiment of selfless love and devotion. His unquestioning loyalty is one of the few flickers of light in the dark universe the play portrays.

HONEST

Like Cordelia, Kent is totally honesty and refuses to flatter. He has no tolerance for falseness and is incapable of telling lies, even when it means his life is at risk. As well as risking Lear's wrath in the opening scene, he is brutally honest when confronted by Cornwall and his entourage after his altercation with Oswald before Gloucester's castle:

Sir, 'tis my occupation to be plain;
I have seen better faces in my time
Than stands on any shoulder that I see
Before me at this instant (2.2.90–3)

He is put in the stocks as a result of his plain speaking. However, some critics have condemned Kent for his bluntness, arguing that he is doing a disservice to the king by making himself helpless at such a crucial point in the drama. But, as with Cordelia, we may also choose to find his honesty and forthrightness admirable and praiseworthy.

CORNWALL

HARDNESS & CRUELTY

Cornwall possesses a terrible streak of hardness and cruelty. This is evident when he tells Gloucester to punish Edgar however he wishes and with his full backing: 'make your own purpose,/ How in my strength you please'. (2.1.111–12) We also see his cruelty when he places Kent in the stocks: 'As I have life and honour,/ There shall he sit till noon'. (2.2.131–2) He seems unconcerned when Gloucester points out that by doing so he will insult the king. (2.2)

Cornwall's cruelty is most evident in his barbaric torture of Gloucester. His cruel blinding of this helpless old man is a despicable act: 'Upon those eyes of thine I'll set my foot … Out vile jelly / Where is thy lustre now?' (3.7.65, 81–2) Perhaps equally despicable is his declaration beforehand that his rage may get the better of him, so he cannot be blamed for his actions: 'our wrath, which men/ May blame but not control'. (3.7.25–7)

Cornwall's decision to blind Gloucester proves to be his undoing, however, as one of his own servants takes exception to his cruelty and defies his orders. (3.7.69–73) In the ensuing fight, Cornwall is fatally wounded. (3.7.95–6) We can only feel that he has met with his just reward.

A SUPPORTIVE HUSBAND?

Cornwall seems to be completely devoted to and supportive of his wife:

- When Regan declares that she will not be at home to welcome Lear, he immediately states that he supports her fully: 'Nor I, assure thee, Regan'. (2.1.105)
- He supports her during her confrontation with Lear in Act 2, Scene 4, brushing aside Lear's objections to Regan's harsh treatment of him: 'Fie, sir, fie!' (2.4.321)
- He seconds his wife's decision to shut the king out, telling Gloucester to 'Shut up your doors, my lord; 'tis a wild night:/ My Regan counsels well'. (2.4.308–9)
- He follows Regan's instructions when she urges him to remove Gloucester's second eye (though it is probable Cornwall intended to do this anyway). (2.7.69)

Cornwall is sometimes portrayed as a weak figure who is dominated by his wife and makes up for this by acting the 'hard man' and committing vicious acts of cruelty. Yet he can also be thought of as a loving and supportive husband who treats his wife as something of an equal, and who aids and abets her plotting in the knowledge that they both will benefit.

THE FOOL

A TELLER OF TRUTH

The Fool plays a unique role in the world of the play. He occupies the lowest rung in society, being only an idiotic jester whose job it is to entertain Lear with his nonsense, songs riddles and rhymes. In a sense. he is little more than Lear's slave, for it seems that the king often has him whipped.

Yet the Fool has a strange power. Because people think of him as a buffoon or harmless idiot, he is allowed to say things that others are not. There is a tradition that fools always spoke the truth as they saw it, however uncomfortable that truth may be for their listeners. The Fool says he cannot lie but wishes that someone would teach him how to. (1.4.167) This is particularly evident in Act 1 when the Fool persistently criticises Lear for giving away his land and power to his daughters. He tells the great king that he has behaved in an incredibly stupid way – something no one else would be allowed to do:

- He says that if we were to give his possessions to his daughters he would at least keep two clown-caps, unlike Lear, who gave everything away. (1.4.96–102)
- He says he will teach Lear a speech about self-control and prudence: 'Have more than thou showest,/ Speak less than thou knowest,/ Lend less than thou owest'. (1.4.107–9) The Fool is obviously criticising Lear's rashness in giving away his land.
- When Lear says that 'nothing can be made out of nothing', the Fool reminds that from now on he will be getting no rents because he has given away his lands (1.4.122–4)
- He patronises Lear, addressing him as 'my boy' and reciting a ditty that suggests he's a 'sweet and bitter fool' for giving away his kingdom. (129–36) He says Lear 'hadst little wit in thy bald crown when thou/ gavest thy golden one away'. (150–2)
- When Lear asks if he is calling him a fool, his reply is bitterly comic. Lear, he says, has given away all his other titles. 'Fool' is the only title he has left, a title that will be with him for life: 'All thy other titles thou hast given away; that thou/ wast born with'. (138–9)
- He suggests Lear's stupidity by singing a song about how wise men have grown foolish. (151–4)
- He says Lear has placed himself in his daughters' power: 'thou madest thy/ daughters thy mothers; for when thou gavest them/ the rod and puttest down thine own breeches'. (157–8)
- All in all, the Fool is the only character who is permitted to openly criticise the king. His lowly status allows him to say things that would see more important people be put to death for uttering.

THE FOOL'S WISDOM

Although his speech takes the form of silly songs and 'nonsense verse', there is much wisdom in the Fool's words. Kent, for instance, sees some wisdom in the Fool's criticisms of Lear: 'This is not altogether fool, my lord'. (139)

The Fool sees immediately that Lear can expect no mercy from either Goneril or Regan. When the king seeks refuge with Regan, the Fool tells him to expect no mercy from her: 'Shalt see thy other daughter will use thee kindly; for/ though she's as like this as a crab is like an apple, yet/ I can tell what I can tell'. (1.5.12–13)

His wisdom is also evident when he and Lear encounter Kent outside Gloucester's castle. He advises Kent not to ask Lear why he has only fifty knights in his retinue. (2.4.62–3) He responds with quick wit to Kent, saying that while he may be a fool, he isn't in the stocks (2.4.84)

LEAR'S AFFECTION FOR THE FOOL

It seems that Lear sometimes gets angry with the Fool's forthright criticisms, referring to him as an annoyance or 'pestilent gall'. (1.4.106) He seems to have the Fool whipped on occasion, and threatens to do so on two occasions in Act 1, Scene 4. (102, 168) In general, however, Lear seems exceptionally fond of the Fool, referring to him affectionately as 'my boy'. The Fool in turn refers affectionately to Lear as his 'nuncle'. He strikes one of Goenril's servants for 'chiding' the Fool. (1.3.1) When Lear returns to Goneril's castle after hunting, one of the first things he does is summon the Fool to his side. (1.4.40) In Act 3, Lear shows the first signs of developing a moral conscience when he expresses concern for the Fool's well-being: 'How dost, my boy? Art cold?' (3.2.69) He urges the Fool to seek shelter in the hovel even before he does: 'In, boy; go first, –/ You houseless poverty –/ Nay, get thee in'. (2.4.26–7)

THE FOOL'S LOYALTY TO LEAR

Although the Fool is very critical of Lear, he is also unquestioningly loyal to him. His criticisms of the king are his way of attempting to alert his master to the realities of the new order that he has created. In Act 1, Scene 5, he tries to cheer Lear up with his jokes and riddles after Goneril has stripped him of half his knights. When Lear is shut out of Gloucester's castle, the Fool stays with him:

But I will tarry; the fool will stay,
And let the wise man fly:
The knave turns fool that runs away;
The fool no knave, perdy (2.4.79–82)

The Fool stays with Lear through the great storm. He urges the king to take shelter from the elements even if it means returning to the castle and asking his daughters to take him in: 'Good nuncle, in, and ask thy daughters' blessing'. (3.2.12) The Fool criticises Kent for his unquestioning loyalty to the king ('Let go thy hold when a great wheel runs/ down a hill, lest it break thy neck with following it'), but in reality he himself shows the same absolute devotion.

THE FOOL'S DECLINE
Lear and the Fool wander through the storm together. In Act 3, Scene 2, the Fool continues to play the role of jester, coming up with amusing nonsense about headpieces and codpieces, and chanting a bizarre 'prophecy'. Yet as Act 3 goes on, the Fool becomes less and less vocal. As Lear slides into insanity, the Fool becomes more and more sorrowful and silent.

He joins in the mock-trial, but after that we hear no more of him. His final words are: 'I'll go to bed at noon'. (3.7.87) This is generally taken to be a statement of the despair and depression he feels at Lear's decline. It's as if the Fool can no longer bear to go on living and wishes to shun the world by taking to his bed. It is often suggested that the Fool dies of a broken heart, his spirit shattered by King Lear's tragic descent into madness. In a sense, Edgar, disguised as 'poor Tom', takes over the Fool's role. Like the Fool ,poor Tom speaks a great deal of nonsense mixed with wit and wisdom.

OSWALD

LOYAL SERVANT
Oswald is Goneril's devoted servant. He carries out her orders diligently and faithfully, and delivers a number of significant letters. In his devotion to his mistress, Oswald can be compared to Kent, another loyal servant. However, whereas Kent has a conscience and is willing to speak out when necessary against his master's foolish wishes, Oswald has no moral qualms about carrying out any of Goneril's commands. He is unquestioningly faithful, and in this regard can be seen as either the perfect servant or a weak and servile man.

If we find Oswald's loyalty to Goneril slightly admirable, and perhaps think that he was a little harshly treated by Kent in the latter's vicious tirades in Act 2, Scene 2, we should also bear in mind that he was perfectly prepared to murder the blind Gloucester in order to advance himself: 'A proclaim'd prize! Most happy!/ That eyeless head of thine was first fram'd flesh/ To raise my fortunes'. (4.6.232–3) It is difficult to feel any pity for his murder at Edgar's hands.

CORNWALL'S SERVANTS & THE OLD MAN

COMPASSIONATE & DECENT
Although the universe in which *King Lear* takes place appears to be dominated by dark forces and brutal violence, there are a few flickers of light occasionally to be seen. One of the most striking and touching examples of this is the compassion shown to Gloucester by Cornwall's servants.

The First Servant is so disgusted by the cruelty displayed by Regan and his master that he feels obliged to voice his protest, regardless of the consequences: 'I have served you ever since I was a child,/ But better service have I never done you/ Than now to bid you hold'. (3.7.74–6) So strongly does he feel, that he fights Cornwall and fatally wounds him. Typically, in the atmosphere of injustice that prevails, he is murdered from behind by Regan. The other two servants express their disgust at what they have witnessed once they are alone, and get the old man to take Gloucester to safety. They also apply egg-white to his eye sockets in order to try and ease his pain.

The old man to whom Gloucester is entrusted also displays great compassion toward his landlord. He ignores Gloucester's warnings that he is putting himself in danger by helping him, and promises to fetch Edgar some clothes: 'I'll bring him the best 'parel that I have,/ Come on't what will'. (4.4.49–50)

These acts of spontaneous compassion and generosity tend to highlight the fact that wanton cruelty and selfishness are most typically found amongst those embroiled in a quest for political power. Shakespeare seems to be suggesting that kindness and decency are still possibilities amongst ordinary humanity.

THEMES

THE GODS & COSMIC JUSTICE

FAITH & APPEALS TO HEAVEN

King Lear is littered with appeals to heaven. Time and time again, characters reveal their faith in the heavens and call upon the gods to help them or to ease their strife. When Lear realises that his daughters are about to betray him, he repeatedly calls on the gods for help:

O heavens,
If you do love old men, if your sweet sway
Allow obedience, if yourselves are old,
Make it your cause; send down and take your part!
(2.4.188–90)

In his hour of need, he abases himself before the heavens, declaring himself to be a helpless old man who is desperate for their aid: 'You see me here, you gods, a poor old man, / As full of grief as age, wretched in both!' (2.4.269–70) As the storm rages around him, he declares that he will do his best to help the poor in order to win the gods' favour. (3.4.36)

Lear's faith in the gods is also apparent in his deluded belief that he and Cordelia will share a blissful future in prison. He tells her that they will be 'God's spies' watching the futile activities of the world from a safe distance. (5.3.17–20) He is utterly convinced that he and his daughter are under heaven's protection ('He that parts us shall bring a brand from heaven').

Kent, Gloucester and Cordelia seem to share Lear's faith. Like Lear, they seem to believe that the gods can and will intervene on their behalves. Each makes several appeals to heaven:

· As Gloucester is blinded, he calls on the gods for help, and declares his hope that 'winged vengeance' will strike Goneril and Regan. (3.7.66)
· He asks the gods to forgive him for treating Edgar badly, and asks them to protect him: 'Kind gods, forgive me that, and prosper him!' (3.7.92)

Kent, meanwhile, calls on the gods to protect Cordelia

after she has been disowned: 'The gods to their dear shelter take thee,/ maid'. (1.1.183)

· When he is placed in the stocks, he takes comfort from the belief that the gods are on his side and that 'heaven's benediction' will keep him from harm. (2.2.159)
· Kent appears to hold onto his faith in the gods' ultimate benevolence. When Gloucester appears and offers them shelter, Kent hopes the gods will repay him: 'The gods reward your kindness!' (3.6.5)
· Cordelia, too, appeals to the gods, asking them to cure her demented father of his madness and mental torture: 'O you kind gods,/ Cure this great breach in his abused nature!' (4.7.15–16)
· Albany also appeals to the Ggods for help. When he learns that Edmund has sent someone to kill Cordelia, he calls on heaven to protect her: 'The gods defend her!' (5.3.256)

An interesting feature of the play is that while the 'good' or sympathetic characters call upon the Gods for help, the wicked ones do not. Of the two sisters, only Regan makes any reference to the gods, claiming to be shocked when Lear curses her sister: 'O the blest gods! So will you wish on me, / When the rash mood is on'. (2.4.167–8) We get the sense, however, that this reference to the gods is not quite genuine. Goneril – the more clinical and ruthless of the two – makes no mention of the gods whatsoever.

Edmund – the other character generally regarded as evil – also has little truck with the gods. He likes to think of himself as a self-made man, and has no time for the belief that gods control humans like puppets on strings. Instead, as we shall see, he worships 'Nature', which he regards as being amoral and indifferent to the ties of love and loyalty that most humans believe in. He seems to believe that he can draw on this cosmic energy and serve his own ends by acting in a completely heartless and ruthless manner.

THE LOSS OF FAITH

One by one, the various characters' faith in the gods is tested or shattered. Their prayers and appeals for help go unanswered. The gods, it seems, are either absent or are indifferent to their various plights:

· Once he is blinded and banished into the wilderness, Gloucester's faith in divine benevolence starts to disintegrate. He comes to believe that the gods torture men for their own amusement: 'As flies to wanton boys, are we to the gods;/ They kill us for their sport'. (4.1.36–7)
· Lear's faith in the gods' goodness appears to crumble when Cordelia is hanged. He enters howling, telling the onlookers that he wants to scream until the heavens themselves are cracked and damaged by the sound: 'Had I your tongues and eyes, I'd use them so/ That heaven's vaults should crack'. (5.3.259–60)
· Kent's belief in the kindness of the gods is also shaken at the play's climax. The sight of his master carrying Cordelia's body makes him wonder if the end of the world has come: 'Is this the promis'd end?' (5.3.265)
· It could also be argued that Cordelia's faith is shattered by the cruel progress of events. When she and her father are brought in as prisoners, she makes no call to the gods. Instead, she makes reference to 'false Fortune's frown'. (5.3.7) She is noticeably silent when her father tries to convince her that they are under heaven's protection.

Edgar's faith, too is tested. Having been falsely accused and hounded into exile, he feels that things can't get much worse: 'The lowest and most dejected thing of fortune,/ Stands still in esperance, lives not in fear'. (4.1.3–4) However, no sooner does he utter these remarks than he sees that his father has been blinded: 'O gods! Who is't can say, 'I am at the worst?'/ I am worse than e'er I was'. (4.1.26–7)

Yet Edgar's attitude to misfortune is one of stoical acceptance. As we shall see, despite his sufferings he retains his faith in divine justice. He refuses to let Gloucester succumb to hopelessness. (4.6.75) His determination to take whatever the world throws at him is summed up by his words of encouragement to his father when the latter wishes to die after learning of the French defeat: 'Men must endure/ Their going hence, even as their coming hither:/ Ripeness is all'. (5.2.9–11) He will not succumb to the temptation to curse heaven or blame the gods for his suffering.

A BELIEF IN DIVINE JUSTICE

Throughout the play, several characters declare a belief in divine justice: a belief that the gods will reward the good and punish the wicked. Edgar, for instance,

seems to suggest that Edmund will lose their duel because he was 'false to thy gods'. (5.3.136)

He also declares that Gloucester deserved his terrible fate because he had sex outside marriage and fathered a bastard child:

The gods are just, and of our pleasant vices
Make instruments to plague us:
The dark and vicious place where thee he got
Cost him his eyes (5.3.172–5)

We might ask ourselves, however, if we find Edgar's dispassionate verdict a little cold and harsh.

Like Edgar, Albany also possesses faith in divine justice. Once he turns against his wife and condemns her cruelty, he declares that humanity will devour itself unless the heavens exact retribution. (4.2.46–50) He finds his faith in heavenly justice affirmed when news is brought that Cornwall has been killed by one of his servants:

This shows you are above,
You justicers, that these our nether crimes
So speedily can venge! (4.2.78–80)

Albany's belief in the gods' righteousness is, like Edgar's, somewhat clinical. When in Act 5 he orders the corpses of Goneril and Regan to be brought out, he declares solemnly that they got what they deserved: 'This judgement of the heavens, that makes us tremble,/ Touches us not with pity'. (5.3.235)

As he lies dying, Edmund, too, seems to declare his faith in divine justice, saying that he has got his just deserts: 'Thou hast spoken right, 'tis true;/ The wheel is come full circle; I am here'. (5.3.176–7) Whether he actually believes this is uncertain. Edmund is nothing if not an actor, and may be playing for sympathy, making the most of his last moment in the limelight.

AN ANGEL & A DEVIL

Cordelia is the character most strongly associated with heaven in the play. In Act 4, her servant describes her as an angelic-like figure: 'There she shook/ The holy water from her heavenly eyes, / And clamour-moisten'd'. (4.3.32–3) When Lear wakes to find her standing over him, he thinks she is a 'soul in bliss', a soul that has ascended into heaven. (4.7.6) Goneril, on the other hand, is so malicious that even her own husband describes her as a devil: 'See thyself, devil!' (4.2.59)

NATURE WORSHIP & SUPERSTITION

Nature is sometimes presented in the play as a kind of goddess, a powerful force that guides people's lives if worshipped correctly. This view of nature is one of the elements that help create what critics have perceived to be a pagan, pre-Christian atmosphere in *King Lear*.

Lear himself is seen as something of a nature worshipper. He calls on the unseen forces of nature to endorse his banishing of Cordelia:

For, by the sacred radiance of the sun,
The mysteries of Hecate, and the night,
By all the operations of the orbs
From whom we do exist and cease to be,
Here I disclaim all paternal care (1.1.109–13)

Lear calls on his goddess Nature to make Goneril barren after she has insulted him: 'Hear, Nature, hear! Dear goddess, hear!/ Suspend thy purpose, if thou didst intend/ To make this creature fruitful!/ Into her womb convey sterility!' (1.4.262–5)

As we have seen, Edmund is the most conspicuous nature worshipper in the play. He has a rather sinister view of nature, regarding it as a powerful and untamed force that has no regard for human morals. During his first soliloquy, he makes it perfectly clear that, as servant of nature, he will be bound only by its laws, disregarding the normal rules of family, loyalty and morality:

Thou, Nature, art my goddess; to thy law
My services are bound (1.2.1–2)

Inspired by what he regards as nature's dynamic, amoral forces, he will let nothing stand in the way of his lust for power.

Perhaps related to nature worship is the notion of superstition. Gloucester is the play's most superstitious character, blaming troubles in the kingdom on 'these late eclipses in the sun and moon'. (1.2.102) Kent seems to share some of Gloucester's faith in astrology. When he learns of Cordelia's compassionate reaction to news of her father's trials, he declares that 'It is the stars,/ The stars above us, govern our conditions'. (4.3.35–6)

DIVINE JUSTICE OR A GODLESS UNIVERSE?

Many readers have suggested that *King Lear* takes place in a cruel and uncaring universe, a world where the gods either do not exist or simply do not care about mankind's suffering. The play has an almost unbearably tragic ending, and is littered with incidents of brutal and gratuitous violence. As we have seen, again and again, characters place their faith in the gods only to meet with tragedy and catastrophe. Again and again, prayers go unanswered.

Other readers favour the view that the gods do govern the play's universe, delivering stern and strict punishment for those who break the rules of morality (as we have seen, this is the outlook expressed by both Albany and Edgar). There are several pieces of evidence that support this view:

· Edmund, Cornwall, Goneril and Regan are all punished with death for their crimes, suggesting that the gods not only exist but punish those who behave immorally.
· The suffering of Lear and Gloucester, it could be argued, is punishment for sins they have committed. Both turn against their good children and reward the wicked ones.
· Order and peace are restored by Albany at the play's conclusion.

Yet it is difficult to understand what Cordelia is being punished for as she behaves in an exemplary fashion throughout the play, showing nothing but love and loyalty to the father who so cruelly disowned her. Furthermore, the suffering endured by both Lear and Gloucester seems out of all proportion to their misdeeds. As Lear himself puts it, he is a 'man / More sinned against than sinning'. (3.2.59–60)

On the whole, then, it is difficult to determine whether the play is set in a world in which the gods dispense divine justice or a universe in which the gods are either absent or completely indifferent to man's plight. Each reader must make up his or her own mind based on the evidence in the play.

LOYALTY & BETRAYAL

The theme of loyalty plays a very crucial role in the play. Depending on their inclinations and motives, characters display either unswerving loyalty to their family and associates, or else betray them in order to further their own ambitions.

FAMILY LOYALTY

In a play dominated by family disloyalty and betrayal, two characters remain steadfastly loyal to their parents: Cordelia and Edgar. When asked at the start of the play to express her love, Cordelia speaks in plain terms about what she understands the relationship between father and daughter to be:

You have begot me, bred me, lov'd me: I
Return those duties back as are right fit,
Obey you, love you, and most honour you (1.1.96–8)

It is terribly ironic that Lear cannot accept this straightforward declaration of the loyalty a child owes its parent. It is not enough for his ego, and he banishes the one daughter who is truly loyal.

Cordelia and Edgar, however, both remain loyal to parents who have wronged them. As such, their loyalty is tested in the harshest possible way. Though she is insulted and publicly disowned by Lear, Cordelia remains loyal to the very end. Edgar, too, stays by his father, helping the blinded man to find his way in life again.

Cordelia's actions following her departure for France are motivated entirely by her loving loyalty to her father. When she receives news of his mistreatment at the hands of her sisters, she is appalled: 'Faith, once or twice she heav'd the name of 'father'/ Pantingly forth, as if it press'd her heart;/ Cried, 'Sisters! Sisters! Shame of ladies! Sisters!' (4.3.27–9) Cordelia makes it perfectly clear that the French invasion has nothing do with any desire to conquer England; it is done purely to rescue Lear: 'No blown ambition doth our arms incite,/ But love, dear love, and our aged father's right'. (4.4.28–9) Her unconditional love for her father and her lack of any resentment at the pain he causes her is summed up when Lear says that she has great reason to hate him. Cordelia's reply is moving simple: 'No cause, no cause'. (4.7.79)

The major difference between the loyalty shown by Cordelia and that of Edgar is that the former acts purely out of love whereas Edgar seems more motivated by a sense of duty. This is best seen in Edgar's 'The gods are just' speech, where he implies that in a certain way he believes Gloucester paid the due penalty for his moral transgressions. Some critics have wondered why Edgar does not reveal his true identity to his father when he finds him blinded, as surely this would be the most direct way to help ease his suffering. Perhaps Edgar thinks his father needs to find his own way to redemption. We cannot be sure.

When that encounter does occur, Edgar exhibits his love for his father by escorting him to Dover and staging the fake attempt at suicide. His motive for doing so is his absolute determination to cure his father's desperate state of mind: 'Why I do trifle thus with his despair/ Is done to cure it'. (4.6.35) Edgar is partly successful in this, and shows even further his love by killing Oswald when the latter is determined to murder Gloucester in order to claim a bounty. (4.4.251–5)

The strength of Edgar's loyalty is proven again by the fact that he is willing to risk his life by taking on Edmund in single combat. His generous nature is on show when he displays forgiveness to his brother and affirms his family tie to the man who would have happily seen him dead: 'Let's exchange charity/ I am no less in blood than thou art, Edmund'. (5.3.170)

FAMILY BETRAYAL

Lear firmly believes that Goneril and Regan will honour what he later describes as 'The office of nature, bond of childhood,/ Effects of courtesy, dues of gratitude'. (2.4.176–8) However, Goneril and Regan feel no real ties of affection or loyalty to their father, the man who has given them everything. They abuse Lear's faith in this natural order of loyalty by lying and pandering to the king's vanity. They receive their due rewards, and through their subsequent actions proceed to show the hollowness of their words.

As well as showing no loyalty to their father, Goneril and Regan also finish by betraying each other. Their common desire for Edmund leads each to view the other with suspicion and distrust, and by the play's climax they have become openly hostile. The absence of any form of loyalty in Goneril is made abundantly clear by her ruthless decision to poison her one-time ally and sister, Regan.

Goneril's act is made appear bitterly ironic by the fact that Edmund in his turn has no deep loyalty to either her or Regan. He views them as mere toys for his amusement and as tools for his own advancement.

The characters associated with evil have no conception of loyalty. They merely enter arrangements of convenience based on necessity, and when circumstances change, they have no hesitation in resorting to betrayal.

Lear himself commits a great crime against ties of natural loyalty by banishing Cordelia, and he pays excessively for it. Gloucester's deeds mirror those of Lear's. Like the king, he ends up disowning the child who genuinely loves him, and views Edgar as an evil aberration: 'Unnatural, detested, brutish villain!/ worse than brutish!' (1.275–6) Gloucester is horrified by what he believes is Edgar's disloyalty:

This villain of mine comes
under the prediction; there's son against father: the
kings falls from bias of nature; there's father
against child (1.2.107–10)

As with Lear, there is a grim irony in the fact that Gloucester views Edmund as being his 'Loyal and natural boy' (2.1.84–5) when the reality is that Edmund is the child who has no respect for conceptions of natural love and loyalty. Edmund not only betrays his father but also his brother Edgar. He betrays the trust that Edgar places in him, duping him into believing that his life is in danger, and making it seem that Edgar is plotting against his own father.

Lear is driven to insanity both by the shock of his daughters' ingratitude and by his need to find an explanation for it. This leads him to stage the mock-trial scene in Act 3, Scene 6, where he is desperate to discover the 'cause in nature that/ makes these hard hearts'. (3.6.81) Unfortunately for the king, he can find none, and his insanity deepens.

Gloucester undergoes a trial very similar to Lear's. He also mistakes his loyal child for his treacherous one, and pays the price. As Lear disowns Cordelia, so Gloucester does Edgar: 'I never got him'. (2.1.78) And much as the king gives power and the realm to his ungrateful daughters, Gloucester promises Edmund that he will inherit everything: 'I'll work the means/ To make thee capable'. (2.1.84–5) As a result of his misjudgement, he ends up betrayed, tortured and exiled. Once again, there are strong parallels with Lear, as Gloucester realises too late which child really loves him: 'Then Edgar was abus'd./ Kind gods, forgive me that, and prosper him!' (3.7.92–3)

The agent of his downfall, Edmund, shows no trace whatsoever of any kind of familial loyalty or love. He contemptuously describes his father as 'credulous', and has no hesitation in betraying him to Cornwall. Edmund is interested only in Gloucester's title and lands. His schemes will 'draw me/ That which my father loses; no less than all'. (3.3.22–3) Edmund see his father purely as an old man who has to be dealt with so that he can take his place: 'The younger rises when the old doth fall'. (3.3.24)

LOYAL SERVICE

The loyalty of servants also plays a huge role in the play. Kent, Oswald and Cornwall's servants display different facets of the ties that bind followers to their masters.

Perhaps the most striking example of unquestioning loyalty in the play is Kent. The king's lifelong servant displays his ferocious love of his master from the very beginning of the play right through to its terrible end. Kent is willing to put his own life at risk by daring to tell Lear that his division of the kingdom is a very foolish act. He does this purely out of concern for Lear's welfare: 'My life I never held but as a pawn/ To wage against thine enemies; nor fear to lose it,/ Thy safety being the motive'. (1.1.156–8)

Knowing that his master is now at risk, he disguises himself in order that he may continue to serve the king. The only reward Kent seeks for his devotion is the hope that Lear will recognise him at the very end of the play. Sadly, this appears to be denied him as Lear is too bereft to register anything around him.

Such is the power of Kent's loyalty that he intends to serve his master even in death, as life holds no meaning for him once Lear is gone: 'I have a journey, sir, shortly to go;/ My master calls me, I must not say no'. (5.3.323–4)

Cornwall's servants provide an interesting example of a mixture of loyalty and betrayal. When they witness their master's brutal treatment of Gloucester, one of them steps forward and objects to the barbarity. He finds himself duelling with Cornwall and inflicts a fatal blow, but is in turn himself killed by Regan. The other two servants come to Gloucester's aid afterwards by applying egg-white to his sockets and finding him an escort to lead him in the countryside. While, technically, the servants may be guilty of betrayal, on another more profound level they are displaying loyalty to common notions of decency and morality.

Similarly, the old man who helps Gloucester initially

does so in spite of the latter's fears for his safety. He has been a tenant of Gloucester and his father for decades, and shows a touching devotion to his landlord. He also takes it upon himself to fetch clothes for Edgar. His loyalty, and the compassion of the servants, is another example of the fact that the universe of the play is not dominated entirely by evil and selfishness. Shakespeare may be suggesting that the very worst excesses of cruelty and heartlessness are displayed by those embroiled in the pitiless quest for political power.

We should also note that the other display of great loyalty in the play comes from Oswald, a character who serves Goneril, an evil and selfish mistress. He obeys her commands without hesitation, and even earns perhaps a slight bit of our admiration for doing so. We might also think that the ferocious tirade Kent pours on him outside Gloucester's castle is a little excessive. After all, isn't Oswald displaying the same kind of loyalty to Goneril as Kent does to Lear?

Although Oswald does accept a little bit of moonlighting from Regan, it seems only fair to note that his dying wish is that Edgar take the letter his mistress entrusted him with and deliver it to Edmund. Unfortunately for Oswald, his last request ends up leading to the revelation of Goneril's treacherous intentions. Oswald's behaviour shows us that loyalty is not necessarily a trait that belongs solely to those characters we associate with goodness and decency.

POWER

The exercise of power, the loss of it and the desire for it feature heavily in *King Lear*. Viewed from one angle, the play can be read as a political morality tale that warns of the consequences that arise from power's wrongful exercise and its deep allure to those who seek it. Different characters deal with power according to their nature and morality.

LEAR & POWER

King Lear is a man defined by power. At the play's beginning, he is an all-powerful autocratic ruler, accustomed to holding unchallengeable authority and commanding complete obedience. We find it difficult to imagine what Lear was like before he became king, so strong is the impression that he has always been a ruler and is nothing else besides.

In many ways, because we have the impression that power is concentrated completely in the hands of one man, it does not seem altogether surprising that Lear's handover of authority leads to disaster. This becomes apparent from the very beginning, when Lear states that he is giving power to his daughters so 'that future strife/ may be prevented now'. While this may appear like a wise move on the surface, the means by which the king goes about his divestment – the love-test – seems flawed.

Lear states that he hopes to prevent further conflict, but he has no sensitivity to the fact that he may be offending Goneril and Regan by declaring that Cordelia is in line to receive 'a third more opulent than your sisters'. (1.1.86) As a result of Cordelia's inability to flatter her father, her two sisters inherit even more power than was intended, and Cordelia removes herself as a political player within the realm. She renders herself incapable of helping her father until she returns with the French forces.

Aside from the flawed division of power, whose consequences will be tragic, the other great difficulty is that Lear seems incapable of truly relinquishing authority. Even after he has technically surrendered power, he still talks and acts like a man in total control. He gives the kingdom to Goneril and Regan in line 130 of Act 1 ('I do invest you jointly with my power'), but still talks about the power he has afterward. He warns Kent not 'to come betwixt our sentence and our power' at line 171, and makes reference to 'the power that made me' at line 208. Even his order that his daughters should each house him and his knights one month at a time seems paradoxical: now that Goneril and Regan have power, why should they do anything he wishes them to do? And, of course, they don't.

Although Goneril is obviously planning to have her father removed altogether, and her word cannot be completely trusted, we feel that she is probably speaking with some measure of truth when she complains that Lear wrongs her day and night. (1.3.3) She sums up Lear's flawed nature perfectly:

Idle old man,
That still would manage those authorites
That he hath given away! (1.3.16–19)

When the one-time king reappears, he still acts and speaks like he is the man who calls the shots: 'Let me not stay a jot for dinner: go, get it ready'. (1.4.8) When Goneril's servants are slow to react, he thinks 'the world's asleep'.

What Lear fails to realise is that the old world he lived in and commanded through his power has vanished thanks to his actions, and that in the new world he has created through his divestment, he occupies a very low place indeed. The Fool is the only character who has the courage and the wisdom to tell Lear this, or at least to hint at it through his songs and riddles, but Lear is either incapable or unwilling to acknowledge the truth of his situation. The Fool summarises the shift in power nicely when he tells Lear that he has 'madest thy daughters thy mothers'. (1.4.157)

Without the power that defined him, Lear is left helpless and without an identity: 'Who is it that can tell me who I am?' (1.4.214) Only when he is exposed to the violence of the storm and the miserable lives led by the poor and the mad, does he begin to think of himself in terms outside of power. He realises that he is only 'a poor, infirm, weak, and despis'd old man'. (3.2.20)

As Lear gains more wisdom through his suffering, he comes to see the injustice that those in power perpetrate. He condemns himself for the lack of care he showed towards the poorest elements in society when he held the throne. When he encounters Gloucester, his views on power and authority have become totally cynical: 'There thou mightst behold the great image of/ authority; a dog's obey'd in office'. (4.6.163) He knows that behind the shield of authority, 'robes and furr'd gowns hide all'. (4.6.170)

Tragically for Lear, he cannot escape the realities of power politics. When being led off to prison with Cordelia, he tells her that for their own amusement they will 'talk of court news' and outlive 'packs and sets of great ones/ That ebb and flow by the moon'. (5.3.18–19) Unfortunately, Edmund views him and Cordelia as potential threats to his newly gained power, and orders them to be executed. Cordelia is hanged and the trauma kills Lear. Ultimately, the one-time king is destroyed by the destructive effects of power.

ABUSE OF POWER

The aim of Goneril and Regan is to gain power and eliminate Lear as a potential threat to their unrestrained exercise of it. They play along with the love-test charade in order to gain their shares in the kingdom, and once they succeed, they show what happens when power falls into the hands of selfish and malicious individuals.

For both sisters, status and authority come solely with power. That is why Lear's expectancy that he will still be treated like a king once he has given away power seems to them ridiculous and absurd. They cannot understand their father's insistence on maintaining a retinue of knights, as they view such a need as unnecessary and, more importantly, as a threat to their own rule. This is why their gradual reduction of the number of knights they are willing to allow Lear in the confrontation scene is of hugely symbolic importance. Without his followers, Lear is just a helpless old man, a charity case reliant on the generosity of his powerful daughters.

Once the sisters are in power, they become very domineering and masculine. The most obvious sign of this is the way in which both treat their husbands. Albany is puzzled by Lear's anger when he comes across his father-in-law railing against his wife because the latter has decided he does not need to know her intentions toward Lear: 'Never afflict yourself to know the cause'. (1.4.276) Goneril views herself as the politician, who has nothing but contempt for Albany's 'milky kindness'.

Much like Lear had little hesitation in banishing Cordelia, Goneril has no moral qualms about viewing Albany as disposable once she grows besotted with Edmund. As an all-powerful ruler, she feels that it is only proper for her to have a husband that matches her in ambition and ruthlessness: 'O! the difference of man and man!/ To thee a woman's services are due:/ My fool usurps my bed'. (4.2.27–9) She goes so far as to encourage Edmund to kill Albany.

Goneril's world starts to fall apart when Albany begins to assert himself. He too now seeks to exercise power, and has nothing but contempt for his wife's selfishness and cruelty. The two become open enemies in the last scene when Goneril tries to defy her husband. Unfortunately for her, Albany is a changed man and will brook none of her insolence. When Albany accuses her of intending to betray him, she makes one final effort to show who's boss: 'the laws are mine, not thine:/ Who can arraign me for 't?' (5.3.160–1) The fact that she no longer wields total control is too much for her. She storms off in a rage and commits suicide.

Regan's attitude toward Cornwall is similar. She cuts across her husband in order to assert her authority in front of others. She asserts herself (and displays her cruelty) by doubling the amount of time Cornwall condemns Kent to spend in the stocks. (2.2.133) Regan is also the one who orders Gloucester to shut his doors on Lear, a command meekly echoed by Cornwall ('My Regan counsels well').

The most brutal expression of Regan's power and dominance over her husband comes when Gloucester is brought before them as a prisoner. She wants him to be hanged immediately and orders the servants to bind his arms tightly. (3.7.33) Regan plucks at Gloucester's beard, and tells her husband to pluck out the prisoner's other eye. (3.7.71) She clearly derives great sadistic enjoyment from her exercise of unlimited power. Outright murder is also of no difficulty to her. When one of the servants dares to intervene on Gloucester's behalf, Regan has no problem in taking up a sword and running him through from behind.

Like Goneril, Regan's grip on power starts to slip when she begins to desire Edmund. She becomes insecure and paranoid, and is ready to make Edmund her lord and master if he will accept her. This is unacceptable to Goneril, who poisons her. In the end, the sisters' lust for power becomes all-consuming and self-destructive.

EDMUND'S QUEST FOR POWER

Edmund is completely dominated by his lust for power. Whereas Goneril and Regan have it delivered into their hands, Edmund has to plot and scheme in order to acquire it. In doing so, he demonstrates what happens when an individual's only goal is to rise to the top, regardless of the consequences.

Like the two sisters, Edmund has no time for family loyalty. He views Gloucester and Edgar as obstacles on his path to power, and has no qualms about disposing of them: 'A credulous father, and a bother noble,/ Whose nature is so far from doing harms/ That he suspects none; on whose foolish honesty/ My practices ride easy!' (1.2.176–9)

Like all shrewd individuals desperate for power, Edmund is also a shameless opportunist. He ingratiates himself with Cornwall and Regan, and impresses the former enough to be taken on as one of his lieutenants. Edmund's most despicable act in the play comes when he betrays his father to his new master. He sees this as being a perfectly natural thing to do, as he believes he is entitled to usurp the aged Gloucester on account of his youth and ability: 'This seems a fair deserving, and must draw me/ That which my father loses; no less than all:/ The younger rises when the old doth fall'. (3.3.22–4) He is rewarded for his treachery when Cornwall makes him the new Earl of Gloucester.

Edmund's ultimate ambition is to wield total power. He manipulates the sisters' desire for him by playing them off against each other in order to further this ambition. He shamelessly swears his loyalty to both of them, and can enjoy speculating which he will take: 'Each jealous of the other, as the stung/ Are of the adder. Which of them shall I take?/ Both? One? or neither? Neither can be enjoy'd/ If both remain alive'. (5.1.56–9) Edmund is happy to see Albany's forces defeat the French and for Goneril to have him removed afterwards. He is a totally pragmatic and unemotional individual.

It is Edmund's determination to safeguard his own position that leads to the play's tragic climax. Although Lear is only a helpless old man, and Cordelia has been defeated in battle, Edmund views them as potential rallying points for the disaffected in the kingdom. The king and his daughter are threats to his political ambition, so must therefore be eliminated.

Edmund's undoing comes as a result of his overconfidence. Once the battle is won, he believes that he has earned the right to wield the same kind of power as Albany. When challenged, he refuses to back down, so sure is he that he can defeat anyone who dares to take him on. The arrogance and conceit that his successful pursuit of power has generated finally leads to his downfall.

THE RIGHTFUL USE OF POWER

Albany represents the morally correct use of power in the play. Although initially a weak and passive figure who does not challenge his wife's authority, Albany undergoes a crisis of conscience that leads to him asserting his rights and taking command over Goneril.

The conflicting calls of power and morality cause Albany great anguish in the lead-up to the battle against the French. According to Edmund, he is 'full of alteration/ And self-reproving'. (5.1.3–4) On the one hand, he does not wish to ally himself with Edmund, Goneril and Regan, yet on the other, he knows that as an English ruler he has a duty to fight the foreign invader.

Before the battle, Albany acknowledges that he has shown a dereliction of duty in his failure to exercise power in a just and lawful manner. He refers to the people who have rallied to Lear and Cordelia ('others; whom the rigour of our state/ Forc'd to cry out'), and admits that have 'just and heavy causes'. (5.1.26–7)

Once the fight against the invader is won, Albany turns his attention to re-establishing a lawful and just rule. His first act is to arrest Edmund on a charge of treason, and then he finally puts Goneril in her place by crushing her attempts to reassert herself ('Shut your mouth, dame').

When Lear and Cordelia reappear, Albany is absolutely determined to fight and overcome the powers of injustice and chaos that have led to tragedy. He announces that Lear will be reinstated: 'we will resign,/ During the life of this old majesty,/ To him our absolute power'. (5.3.300–2) He also promises to elevate Kent and Edgar. His vision is that 'All friends shall taste/ The wages of their virtue, and all foes/ the cup of their deservings'. (5.3.305–7)

Even Lear's death does not stop him in his quest to see justice done. He announces that Kent and Edgar will rule with him, and promises to institute a new era where honesty will be the norm: 'Speak what we feel, not what we ought to say'. (5.3.325–6) The prospect of Albany as a king of the land is one of the more hopeful outcomes of the play.

CIVILISATION & NATURE

King Lear draws a powerful contrast between civilisation and nature. Civilised society is depicted as false and deceitful, as corrupt and corrupting. The play suggests that we can only gain wisdom and insight when we leave the comforts of civilisation behind and lose ourselves in the natural world.

Lear, Edgar and Gloucester are banished from 'civilised' society with its lies, power-games and corruption. All three are stripped of their power and cast out into the wilderness. Both Lear and Gloucester are thrown out of Gloucester's castle and are left at the tender mercy of the elements. Suddenly, Lear goes from being a king attended by a hundred knights to being a 'poor, infirm, weak, and despis'd old man'. (3.2.20) Similarly, the blind and helpless Gloucester is stripped of his earldom and turned out of doors. Meanwhile, Edgar, once the heir of a powerful earl, becomes a hunted fugitive who is forced to hide in a tree, cover himself with mud and pretend to be a half-naked madman.

All three lose their power and prestige and are sent from civilisation into nature. Yet it is through being cast out of society that these characters acquire wisdom. As they wander the bleak environment of the heath, they gain powerful insights into themselves and into the society they live in.

Lear, for instance, realises that the kingdom is full of 'poor naked wretches' and that he was wrong not to address this issue during his reign: 'O! I have ta'en/ Too little care of this'. (3.4.32–3) Gloucester comes to a similar realisation. He condemns those who run society for being greedy and gluttonous, for being 'superfluous and lust-dieted man'. (4.1.69–72) They live lives of plenty while the poor starve. He gives Edgar his purse, declaring that each person should have only what they need to survive: 'So distribution should undo excess,/ And each man have enough'. (4.1.71–2) Edgar, too, comes to realise how divided his society is. His experience as 'poor Tom' teaches him what life is like for the 'lowest and most dejected' in society. (4.1.3)

All three come to understand how vulnerable and weak we human beings actually are. Lear realises that even rich and powerful people are in reality as vulnerable as the naked poor Tom because fate can destroy them in an instant:

thou art the thing itself;
unaccommodated man is no more but such a poor,
bare, forked animal as thou art. (3.4.108–10)

Lear tries to demonstrate this new understanding by taking off his clothes. He seems to regard wearing clothes as dishonest because it disguises how frail and defenceless we all actually are.

Gloucester comes to a similar realisation. He comes to understand that while our material possessions give us a false sense, we are always at the mercy of fate: 'Full oft 'tis seen,/ Our means secure us, and our mere defects/ Prove our commodities'. (4.1.18–21) He puts this new-found realisation in memorable terms: 'As flies to wanton boys we are to the Gods/ They kill us for their sport'.

It could be argued that Edgar, too, gains this insight. His experience of going from favoured son to hunted fugitive teaches him how fickle fate, or the gods, can really be. Living the life of an outcast, he declares that things can get no worse – until that moment when he encounters the sight of his blinded father: 'O gods! Who is't can say, 'I am at the worst?'/ I am worse than e'er I was'. (4.1.26–7)

Both Lear and Gloucester also come to understand the deceit, hypocrisy and falseness that characterise life at court. Lear refers to this kind of hypocrisy during the storm when he rants about those 'that under covert and convenient seeming/ Hast practis'd on man's life'. (3.2.56)

The play, then, presents civilised society as a place of corruption. It is only by leaving civilisation behind that we can gain wisdom, insight and redemption. This journey undertaken by Lear, Gloucester and Edgar is one that has echoes throughout history and literature. All three are powerful wealthy characters who lose their possessions and influence, leave society behind and gain wisdom in the wilds of nature. In this regard, their experience recalls that of Jesus, the Buddha and other wise figures from the past who gained insight by leaving civilisation behind and finding themselves in the wilderness.

A BLEAK VIEW OF HUMAN NATURE

The issue of the evil and malignancy latent in human nature also comes under close examination during the play. There is a very strong sense that with the collapse of the social order that Lear's division of power brings about, human nature takes a turn for the worst. Gloucester refers to the fact that with recent tumultuous events, 'nature finds itself scourged by/ the sequent effects'. (1.2.104–5) Edgar find himself having to adapt a disguise 'in contempt of man' in order to escape the consequences of his brother's evil acts. (2.3.8) Gloucester later comments on the general darkness that has overwhelmed the land by saying that 'Our flesh and blood, my lord, is grown so vile,/ That it doth hate what gets it'. (3.4.149–50)

The unnatural degree of cruelty and selfishness shown by his daughters leads Lear to demand that the cause be found: 'Then let them anatomise Regan, see what breeds/ about her heart. Is there any cause in nature that/ makes these hard hearts?' (3.6.80–2) Similarly, after he has been blinded, Gloucester calls in vain for nature to redress the balance of good versus evil: 'Edmund, enkindle all the sparks of nature/ To quit this horrid act'. (3.7.86) Unfortunately, it is Edmund – who has no respect for the conventional concepts of human nature – who is responsible for his suffering.

The rampant evil and selfishness of the new rulers leads some to wonder if human nature is not taking a permanent turn toward darkness. After witnessing Regan's cruelty in blinding Gloucester, one of

Cornwall's servants remarks on the necessity for her to be punished and the dire consequences if she is not: 'If she livelong,/ And, in the end, meet the old course of death,/ Women will all turn monsters'. (3.7.100–2)

Albany expresses similar fears when he openly confronts Goneril over her savagery: 'I fear your disposition:/ That nature, which contemns its origin,/ cannot be border'd certain in itself'. (4.2.31–3) He fears the self-destructive potential in her character if she is so heartless: 'She that herself will sliver and disbranch/ From her material sap, perforce must wither/ And come to deadly use'. (4.2.44–6) Goneril's suicide later proves his fears to be accurate.

Albany tells his wife that her actions are more befitting to wild animals than to human beings: 'Tigers, not daughters, what have you perform'd?' He believes, like Cornwall's servant, that if justice is not done, humanity 'must perforce prey on itself,/ Like monsters of the deep'. (4.2.49–50)

Lear's sufferings and the recognition of his own selfishness and hypocrisy when he was king lead him to despise his own human nature. When Gloucester asks for his hand, he replies: 'Let me wipe it first; it smells of mortality'. (4.6.137) Gloucester replies in terms that hint at the end of the world: 'O ruin'd piece of nature! This great world/ Shall so wear out to nought'. (4.6.138)

POVERTY & NOTHINGNESS

The play draws a powerful contrast between the poor and the wealthy in the society it depicts. There are several depictions of poverty in the play. Lear himself refers to the 'poor naked wretches' who inhabit his kingdom and are exposed to the storm's rage.

The old man who helps the blinded Gloucester in Act 4 is perhaps one of these wretches. Another wretch is the captain who follows Edmund's orders to have Lear and Cordelia executed. The captain has no desire to carry out this brutal act, but is too poor to do otherwise: 'I cannot draw a cart nor eat dried oats/ If it be man's work I will do it'. (5.2.39–40)

At the beginning of the play, the main characters are untroubled by poverty. They live lives of relative plenty in their palaces and castles. One of the play's most distinguishing features is that three of these wealthy characters are thrust into poverty and learn what it is like to have nothing.

Lear, Edgar and Gloucester are banished from the higher echelons of society. All three are stripped of their power and reduced to nothing. Both Lear and Gloucester are thrown out of Gloucester's castle and are left at the tender mercy of the elements. Suddenly, Lear goes from being a king attended by a hundred knights to being a 'poor, infirm, weak, and despis'd old man'. (3.2.20) Similarly, the blind and helpless Gloucester is stripped of his earldom and turned out of doors. Meanwhile, Edgar – once the heir of a powerful earl – becomes a hunted fugitive who is forced to hide in a tree, cover himself with mud and pretend to be a half-naked madman.

Yet poverty does these characters a lot of good. Both Lear and Gloucester develop a sense of social justice. Once Lear becomes a helpless and socially insignificant exile, he acknowledges for the first time the existence of the poor, who are usually invisible to those who hold power. His new position at the bottom of the ladder makes him realise how negligent he was with regard to these, his most vulnerable subjects: 'O! I have ta'en/ Too little care of this'. (3.4.32–3)

Gloucester, meanwhile, learns to condemn the typical 'superfluous and lust-dieted man' at the top of society who has no awareness of the realities of life for the poor majority. (4.1.69–72) His experience of poverty causes him to declare that each person should have only what they need to survive: 'So distribution should undo excess, / And each man have enough'. (4.1.71–2) Edgar, too, learns what it is like to be poor. His experience as 'poor Tom' teaches him what life is like for the 'lowest and most dejected' in society. (4.1.3)

Through their experiences of poverty, both Lear and Gloucester understand how vulnerable and weak we human beings actually are. Gloucester realises that while our material possessions give us a false sense, we are always at the mercy of fate: 'Full oft 'tis seen,/ Our means secure us, and our mere defects/ Prove our commodities'. (4.1.18–21)

Lear's ordeal on the heath leads him to realise that human beings are weak and vulnerable, little more than 'bare, forked animals' at the mercy of forced beyond our control. Poor Tom, he declares, is true to himself because he makes no attempt to conceal these vulnerabilities and frailties. Poor Tom, according to Lear, is the 'thing itself'. He shoes us how:

thou art the thing itself;
unaccommodated man is no more but such a poor,
bare, forked animal as thou art. (3.4.108–10)

Lear tries to demonstrate this new understanding by taking off his clothes. He seems to regard wearing clothes as dishonest because it disguises how frail and defenceless we all actually are, and he no longer has interest in wearing these 'lendings' from animals and insects. (3.4.98–100)

It is through their experience of poverty, then, that Gloucester and Lear gain new insights into themselves, their society and the world we live in. By becoming 'nothing', they undergo a terrible penance for the wrongs they have committed, and they prepare themselves for reconciliation with the loved ones they have treated so badly. It is a wiser, humbler Lear who begs Cordelia's forgiveness in Act 4, Scene 7. This wisdom and humility stems to a large extent from his experience of poverty.

LANGUAGE & IMAGERY

ANIMALS & MONSTERS

King Lear contains numerous images of animals and savage monsters. Humans in their cruelty are often compared to vicious beasts that prey on their innocent victims. In particular, animal imagery is often used in connection with Goneril and Regan.

GONERIL & REGAN COMPARED TO ANIMALS & MONSTERS

Throughout the play, Goneril and Regan are compared unfavourably to animals and monsters. Lear often uses animal and monster metaphors when describing his daughters' cruelness and heartlessness. In Act 1, Scene 4, he calls Goneril a 'marble-hearted fiend', and says that her ingratitude is more hideous than that of a sea-monster. (1.4.247) Shortly afterwards, he calls her a 'Detested kite', referring to a particular bird of prey. (1.4.248) The king also describes his eldest daughter as having a 'wolfish visage'. (1.4.294)

Lear says that the pain of ingratitude is 'sharper than a serpent's tooth'. (1.4.274) He returns to this image later, telling Regan that her sister 'struck me with her tongue,/ Most serpent-like'. (2.4.57–8) Interestingly, Albany uses the same image when arresting Goneril at the play's climax, calling her a 'gilded serpent'. (5.3.85)

Before he exits into the storm, Lear calls his daughters 'unnatural hags' (2.4.176) He says that he would rather 'be a comrade with the wolf and owl' than return to Goneril. (2.4.208) Inside Edgar's hovel, Lear calls Goneril and Regan 'those pelican daughters'. (3.4.75) Pelicans were reputed to feed on the blood of their parents.

When Albany condemns the cruelty of Goneril and Regan, he says that they are 'tigers, not daughters'. (4.2.40) He goes on to say that if the gods do not punish their savagery, 'Humanity must perforce prey on itself,/ Like monsters of the deep'. (4.2.49–50) Albany warns his wife to 'be-monster not thy feature'. (4.2.64) He goes on to claim that Goneril is a devil in disguise: 'thou art a fiend, a woman's shape doth shield thee'. (4.2.67–8)

Kent describes Goneril and Regan as being the king's 'dog-hearted daughters'. (4.3.48) Before he is blinded, Gloucester says he will not have Goneril 'In his [Lear's] anointed flesh stick boarish fangs'. (3.7.58) One of Cornwall's servants says that if Regan lives to die a natural death, 'Women will turn all monsters'. (3.7.102)

HUMANS BEINGS COMPARED TO ANIMALS & MONSTERS
Human beings are sometimes compared to animals and beasts in *King Lear*. Sometimes, this comparison is intended to highlight mankind's capacity for cruelty and savagery. Edgar, in the guise of poor Tom, uses a set of animal metaphors to describe the worst tendencies in humanity: 'hog in sloth, fox in stealth, wolf in greediness, dog in madness, lion in prey'. (3.4.92–3) Lear's rage and bitterness at his daughters' cruelty leads him to curse female sexuality: 'Down from the waist they are Centaurs,/ Though women all above'. (4.6.127–8)

King Lear also highlights the fact that beneath his clothes, man is no more than a vulnerable animal: 'Unaccommodated man is no more but such a poor, bare, forked animal as thou art'. (3.4.105) Lear comes to realise that people use fancy clothing and riches to disguise the fact that they little more than beasts: 'Allow not nature more than nature needs,/ Man's life is cheap as beasts'. (2.2.455–6)

VIOLENCE
....

King Lear is set in a brutal and savage prehistoric world, a Britain where violence, torture and physical suffering are all so commonplace as to be unremarkable. It is little wonder when King Lear himself declares that 'Man's life is cheap as beast's'. (2.4.265)

LEAR & VIOLENCE
Throughout the play, Lear regularly uses violent images in his speech, threatening his enemies and those who displease him with violent retribution:

- He declares that a barbarian who eats his own young would be more dear to him than Cordelia is now, referring to 'the barbarous Scythian,/ Or he that makes his generation messes/ To gorge his appetite'. (1.1.117–20)
- Shortly afterwards, he threatens Kent with violence for daring to question him: 'Come not between the dragon and his wrath … Kent, on thy life, no more'. (1.1.122–54) He then declares Kent exiled, and says that he will be killed if he is found within the kingdom after ten days have passed. (1.1.177–9)
- He also threatens Goneril with violence, saying he is sure that Regan will attack her for treating him badly: 'with her nails/ She'll flay thy wolvish visage'. (1.4.293–4)
- The king calls on nature to physically strike Goneril down as punishment for her ingratitude: 'strike her young bones … You nimble lightnings, dart your blinding flames/ Into her scornful eyes!' (2.4.160–4)
- Similarly, he calls for 'Vengeance! Plague! Death! Confusion!' to strike Regan and Cornwall when they refuse to see him at Gloucester's castle (2.4.92)
- As he wanders the heath in the midst of the storm, he invokes nature's violent and destructive forces when he calls on the storm to destroy 'ingrateful man' once and for all. (3.2.1–9)
- When Lear is trying to reassure Cordelia that they are under heavenly protection, he says that the 'goujeres' (misfortune and disease) will attack their enemies and 'devour them, flesh and fell'. (5.3.25)
- During the mock-trial, Lear expresses his desire to 'anatomize' or dissect Regan in order to find the cause of her cruelty. (3.6.80)
- Perhaps the king's most disturbing cry for violence comes when he raves at Gloucester about his desire for vengeance against Albany and Cornwall: 'And when I have stolen upon these sons-in-law,/ Then, kill, kill, kill, kill, kill, kill!' (4.6.192)

It is Lear who first commits an act of physical violence in the play when he strikes one of Goneril's servants for giving out to his fool. (2.3.1) Shortly afterwards, he and Kent commit a further act of violence when they strike, trip and kick Oswald. (1.4.79–85)

COMBAT

There are several instances of combat in the play. Edmund stages a mock-duel with Edgar, cutting himself in order to fool his father. (2.1.33) The quarrel between the two is resolved by a real duel in the play's final scene, with Edgar mortally wounding his brother. (5.2.146)

Kent insists on fighting a duel with Oswald, and when the latter refuses, starts to beat him. (2.2.35–40) Later, Oswald fights and is killed by Edgar. (4.3.242) There is also a brief skirmish between Cornwall and his rebellious servant, which is resolved when Regan stabs the servant in the back. (3.7.70–80)

The most large-scale combat is the battle between the French and English forces. This takes place off-stage, though we do see the armies riding into battle in Act 5, Scene 2. The final and most pitiful instance of combat comes when Lear kills the captain who has hanged Cordelia: 'I killed the slave that was a-hanging thee'. (5.3.275)

TORTURE & EXECUTION

Torture also features widely in the bloody universe of *King Lear*. The Fool implies that he has been whipped somewhat regularly by the king: 'thou'lt have me/ whipped for speaking true, thou'lt have me/ whipped for lying'. (1.5.167–8) Kent, meanwhile, is placed in the stocks, a barbaric and degrading form of torture that prevents its victims from moving. (2.2.137) He will be left there cramped and immobile until noon, or, if Regan has her way, for nearly twenty-four hours. (2.2.133) When Gloucester is Regan's prisoner, he defies her, saying that he will not let her and Regan torture Lear: 'Because I would not see thy cruel nails,/ Pluck out his poor old eyes; nor thy fierce sister/ In his anointed flesh stick boarish fangs'. (3.7.56–8)

Yet the most graphic example of torture is, of course, the blinding of Gloucester in Act 3, Scene 7. He has his arms bound tightly, his beard plucked, and is blinded in both eyes: 'Upon those eyes of thine I'll set my foot ... Out vile jelly / Where is thy lustre now?' (3.7.65, 81–2) Gloucester is also psychologically tortured when Regan reveals that it was Edmund who betrayed him, and that he showed no mercy in doing so: 'it was he/ That made the overture of thy treasons to us,/ Who is too good to pity thee'. (3.3.88–90) In a further act of cruelty, the blinded Gloucester is

thrown out of the castle and left to fend for himself: 'Go thrust him out at gates, and let him smell/ His way to Dover'. (3.7.93)

Torture imagery is also used to depict Lear's own suffering. When he realises that he has mistreated Cordelia, he uses the imagery of the rack to describe the regret that ravages his mind: 'Which like an engine, wrenched my frame of nature/ From the fix'd place'. (1.4.254–5) Similarly, when he awakes to find Cordelia standing over him, he says 'I am bound/ Upon a wheel of fire'. (4.7.47) The image of the rack features again when Kent expresses his wish that Lear should be let die. The king's trials are once again described using a metaphor of physical torture: 'he hates him/ That would upon the rack of this tough world/ Stretch him out longer'. (5.3.314–16)

Summary executions, without trial or hearing, are a feature of life in the Britain of *King Lear*. As we have seen, Kent is threatened with execution if he remains in the kingdom for longer than ten days. Gloucester, meanwhile, has no hesitation in pronouncing a death sentence on Edgar when he believes that the latter tried to kill him. (2.1.58) When Gloucester falls into Regan's power, she wants him executed immediately: 'Hang him instantly'. (3.7.4) Yet the most tragic and moving instance of execution comes at the end of the play, when Cordelia is hanged on Edmund's orders. (5.3.37–9, 258) This takes place off-stage, but the sight of Lear returning with Cordelia's body is one of the most tragic moments in literature.

SUICIDE

As if all this murder and mayhem wasn't enough, there are also two suicide attempts in the play. Gloucester, in despair after his blinding, attempts to commit suicide by jumping from what he believes to be the Cliffs of Dover. (4.6.41–50) Goneril successfully commits suicide by stabbing herself after her beloved Edmund has been killed and her desire to dominate the kingdom have come to nothing. (5.3.240–2)

VISION & BLINDNESS

METAPHORICAL BLINDNESS

At the beginning of the play. blindness is used as a metaphor for Lear's poor judgement in giving away his kingdom. When Kent tells Lear to 'See better' and asks to be let remain 'The true blank of thine eye', (1.1.158–9) he is referring to the fact that the king cannot see the truth of his eldest daughters' greed. Perhaps a similar blindness to reality is suggested when Lear wonders where his eyes are after he has been insulted by Goneril: 'Where are his eyes?' (1.4.211) Lear makes sarcastic references to sight and blindness when he encounters Gloucester. He seems to berate himself for his own previous blindness to reality: 'I remember thine eyes well enough./ Does thou squiny at me? No, do thy worst, blind/ Cupid: I'll not love'. (4.6.140–2)

Gloucester, too, realises that he was blind to reality when he failed to recognise that Edgar was really his loyal son. Ironically, it is only when he is blinded by Cornwall that he realises this important truth. Gloucester's blinding and subsequent suffering give him a new wisdom and insight. As he puts it: 'I stumbled when I saw'. (4.1.18–19)

The half-deranged Lear echoes this sentiment when he meets the blinded Gloucester near the French camp. He tells Gloucester that a man does not need sight to understand the world: 'A man may see how this world goes with no eyes. Look with thine ears'. (4.6.148–9) Lear actually seems to devalue sight, saying those that possess it are led astray, becoming nothing but liars and hypocrites: 'Get thee glass eyes;/ And, like a scurvy politician, seem/ To see the things thou dost not'. (4.6.168–70)

THE EYES AS INDICATORS OF PERSONALITY

Lear's three daughters' personalities are suggested by descriptions of their eyes. Cordelia leaves her father tearfully, with 'wash'd eyes'. (1.1.269) She is later described as having 'heavenly eyes' from which holy water pours. (4.3.32) Such language reinforces the image of her as an angelic force of goodness and truth. Lear suggests Goneril's aggressive and ruthless personality by saying that 'her eyes are fierce'. Unfortunately, he deludes himself into thinking that Regan's 'do comfort and not burn'. (2.4.47–8) In the event, Regan will turn out to be every bit as 'fierce' as Goneril.

BLINDING

The world of *King Lear* is a violent, brutal world, and there are several references to characters having their eyes plucked out. Lear calls on nature to blind Goneril as punishment for her ingratitude: 'strike her young bones … You nimble lightnings, dart your blinding flames/ Into her scornful eyes!' (2.4.160–4) When Lear's retinue of knights is reduced by Goneril, he is so filled with despair and rage that he threatens to blind himself: 'Old fond eyes,/ Beweep this cause again,/ I'll pluck ye out'. (1.4.287–8) Later, when he meets the

blinded Gloucester near the French camp, he seems to offer to take out his eyes and give them to him: 'If thou wilt weep my fortunes, take my eyes'. (4.6.81)

Gloucester says that he will not let Regan and Goneril torture Lear by tearing out his eyes: with 'thy cruel nails,/ Pluck out his poor old eyes'. (3.7.56–7) Gloucester himself has his eyes torn out by Cornwall in Act 3, Scene 7: 'Upon those eyes of thine I'll set my foot … Out vile jelly / Where is thy lustre now?' (3.7.65, 81–2) We are filled with horror as this poor old man declares that 'all is dark and comfortless'. (2.7.83)

CLOTHING, NAKEDNESS & DISGUISE

FANCY CLOTHING

Throughout the play, fancy clothing tends to be associated with insincerity and falsity. The clothes of the rich, especially those in power, are typically seen as a symbol of hypocrisy and insincerity. Those who dress in beautiful clothes are often the most corrupt. The expensive and elaborate garments they wear serve as an effective disguise and protect them from rule of law. Lear describes how the well-dressed man will invariably be treated more leniently than the man dressed in rags: 'Through tatter'd clothers small vices do appear;/ Robed and furr'd gowns hide all. Plate sin with gold,/ And the strong lance of justice hurtles breaks'. (4.6.169–71)

DISGUISE

For the characters that live by a virtuous moral code, disguise becomes necessary in order to survive and function. Honesty and loyalty are qualities not appreciated in the social reality of the play. In order to escape the death sentence passed on him, Kent is forced to disguise himself. He puts on a false accent and has 'raz'd my likeness' in order to serve the king. (1.4.4) In similar fashion, Edgar is obliged to disguise himself as poor Tom to protect his life. As poor Tom, he is 'something'; as Edgar, 'I nothing am'. (2.3.20–1) He later disguises himself as a peasant when he is leading Gloucester to Dover. After his father's 'suicide attempt', he changes accents again to disguise his trickery.

NAKEDNESS

Kent tells us how Lear raves against the elements 'unbonneted' and 'bareheaded'. Exposed to the violence of the storm, Lear begins to realise the plight of those at the bottom of the social ladder, who don't have the proper clothes to wear. He refers to the 'poor naked wretches' that have to endure nature's miseries. (3.4.28) When the king encounters poor Tom, he sees in him the essence of humanity stripped of its covering: 'unaccommodated man is no more but such a poor,/ bare, forked animal as thou art'.

In order to show his new solidarity with the repressed, Lear strips himself of his clothes: 'Off, off, you/ lendings! Come; unbutton here'. (3.4.110–11) Lear later crowns himself with a variety of weeds, flowers and nettles in order to show his new unity with nature and his contempt for his former regal clothing. (4.4.3–6)

Edgar is the other figure most closely associated with a symbolic removal of clothes and an exposure to the elements. He disguises himself as poor Tom by wearing only the bare minimum 'in contempt of man', and says that he will 'with presented naked-ness outface/ The winds and persecutions of the sky'. (2.3.11–12) When Lear enters his hovel, he makes us aware of the suffering that comes from such a reduc-tion, repeating the line 'Poor Tom's a-cold', which arouses Gloucester's pity. (3.4.178–9) This motif is repeated later, when the blind Gloucester asks his old tenant to bring 'some covering for this naked soul'. (4.1.45) The tenant promises to bring 'the best 'parel that I have'.

The truth that the essence of a man can shine through regardless of the clothes he wears, however, is best illustrated after Edgar defeats Edmund in battle. Albany tells him that 'thy very gait did prophesy/ A royal nobleness'. (5.3.178) In spite of the clothes he was wearing as a disguise, Edgar's upright character was still apparent.

WHAT IS TRAGEDY?

Tragedy is typically defined as a drama or literary work in which the main character is brought to ruin or suffers extreme sorrow, especially as a consequence of a tragic flaw, moral weakness, or inability to cope with unfavourable circumstances. Tragic drama often shows us that we are terrible limited beings, powerless to control and determine our own fates. A hidden or malevolent god, blind fate, or the brute fury of our animal instincts waits for us in ambush, bringing about our downfall and destroying our hopes and dreams.

A tragedy often contains the following elements:

· It tells of a person who is highly renowned and prosperous and who falls as a result of some error or frailty, because of external or internal forces, or both.
· The tragic hero's powerful wish to achieve some goal inevitably encounters limits, usually those of human frailty, the gods or nature.
· The tragic hero should have a flaw and/or make some mistake.
· The hero need not die at the end, but he must undergo a change in fortune.
· In addition, the tragic hero may achieve some rev-elation or recognition about human fate, destiny and the will of the gods.

WHY IS KING LEAR A TRAGEDY?

King Lear is a tragedy because it conforms to the above criteria:

· It tells the story of an enormously powerful but flawed individual. At the start of the play, Lear is king, but he acts in a foolish and short-sighted manner. He gives up his power and land, and entrusts his care to his ungrateful daughters after banishing the one daughter who genuinely loves him.
· Lear's goal is to retire from the office of king but to be still treated like a king. This goal is met with stern opposition from Goneril and Regan.
· Lear undergoes a dramatic change of fortune. He goes from being a powerful king to being a power-less, frail old man. Locked out of the castle in a violent storm, Lear gains insight into the human condition and the error of his ways.
· *King Lear* is an especially tragic play because it allows for no redemption. When Lear learns the errors of his ways, he is destined to suffer further. After a brief and happy reunion with Cordelia, he must live to see his beloved daughter murdered. He dies in the end, leaving behind a world marked by cruelty and violence.